The Beauty and Glory
of the Holy Spirit

The Beauty and Glory of the Holy Spirit

Edited by
Joel R. Beeke and Joseph A. Pipa

Reformation Heritage Books
Grand Rapids, Michigan

Published by
Reformation Heritage Books
2965 Leonard St. NE
Grand Rapids, MI 49525
616-977-0889 / Fax 616-285-3246
e-mail: orders@heritagebooks.org
website: www.heritagebooks.org

Printed in the United States of America
12 13 14 15 16 17/10 9 8 7 6 5 4 3 2 1

Library of Congress Cataloging-in-Publication Data

The beauty and glory of the Holy Spirit / edited by Joel R. Beeke and Joseph A. Pipa.
    p. cm.
  Includes bibliographical references.
  ISBN 978-1-60178-184-0 (hardcover : alk. paper) 1. Holy Spirit. I. Beeke, Joel R., 1952- II. Pipa, Joseph A.
  BT121.3.B44 2011
  231'.3—dc23
                          2012025811

---

*For additional Reformed literature, request a free book list
from Reformation Heritage Books at the above address.*

With heartfelt appreciation for

Rev. Mark Kelderman

faithful preacher and pastor;
my spiritual son of thirty years, theological student for four years,
and colleague in the ministry for thirteen years, and now,
I look forward to co-laboring with you in Puritan Reformed
Theological Seminary, as you serve as Dean of Students
and Spiritual Formation (2 Tim. 2:2).

—JRB

⸻ ⋙•⋘ ⸻

With thanksgiving for

Dr. George W. Knight

chairman of the Board of Trustees
of Greenville Presbyterian Theological Seminary
and Adjunct Professor of New Testament;
a friend, counselor, and colleague;
a promoter of a gracious Calvinism and defender of the truth;
a sterling example of a Christian gentleman.

—JAP

Contents

Preface

We need the Holy Spirit. It is impossible to overestimate the significance of the Spirit of God for the lives of Christians. In the words of Jesus, the Spirit is the "living water" who satisfies our deepest desires with the streams of Christ's redemptive glory (John 4:10–14; 7:37–39). Jonathan Edwards (1703–1758) said, "The sum of the blessings Christ sought, by what he did and suffered in the work of redemption, was the Holy Spirit."[1] Christ died to take away the curse and to give us the Spirit (Gal. 3:13–14).

This emphasis on the Spirit, if handled biblically, does not detract from the glory of Christ. The Spirit is the glorifier of Christ (John 16:14). Just as His Person cannot be separated from the Father and the Son in the blessed Trinity, so His work is essential to the salvation of those whom the Father chose and the Son purchased by His precious blood.

Christians of the Reformed and Presbyterian tradition have long adored the Person and cherished the work of the Holy Spirit. Benjamin Warfield said that John Calvin (1509–1564) could rightfully be named, "the theologian of the Holy Spirit."[2] The Reformed and Puritan heritage pulsates with the ministry of the Spirit of the living God.

This book springs from two conferences rooted in that heritage. In March 2011 Greenville Presbyterian Theological Seminary held a conference on "The Person and Work of the Holy Spirit." In August of that same year, Puritan Reformed Theological Seminary held its conference on "The Beauty and Glory of the Holy Spirit." This book

---

1. Jonathan Edwards, *An Humble Attempt to Promote Explicit Agreement and Visible Union of God's People in Extraordinary Prayer,* in *The Works of Jonathan Edwards, Volume 5, Apocalyptic Writings,* ed. Stephen J. Stein (New Haven: Yale University Press, 1977), 341.

2. Benjamin B. Warfield, *Calvin and Augustine,* ed. Samuel G. Craig (Philadelphia: Presbyterian and Reformed, 1956), 487.

is the result of the two schools, already joined by common confessions of faith and strong bonds of friendship, deciding to publish the conference messages combined under a single title.

In the first part of the book, you will find a number of biblical studies. In the opening conference sermon, David Murray explores how Solomon's dedication of the temple was an Old Testament revival by the Spirit (1 Kings 8). Geoffrey Thomas calls believers to seek the promise of the Holy Spirit from a loving and generous Father (Luke 11). John Thackway offers sweet consolation through Christ's words that the Spirit is "another Comforter" (John 14). Malcolm Watts summons us to boldly pursue the knowledge of the Lord through the Spirit's ministry of glorifying Christ (John 16). Gerald Bilkes traces the foreshadowing of Pentecost in Old Testament figures like Moses (Num. 11) and Elijah (2 Kings 2).

Next the book dives into the New Testament revelation concerning the Spirit. Michael Barrett explores the meaning of the outpouring of the Spirit at Pentecost by the ascended Christ (Joel 2; Acts 2). George Knight argues from New Testament texts that all Christians are baptized with the Spirit and that extraordinary gifts such as apostleship, prophecy, tongues, and healing have ceased. John Thackway lifts our eyes to Christ to meet the needs of suffering saints by "the supply of the Spirit of Jesus Christ" (Phil. 1:19).

The second part of the book sheds light on the doctrine of the Holy Spirit. Morton Smith walks through dozens of Scripture texts to show that the Spirit is indeed a Person, not just a power. Geoffrey Thomas gives us a heart-warming glimpse of the Spirit's jealous love over the souls of those whom He indwells. Ian Hamilton helps us treasure the precious works of regeneration and sanctification by the Holy Spirit. William Shishko investigates the meaning of the Spirit's objective sealing for believers in regeneration. And Malcolm Watts guides us in meditating on the witness of the Spirit to assure the Christian of his salvation, sometimes with a quiet, steady peace and sometimes with extraordinary power. Watts's focus is on the believer's growing, subjective consciousness of being sealed by the Spirit.

The third section of the book explores historical figures and movements. William VanDoodewaard uncovers evidences of the Holy Spirit's work in the early church in the preservation, proclamation, and powerful application of the Scriptures. Joel Beeke mines the writings of Richard Sibbes (1577–1635) for rare gems about making our hearts a hospitable home for the divine guest: "entertaining the Spirit." Joseph Morecraft studies the many-faceted doctrine of the Spirit in the Westminster Confession and Catechisms. Ryan McGraw movingly presents the teachings of John Owen (1616–1683) on the Spirit with respect to the Trinity, Christ's humanity, and our lives today. John Carrick stirs our hopes for "times of refreshing" (Acts 3:19) with a historical study of seasons of revival.

Lastly, the book concludes with a study by Joseph Pipa on the Holy Spirit's anointing for powerful preaching. In the appendix, one also finds an engaging essay by Michael Barrett on the King James Version of the Bible—a tribute to its 400th anniversary. While we as editors do not necessarily agree with all the exegetical nuances of every article and in fact there are some minor doctrinal differences between a few of the authors, all of the positions stated in the book are part of the orthodox Reformed tradition.

There is a richness to this subject of the Holy Spirit that defies our attempts to plumb its depth. All eternity will not exhaust our meditation, for the Spirit is the fullness of God for us in Christ. Edwards said, "The Holy Spirit, in his indwelling, his influences and fruits, is the sum of all grace, holiness, comfort and joy, or in one word, of all the spiritual good Christ purchased for men in this world: and is also the sum of all perfection, glory and eternal joy, that he purchased for them in another world."[3]

We are grateful to the staffs of PRTS and GPTS for organizing these conferences. If you weren't able to attend our schools' conferences in the past, after reading the wealth of spiritual nourishment in this book we hope you will consider joining us for future conferences in Greenville, South Carolina, and in Grand Rapids, Michigan.[4]

We heartily thank all the speakers for diligent work on their excellent addresses. We thank Gary den Hollander and Irene VandenBerg for their meticulous proofreading, Linda den Hollander for her able typesetting, and Amy Zevenbergen for the attractive cover design. Thanks, too, to Lois Haley for transcribing several of the addresses. We also thank our sweet wives, living epistles of Christ written by the ink of the Spirit, in whom we daily see the image of the triune God writ large before our eyes.

—Joel R. Beeke & Joseph A. Pipa

---

3. Edwards, *Humble Attempt,* in *Works,* 5:341.
4. For more information, see www.gpts.edu and www.puritanseminary.org.

BIBLICAL STUDIES

CHAPTER 1

The Old Testament Pentecost

David Murray

Revival is a sovereign, powerful, concentrated, and rare work of the Holy Spirit that renews and multiplies God's people. Revivals occurred regularly in Bible times, and maybe especially in Old Testament times. Horatius Bonar identified fourteen Old Testament events that could be described as revivals. Others identify eight to ten. However many there are, Wilbur Smith noted a number of common features. For the most part, each of them had a background of moral darkness and national depression; started in the heart of one special servant of God, who became the energizing power behind it; sparked a new and powerful proclamation of God's Word; saw a return to the worship of God; included the destruction of idols; created a deep sense of sin and its consequences, and a desire to separate from it and all its causes; brought a return to offerings of blood sacrifices and their prophetic picturing of the Messiah's atonement; saw a restoration of great joy and gladness; and were followed by a period of national productivity and prosperity.[1] We might sum up these features as increased spiritual knowledge, deepened spiritual feeling, and wider spiritual obedience, all of which are caused by the Holy Spirit.

It is true that few of the Old Testament revivals mention the Holy Spirit. However, we know that there is no such thing as a spiritual revival without the Holy Spirit. And although those involved in these revivals did not have such a developed pneumatology (theology of the Holy Spirit) as we do, they certainly knew that what was happening was the result of an outside and higher spiritual power.

---

1. Wilbur M. Smith, *The Glorious Revival under King Hezekiah* (Grand Rapids: Zondervan, 1937), vi–vii.

Let us take a look at one of these Old Testament revivals, one that has been called the greatest Old Testament revival, or the "Old Testament Pentecost": the revival under King Solomon when the temple was dedicated.

The main point I want to emphasize as we look at this event is that spiritual revival is rooted in united prayer. We see that in the New Testament Pentecost also; it was when the disciples "were all with one accord in one place"—surely a description of corporate prayer—that the Holy Spirit fell upon them (Acts 2:1–4). And we see that in the Old Testament Pentecost in 1 Kings 8 (as well as its parallel account in 2 Chronicles 6–7).

Solomon Prepared by the Spirit (vv. 1–11)
Solomon was prepared by God
We shall look at how Solomon prepared for this revival, but we must also recognize that Solomon was himself prepared by God. When Horatius Bonar surveyed the history of revival in the Bible and in church history, he found that God usually uses certain kind of men for this great work.[2]

> They were men of great earnestness in ministry. They felt their infinite responsibility as stewards of the mysteries of God, and shepherds appointed by the Chief Shepherd to gather in and watch over souls. They lived and labored and preached like men on whose lips the immortality of thousands hung. Everything they did and spoke bore the stamp of earnestness, and proclaimed to all with whom they came into contact that the matters about which they had been sent to speak were of infinite moment, admitting of no indifference, no postponement even for a day.

These men were also optimistic about success: "As warriors, they set their hearts on victory, and fought with the believing anticipation of triumph, under the guidance of such a Captain as their head."

They were men of faith: they had confidence in the God who saved them, in the Savior who commissioned them, in the Holy Spirit who empowered them, in the Word they proclaimed.

---

2. Quotations in this section are from Horatius Bonar, editor's preface to *Historical Collections Relating to Remarkable Periods of the Success of the Gospel*, comp. John Gillies (Kelso, Great Britain: John Rutherfurd, 1845), vi–xi.

They were men of labor: "Their lives are the annals of incessant, unwearied toil of body and soul: time, strength, substance, health, all they were and possessed, they freely offered to the Lord, keeping back nothing, grudging nothing, joyfully, thankfully, surrendering all to Him who loved them and washed them from their sins in His own blood.... They laboured for eternity, and as men who knew that time was short and the day of recompense at hand."

These men were patient: "They were not discouraged, though they had to labour long without seeing all the fruit they desired.... Attempts have been made to force on a revival by men who were impatient at the slow progress of the work in their hand; and seldom have these ended in anything but calamitous failure, or at best a momentary excitement which scorched and sterilised a soil from which a little more patient toil would have reaped an abundant harvest."

They were men of boldness and determination: "Adversaries might contend and oppose, timid friends might hesitate, but they pressed forward, in nothing terrified by difficulty or opposition."

They were men of prayer:

> It is true that they laboured much, visited much, studied much, but they also prayed much. In this they abounded. They were much alone with God, replenishing their own souls out of the living fountain that out of them might flow to their people rivers of living water.... Were more of each returning Saturday spent in fellowship with God, in solemn intercession for the people, in humiliation for sin, and supplication for the outpouring of the Spirit, — our Sabbaths would be far more blest, our sermons would be far more successful, our faces would shine as did the face of Moses, a more solemn awe and reverence would be over all our assemblies, and there would be fewer complaints of labouring in vain, or spending strength for nought. What might be lost in elaborate composition, or critical exactness of style or argument, would be far more than compensated for by the "double portion of the Spirit" we might then expect to receive.

These men were men of solemn deportment: "Their daily walk furnished the best attestation and illustration of the truth they preached. They were always ministers of Christ, wherever they were to be found or seen. No frivolity, no flippancy, no gaiety, no worldly conviviality or companionships neutralised their public preaching, or marred the work they were seeking to accomplish."

All such characteristics are the work of God's Spirit. Many of them can be found in Solomon. When God begins to shape and form men like this, then we may have hope that He is preparing men for great work in His church, and perhaps even to be instruments of revival.

Solomon prepared for God
We not only see God preparing Solomon with these Spirit-wrought characteristics, but we also see Solomon preparing for God. It took four years to prepare the temple materials and seven to build it. Once it was built, Solomon waited eleven months for the dedication so that it would coincide with the Feast of Tabernacles, a festival that reminded the Israelites of their journey through the wilderness.

1. The ark comes to the temple (vv. 1–9)

The ark of the covenant had led the people through the wilderness and had been closely associated with the tabernacle, the place where God met with and dwelt among His people. The ark was now making its final journey to rest in the temple on Mount Moriah, signifying that God was now transferring His special presence to the temple.

Although this account reminds us of David's transfer of the ark to Jerusalem (2 Sam. 6:12–19), this is on a far grander scale. The ark was being brought not to a tent but to a magnificent temple, and the sacrifices were innumerable.

2. God comes to the temple (vv. 10–11)

When the ark entered the temple, so did God. The priests who had carried the ark exited, and the glory cloud of God's presence entered and filled the building, making it impossible for the priests to perform their service.

Something very similar happened at the initial setup of the tabernacle (Ex. 40:34–35). Both times the glory cloud entered, filled, and overwhelmed, indicating God's acceptance and approval of what had been done. He was not just beside or above, but in the temple.

Solomon Preaches by the Spirit (vv. 12–21)

Solomon's "sermon" reminded the people of God's promise of the temple and of His purpose for it.

1. God's promise of the temple (vv. 12–19)

Solomon reviewed God's faithfulness to the nation and reminded the people that God had fulfilled with His mouth what He had spoken with His mouth (v. 15). God had shown His words perfectly trustworthy.

Solomon could say, "Blessed be the LORD, that hath given rest unto his people Israel, according to all that he promised: there hath not failed one word of all his good promise, which he promised by the hand of Moses his servant" (1 Kings 8:56).

How reminiscent this is of the New Testament Pentecost, when the apostles also celebrated God's kept promise through His prophets of the temple of His Son (Acts 2:16ff.).

2. God's purpose for the temple (vv. 20–21)

The temple had a double purpose. First, it was to honor God's name (v. 20). It was a house for the name of Yahweh (vv. 17, 20), an important idea in the following prayer. This meant it would be a place where God's character would be revealed. Second, it was to house God's ark (v. 21). The ark was the special symbol of God's presence, the throne on which He chose to "sit." The temple was the place where God revealed His character and the place He lived.

Solomon Prays by the Spirit (vv. 22–53)

Remember, the emphasis of this chapter is "Spiritual revival is rooted in corporate prayer." Therefore, I want to pause here and highlight five important features of Solomon's prayer.

First, it was a corporate prayer. One of the marks of spiritual revival throughout church history has always been a coming together of God's people for prayer and a united longing for God's work in their midst.

Second, it was a comprehensive prayer. The Bible often uses the number seven to express completeness. Here we have seven petitions covering all aspects of national life, from war to famine to interpersonal disputes. These seven petitions are samples of all possible situations that call for prayer. This is another mark of true spiritual revival; prayers become much less selfish and narrow, and instead become more comprehensive and concerned for all aspects of life.

Third, it was a contrite prayer. Solomon came before the Lord humbly as "thy servant" (v. 28), not as the king. There was a spirit of deep humility and lowliness of mind. Eight times he spoke of sin (once he described it as the plague of his heart, v. 38) and five times he begged for forgiveness. In verses 46–50, he set forth repentance as the basis for the hoped-for forgiveness and restoration of blessing after the people's disobedience and failure.

Solomon knew his Bible and based his prayer on the predicted covenant blessings and curses of Leviticus 26 and Deuteronomy 28–30. Remember, 1 and 2 Kings were written to Israelites who were then in Babylonian exile, asking: "What about God's covenant promises? Has God broken His Word to us?" Solomon's prayer was recorded here to remind them that God had indeed kept His covenant as set out in Leviticus and Deuteronomy. He had dealt justly with them. The exiles were being invited to share in Solomon's humble words and repentant spirit.

However, the exiles were also being encouraged by Solomon's rehearsal of the conditions of restoration to the land: a change of heart, a turning back to God with all their heart and soul, and praying toward the land of their fathers and the temple. God kept His covenant Word (v. 24) and showed His covenant love (v. 23).

There was neither hyper-Calvinistic fatalism nor Arminian activism here. Solomon avoided simply waiting and he avoided simply demanding. There was boldness and there was caution. He recognized that God alone has the sovereign right to decide what prayers He should answer, but he also recognized that God usually acts in response to means He has appointed (2 Chron. 7:14). This must not be allowed to degenerate into a mechanical, "If we do this, then God will do that." Iain Murray noted how those who have lived through revivals "have been the first to say how there was so much which left them amazed and conscious of mystery."[3]

Fourth, it was a cosmic prayer. Solomon not only showed concern for the foreigner (vv. 41–43), but also desired that ultimately all the peoples of the earth might know that Jehovah is the only true God (vv. 43, 60). Similarly in the New Testament Pentecost, the work of the Spirit turned the inward-looking disciples outward and made them pray for the nations and go to them.

---

3. Iain H. Murray, *Pentecost Today* (Edinburgh: Banner of Truth, 1998), 5.

Fifth, it was a Christ-centered prayer. Like the tabernacle, the temple and all its furniture, officials, and rituals revealed the coming Messiah to the Israelites. It was one large picture of the coming Christ, with lots of small pictures in there, too.

That is why, when Christ came, He described Himself as the temple of God (John 3:19–22). Like the temple, Christ is the One in whom God's glory dwells, the One in whom God puts His name, the One through whom God hears prayer, the One whom God calls us to look toward, the One in whom we find forgiveness. When Solomon asked the question "Will God indeed dwell [with men] on the earth?" (v. 27), we are to hear it as rhetorical, and as ultimately fulfilled by the great divine "Yes" in Christ.

Look at the number of sacrifices offered: 22,000 oxen and 120,000 sheep. That is seven sacrifices a minute! Yet, the blood of bulls and goats could never take away sin. So why offer them? It was to express their faith in and hope of a coming suffering sacrifice that would take their deserved place of punishment.

Solomon Praises by the Spirit (vv. 54–61)

The prayer concluded with paeans of praise. The "vast assembly" (v. 8), which included people of distant lands, celebrated for two weeks before going home full of joy. What a Spirit-wrought revival! Divine preparation, inspired preaching, Christ-centered prayer, and spiritual worship abounded.

Conclusions

Although there are two accounts of the Old Testament Pentecost in Kings and Chronicles, they were written for different audiences and different purposes.

As we have seen, 1 and 2 Kings was written for the children of Israel in Babylonian exile. Their question was, "Why did this happen to us?" Kings was written to answer that question and to show that the exile was a just and predicted act of God. The writer was calling the people to consider the great events of the past to bring them to repentance. Let us also trace the great revivals of the past that they might humble us, convict us, and impress on us the justice of God's present withdrawal of His reviving Spirit.

Chronicles was written after the exile to encourage more Israelites to return to Jerusalem and rebuild the nation. Their question was, "Is there any hope?" In the Chronicler's account of these events, therefore, he emphasized the glories of the past to kindle hope and expectation, especially in a renewal of the Davidic King. Let us read revival accounts to kindle our hope in the rebuilding of the church and the future glory of the Davidic King.

Above all, let us kindle hope that if such things can happen in Old Testament times, when the Holy Spirit's work was not yet at its fullest, we might expect much more in our days, when the Spirit has been promised in even greater measure.

CHAPTER 2

The Father's Gift of the Spirit

Geoffrey Thomas

And I say unto you, Ask, and it shall be given you; seek, and ye shall find; knock, and it shall be opened unto you. For every one that asketh receiveth; and he that seeketh findeth; and to him that knocketh it shall be opened. If a son shall ask bread of any of you that is a father, will he give him a stone? or if he ask a fish, will he for a fish give him a serpent? Or if he shall ask an egg, will he offer him a scorpion? If ye then, being evil, know how to give good gifts unto your children: how much more shall your heavenly Father give the Holy Spirit to them that ask him?

—Luke 11:9–13

When we read the first three Gospels, Matthew, Mark, and Luke (the "Synoptic Gospels"), we are conscious at first of the old covenant atmosphere of those books. Luke, for example, begins with an actual priest named Zacharias, serving in the temple and burning incense. Then the priest is told by a messenger from God that his wife is going to have a son who "will be filled with the Holy Spirit even from birth" (Luke 1:15). In other words, from the very beginning of his life, the baby will know that his vocation is to be one of the Lord's prophets, that he has the charisma of prophecy, and it is for this work that the Spirit of God is in him. Soon Zacharias is also filled with the Holy Spirit and so is enabled to make a long prophecy. Soon we are also told of the Spirit of God coming upon a man called Simeon and moving him to enter the temple to meet with Joseph, Mary, and the baby Jesus. He, too, is filled with the Spirit and he, too, prophesies. This is an old covenant picture of the Spirit anointing gifted men of office, such as prophets and kings, for particular works God gives them to do.

Then thirty years pass and John the Baptist and Jesus begin their public ministries. "The promised one is coming," cries John, "the one the prophets spoke of who is going to pour out the Holy Spirit." Then Jesus leaves Nazareth and goes to the River Jordan, and the Spirit of God comes upon Him at His baptism. Jesus' great theme, as He begins to preach, is that the kingdom of God has arrived. This is a critical moment in human history, a time of decision for the people of the Old Testament, when that covenant at last finds its complete fulfillment. This is the time that has been prophesied by the Spirit-filled men of the older dispensation with such expectancy, apprehension, and longing.

They knew that they were living in the age of decision and crisis. The time had finally come; the hour was at last fulfilled. The Spirit of God was going to be poured out on all flesh, no longer on the Jews alone, and not only upon kings, prophets, and priests for their work, but on every believer, even servants and maidservants, both old and young. The last days were dawning, the days in which we still live today, the time between the first and second comings of Christ. We are those upon whom the ends of the ages have come (1 Cor. 10:11); we have tasted the powers of the world to come (Heb. 6:5); we are living in the age of the Spirit because the Lord has come with redeeming power and might, and when He is exalted He is going to baptize the nations far and wide with the Spirit. Death has been conquered and the guilt of sin has been removed.

So, the ministry of Christ begins with the declaration that the King has already come and His Spirit is soon about to come. Luke's gospel ends with the last words of Jesus: "And, behold, I send the promise of my Father upon you: but tarry ye in the city of Jerusalem, until ye be endued with power from on high" (24:49). Then, in the opening chapter of Acts, the promise of the coming of the Spirit is given a remarkable immediacy: "ye shall be baptized with the Holy Ghost not many days hence" (1:5).

The Gospels, then, are as much books of anticipation about the coming of the Spirit as the Old Testament prophecies. So, there is a cluster of teachings about the Spirit at the birth of Christ, both in the prophecies and in the overshadowing of Mary in Jesus' incarnation, but there are few other references to the Spirit of God in the first three Gospels except those that look forward to Pentecost. That is why the words of our text are so fascinating. In them the Spirit is made accessible to us; we can make connection with Him. Jesus says, "If ye then, being evil, know how to give good gifts unto your children: how much more shall your heavenly Father give the Holy Spirit to them that ask him?" (Luke 11:13).

A Promise to God's Own Children

In this passage, we have a wonderful promise, a pearl of a promise; in fact, a series of very great promises building up in earnestness and affection: "And I say unto you, Ask, and it shall be given you; seek, and ye shall find; knock, and it shall be opened unto you. For every one that asketh receiveth; and he that seeketh findeth; and to him that knocketh it shall be opened" (Luke 11:9–10). But these assurances do not belong to all men indiscriminately. We cannot put these words of Jesus on a notice board outside a church, "Ask and it will be given to you," for a man walking by in the street to consider that such a promise is for him: "'Ask, and I will receive'? Sounds good to me. All right, then I will ask that I'll have that woman.... I'll ask for money to take a holiday in Las Vegas.... I'll ask that I'll win the lottery this Saturday. I'm encouraged to believe I'll win it because God says, 'Ask and it will be given to you.'" No, that is wrong; these are not promiscuous promises. We need to see how carefully they are curtailed in our text: "how much more shall your heavenly Father give the Holy Spirit to them that ask him?" (v. 13).

These words are spoken to Jesus' disciples. They are part of a discourse on prayer. His followers have asked Him to teach them to pray, and these words are about what the heavenly Father will do for those who are His own children. If you today are a child of God, these are your promises. If you have received God's Son as Messiah and Savior, becoming His disciple, you have been given the right to be called a son of God. He is your Father in heaven, and these promises are your very own promises. However, if you spurn the Lord Jesus Christ and obey another lord, and if you reject the privilege of adoption into God's family, these are not your promises. They are promises for the sons of the heavenly Father. So, there are multitudes of men and women who can take no comfort from these words. It is not at all true that if they ask for something that God is bound to give it to them.

So, we must ask ourselves: "Have we any claims whatsoever on these promises? Are we God's children? Are we the disciples of Christ who want to be taught by Him concerning how to pray properly?" There is a very real possibility that men pray to God and He will not answer because they are asking amiss; they are asking for things in order to consume them to satisfy their own lusts; they are asking while tenderly regarding sin in their own hearts; they are asking God for forgiveness and mercy while they entertain no mercy at all for those who have offended them. We are told that in such cases God will not hear us, and so we have no right to take these great words—which everyone can quote—and believe they are an assurance that our whims and fancies will be met, because these are great family promises for the household of faith. When God's own children ask for those things that are pleasing to their Father, God will give them to them.

Unbelievers Welcome to Come to a Seeking Christ

I want to give every encouragement to men and women to attend worship services and hear the Word of God preached, seeking to listen intently, to understand, to learn, and to obey what God says. If you are asking God for a closer walk with Him and for greater trust in Him, and knocking for entry into the deepest fellowship with Him, keep on doing that. Indeed, I believe that in such longings and yearnings—in that actual asking, seeking, and knocking—there is saving faith and the possession of Christ's salvation. So, seek the Lord while He may be found and where He may be found, and that is where people gather together in His name and hear His Word. There He is near.

Yet I do not believe that this particular passage is saying to men and women who are still in unbelief that their salvation depends on their endlessly seeking Christ. Indeed, I think that the New Testament language is quite the opposite, that it does not show us people seeking Christ; in fact, it says quite categorically that none are seeking God. What we find in the Bible is the Lord seeking men and women. I find it saying: "God is seeking you. He is seeking you in the testimony of your friends, in the preaching of the gospel, in the offer of pardon and forgiveness through Christ, in the prayers of your parents and friends, in the Bible you read and the Christian books you have been given, in a host of providences that have made this world less and less satisfying, and in your satisfaction at being in the presence of other

Christians. In all of that God is showing evidence that He is seeking you. For some of you, I am afraid that a great deal of what you refer to as your "seeking" is the seeking of a better invitation than you have had so far. You are wanting to hear the gospel with more excitement. You are wanting to feel it more deeply. You are wanting to hear it more persuasively so that you won't have to make that painful, lonely, personal commitment to entrust yourself to Jesus Christ forever.

The Lord Jesus Christ is not an object that you have to search for as if He were somehow lost and buried away in some mysterious place, in a cave in the Himalayas that required a trip to Nepal, on a distant island in the South Seas, off in some lonely cell behind granite walls in Scotland, or in some such inaccessible and forbidding spot. It is not true that the Savior or the Holy Spirit is so far from you that you must seek Him endlessly, because in the preaching of the Bible He is near you; He is in the word of faith that we preach, and that word is nigh you (Rom. 10:8). Your task, your obligation, and your privilege is not to be shaking your head sadly that it is so difficult to find Jesus Christ. No, He is the one seeking, and He is seeking you now. He says, "I am here, so come to Me now." He is here because He is seeking for you. He is not seeking your seeking, more intense seeking, more emotional seeking, more weepy seeking, or more sighing seeking. He is watching to see if you are receiving Him as your Prophet, Priest, and King. He is saying to you to come to Him, to enter the kingdom of God by the door, and He is the door that He sets before you. Enter! He is not saying you must keep seeking for the door. No, He is saying: "Here is the door, right before you. I am that door, and you must enter through it."

God's Children Should Ask Him to Fulfill His Promises

What should we as Christians ask? What should we plead? For what should we knock on the gates of heaven? We should ask God to fulfill all His promises. We should ask ourselves, as we start to pray, whether we have a promise. I do not mean at all whether we have one emotionally, one that grips us, makes us weep, takes all our strength from us, and touches us very deeply. There are such consequences to reading and especially to hearing the Word of God preached with the Holy Spirit sent down from heaven, and we should thank God for that. But these are not my concern now. In this great inspired

Word that comes from another, better place, which in its jots and tittles is inspired by God, of which the Savior said, "Thy word is truth" (John 17:17b), is there a promise? And is that promise mine simply on the basis that I am a child of God? Yes, there is such a promise; indeed, there are many exceedingly great and precious promises in the Bible, and they are all yea and amen in Christ Jesus (2 Cor. 1:20). These promises are ours, and when we worship God we can pray with the confidence that God will fulfill what He has promised to every Christian.

Such promises are the limits of God's obligations. What He has promised He will give, but no more than that. For example, He has not promised that we will get A grades on all our exams, or even that we will pass every one of our exams, or even that we will pass our driving tests. He has not promised that we will be cured of every ailment and disease we contract. He has not promised us riches, marriage, children, or long life. He has not promised us a mighty religious awakening in our own lifetimes. Where there are no promises, there God has not bound Himself to us. But every promise that He has made He will fulfill, such as, that He will work all things together for our good (Rom. 1:28), that He will supply all our needs according to His riches in glory in Christ Jesus (Phil. 4:19), that nothing shall ever separate us from His love in Christ (Rom. 8:38–39), that we will be able to do all things through Christ who strengthens us (Phil. 4:13), that I will learn in whatsoever state I am in to be content (Phil. 4:11), and that the good work He has begun in me He will complete in the day of Christ (Phil. 1:6). What He has promised He will perform infallibly, and that is what we are to pray for. All our certainty and assurance must be based on such promises. Our heavenly Father is saying to every one of His children: "You may ask Me for the fulfillment of any promise. You may plead for its fulfillment now. Knock on the door of these promises and that door will be opened to you."

I am saying that for every expectation and all our confidence, we must have a promise, and we can begin to doubt our God and question His faithfulness when we discover Him breaking His promises. It is not when He fails our expectations or does not grant our whims that we are justified in being angry with Him; it is when His solemn promises begin to fail that we may doubt Him.

So, has God made promises about the Holy Spirit? Indeed He has, for example, through the prophet Joel: "I will pour out my Spirit upon all flesh; and your sons and your daughters shall prophesy, your old men shall dream dreams, your young men shall see visions; and also upon the servants and upon the handmaids in those days will I pour out my spirit" (Joel 2:28, 29). Here is a promise to all God's people, to old men and young men, even to male and female servants. The Lord says, "I will pour out My Spirit in those days, that is, the days of fulfillment when the Christ, the Anointed One comes." So, we can go to God and ask Him to pour out His Spirit upon us, and we can say to Him: "Thou hast promised Thou wilt do this. I read Thy word in Joel 2:28–29 and I am holding Thee to Thy word to fulfill that for me. I am dead and I need the Spirit's life. I am blind and I need the Spirit's illumination. I am ignorant and I need the Spirit's understanding. Please give to me what Thou hast promised."

Then we read another promise about the Holy Spirit in our text. The Lord Jesus says: "If a son shall ask bread of any of you that is a father, will he give him a stone? or if he ask a fish, will he for a fish give him a serpent? Or if he shall ask an egg, will he offer him a scorpion? If ye then, being evil, know how to give good gifts unto your children: how much more shall your heavenly Father give the Holy Spirit to them that ask him?" (Luke 11:11–13). We see the Savior's argument; He spells it out in a fascinating way to encourage us to address our heavenly Father about giving us the Spirit: "Your little boy is hungry. 'Daddy, give me some fish,' he cries. 'I'll give you something,' you snarl at him, and you throw at him a viper. Or he asks you for a hard-boiled egg, and you drop into his hands a scorpion with its stinging tail. 'Never,' you protest. 'We wouldn't treat our children in that way. We would give them bread and eggs. We would give them good gifts, not evil.' You are evil men by nature. You are the sons of Adam and have gone astray from the womb, telling lies. You drink iniquity like water; in your flesh there is absolutely no good thing to be found. Yet you know how to give good gifts to your children. How much more will your heavenly Father give the Holy Spirit to those who ask Him?" That is what the Lord is saying. He is giving a promise to us, that whoever asks for the Spirit will receive Him.

What does our Lord say? Agonize for Him? Be totally yielded for Him? Make full surrender to have Him? Be completely dedicated to get Him? Renounce all sin? Lay all on the altar for Him? Yield body, soul, and spirit? Make a perfect consecration of our entire beings to Him? Struggle for Him? Ask in intensive and persevering prayer, and then we might have the Spirit? No. He simply says, "*Ask* for Him!" He says that the Father *gives* the Holy Spirit. He does not have to be wrested out of the Father's reluctant hands. The Spirit is *given*, and a gift is not earned or won by price or merit.

When I paid the miners of Cynheidre colliery on a Friday morning when I worked for the National Coal Board, they did not grovel at the pay desk and thank me with tears in their eyes for their pay packets. They picked them up without a word because they had worked hard for them. I was giving them nothing; they had earned their pay. God does not make us work to have the Holy Spirit. He is a gracious, God-sent gift that we receive by faith alone. At the beginning of Acts 2, the history of the coming of the Spirit on the day of Pentecost, we are not told that the church was agonizing, meeting all the conditions, and fully paying the price of Pentecost, and thus the Spirit came suddenly from heaven. There was just one divine request—that they not leave Jerusalem. All we are told about them was that they were in one accord and in one place, and then He came as the Lord had promised. He came to Peter not by works of righteousness that Peter had done. He came to the hundred and twenty not because of their own holiness and merit, not as a reward for their fasting and praying, but as a free gift of Christ's infinite grace, just as had been promised through the prophet Joel. The Spirit who came into them and upon them came without money and without price as they waited for His coming, as they appropriated Him, and as they received Him as their own. Let us ask God to fulfill His promise and give us His Spirit.

God's Children Should Ask for the Spirit
to Live the Christian Life

We see the context of these promises. They are found at the close of a sermon of our Lord on the most difficult thing any Christian will ever be asked to do, namely, to pray. Jesus begins by teaching the disciples the Lord's Prayer. Then He gives them a simple parable to make prayer come alive. Finally, He makes these great promises that God hears us when we ask, sees us when we seek, and opens to us when we knock. We are kind to our children, but how much kinder is our heavenly Father to those who ask Him for His Spirit? The road is exceedingly long and is hard-going. Disciples must love God with all their hearts and love their neighbors as themselves, and never stop. They must present their bodies as living sacrifices to God every day. They must be filled with the Spirit. They must take up their crosses, deny themselves, and follow the Lord.

The Christian life is one of great ethical stringency; it is one of severe, demanding, relentless, and arduous labor. The burden we bear is heavy, and we who are strong must bear the burdens of the weak. The Lord Jesus lays down principle upon principle, precept upon precept, regarding church life, family life, life before the watching world, and life with enemies, and He tells them this is the road to heaven; it is the only road. They are starting to think, "Who then can be saved? How can any man live like this?" That is why He ends His sermon with our text: "Ask and you shall receive; seek and you shall find; knock and it will be opened to you. Seek the grace to pray as I have taught you, to obey this principle and attend to these standards."

We often forget that the energy to live the Christian life comes to us by the Holy Spirit. We look at the Christian ethic and the issue of holiness of life, and we are often overwhelmed by our failures: "Lord, I cannot be that kind of Christian. I cannot be a preacher. I cannot be a husband. I cannot be a church member. I cannot, Lord." We are told that the Savior knew what men were thinking, and with His teaching on the life of prayer, He is encouraging the disciples with this great promise. He can read their thoughts: "The things He demands from us are impossible!" So, Jesus says to them: "Ask... seek...knock, and you will get what you want. Ask for the Spirit of God to assist you." The Christian life is not an impossibly unattainable life. It is the road stretching out before each one of us who is a child of God. It is the only road to glory, and if we are not walking it we will not reach glory. When the Lord teaches us about praying, it is not in order that we should admire the meditative life, but so that we live it and follow it.

We are being challenged as to what is our chief commitment and primary concern. Do we hunger and thirst for righteousness? Do we assert that for us to live is Christ? How committed are we? Do we say, "This one thing I do?" If not, why not? What is more important than glorifying God and enjoying Him? Do we say, "Take my life and let it be/Consecrated Lord to Thee"?

If not, we should ask for grace to live like that; to be that kind of man or woman; to be a proper Christian boy or girl. We cannot be half Christian and half follower of the world. The promise of the Holy Spirit has nothing to do with tongue speaking or being the most eloquent preacher in the land. Jesus is not telling us that we are going to be healed of our illnesses. Such promises are not about problems with our health, getting a job, or getting some recognition. This is a promise about sustained energy to walk the holy road that leads to God.

The Father Promises the Spirit Will Be Given to Those Who Ask Him

We can sit for years moping that the church is in decline and that we are living in a day of small things. We can have our meetings and confer together, discussing all the depressing pressures being brought to bear on the church, forgetting the one great remedy, God the Holy Spirit, the third member of the Godhead. Is that central to our thinking? Christ is saying to His disciples: "What you men need now is the Spirit of God. Ask God to send God to you." What we Christians need, and need more of, and always need more of, is the Spirit. We need His comfort, His courage, His morale-boosting ministry, His energizing, His fruitfulness, His leading, and His perseverance. It is not enough to know that there are problems and that we have wise friends and special inspirational speakers to help us. We have the great remedy for all our ills and infirmities in God's gift of the Holy Spirit.

The teaching is not at all that we can manage the small things, but for the great awakenings we need Holy Spirit-sent revival. We need the Holy Spirit for everything we do as Christians, so we are asking God, "Help me prepare this meal, spend my housekeeping money well, decide what to do in the garden, call the children who are away in college, heal the kids of their head lice, and answer their questions about movies." We need the Holy Spirit for every decision, and so we have to ask God for everything. Without the Holy Spirit, we can do nothing. We will get nowhere in our Christian lives by our own wits and energy.

So often our praying is a protest against the very nature of the Christian life—entering many disappointments and heartaches. We forget that our usefulness in Christ's service and our profitableness in the work of the church depend on our going through trials from which our flesh shrinks. I am saying that often our prayers can be a protest against our providence, and we have to keep going to our Father with our requests. God is our Father, a God who pities His children. We hear our little children, and they are worried. They do not want to go to school, having some mysterious struggle with a teacher perhaps, or with some other children. We do not know; the children will not tell us. They simply cry, tell us they are ill, or ask us to home-school them, and we pity them because they are so weak and vulnerable. In the end, they are going to do what we decide, and we pity them in their helplessness. As a father pities His children, so our Father pities us; He sends for our survival His grace and His Spirit. He knows what we need, what is absolutely indispensable.

How marvelous is God's love; how willing He is to give grace to us, and with Him there are no mistakes. We are all aware of the spoiled child syndrome, the little boy who has been spoiled by getting all he clamors for and has turned into an utter brat. God makes no mistakes like that. With Him, there are no moods; it is never inconvenient for God to get involved in our lives. If we are in the depths and cry to Him from there, He hears and comes to our assistance. He commands the Spirit to go forth into the darkest, dirtiest, hottest, most unfriendly, most hostile, most remote places in the world to help us, where we send sewerage workers, riot police, or morticians. These are all necessary and noble jobs, even if they are not ones we might choose. But the Holy Spirit operates in the darkest places on earth.

Conclusion

I will close with this, returning to my two fundamental principles. First, to those of us who are Christians, we have to follow the Lord Jesus Christ as His disciples each day. To live this life, we need the Holy Spirit and His graces. We have to go to Him and seek the grace to live the life of a follower of the Lamb of God, and God promises that if we seek Him then we will find Him.

Second, to those of you who are not yet Christians, you may know better than I do who are and who are not believers in Jesus Christ. I am saying to you that you have nothing to do with this particular promise. You may protest and ask, "Is there nothing for me?" There is a great deal for you, for the living God is seeking you. You would not be reading these words if He had not worked His providential will in orchestrating everything, so that you are thinking of His claims over your life. God is seeking for you, and is that not marvelous? At times you have almost given up on yourself, and maybe your closest relatives and friends have been tempted to give up on you, but God has not given up. You were a lost sheep, but He abandoned all the safe sheep and set out searching for you, and He kept seeking until He found you, and this is where He has found you today. I am saying to you, "By grace, take Him, in all the glory of His person and in the perfection of all He has done for sinners, as He offers Himself to you in the gospel. Enter in at the narrow gate. It is open for you now."

So, there are two kinds of people. To those who are saved I say, "Seek!" To those who are not saved I say, "Take!" However paradoxical it may seem, that is the biblical order in the context of Luke 11. The Lord's people are to ask God for the Holy Spirit to help them day by day, and those who are not Christians are to take His free salvation.

CHAPTER 3

How the Holy Spirit Is Another Comforter

John P. Thackway

And I will pray the father, and he shall give you another Comforter, that he may abide with you for ever.... I will not leave you comfortless: I will come to you.

—John 14:16, 18

John 13–16 is a passage that is particularly treasured by God's people. In it, the Lord reveals His heart and shows that He "loved his own which were in the world" (13:1). However, He has to tell His disciples that He must leave them. He has in view His death, resurrection, and ascension to heaven after forty days. This, of course, is our Lord removing His bodily, visible presence from the disciples.

It cannot be worse news for them. They have given up all to follow Christ and be with Him. For three years, He has been everything to them: their Savior, their Master, their Lord, and their dearest Friend. Now they will have Him no longer.

Knowing their hearts, He breaks the news gently. How tenderly He does this: "Little children, yet a little while I am with you. Ye shall seek me: and as I said unto the Jews, Whither I go, ye cannot come; so now I say to you" (13:33); "In my father's house are many mansions: if it were not so, I would have told you. I go to prepare a place for you" (14:2); "I will not leave you comfortless: I will come to you" (14:18); "Peace I leave with you, my peace I give unto you: not as the world giveth, give I unto you. Let not your heart be troubled, neither let it be afraid. Ye have heard how I said unto you, I go away, and come again unto you. If ye loved me, ye would rejoice, because I said, I go unto the Father: for my Father is greater than I" (14:27, 28).

We know it is the way of love tenderly to spare the feelings of others and to reassure them. Our dear Lord is infinitely like this; He does not break the bruised reed (Matt. 12:20). We should always seek to be like this in our treatment of others, and love our fellow Christians as He has loved us (John 13:34).

Out of this concern, the Lord does not leave His disciples in the world before He has thoroughly prepared them for the change that is coming. In this, He looks beyond these men to us as well. As E. W. Hengstenberg put it: "In the prospect of His passion, He prepared His disciples for His coming departure, thus furnishing for His Church of all times a rich treasure of consolation."[1]

However, the Redeemer is doing more than gently breaking bad news—He is also firmly assuring His disciples that His departure will not deprive them. The removal of His physical presence will not be a loss: it will be a *gain*. He will be nearer and dearer to them than was possible before. To see the precious truth of this for us all, let us consider the following.

How This Can Be

In John 14:16, the Lord speaks of asking the Father to give the disciples "another Comforter." Someone whom He calls "the Spirit of truth" is coming to take His place. Yet, Jesus identifies the Newcomer with Himself: "ye know him; for he dwelleth with you"—the Lord, whom they have known all this time. Then He says: "and shall be in you" (v. 17). This can only mean that *He* will be in them by means of the Newcomer! Therefore, what is in view is a new and closer relationship, deeper than was possible in the flesh.

Alexander Maclaren, in his exposition of this passage, said:

> Who was the other but the Master who was speaking? So all that that handful of men had found of sweetness and shelter and assured guidance, and stay for their weakness, and enlightenment for their darkness, and companionship for their solitude, and a breast on which to rest their heads, and love in which to bathe their hearts, all these this divine Spirit will bring to each of us if we will.[2]

---

1. E. W. Hengstenberg, *Commentary on the Gospel of St John* (Edinburgh: T & T Clark, 1865), 2:133.
2. Alexander Maclaren, *The Gospel According to St. John, Chapter IX to XIV* (New York: A. C. Armstrong, 1908), 326.

His new relation to us is through the indwelling Spirit
He will fully come on the day of Pentecost. And because the Spirit and Christ are one, His indwelling us will be *Christ* indwelling us. The Spirit will become the medium of a spiritual union with the Lord, who will be nearer than ever. Therefore, Jesus can say, "I will not leave you comfortless: I will come to you" (v. 18). None other than the dear Lord Himself! And His coming to us covers no distance: He is *in us*! All He needs to do is to "manifest" Himself to us (v. 21).

This is how He is with His people now
He is in us by His Holy Spirit. We must not confuse the two: Christ and the Spirit are distinct. Yet they are one, and so the indwelling Spirit is the indwelling Christ. The Master's bodily presence is in heaven, but He is also in us by His divine nature through the Spirit. The Spirit is Christ in the soul. This is how Paul can say, "Christ liveth in me" (Gal. 2:20). This once came sweetly home to Fred Mitchell, former home director of the China Inland Mission. In 1921, his biographer tells us:

> He was returning by train to Bradford one Monday morning, and alighting at that station, he walked along towards the barrier, when the words came quietly but with overwhelming power to his mind: "Christ liveth in me." For months, if not years, he had believed it, but this Monday morning, amidst the smoke and clangour and bustle of the station, the holy, awe-inspiring reality dawned upon him. Christ Himself…was dwelling in him.[3]

The same wondrous truth is in Colossians 1:27: "Christ in you, the hope of glory."

This is better than His bodily presence
He is so much closer to us now—and to all His people at the same time. It was "expedient" that our Lord went away (John 16:7), that He might now be one with us in an indissoluble union. Therefore, the Holy Spirit is "another Comforter" because He is none other than Christ within us. This is how our blessed Lord is now present with us! And this is why Paul can say that he and his fellow apostles

---

3. Phyllis Thompson, *Climbing on Track: A Biography of Fred Mitchell* (London: China Inland Mission, 1953), 58.

"henceforth know [Christ after the flesh] no more" (2 Cor. 5:16). That apostle's favorite term for this new relationship is "in Christ" (Rom. 8:1; 16:3, 10, etc.)—which is only another way of saying "Christ…in you" (Rom. 8:9, 10).

How This Will Be

Jesus says, "I will not leave you comfortless, I will come to you" (John 14:18). "Comfortless" means "orphans." He calls His disciples "Little children" (13:33), and they will be like orphans without our Lord—bereaved, desolate, alone. His coming by the Spirit prevents this—by giving us more of Him than was ever possible before.

First, when Jesus says in verse 16, "I will pray the Father, and he shall give you another Comforter," what kind of "another" does He mean? We can answer this by saying that everything the Lord has been to the disciples until now—Savior, Master, Lord, dearest Friend—"another" will be to them.

Now, there are two words in the Greek for "another:" another of a *different* kind (*heteros*) and another of *the same* kind (*allos*). Our Lord uses *allos:* another of the same kind for "another Comforter." The Holy Spirit is no unknown, strange Comforter, but the same as the Lord Jesus. We can say, then, that the coming Holy Spirit is our Lord Himself, who will indwell His people to be their Comforter.

Second, what is the meaning of "Comforter"? It is *paraklētos*, sometimes turned into English as "Paraclete." The noun form of this word is found only in the writings of John. Usually it is translated "Comforter," but it is such a rich, deep word that commentators offer an array of suggestions as to how it should be understood: "no one English term expresses the full semantic range of Paraklētos."[4]

Paraklētos can be translated "Advocate." It is rendered this way in 1 John 2:1: "And if any man sin, we have an Advocate with the Father, Jesus Christ the righteous." Here, it is in a legal setting; the court of heaven is in view. When we sin, there is one who cries up our guilt against us, who is called "the accuser of the brethren" (Rev. 12:10). However, in heaven there is also One who answers for us: "an Advocate," our best Friend—more than a legal representative.

---

4. Stephen D. Renn, ed., *Expository Dictionary of Bible Words: Word Studies for Key English Bible Words* (Peabody, Mass.: Hendrickson, 2005), 196.

Notice, He is called "Jesus Christ the righteous." This refers to our Lord's perfect obedience of God's law for us, that He might give this to be *our* righteousness. God imputes it to us when we believe, and then we stand before Him as righteous, as accepted, as welcome, as entitled to heaven as our Lord Himself!

For our comfort, therefore, we can reason like this: I am not righteous, but He is. My Redeemer suffered the law's penalty and fulfilled all its precepts. When I confess my sin, it is instantly pardoned because our Lord presents His atonement to the Father; I am still counted righteous because "The LORD our righteousness" (Jer. 23:6) is before the Father for me. And the beloved apostle does not say, "*There is* an Advocate..." but "*We have* an Advocate..." He is there and is mine personally to plead my cause—*my* Righteousness and *my* Defender!

However, even when we do *not* sin, Satan still accuses us, because he is our slanderer before God. We feel this in the court of conscience—in the form of nagging feelings of guilt, "if our heart condemn us" (1 John 3:20). Satan knows we will not be condemned, but he can make us *feel* condemned, although innocent, to spoil our peace. But our Lord, by His Spirit, can reflect His heavenly advocacy in our hearts. He reveals to us, for our comfort, that He is our devoted Defense Attorney who wins every case for His clients: "He shall stand at the right hand of the poor, to save him from those that condemn his soul" (Ps. 109:31). And He persuades us that the Father is biased in our favor through grace, and that He gladly accepts our Lord's advocacy.

The author of a helpful book touches on this and gives her testimony:

> When a Christian recognises that Satan is accusing, and he is not sure whether the thing about which he is being accused is, in fact, right or wrong, he must know how to silence his accuser, otherwise the pain and conflict may continue for a long period of time and actually cause mental tension.
>
> I would like to share what I have found.... I believe that Jesus, having died for me and taken up my cause before the Father, has become my Advocate and I believe He gives me permission to refer my cause to Him even as I would to a human advocate. If I had an enemy who repeatedly came to accuse me, I would put my case into the hand of the best advocate I could find, and

then whenever my enemy would turn up to accuse me I would say, "I've handed over my case to another, please go and talk to my advocate, he'll answer for me." This is how I now face Satan; whenever he starts to accuse, I say something like this to him, "Satan, I have put my case into the hands of Another, I really do not know whether I've done wrong or not, but He knows; go and tell Him what you think. If He knows I've done wrong He can tell me. I am not dealing with you except through my Advocate." And then I quietly get on with my work. I find that in the majority of cases I never hear anything more about the matter![5]

Putting it all together, we can say this: in heaven, He answers for me to His Father and my Father—that is comfort. In my heart as "another Comforter," He answers for me to my conscience—this is comfort sealed to me. Let us remember, then, that we have an Advocate at God's right hand—and at *our* right hand. Lay hold of the wonderful truth that God listens to your Advocate above, and to the equally wonderful truth that you can listen to your Advocate within. Therefore, let us complete the verse quoted earlier: "If our heart condemn us, God is greater than our heart, and knoweth all things."

Paraklētos is sometimes understood as "Helper." Our Lord by His Spirit can strengthen us. Paul experienced this when he said, "I can do all things through Christ which strengtheneth me" (Phil. 4:13); literally the word is "in-strengthen." Christ by the Spirit was an inward helper to the apostle's weakness and made him strong. Paul teaches that the Spirit can give this help to our prayers also: "Likewise the Spirit also helpeth our infirmities: for we know not what we should pray for as we ought" (Rom. 8:26). Christ by His Spirit gives us strength for any work that we do for Him: "I also labour, striving according to his working, which worketh in me mightily" (Col. 1:29). Notice here that we are to "labour" and "strive," yet as we do so we find that He "worketh" in us "mightily" to enable us. Believe that as we do our part, He does His, and we will be amazed at what we can accomplish.

This is wonderfully illustrated by a touching picture the French artist Emile Renouf painted in 1881 entitled, "The Helping Hand."[6]

---

5. Marion Ashton, *A Mind at Ease* (Fort Washington, Pa.: The Christian Literature Crusade, 1969), 39.

6. See it here: http://www.tyronehistory.org/wcp_helping.html (accessed May 4, 2012).

In a large rowing boat, a grandfather sits next to his granddaughter. Both have their hands on a huge oar—his large hands pulling the oar, and her little fingers that do not even go round the thick wood. He looks down fondly and lovingly at her, while she is so serious, pulling away at the oar. Of course, all the strength is the old man's, but the little girl is doing her part! And he loves her for it! It is like that when we faithfully exert ourselves in the ways of God—it is in the strength of a loving Helper who strengthens us within. We then find that "the way of the LORD is strength to the upright" (Prov. 10:29) and we have "wrought with God" (1 Sam. 14:45).

Paraklētos can be understood as "Consoler." One dictionary offers this definition of *paraklētos*: "One who stands alongside another in order to offer encouragement, comfort."[7] It is interesting that Jesus emphasizes this side of things here. He does so because we need this so much. Charles H. Spurgeon once said that the fall of man introduced a new vocabulary that we would not otherwise have heard, words such as *sorrow, suffering, death*, etc. *Comfort* is also one of these, but comfort is what Jesus by His Spirit gives us. John Owen taught that comfort is the Spirit's chief work.

Christ, by His Spirit, comforts us by divine teaching
John 14:26 says, "he shall teach you all things." In the apostles' case, of course, it was in order to write the New Testament Scriptures. In our case, it is spiritually to understand them. The Spirit enlightens our minds and enlivens our hearts in the knowledge of the truth. And He enables us to be doers of the word. As Thomas Watson wrote:

> The natural man may have excellent notions in divinity, but God must teach us to know the mysteries of the Gospel after a spiritual manner. A man may see the figures upon a (sun)dial, but he cannot tell how the day goes unless the sun shines; so we may read many truths in the Bible, but we cannot know them savingly, till God by His Spirit shines upon our soul…. He not only informs our mind, but inclines our will.[8]

We need to get beyond the cerebral to the experiential. As one hymn writer put it, "We have listened to the preacher—/Truth by

---

7. Renn, ed., *Expository Dictionary of Bible Words*, 195.
8. Thomas Watson, *The Lord's Prayer* (Edinburgh: Banner of Truth, 1965), 15–16.

him has now been shown;/But we want a Greater Teacher/From the everlasting throne:/Application is the work of God alone."[9]

This includes the recall of wonderful truths that we know. He will "bring all things to your remembrance" (John 14:26), sometimes "out of the blue" and just when we need them. This especially applies to the promises. How often has a choice promise of God come to us and met our case! We never really forget Scripture passages, sermons, things we read. In prayer, when we are especially sensitive to divine things, some fragment of truth comes to mind in sweet application, and we are wonderfully blessed! Sometimes it is even when we are going about our daily duties and not particularly thinking about spiritual things—then a truth or promise will dart into our minds. John Bunyan experienced this:

> One day, as I was passing into the field, suddenly this sentence fell upon my soul: "Thy righteousness is in heaven." And I thought that I could see Jesus Christ at God's right hand. Yes, there indeed was my righteousness, so that wherever I was, or whatever I was doing, God could not say about me that I did not have righteousness, for it was standing there before Him.
>
> I also saw that it was not my good feelings that made my righteousness better, and that my bad feelings did not make my righteousness worse, for my righteousness was Jesus Christ Himself, "the same yesterday, and today, and forever," (Hebrews 13:8).
>
> Now indeed the chains fell off my legs, and I was loosened from my afflictions and irons.[10]

Christ by His Spirit comforts us by His felt presence

"I will not leave you comfortless: I will come to you." Our Lord perfectly understood how His disciples would feel when He had to leave them. And He perfectly understands our needs and how we love to feel Him near. He promises to continue His presence in this new way. Nothing makes the Holy Spirit more beautiful and glorious than this side of His ministry—making Christ real to our souls. The Spirit manifests the Lord Jesus to us, not like a portrait to admire,

---

9. Joseph Irons, "May the Holy Ghost descending," in *Trinity Hymns for the Worship of the Three-One Jehovah in Faith and Love* (London: Trinity Chapel, 1876), #1278.

10. John Bunyan, *Grace Abounding to the Chief of Sinners*, sec. 229–30. See *The Whole Works of John Bunyan*, ed. George Offor (Edinburgh: Banner of Truth, 1991), 1:35–36.

but by revealing Christ as a living and real Person, the "Beloved of our souls," One whom we can know and love for ourselves. His felt presence and love is our heaven begun below, which only heaven itself can surpass.

Christ by His Spirit comforts us by meeting all our needs
His disciples can expect everything they had in Him before, but so much more now. We can expect the same: the inward and felt equivalent of what He literally was to His disciples. Hear His word to them—and to us—to allay their fears in the storms of life: "Be of good cheer; it is I; be not afraid" (Matt. 14:27). Also, the timely word to a father who had just heard that his only daughter had died: "As soon as Jesus heard the word that was spoken, he saith unto the ruler of the synagogue, Be not afraid, only believe" (Mark 5:36). And His defense of a good woman who was criticized: "And Jesus said, let her alone; why trouble ye her? she hath wrought a good work on me... she hath done what she could" (Mark 14:6, 8).

In all this sweet work, we find that while the Spirit is the Comforter, Jesus is the Comfort. Robert Murray M'Cheyne once said, "His human heart beats towards us just as if He were sitting by our side."[11] Horatius Bonar puts it like this:

> *Christ is our CONSOLATION.* Though the Holy Ghost be "the Comforter," yet it is out of Christ that the consolation is drawn, with which He comforts the sorrowful. It is by unfolding the unsearchable riches of Christ, that He comforts. Christ is the well, out of which He brings the draughts of abundant consolation, with which He refreshes and revives us in our weariness. "Consolation in Christ"; nay, Christ Himself is our consolation, this is what the Gospel reveals. It was in acquaintanceship with Him that our first consolation began, when forgiveness dawned upon us; and it is, in continued and increasing acquaintanceship with Him, that our consolation is perpetuated, in spite of a thousand evils daily occurring to mar it. In fellowship with Him, we find ourselves wondrously lifted up out of the dust: "With Him conversing, we forget all care"; sorrow takes wings to itself and flies away. His words reveal Himself, and His words are such as

---

11. Letter to A. S. L. (August 16, 1840), in *Memoir and Remains of the Rev. Robert Murray M'Cheyne* (Edinburgh: Banner of Truth, 1966), 286.

these: "Let not your heart be troubled, neither let it be afraid; ye believe in God, believe also in me."[12]

Christ by His Spirit also comforts us at special times of need
He comforts in the church. By His divine and manifested presence, He promises to be in the midst of every assembly of His people (Matt. 18:20; 28:20). Every service and meeting can be like the one in the upper room, when our Lord came and showed Himself, and, "Then were the disciples glad, when they saw the Lord" (John 20:20).

He comforts when others fail us. And they will, but never mind, Jesus will not. The man born blind, whom the Lord cured, was abandoned by his parents and excommunicated by the Jews. However, "Jesus heard that they had cast him out; and when he had found him, he said unto him, Dost thou believe on the Son of God?" (John 9:35). In this He fulfills that lovely promise, "When my father and my mother forsake me, then the LORD will take me up" (Ps. 27:10).

He comforts in our loneliness. We may live alone, be bereaved of a loved one, lack family and numerous friends. However, we are not alone. One there is who sticks closer than a brother, and says, "I will not leave you comfortless, I will come to you." Then, plead the promise. Plead it for yourself. He is the "I," put yourself in the "you."

Conclusion
Be careful not to grieve the Spirit (Eph. 4:30; Ps. 51:11). Only He can make Christ real to us; without Him, our Lord will seem a Stranger. Then seek only to please Him. Later in the chapter He says, "He that hath my commandments, and keepeth them, he it is that loveth me: and he that loveth me shall be loved of my father, and I will love him, and will manifest myself to him" (John 14:21).

This is the ultimate reward of being obedient to the Lord. Do not balk at it if it seems hard and costly. As someone once said, "Obey, and let heaven answer for the rest."[13] Heaven's answer will include more of Christ than you have ever known.

---

12. Horatius Bonar, preface to Thomas Wilcox, *Christ is All and Saving Faith Discovered* (Kelso: J. & J. H. Rutherfurd, 1855), xxv–xxvii.

13. Quoted in Ashbel Green, *Lectures on the Shorter Catechism of the Presbyterian Church in the United States of America* (Philadelphia: Presbyterian Board of Publication, 1841), 1:43.

In putting the Lord first, others may not be pleased. Yet, if the Lord smiles, it matters not who frowns. This is our consolation and joy. The Lord gives Himself to us in all the fullness of His promise to be "another Comforter," who is hardly another because by His Spirit He is "this same Jesus"—nearer and dearer than before.

CHAPTER 4

The Ministry of the Spirit in Glorifying Christ

Malcolm H. Watts

The public ministry of the Lord Jesus is over. It is the Thursday evening before His death, and the Lord meets for the last time with His beloved disciples, mainly to pass on to them His tender words of comfort and consolation. These last words of His are recorded only by John (John 13–16) in what is generally known as the Upper Room Discourse. One commentator has rightly called this discourse the "most sacred legacy which the Lord has left to the disciples." He continues, "[it] can never be interpreted except by the heart which enters into the secret place of the Most High."[1]

Our Lord is only too aware of the great sorrow in the disciples' hearts (John 13:21, 33; 14:1; 16:6), and although His own sorrow is far greater, it is remarkable that He seeks no comfort for Himself and desires only to impart it to them. To do this, He touches on many things, yet we cannot but observe that time and again He refers them to the blessed ministry of the Holy Spirit (14:26; 15:26; 16:7). Indeed, He goes so far as to say that His own near departure, which seems so dark and grievous to them, will actually be the means of bringing much-needed comfort, for the great atonement having been made, there could be both an expected *and* an experienced fullness of blessing through the presence, power, and grace of the Holy Spirit (16:7).

The Spirit will be the "Comforter" (*parakletos*: from *kaleo*, "to call," and *para*, "beside": hence, "one called to our side"). Our Lord says He will come: the primary reference must be to Pentecost, but this in no way precludes other and subsequent visitations or manifestations.

---

1. Lyman Abbott, *An Illustrated Commentary on The Gospels: The Gospel according to St. John* (New York: A.S. Barnes & Co., 1906), 162.

Now "when he is come" (16:8), He will minister in the world (vv. 8–11) and in the church (vv. 12–15).

Ministry in the World (vv. 8–11)

First, the Spirit will minister in the world. He will convince of sin in such a way as to convict of wrongdoing. This has to be His first work (Job 36:9, 10). By it, He will: (1) impress upon hearts that God's holy, moral law has been violated (Rom. 3:19; 4:15), sin being, in the words of the Shorter Catechism, "any want of conformity unto or transgression of the law of God";[2] (2) make us feel our sad and sorry state due to both original and actual sin (Matt. 15:19; cf. Ps. 51:5; Rom. 3:19–21); and (3) alert us to our great danger (Rom. 7:7, 8), make us feel our need of Christ (Gal. 3:24), and then incite us to seek salvation through the gospel (Acts 2:37).

Observe that the sin of unbelief is particularly emphasized. This is because it is the worst of all sins (Matt. 11:24). It is also against divine mercy and the remedy (1 John 3:23). Furthermore, it binds all other sins upon us (John 3:18; 8:24).

Second, the Spirit will also persuade of "righteousness," which, unlike sin, does not pertain to sinners but to Christ (compare "sin, because *they* believe not," [v. 9] and "righteousness, because *I* go to my Father" [v. 10]). By this work He will: (1) show that Christ undertook to provide a righteousness for us (Jer. 23:6; Matt. 3:15) in the holiness of His human nature (Luke 1:35; Heb. 7:26), the perfect obedience of His life (Matt. 5:17; Phil. 2:7), and the suffering that climaxed in His death (Luke 24:26; Eph. 5:2); (2) demonstrate that this righteousness, all-sufficient, was wrought for us, in our name and place (Jer. 23:6; Rom. 5:19; 1 Cor. 1:30); and (3) make us see that this righteousness is revealed in the gospel as a gift to all believers (Rom. 1:17; 9:30), being "imputed" (or "credited") to such (Rom. 4:6, 11), so that, in God's sight, they are presented perfect and entitled to eternal life (Isa. 45:24, 25; 61:10; Rom. 5:21).

This righteousness is proved, or declared, by Christ's return to the Father: "because I go to my Father." His exaltation is designed to show that He has rendered full satisfaction to the law, leaving

---

2. Question 14 in *The Confession of Faith; the Larger and Shorter Catechisms: together with The Sum of Saving Knowledge* (Edinburgh: D. Hunter Blair and M.S. Tyndall Bruce, 1841), 403.

nothing undone (John 19:30). It makes clear, too, that what He has accomplished in His birth, life, and death, He has accomplished marvellously well (1 Tim. 3:16; Acts 2:33). There is just one further and comforting thought. As our Representative—and therefore in our name—He is able now to enter the world above and to claim for us the reward of a glorious and eternal inheritance (Ps. 15:1, 2; John 14:19; Heb. 6:19, 20).

The truth is most beautifully stated by John Bunyan when, describing his own experience, he writes: "One day, as I was passing in the field, and that too with some dashes on my conscience, fearing lest yet all was not right, suddenly this sentence fell upon my soul, 'Thy righteousness is in heaven'; and methought withal, I saw, with the eyes of my soul, Jesus Christ at God's right hand; there, I say, as my righteousness; so that wherever I was, or whatever I was adoing, God could not say of me, He wants ['lacks'] my righteousness, for that was just before him…. My righteousness was Jesus Christ himself, the same yesterday, to-day, and for ever."[3]

Third, the Spirit makes known "judgment." This is to make clear that judgment has not yet taken place, so there is still time in which to be saved (2 Peter 3:9). In view of that tremendous day, sinners must prepare by believing in the Savior (John 3:16; 5:24), for we are assured in God's Word that sin will be punished and righteousness rewarded (Matt. 25:41, 46; Rom. 8:34; Phil. 3:9).

The stated reason for this is "because the prince of this world is judged" (v. 11); in other words, because Christ has evidently triumphed, His archenemy has been brought down, and therefore all his subjects will be condemned, too (although Christ's people will share His heavenly glory). The meaning is brought out well by E. W. Hengstenberg, who writes: "It is a perilous thing to continue a subject of an already condemned prince, and to refuse submission to Him who hath condemned that prince. If the prince of this world is judged, the cry rings out, 'Save yourselves from this untoward generation,' Acts 2:40—a generation which has Satan for its lord, ch. 8:44."[4]

---

3. John Bunyan, "Grace Abounding to the Chief of Sinners," in *The Works of John Bunyan* (Glasgow: Blackie and Son, 1854), 1:35, 36.

4. E. W. Hengstenberg, *Commentary on the Gospel of St John* (Edinburgh: T & T Clark, 1865), 2:282.

Ministry in the Church (vv. 12–15)

In the church, the ministry of the Spirit will be to draw our attention to Christ, to make known His preciousness, and to evoke praise to His wonderful name. After saying that He cannot teach them more at that time, our Lord promises that the Spirit, who is "the Spirit of truth" (14:17; 1 John 4:6)—the perfect Possessor and Revealer of the knowledge of God in Christ—will graciously "guide" them (gradually and gently, Matt. 15:14; Luke 6:39; Acts 8:31) into "all truth," which must be, at least in the first place, the absolute truth that is in Christ Himself (John 1:14; 14:6; 1 John 5:20). He will not, in any way, speak independently of Christ (cf. 12:49), but He will speak to make known His mind (and the mind of His Father), and He will particularly unveil "things to come," literally, "the coming things," concerning Christ and His future kingdom (vv. 12, 13).

"He shall glorify me": that is, the Spirit's ministry in the church will be Christocentric. It will be, as R. C. H. Lenski says, "to place Jesus before the eyes and into the hearts of men, to make His Person and His work shine before them in all the excellencies of both."[5] In order to make Him most glorious to men, the Spirit will take Christ's most precious treasures—those of His Person, works, and benefits—and display them to men's souls in all their resplendent beauty and splendor. We will understand this further by considering the One possessing the glory, the One revealing the glory, and the one viewing the glory.

The One possessing the glory

"Glory," in the Hebrew, is *kabod*, derived from a root that means "weight" (Gen. 45:13; Ex. 2:37), the idea suggesting someone's solid worth. "Glory" also translates the Greek *doxa*, which originally meant "estimation" or "opinion." The basic idea with both terms is that of "excellence." This excellence may be either what is called His essential glory, the glory Christ ever had as God (Isa. 9:6; John 16:15; Rom. 9:5; Phil. 2:6), or His mediatorial glory, the glory He now has by office, as the God-man (John 3:13; Col. 1:19; 1 Tim. 2:5).

In eternity past, His essential glory was manifested within the Godhead (Prov. 8:22–26; John 1:1, 2; 17:5), when His perfections were

---

5. R. C. H. Lenski, *The Interpretation of St. John's Gospel* (Minneapolis, Minn.: Augsburg, 1961), 1092.

in evidence (John 3:35; 14:21; Rom. 15:30) and He shared thoughts, desires, and purposes with the other divine Persons (Isa. 9:6; Zech. 6:3; Col. 2:3). His mediatorial glory was also made known by His acceptance, from everlasting, of the divine will (Isa. 42:1; John 10:18; 14:31) and His undertaking to perform the essential redeeming work on behalf of elect sinners (Isa. 49:8; John 6:38, 39; Heb. 7:22). He Himself referred to "the glory which I had with thee [the Father] before the world was" (John 17:5).

At creation, when time began its course, His glory was revealed to men and women. Even in Old Testament times this was so (Mic. 5:2—"[His] goings forth have been from of old"; Gen. 17:1—"the God of glory appeared unto our father Abraham"), as He appeared to certain individuals as Mediator, teaching truth as a Prophet (Ex. 3:1–22); making typical sacrifice as Priest (Gen. 3:21; Judg. 6:19–24), and exercising universal dominion as King (Ps. 99:1–5; Prov. 8:15, 16). In New Testament times, there was a very much fuller and clearer disclosure. He appeared in His humanity (John 1:14; Heb. 9:26), and personally, in the flesh, fulfilled these same offices (Mark 1:14, 15; Eph. 5:2; Heb. 10:12, 13). How amazing the revelation! Writes the apostle John, "We beheld his glory, the glory as of the only begotten of the Father" (John 1:14).

Puritan Ralph Robinson wrote: "There must be a resplendency and shining forth of that eminence, else it cannot be glorious. Pearls in the sea are precious, but not glorious, till they be polished and sparkle out their brightness. The sun is not glorious when obscured by a cloud, but when the beams shine out. A bright shining day we call a glorious day."[6]

The Lord appeared particularly glorious in His wonderful achievements. He appeared as the last Adam, in the holiness of His nature (Luke 1:35; Heb. 7:26), and fulfilled perfect obedience (Matt. 5:18; Rom. 5:19), enduring both condemnation and execution (Isa. 50:6; Gal. 3:13). Thereby He brought deliverance from the law as a covenant, removed from sinners dreadful guilt, and obtained for them victory over death (Rom. 6:14; Col. 2:13, 14; Heb. 2:14, 15). Our Lord, anticipating His final achievement, said, "The hour is come, that the Son of man should be glorified" (John 12:23). Was He glorious then? Yes, indeed He was—most glorious!

---

6. Ralph Robinson, *Christ All and in All* (Woolwich, U.K.: T. Sharp, 1827), 384.

After being brought low, to a condition of abject humiliation, He was lifted up, through resurrection, ascension, and enthronement, to *a state of the highest and most splendid exaltation.* In His divine nature He then fully displayed infinite perfection; in His human nature, He appeared with both beauty and renown. Alluding to this, He once said to His beloved disciples, "Ought not Christ to have suffered these things, and to enter into his glory?" (Luke 24:26). The apostle later writes, "we see Jesus, who was made a little lower than the angels for the suffering of death, crowned with glory and honour" (Heb. 2:9). The ignominy removed, there was bestowed on Him resplendent majesty and surpassing praise.

Now, in heaven, elect angels and redeemed men behold "the Lord of glory" (1 Cor. 2:8). The One who was ever God became the God-man, and, as such, represents His people in the world above (Heb. 9:24); He meets their needs (Col. 1:19), defends them from evil (1 Peter 3:22), cares for them (1 Peter 5:7), and receives them in the hour of death into His kingdom (Acts 7:59). So now, as we view Him by faith, what a glorious person He appears to be—"Lord of all" and "King of saints" (Acts 10:36; Rev. 15:3)!

In the heavenly world, His glory is continually made known to the saints in light, streaming forth from His person, to those adoring spectators who know that He is "chiefest among ten thousand" (Song 5:10), unfading and unfailing in His beauty as "the same…for ever" (Heb. 13:8). There, He finds satisfaction in His own benevolent and beneficent love; indeed, He delights in this love (Isa. 53:11), as He does in the company of the Father and the Holy Spirit (2 Cor. 13:14; Rev. 1:4, 5), the cherubim, the seraphim, and all the angels (Ps. 80:1; Isa. 6:1–3, cf. John 12:37–41; Rev. 5:11–13). He is incomparable. There is no one like Him. Behold Him: there is about Him nothing unpleasant (1 Peter 2:22) but everything pleasant (Col. 1:19), and this to a transcendent degree—He is "fairer than the children of men" (Ps. 45:2).

The ultimate glorious sight of Christ is held out until last, even as the best wine is kept to the end. What a day it will be when men "shall see the Son of man coming in the clouds of heaven with power and great glory" (Matt. 24:30).

The promise reads: "Thine eyes shall see the king in his beauty: they shall behold the land that is very far off" (Isa. 33:17). Christ prayed for this, "that they may behold my glory" (John 17:24). That, of course, will be more than sight: it will be access, favor, comfort, and ultimate, everlasting delight.

All heaven will then and forever be before Him, singing His infinite and inexhaustible praise. "Worthy is the lamb that was slain to receive power, and riches, and wisdom, and strength, and honour, and glory, and blessing" (Rev. 5:12).

The One revealing the glory
The Spirit reveals the glory of the Son of God, which perhaps explains why He is several times called "the Spirit of Christ" (Rom. 8:9; Gal. 4:6; 1 Peter 1:11). Evidently He sustains a special relationship with the Lord Jesus Christ, but H. C. G. Moule is undoubtedly correct when he writes, "the emphasis of the words here (is) on the *work* of the Holy Ghost as *the Revealer of Christ* to the soul."[7]

Should we ask why it is the Spirit who performs this work? Several answers may be given: the Spirit is one with Him in essential union (2 Cor. 12:13; 1 John 5:7); He dwelt in Christ, in fullness and without measure (John 3:34); He is granted to us on account of Christ's redeeming work (Gal. 3:13, 14); He was sent by Christ to perform His special ministry (John 15:26); He is responsible for applying to men the benefits of Christ (Eph. 1:17); He manifests Christ's presence in the soul (John 14:16–18); and He is the great "promise" of Christ's gospel (Gal. 3:14).

It is important to observe that the Spirit's work is not, in any way, to enhance the Lord's glory, but simply to throw light upon it, bringing it wonderfully into view. In this respect, it is akin to what happens in the natural world. The scenery in some given place may be very beautiful, and the sun, when it comes out, does not intrinsically change or improve it; yet its light does make a difference, transfiguring it by bringing out more fully its delightful loveliness. As the psalmist says, "With thee is the fountain of life: in thy light shall we see light" (Ps. 36:9).

The Spirit is moved to exercise His ministry. What exactly motivates and encourages Him in this? Since Scripture refers to "the love of the Spirit" (Rom. 15:30), no doubt His own eternal love for the Son is a major factor, and "to have an opportunity of letting His love go

---

7. H. C. G. Moule, *The Epistle of Paul the Apostle to the Romans* (Cambridge: Cambridge University Press, 1892), 144.

forth towards Him, in an exuberance of joy and affection is only what we might expect. He glorifies Christ."[8] In particular, it is evident that the Spirit is lovingly concerned to redress the wrong done to the Son in the time of His humiliation, when, "despised and rejected of men" (Isa. 53:3), He was held up to dreadful indignity and shame (Matt. 26:67; Gal. 3:13; Heb. 12:2). The Spirit has ever been the One to vindicate the Lord Jesus Christ (see 1 Tim. 3:16—"justified in the Spirit").

Then there are His own covenant obligations. In eternity past, when the covenant was agreed by the eternal Three, the Father and the Son had major parts to play (Zech. 6:13). The Father's part chiefly concerned the promise; the Son's, the condition; but the Spirit was also involved, consenting to apply covenant blessing to the elect of God. In order to fulfil this, His role, the Spirit agreed to become "the spirit of faith" (2 Cor. 4:13), granting to sinners believing and enriching sights of Christ (John 16:14, 15; Eph. 1:17).

The Spirit is Himself the great gospel promise: hence, He is called "the promise of my Father" (Luke 24:49), and this "promise" is to "as many as the Lord our God shall call" (Acts 2:39). As *the* blessing to elect believers, the Spirit is concerned to lead them into truth, sanctify them unto holiness, and provide precious comfort for them. But how shall He perform this last ministry? He will perform it by enabling them to comprehend the Lord's incomprehensible glory (cf. Matt. 16:21–17:8; Rev. 1:9–16).

Proceeding further now, we should observe that there is *objective* revelation in the gospel, but this ministry of the Spirit concerns subjective revelation (or illumination), which means for us a spiritual experience and appreciation. Alluding to what happened to Him in the past, Paul wrote, "it pleased God…to reveal his Son in me." As John Eadie explains, Paul meant "in my soul, in my inner self" (Gal. 1:15, 16).[9] According to 1 Corinthians 2:10–12, the blessed Holy Spirit alone can do this: "God hath revealed them [divine things] unto us by his Spirit." How? Well, He so blesses the gospel that Christ is vividly presented to our souls, and then He so blesses our souls that they are enlightened or illuminated (Acts 26:18; 1 John 5:20).

---

8. James Elder Cumming, *"Through the Eternal Spirit": a Bible Study on the Holy Ghost* (Stirling, U.K.: Drummond's Tract Depot; London: S.W. Partridge, n.d.), 191.

9. John Eadie, *Commentary on the Epistle of Paul to the Galatians* (Edinburgh: T. & T. Clark, 1884), 43.

Deserving emphasis is the point that this ministry of the Spirit is not separate from ordinary means but attends those means, particularly the preaching of the Word and the administration of the sacraments. The apostle's "speech" and "preaching" is said to have been "in demonstration of the Spirit and of power," which appears to mean that the Spirit, by His powerful working, demonstrated to the hearers the truth of Jesus Christ in the gospel (1 Cor. 2:4; cf. 2 Cor. 3:6; 1 Thess. 1:5). The same could be said of those visible sermons, the sacraments (Rom. 6:4; 1 Cor. 11:26).

The means of grace are linked to the grace of means, and the means are blessed in such a way that Christ is made very real to us and our sight of Him is vivid indeed. "Therefore my people shall know my name: therefore they shall know in that day that I am he that doth speak: behold, it is I" (Isa. 52:6).

At this time, an associated ministry is the quickening and reviving of our graces, such as faith, hope, and love. To this reference is made in the Song of Solomon: "Awake, O north wind; come, thou south; blow upon my garden that the spices thereof may flow out" (4:16). Among these spices, faith will always be conspicuous, faith through which we seek the Lord and draw near to Him (Zech. 12:10; John 6:44, 45).

Thus it is that we are brought to Christ and then afforded a new vision of Him, clearer and more vivid than anything we have seen before. We become somewhat like our "father Abraham," who, the Lord said, "rejoiced to see my day: and he saw it, and was glad" (John 8:56), and a little like the disciples in the upper room, of whom it is written, "Then were the disciples glad when they saw the Lord" (John 20:20).

Thereafter, the more we have of the Spirit, the more wonderful the Lord will be to us, both in our perception of Him and our experience of Him. No wonder the apostle exhorts the early Christians to "be filled with the Spirit" (Eph. 5:18). In one of His sermons, Charles Spurgeon says, "The Spirit of God will…fill your heart with Christ," and "the more you have of that Spirit, the more intense will be your love of the Saviour, until at last you will be able to say, 'Jesus, the very thought of thee/With sweetness fills my breast.'"[10] Little wonder,

---

10. Charles Spurgeon, *The Metropolitan Tabernacle Pulpit* (Pasadena, Texas: Pilgrim Publications, 1978), 35:509.

then, that in the Ephesians passage, the apostle proceeds with the words "making melody in your heart to the Lord" (v. 19).

Before concluding this point, let us return for a moment to the words of our text: "He shall glorify me: for he shall receive of mine, and shall shew it unto you" (John 16:14). Among the glories of Christ shown to us, are: the beauty of His person (Ps. 45:1, 2), the uniqueness of His office (1 Tim. 2:5), the condescension of His Spirit (Matt. 11:29), the wonder of His love (Eph. 3:17–19), the efficacy of His atonement (Rom. 5:11), the power of His resurrection (Phil. 3:10), the splendor of His enthronement (Mark 16:19), the prevalence of His intercession (Heb. 7:25), the fullness of His bounty (John 1:16), and the consolation of His promise (John 14:3). There is more, so much more. The Spirit shows us our right to, and our interest in, all these things, and, when He does, Christ is more precious to us than a thousand worlds. David says: "Whom have I in heaven but thee? And there is none upon earth that I desire beside thee" (Ps. 73:25). And Paul says, "Christ is all, and in all" (Col. 3:11). That is the truth for Spirit-blessed believers: Christ is everything in everyone.

The one viewing the glory
How do believers view Christ's glory? They look through the eye of faith, which faith is called "the substance of things hoped for," because it brings Christ near to our souls, and "the evidence of things not seen," because by it Christ, although unseen, is shown to be a reality (Heb. 11:1). Most important to grasp is the fact that faith does not communicate anything to its object: it is simply the medium that renders Him conspicuous. It merely receives and believes the divine revelation (John 1:12; Col. 2:6).

Although we are able, to some extent, to see something of Christ in the outward works of creation and providence (Ps. 19:1; Rom. 1:20; Ps. 90:16) and in the inward works of regeneration and sanctification (Acts 8:21; Gal. 4:19), it is through the ordained means, and chiefly the Scriptures, that we see the Lord in all His saving power and grace. Says the apostle, "We all with open face, beholding as in a glass ['he compareth the gospel to a glass'[11]] the glory of the Lord, are changed into the same image, from glory to glory, even as by the

---

11. Westminster Divines, *The Second Volume of the Annotations upon all the Books of the Old and New Testament* (London: Evan Tyler, 1657), on 2 Corinthians 3:18.

Spirit of the Lord" (2 Cor. 3:18). Prior to the writing of those words, the Lord Himself said to the Jews, "Search the Scriptures...they are they which testify of me" (John 5:39). On this subject, Ralph Erskine, minister in the Scottish Secession Church, makes the following comment: "All the believing views of Christ and sights of him here-away are mediate, through the intervention of means and ordinances; not immediate, as they shall be above.... The time comes, when the glasses shall be broken, and believers shall see him face to face, and see him as he is."[12]

This is, for the believer, vital religion: a sight of Christ, the Lord of glory, concealed from unanointed, darkened eyes, but discovered to spiritual eyes, which convey to our souls not only wonder but also love and praise. Simeon came "by the Spirit" into the temple, and it had been revealed to him that he would not die before he had "seen the Lord's Christ"; and when he eventually saw Him—with more than natural sight—he "blessed God," and describing what he saw, he said, "A light to lighten the Gentiles, and the glory of thy people Israel" (Luke 2:25–32). O what a sight it must have been to behold the One who is "*the* consolation!" Ralph Robinson speaks eloquently of Christ when he says: "All a Christian's glory may be summed up in this short sentence, *Christ is mine*. Take away Christ and you have stript a Christian of all his glory, Christ is all in all (Col 3:11)." Further on he says, "Let men revile, defame, and study to put all the ignominy that they can upon a Christian, while Christ is his glory, they can never take away his Crown."[13]

There are times when we can have amazingly clear views of Christ. The day of conversion is one such time, when we "behold the Lamb of God" (John 1:29). The day of prayer is another, when we pray, as Moses did, "I beseech thee, shew me thy glory," and the answer comes as it came to him, "the LORD passed by before him" (Ex. 33:18, 19; 34:6). Then there may be the day that Jacob experienced when he left his home to begin an exile of twenty years; on the way to Haran, he was given a dream in which he saw a beautiful emblem of the Mediator, "a ladder set up on the earth, and the top of it reached to heaven" (Gen. 28:12). The day of recovery may be

---

12. Ralph Erskine, *The Sermons and other Practical Works of the Reverend and Learned Ralph Erskine M.A.* (London: R. Baynes, 1821), 4:348.
13. Robinson, *Christ All in All*, 385, 389.

another such day, for then "thou shalt lift up thy face without spot; yea, thou shalt be stedfast, and shalt not fear" (Job 11:15). It may even be the day of death, because God may give us to say with Stephen the martyr, "Behold I see the heavens opened, and the Son of man standing on the right hand of God" (Acts 7:55).

Whenever it is, what a sight we may have of Christ! It is such a sight as throws this world into darkness, thereby making it appear most unattractive and undesirable. Of Moses it is written that "he endured, as seeing him who is invisible," and further it is said he was one "esteeming the reproach of Christ greater riches than the treasures in Egypt" (Heb. 11:24–27). But this sight, enabling us to say "we beheld his glory" (John 1:14; cf. 2 Cor. 3:18), being a preview of what one day will be seen—"that they may behold my glory" (John 17:24)—greatly brightens our prospects and draws our hearts to that world that is presently beyond us. The Lord bids us to "set [our] affection on things above, not on things on the earth" (Col. 3:2), and true Christians respond, confessing, "Here have we no continuing city, but we seek one to come" (Heb. 13:14; cf. 11:8–10).

Thus, the sight has a wonderfully sanctifying effect upon us and, in addition to what has been said, strongly moves us to the discovery of peace. When, after the resurrection, the Lord Jesus appeared to His disciples in the flesh, He spoke to their hearts, saying, "Peace be unto you" (John 20:19). Truly, "this man shall be the peace" (Mic. 5:5). There is nothing in this world more comforting than a spiritual view of Him whom our souls love. To see Him spiritually as the God-man and our Mediator, Redeemer, Husband, Brother, and Friend, what peace the sight affords! What relief, confidence, rest, satisfaction, and security! But recall what is written immediately afterward: "Then were the disciples glad when they saw the Lord" (John 20:20). Such a sight as we are considering will surely lead us to "delight" in the Lord (Ps. 37:4), and the hearts that delight in Him find their happiness in the "secret" of communion (Ps. 25:14), in discovering, knowing, loving, enjoying, and praising His wonderful name.

Why, it may even be a sight to break our hearts. How can that be possible? Well, we may see Him as the One we have neglected and deeply grieved. That sight affects us so much, moving us to sigh after Him and to cry before Him. It makes our eyes to overflow with tears; it makes our souls to fall at His feet in godly sorrow and true penitence: "And the Lord turned, and looked upon Peter.... And Peter went out and wept bitterly" (Luke 22:61, 62).

The sight also, of course, can be restoring: "They looked unto him, and were lightened: and their faces were not ashamed.... The Lord is nigh unto them that are of a broken heart; and saveth such as be of a contrite spirit" (Ps. 34:5, 18).

Finally, this sight can bring greater devotion and holiness. In the words of John Swanston, an eighteenth-century secession minister in Kinrose, Scotland: "A sight of the Lord produces holiness and conformity to the object.... According to the measure of the manifestation of Christ's glory to the soul, so is the degree of likeness to him: perfect views of his glory produce perfect likeness; 1 John 3:2. *'When he shall appear, we shall be like him; for we shall see him as he is.'*"[14]

As we draw near to the ends of our lives with the Savior often in our view, the world may well become to us a sadder place and heaven a happier place by far. But whether here or there, He is ever before us: "Whom have I in heaven but thee? And there is none upon earth that I desire beside thee" (Ps. 73:25). Who can doubt that, when "the silver cord be loosed," we shall see the Lord as we have never ever seen Him before; we shall see Him in all His beauty and glory — "Thine eyes shall see the king in his beauty," and as the Lord prayed, "Father, I will...that they may behold my glory" (Isa. 33:17; John 17:24). We shall then see Him, not as our visions in this life, through faith, and with mind and heart; but while still seeing spiritually — but no longer partially, obscurely, and transiently — we shall also see with our eyes, beholding the wonderful and heavenly form of our beloved Redeemer (Job 19:26, 27; 1 John 3:2; Rev. 22:4).

John Owen, the Puritan, once wrote, "In the vision which we shall have *above*, the whole glory of Christ will be at *once* and *always* represented to us; and we shall be enabled in one act of the light of glory to comprehend it."[15] After this he wrote: "In the resurrection of the body, upon its full redemption, it shall be so purified, sanctified, glorified, as to give no obstruction unto the soul in its operations, but be a blessed organ of its highest and most spiritual actings. The body

---

14. John Swanston, *Sermons on Several Important Subjects* (Glasgow: William Smith, 1773), 268.

15. John Owen, "Meditations and Discourses on the Glory of Christ," in *The Works of John Owen* (repr., Banner of Truth, 1965), 1:410.

shall never be a trouble, a burden unto the soul, but *an assistant* in its operations, and participant of its blessedness. Our eyes were made to see our Redeemer, and our other senses to receive impressions from him, according unto their capacity."[16]

Just before Owen died, he was visited by Thomas Payne, a minister from Saffron Waldon, in Essex, who had been entrusted with the publication of *Meditations on the Glory of Christ*. "O! brother Payne!" Owen exclaimed, "the long wished for day has come at last, in which I shall see that glory in another manner than I have ever done, or was capable of doing in this world."[17]

May we be granted such grace as to see more and more of Him on earth; and then such glory, as to see Him to our everlasting happiness in the kingdom of heaven. At the last, rejoice: there is for us the beatific vision!

---

16. Owen, "Meditations," 1:412.

17. William Orme, *The Memoirs of the Life, Writings, and Religious Connexions, of John Owen, D.D.* (London: T. Hamilton, 1820), 448.

CHAPTER 5

Precursors to Pentecost

Gerald Bilkes

On a spring Lord's Day morning in Jerusalem some two thousand years ago, while 120 believers were together in Jerusalem in or near the temple complex, God the Holy Spirit came down and "filled all the house where they were sitting" (Acts 2:2).[1] These believers had been persevering in prayer since their Savior had ascended into heaven. He had instructed them to wait until power came upon them from on high. Their praying together had bound them together; we read that they were "with one accord" (Acts 2:1). Matthew Henry writes: "They had prayed more together of late than usual (chp. 1:14), and this made them love one another better. By his grace he thus prepared them for the gift of the Holy Ghost…for, where *brethren dwell together in unity,* there it is that *the Lord commands his blessing.*"[2]

The blessing that God commanded took place on the occasion of the Feast of Pentecost, and is now known as Pentecost.[3] George Smeaton describes Pentecost this way: "The greatest event in all history,

1. I gratefully acknowledge Michael Borg's able assistance in bringing this chapter into its current form.

2. Matthew Henry, *Matthew Henry's Commentary on the Whole Bible Complete and Unabridged in One Volume* (Peabody, Mass.: Hendrickson, 1991), 2066.

3. Pentecost was the second of the three harvest feasts. It was held seven weeks after Passover (the first of the harvest feasts) and was followed some months later by the Feast of Tabernacles (the final harvest feast). As part of the feast being celebrated on the day of Pentecost, two loaves made with firstfruits from the wheat harvest were baked and offered to the Lord by waving them before Him (Lev. 23:17). Many have observed that this ceremony was fulfilled in a glorious way on the day of Pentecost, as three thousand souls were harvested, and were—as it were—waved before the Lord as the firstfruits of the early church through the gift of the Spirit, who Himself is called the firstfruits (2 Cor. 1:22; Eph. 1:13–14) of the redemption of God. See Patrick Fairbairn, *Typology of Scripture* (Grand Rapids: Kregel Publications, 1989), 36.

next to the incarnation and atonement, was the mission of the Comforter; for it will continue, while the world lasts, to diffuse among men the stream of the divine life."[4] Luke highlights this truth by the place he gives to the outpouring of the Spirit. He records the event practically at the head of his second book (Acts 2), just as he describes the coming of the Son of God at the head of his first book (Luke 2).

Luke begins his account of the Spirit's coming by writing of the unusual signs that accompanied it. He notes the elements of wind and fire: "There came a sound from heaven as of a rushing mighty wind, and it filled all the house where they were sitting. And there appeared unto them cloven tongues like as of fire, and it sat upon each of them" (Acts 2:2–3).

Miraculously, representatives from the surrounding nations, each in his own language, heard the same message: the wonderful works of God (Acts 2:11).[5] How different this event was from that of the tower of Babel (Gen. 11:1–9), a few hundred miles to the east from this very spot. There, in the Valley of Shinar in Mesopotamia, people had vainly attempted to avoid being "scattered abroad" (Gen. 11:4) by building something they hoped would reach to heaven. Then a curse had come down—the curse of confusion and separation. Now, on the occasion of Pentecost, the blessing of illumination and salvation descended! By the end of this day, a few thousand believers—diverse as they were—enjoyed fellowship together (Acts 2:42). Miraculously, this was not the kind of fellowship that would be bound to one geographical place. The blessing that began in Jerusalem would be conveyed and dispersed throughout the world, even unto the uttermost parts of the earth. It would reach into all the corners of the world affected by the curse, for such would be the magnitude of its power. God was fulfilling His promise to Abraham: "And in thee shall all the families of the earth be blessed" (Gen. 12:3).

Near the end of the same chapter, Luke goes on to describe the *effects* of the Spirit's coming: conversion, baptism, fellowship, fear,

---

4. George Smeaton, *The Doctrine of the Holy Spirit*, 4th ed. (Edinburgh: Banner of Truth, 1958), 48.

5. For a detailed look at the connections between Babel and Pentecost, see G. K. Beale, "The Descent of the Eschatological Temple in the Form of the Spirit at Pentecost: Part 1: The Clearest Evidence," *Tyndale Bulletin* 56 (2005): 76–83.

and praise (Acts 2:37–47). People who had arrived in the morning as strangers to grace left that evening having come through the waters of baptism. God parted for them the seas of impossibility in their lives that kept them bound to sin and death (cf. Rom. 8:1–4), and by His grace, symbolized in baptism, led them into the realm of grace, liberty, peace, and life.

Between the signs of the Spirit's coming and the effects of His coming, Luke depicts the disciples being filled like empty vessels. He uses the passive voice: "they were filled" (Acts 2:4). Standing behind this filling is the active work of Jesus Christ. Peter quotes Joel 2:28: "I will pour out of my Spirit" (2:17), showing that through Christ, God is continuing His work among His disciples. The coming of the Spirit is Christ's work of lavishly filling the emptiness of the disciples who are awaiting this coming promise. This is how the Spirit has seen fit to record the remarkable event of His own coming to the church fifty days after Christ's resurrection.

Clearly, Pentecost was not a minor event—simply one of many revivals in history. After all, the fullness of time had come and Christ had appeared "in the end of the world," "once for all" (Heb. 9:26), to atone for sin. Would a common occurrence accompany the giving of the Holy Spirit? Any expectation among the believers of a unique and superlative event did not go unrewarded; even reverberations were notable.[6]

If we should interpret later outpourings as reverberations, how should we view antecedent outpourings and other events that bear some relationship to Pentecost across the landscape of redemptive history?[7] Were there any events in Israelite history which pointed the way to an understanding of Pentecost that helped cultivate an expectation and longing for the outpouring of the Spirit? Some believe

---

6. According to the book of Acts, Pentecost had subsequent reverberations. Besides this notable outpouring of the Spirit after Christ's death, there were subsequent outpourings (2:1–4; 8:14–17; 10:44–46; 19:6). These events related to the fulfillment of Christ's promise that the gospel would be preached throughout Jerusalem, Samaria, and to the uttermost parts of the earth (1:8). Each time the gospel crossed one of these boundaries, the Spirit showed Himself in a way that echoed the first and primary event in Jerusalem, fifty days after the resurrection.

7. Pentecost was clearly announced ahead of time. God does nothing without letting His prophets in on the secret (Amos 3:8). And so God's pouring out of His Spirit was in accordance with the promises of the OT (see Joel 2:28, 29; Zech. 12:10a; Ezek. 36:25).

that it takes away from the uniqueness of Pentecost to say that any prior event paralleled the outpouring of the Spirit.[8] Yet just as the Holy Spirit, through the inspired authors, gave us small glimpses into the extraordinary events of Jesus' life, death, and resurrection before these events occurred, so, too, the Holy Spirit gave us small foretastes of Christ pouring out His Spirit on the day of Pentecost.

In Reformed Bible scholarship, there is considerable agreement that the coming of Christ in the New Testament was prefigured in the Old Testament in types and shadows.[9] Reformed hermeneutics recognizes that Scripture often prepares and anticipates certain redemptive-historical events through events that mirror or foreshadow later events.[10] The same holds true for the event of Pentecost.[11] Pentecost may have been the Spirit's official entrance

---

8. See Brian Edwards, *Can We Pray for Revival?* (Darlington, U.K.: Evangelical Press, 2001), 33–36.

9. The past few decades have seen a proliferation of books arguing for and elaborating on a biblical perspective of typology. See Michael Lawrence, *Biblical Theology in the Life of the Church* (Wheaton, Ill.: Crossway Books, 2010), 69–84; Gregory K. Beale and D. A. Carson, *Commentary on the New Testament Use of the Old Testament* (Grand Rapids: Baker Academic, 2007), xxii–xxviii; Graeme Goldsworthy, *Gospel-Centered Hermeneutics* (Downers Grove, Ill.: InterVarsity Press, 2006), 234–57; Edmund P. Clowney, *Preaching Christ in All of Scripture* (Wheaton, Ill.: Crossway Books, 2003), 11–44; Sidney Greidanus, *Preaching Christ From the Old Testament: A Contemporary Hermeneutical Method* (Grand Rapids: Eerdmans, 1999); G. K. Beale, ed., *The Right Doctrine from the Wrong Texts? Essays on the Use of the Old Testament in the New* (Grand Rapids: Baker Academic, 1994), 313–74; Jonathan Edwards, *The Works of Jonathan Edwards: Typological Writings,* vol. 11, ed. Harry S. Stout (New Haven, Conn.: Yale University Press, 1993); Vern S. Poythress, *The Shadow of Christ in the Law of Moses* (Phillipsburg, N.J.: P&R Publishing, 1991); Fairbairn, *Typology of Scripture;* Edmund P. Clowney, *The Unfolding Mystery: Discovering Christ in the Old Testament* (Colorado Springs, Colo.: NavPress, 1988); Edward Burgess, *Christ, the Crown of the Torah/Christ in the First Five Books of the Bible* (Grand Rapids: Zondervan, 1986); Leonhard Goppelt, *Typos: The Typological Interpretation of the Old Testament in the New,* trans. Donald H. Madvig (Grand Rapids: Eerdmans, 1982); Ada R. Habershon, *The Study of Types* (Grand Rapids: Kregel, 1967); Geerhardus Vos, *The Teaching of the Epistle to the Hebrews* (Phillipsburg, N.J.: P&R Publishing, 1956), 55–87.

10. There were events that preceded and pointed toward each of these special redemptive happenings. Isaac's miraculous birth anticipated Christ's miraculous birth. The near-sacrifice of Isaac on Mount Moriah foreshadowed the crucifixion of Christ, which would take place in a nearby spot two thousand years later. The return of the nation of Israel as from the grave of the exile anticipated the resurrection of Christ.

11. Jonathan Edwards writes, "Though there be a more constant influence of God's Spirit always in some degree attending his ordinances; yet the way in which

into the world in the economy of redemption. It may have been, as Thomas Goodwin says, "his coming in state, in a solemn and visible manner, accompanied with visible effects as well as Christ had, and whereof all the Jews should be, and were witnesses."[12] However, throughout the Old Testament, there were visits of the Spirit in a less-visible manner that pointed ahead to His glorious coming at Pentecost, together helping shape the expectation of Pentecost and helping explain Pentecost when it took place. One might say that the Lord, for our sakes, drew a pencil sketch of Pentecost in events beforehand, before painting the final version—the event itself—on the canvas of world history.[13] However, none of this was for its own sake, but rather that by it, the church would know and have something of the unending riches in God for the sake of Christ through the Spirit (see Eph. 1:13–14).

A Precursor with Moses

The book of Exodus describes a remarkable time period in world history, when God showed His saving power in redeeming a people from bondage to serve Him and to enter a promised land. It should not surprise us that the Spirit saw fit to make an entrance into these events. Indeed, throughout the Scripture narratives about Moses, there are many symbols that point to the Spirit of God. They are particularly the emblems of fire and wind—the same emblems that were present on the day of Pentecost.

Notice first that when God called Moses, He did so from the burning bush, where tongues of fire mysteriously appeared without consuming the bush (Exodus 3). This burning bush represented the Lord's presence with His people, which was bestowed through the Spirit. Likewise, He led His people through the Red Sea by the breath of His mouth, which parted the waters before them. This must have been not unlike the rushing mighty wind on the day of Pentecost

---

the greatest things have been done towards carrying on this work, always has been by remarkable effusions of the Spirit at special seasons of mercy." *A History of the Work of Redemption* (Edinburgh: Banner of Truth Trust, 2003), 7.

12. Thomas Goodwin, *The Work of the Holy Ghost in Our Salvation*, in *Works of Thomas Goodwin* (Grand Rapids: Reformation Heritage Books, 2006), 6:8.

13. Other incidents could be considered as well, such as the conversion of the Ninevites under Jonah, the revival that occurred under King Hezekiah, the awakening under Ezra, etc.

(Ex. 14:21). Also, on their journey through the wilderness, God led his people with a pillar of fire and cloud (Ex. 13:21), much like believers "are led by the Spirit of God" (Rom. 8:14). It is no wonder that, in Nehemiah 9, Israel's journey is spoken of this way: "Thou gavest also thy good Spirit to instruct them" (v. 20).

We should also keep in mind that the Feast of Weeks celebrated by the Israelites, in addition to being a harvest festival, was also a remembrance of the giving of the law at Sinai. In fact, some believe that God's giving of that law to Moses happened precisely fifty days after the Passover, in order to coincide with the day of Pentecost as it would happen thousands of years later. Matthew Henry wrote: "This feast…was kept in remembrance of the giving of the law upon Mount Sinai. Fitly, therefore, is the Holy Ghost given at that feast, in fire and in tongues, for the promulgation of the evangelical law, not as that to one nation, but to every creature."[14]

Clearly, there were many differences between what happened at Sinai and what happened on the day of Pentecost. However, at both times, God spoke to His people with power, binding them to Himself in service. At Sinai, He engaged them to be a consecrated people, wholly His, a kingdom of priests, a holy nation. Similarly, the early church was bound to the Lord in one Spirit at Pentecost, through the preaching of the message of redemption through Christ crucified and risen.

Psalm 68, which recalls and celebrates the Exodus, gives us an interesting link between Sinai and the Spirit.[15] In verses 9–11, the

---

14. Matthew Henry, *Commentary*, 2066. See also, James C. VanderKam, "Covenant and Pentecost," *Calvin Theological Journal* 37 (2002): 239–54 (esp. 252–53).

15. There is considerable evidence that Acts 2:32–33 alludes to Psalm 68. This view was first introduced by F. H. Chase (1902), who argued "that the connection between Christ's ascent to heaven and his exaltation to the right hand of God mentioned in the following verse (Acts 2:34) was best explained if the tradition behind 2:33 originally contained a citation of Ps. 68:19, which had become virtually unrecognizable in the existing redaction." Chase suggested Psalm 68:19 as the source of the quotation in the underlying tradition not only because of the sequence of thought, but on the basis of the actual language of Acts 2:33–34, which used similar Greek words (W. Hall Harris III, *The Descent of Christ: Ephesians 4:7–11 & Traditional Hebrew Imagery* [Leiden: Brill, 1996], 161). While this thesis has been developed, it has also been challenged (see D. L. Bock, *Proclamation from Prophecy and Pattern: Lucan Old Testament Christology* [Sheffield, Eng.: Sheffield Academic Press, 1987]). On the whole, Harris agrees "that an allusion to Ps. 68:19 was present in the underlying tradition used by Luke in Acts 2" (Harris, *Descent of Christ*, 169). He argues throughout his

psalmist recalls the following: "Thou, O God, didst send a plentiful rain, whereby thou didst confirm thine inheritance, when it was weary. Thy congregation hath dwelt therein: thou, O God, hast prepared of thy goodness for the poor. The Lord gave the word: great was the company of those that published it" (vv. 9–11).[16] Jonathan Edwards and others believed that this plentiful rain referred to the Spirit being effused at Mount Sinai.[17]

---

book, *The Descent of Christ: Ephesians 4:7–11 and Traditional Hebrew Imagery*, that Paul's quotation of Psalm 68 is in fact referring to the Sinai event. Harris focuses on this passage: "Wherefore he saith, When he ascended up on high, he led captivity captive, and gave gifts unto men. (Now that he ascended, what is it but that he also descended first into the lower parts of the earth?)" (Eph. 4:8–9). He argues that commonly this verse (a citation of Psalm 68) has been seen as though the descent happened prior to the ascent. He argues (as does A. T. Lincoln) that the descent actually happened subsequent to the ascent, and this descent is nothing other than Pentecost. Thus, Paul's citation from Psalm 68 shows that this psalm is closely linked with Pentecost.

16. The largest exegetical problem in Ephesians 4 is Paul's usage of "gave gifts to men," whereas the Hebrew seems to read, "received gifts from men." Harris argues: "The author of Ephesians was aware of the targumic interpretation of Ps 68:19...and adapted it for his own purposes. Use of such a tradition by the author of Ephesians is particularly significant for the interpretation of the descent mentioned in Eph 4:9–10. *Tg.* Psalms interpreted Ps 68:19 as a reference to Moses, who first ascended Mt. Sinai and 'captured' the words of Torah, which he then brought down and gave as gifts to 'the sons of men.' Since Moses' descent from Sinai to distribute to men the 'gifts' he had obtained there necessarily followed his ascent, use of this tradition by the author of Ephesians would explain why he found it necessary to deduce from the text of Ps 68:19 (as quoted in Eph 4:8) a descent not explicitly mentioned in the Psalm, followed by the distribution of the gifts mentioned in Eph 4:11–16" (Harris, *Descent of Christ*, 143). Harris gives other evidence from intertestamental times that Psalm 68 may well have been connected with the feast of Pentecost (Harris, *Descent of Christ*, 159ff.).

17. George B. Davis summarizes *how* we can see a Sinai and Pentecost connection in his article "Acts 2 and the Old Testament: The Pentecost Event in Light of Sinai, Babel, and the Table of Nations," *Criswell Theological Review* 7, no. 1 (2009), 29–48. The Sinai/Pentecost interpretation has been maintained by people such as Cyprian, Jerome, Augustine, Leo, Bede, Archbishop of Canterbury Tillotson, Jonathan Edwards, Henry, Clarke, Bengel, and G. K. Beale. Likewise, Edwards says: "Thus the two great feasts of the Jews that followed the Passover, represent the two great seasons consequent on the death of Christ, which was at the passover of the communication of the benefits of Christ's redemption to his church on earth; one that which was in primitive ages of the Christian church, which began in the day of Pentecost, on which the Holy Ghost was not only given in the ordinary sanctifying, saving influences, but also given in extraordinary gifts of inspiration for the revealing the mind and will of God, and establishing the standing rule of the faith, worship, and manners of the Christian church, which answered to the giving of the law at mount Sinai, which was on the feast of Pentecost: the other is that which shall follow the destruction of antichrist, which answers to the setting up the tabernacle

So, we see that there is an abundance of Holy Spirit symbolism during the time of Moses. However, none of the Scripture narratives of events we have mentioned so far specifically mention the Holy Spirit. Let us look now at a narrative in which the Spirit is specifically highlighted.

Numbers 11:24–30 directly relates the work of the Holy Spirit among God's people in the time of Moses. It is important to note the context of this precursor to Pentecost. Israel is complaining about the manna, instead desiring flesh to eat. The people directed their anger and bitterness against Moses, who in turn complained to the Lord that the people were too heavy for him, and asked to die (11:14–15). Curiously, the Lord did two things in response to this situation. He sent a wind to bring quail to the people—a remarkable judgment upon them for kindling His wrath by their dreadful desires. But He also took of the Spirit that rested upon Moses and gave it also to seventy elders: "the LORD came down in a cloud, and spake unto him [Moses], and took of the spirit that was upon him, and gave it unto the seventy elders" (v. 25).

It is worth underlining that the coming of the Spirit took place in the context of the Israelites rejecting God's provision and despising God's mediator. It was also a context of judgment upon the unbelief of the people. Precisely in the midst of these circumstances of sin, unbelief, and death, the Lord deemed fit to send a manifestation of Pentecost, not unlike it would be many centuries later when "Pentecost was fully come" (Acts 2:1). Then the people had rejected not just the manna that God had provided, but even the mediator whom God had sent. His judgments would come as a result of this, but before they did, God would pour out His Spirit and show his power and grace in a miraculous way.[18]

The consequence of God the Spirit coming in Numbers 11 is that the elders prophesied. It seems that most of the elders (sixty-eight of them) prophesied in the tabernacle sanctuary, but two of them

---

in the wilderness, and the gifts, sacrificings, and rejoicings that were on that occasion, which was on the same day of the year that the feast of tabernacles was" (*Works of Jonathan Edwards*, 2:776).

18. Based on passages such as Deuteronomy 28:49, Isaiah 28:9ff., and Jeremiah 5:15, O. Palmer Robertson rightly sees the giving of the Spirit at Pentecost (especially the gift of tongues) through the lens of both blessing and curse. See O. Palmer Robertson, *Final Word* (Edinburgh: Banner of Truth, 1993), 43ff.

remained among the people, out in the camp, prophesying there: "There remained two of the men in the camp, the name of the one was Eldad, and the name of the other Medad: and the spirit rested upon them; and they were of them that were written, but went not out unto the tabernacle: and they prophesied in the camp" (Num. 11:26). When Joshua heard about this, he urged Moses to forbid these men from prophesying in the midst of the camp. However, Moses' wise reply shows the desire of his heart for an outpouring of the Spirit: "Enviest thou for my sake? would God that all the LORD's people were prophets, and that the LORD would put his spirit upon them!" (v. 29). So, Moses and the elders of Israel went out into the camp as well (v. 30). You could say that the heart of the Old Testament mediator, Moses, was longing for a day when the Spirit would be poured out upon all the people. How fitting that the Mediator of the New Testament, Christ Jesus, would secure and fulfill this desire.

It is a mark of a true knowledge of and love for the Spirit of Pentecost when the desire that Moses expresses here burns in our own hearts, and we long to see Christ glorified and honored through His Spirit's presence in the church today. But the opposite is true as well; when we lack the longing for the Spirit's presence in His church, it is evidence that we ourselves are not filled with that Spirit. How shortsighted we often are about the work of the Lord! We imagine that the Lord is limited to how we think things should go. Moses prays here for the day when "they shall teach no more every man his neighbour, and every man his brother, saying, Know the LORD: for they shall all know me, from the least of them unto the greatest of them" (Jer. 31:34).

The parallels between the precursor and the real event are remarkable. Just as the seventy elders received the Spirit from Moses, the Old Testament mediator, so the disciples received the Spirit from the New Testament Mediator—Christ. As Moses and the elders stood before the tabernacle of God, God came down in a cloud and gave of the Spirit that rested upon Moses to the seventy elders. So, too, as Christ was lifted up and brought forth through the heavenly tabernacle, He gave gifts to men, namely, His own Spirit. Having secured forever a better covenant than the covenant of Moses, Christ lavishly poured His Spirit down upon all flesh.

Just as the seventy elders received the Spirit after Israel rejected the manna and murmured against Moses, so the disciples received the Spirit after the world and the church both had crucified Christ. In both cases, the abundant giving of the Spirit was marked first by a rejection of God and His Word. In both cases, the irony of this gracious gift is highlighted all the more in the people's rejection of the Lord and His Anointed. In both cases, mouths were stopped at this wonderful act of mercy. The Spirit worked in and through a rebellious people, effectually working sanctification in their hearts and lives.

Just as the seventy prophesied in a way that was a public testimony, so the disciples spoke the marvelous deeds of God as evidence of the Spirit's outpouring upon them for many to witness. Condoning the actions of the two elders, Moses brought the other sixty-eight into the camp. There they stood and prophesied. Imagine the power and influence of seventy men, at one time, proclaiming the amazing works of God in the midst of the congregation! How could their hearts not have been affected? On the day of Pentecost, the crowds gathered, hearing of God's works in their own languages. In both cases, the coming of the Spirit was accompanied by the visible, tangible, and expressed words of God. He did not come in secrecy; rather, He came for all to behold, as an open proclamation of God's great redemption.

Just as the power of the Spirit moved outward from the tabernacle to the camp, so, too, the Spirit propelled the disciples outward into the world. Moses was not content to veil from the public such a great outpouring of God's Spirit. Compelled by the glory of it all, Moses urged the elders to go about the camp. In like manner, the glory of Christ's kingship and the coming of the Spirit are forces claiming disciples from every nation.

Moses foresaw a day when all should share in the blessing of his inheritance. He did not desire to keep such a gift to himself, but with eager expectation prophesied and prayed for the Spirit to be imparted on the whole company of God's people to the greater glory of God. So, too, Christ desired that His people would have that glory by the Spirit in earnest now, while the fullness of it awaits His return.

A Precursor with Elijah

A second precursor to Pentecost occurs in the life of Elijah. Here again we do not have merely a prophecy or picture but an event that prefigures the Spirit's coming on the day of Pentecost.

Frequent symbolic references throughout the Elijah narratives point us in the direction of the Holy Spirit, namely, the use of fire, clouds, and water. For example, we read of fire that came on Mount Carmel and consumed Elijah's sacrifice as he stood against Baal and his false prophets (1 Kings 18:20–40). Later that same day, God brought the drought that affected the whole country to an end. The land of Israel had suffered under the reign of Ahab and Jezebel. The Spirit had removed much of Elijah's influence to the point that there was little to no teaching ministry (compare 1 Kings 19:10). Nevertheless, Elijah had seen a cloud the size of a man's hand, the indication that the drought of the Word of God was coming to an end. God would again rain down His covenantal blessing upon His people by His Spirit.

Thus, the Elijah narratives contain the symbolism of the Spirit. However, in the passage that recounts Elijah's ascension into heaven (2 Kings 2), there is an explicit mention of the Spirit of God.[19] The narrative describes the Spirit, which had rested upon Elijah, falling upon his successor, Elisha. As the time came near for Elijah to be taken from this world, he went at the Lord's bidding from Gilgal to two other cities in the northern kingdom—Bethel and Jericho. Initially at Gilgal and then again at Bethel, Elijah put Elisha to the test by urging him to stay behind rather than accompany him (2:2, 4, 6). But Elisha was determined to stay with his master. This meant a difficult walk over steep hilly terrain before reaching the Jordan River.[20]

---

19. See J. Severino Croatto, "Jesus, Prophet Like Elijah, and Prophet-Teacher Like Moses in Luke-Acts," *Journal of Biblical Literature* 124, no. 3 (2005): 451–65 (esp. 456–58).

20. Each of these towns had historical importance in the life of Israel, especially in terms of when Israel conquered the Promised Land (Josh. 2:1; 4:19–20; 7:2). Gilgal was the place where the people prepared for battle by rededicating themselves to the Lord and having the Lord take away their reproach. Bethel was the place where God had appeared to Jacob (Gen. 28:16–19). It was to be the place of worship, but it had become a place of shame (cf. 1 Kings 12:33 and Amos 4:4; 7:13). Jericho was the place where the Lord had shown the might of His hosts against the strong fortified enemy behind those strong walls—the first city that Israel conquered in the Promised Land. In summary, Gilgal was the place of *rededication*; Bethel the place of

As Elijah and Elisha journeyed toward the Jordan from Jericho, we read, "Fifty men of the sons of the prophets went, and stood to view afar off: and they two stood by Jordan" (2:7). These sons of the prophets, in both Bethel and Jericho, knowing that Elijah's time had come, told Elisha of his approaching dismissal. Heading down to the Jordan, fifty sons of the prophets stood afar to watch Elijah's ascension. These fifty prophets did not cross the Jordan to see the miraculous event that Elisha saw, with the heavens opening and Elijah ascending. Elisha alone journeyed with Elijah. Elisha alone had been chosen to be Elijah's successor. The Spirit, in some measure, would be withheld from these fifty prophets, as Elisha stood to inherit the double portion.

When they reached the Jordan, Elijah struck the water with his mantle, and the waters parted for them (2:8). This crossing of the Jordan is pregnant with symbolic meaning.[21] The parting of the Jordan River recalls Israel's crossing of the Jordan in Joshua 3. Around that same time, Moses had died and appointed a successor to fulfill his ministry. Joshua declared to the people that God would be in their midst and go before them. God's parting of the Jordan River was also reminiscent of the crossing of the Red Sea (see Ps. 114:1–3). As the Israelites walked on dry ground, God was confirming His covenant with His people.

The whole journey was more than twenty-five miles over rugged and difficult terrain; no easy journey for either Elijah or Elisha. It must have taken a toll on Elisha. But journeying with his teacher, he was willing to endure the difficulties presented to him. In a real sense, Elisha endured through the hope of glory to be revealed to him in the inheritance of Elijah's spirit (cf. 1 Peter 1:13).

Think of how, on many occasions, Christ also tested the resolve of His disciples as they journeyed up and down the Promised Land with Him during His time on earth. Would they persevere? Or would they leave Him like many of the multitudes did? The question He asked them on one occasion sought to test their perseverance: "Will

---

worship; and Jericho the place of *battle*. Each of these was a place that pointed to the Lord's grace and glory in the past, and Elijah took Elisha through these places on this last journey before they would part.

21. See J. V. Fesko, *Word, Water, and Spirit: A Reformed Perspective on Baptism* (Grand Rapids: Reformation Heritage Books, 2010), 213.

you also go away?" (John 6:67). The disciples were resolved to follow Jesus, even to death (cf. John 11:16). They had their failings but, except for Judas, His disciples did persevere.

We are left with a valuable lesson through the example of Elisha and the disciples. If we, too, desire an outpouring of the Holy Spirit in our lives, we, too, will find our resolves tested. The journey may be long and difficult. We may not be called to traverse the rugged Middle Eastern terrain, but our journey will cost us something—and it is a journey in which we must persevere.

After being invited by Elijah to ask for something, Elisha replied: "I pray thee, let a double portion of thy spirit be upon me" (2 Kings 2:9). This term "double portion" was "inheritance language" of that day.[22] In the laws of Leviticus and Deuteronomy, we read that when a father left an inheritance to his children, the firstborn would get a double portion (cf. Deut. 21:17). That meant that if a father had nine sons, he would divide his inheritance into ten parts. Every son would get one part except for the eldest, who would get two parts—a double portion. Thus, Elisha requested the favored part of the inheritance—the portion that an oldest son would get.

Elijah responded by saying: "Thou hast asked a hard thing; nevertheless, if thou see me when I am taken from thee, it shall be so unto thee, but if not, it shall not be so" (2 Kings 2:10). This was an intriguing answer. Elijah's point was that the Spirit was not his to give Elisha. Yet he did give a further direction to Elisha. He said, "If you see me when I am taken from you, you will have this double portion, and if not, then no—you will not have it."

The point Elijah was making to Elisha was something like this: "Your eyes need to be opened to a critical reality at a critical moment—to see something you've never seen before. In order to receive this double portion of the Spirit, you need to see the reality of God's kingdom—God on the throne, His blazing glory and holiness, His power and might, and the fact that He appears with and for His people." This is similar to the theophany that both Moses and Isaiah

---

22. G. K. Beale notes that often in the Ancient Near East, articles of clothing were given as representing an inheritance. See G. K. Beale, *The Temple and the Church's Mission: A Biblical Theology of the Dwelling Place of God* (Downers Grove, Ill.: InterVarsity Press, 2004), 30. Elijah's bestowal of his garment to Elisha underscores this inheritance idea.

received when they were called to speak on behalf of God (Ex. 3:1–5; Isa. 6:1–4). Elijah was saying, in effect: "This is not a vision I can give you. But if you have it, then you can know that you have received a double portion of the Spirit."[23]

Thus, as the men were going on and talking, a chariot of fire and horses of fire appeared (2 Kings 2:11). This chariot came between them, and a whirlwind (a tunnel wind) came down.[24] Elijah was drawn up, higher and higher, until he was out of sight. Soon it was clear to Elisha that Elijah had ascended into heaven. Like Enoch before him, and like the believers who will be alive at Christ's coming, Elijah bypassed death.

As Elijah was taken up, the reality of Paul's encouragement and the Spirit's decree came true. Mortality put on immortality, and the corruptible put on incorruption (1 Cor. 15:42–44). As Elijah was carried up to his eternal resting place, he was, in a sense, transfigured before the eyes of Elisha. The chariot and horses served to confirm Elisha as the successor of Elijah. As Elisha beheld this awesome vision, he cried: "My father, the chariot of Israel, and the horsemen thereof" (2 Kings 2:12). Notice that Elijah did not go to heaven in the chariot. He went up through a whirlwind into heaven. The horses and the chariot appeared for the benefit of Elisha, whose eyes were opened to see in them a symbol of God's presence and protection.

Elisha was profoundly affected by the absence of his "spiritual father." Elijah was taken from his midst. At such a glorious moment in time, one in which we might say that "heaven kissed earth," with the glorious appearing of the angelic host, Elisha lost a dear and intimate friend. But he lamented as well that Israel had lost her chief warrior. Elijah was of greater benefit to Israel than an army of five hundred thousand. His prayers were more powerful than all the weaponry of Israel. A great man and blessing had been removed. Yet, at that moment, Elisha was to take up Elijah's mantle, having been confirmed as the prophet's great successor. The Lord did not leave Israel in her sin. The ascension of Elijah showed the Lord's

---

23. Some years later, Elisha himself would pray that his own servant would see something: "LORD, I pray thee, open his eyes, that he may see. And the LORD opened the eyes of the young man, and he saw, and behold the mountain was full of horses and chariots of fire round about Elisha" (2 Kings 6:17).

24. The word translated as "whirlwind" literally means "a gust of wind, a windy moment."

favor, vindicating Elijah's ministry and launching Elisha's. Elisha would carry forward the cause of the Lord in Israel in a continued demonstration of grace and judgment.

Next, the narrative shows us the gift of the Spirit, symbolized by the mantle. We read: "He took up also the mantle of Elijah that fell from him, and went back, and stood by the bank of Jordan. And he took the mantle of Elijah that fell from him, and smote the waters, and said: Where is the LORD God of Elijah?" (2 Kings 2:14). This cry for God was evidence that the Spirit of Elijah already had fallen on Elisha. Through the Spirit, Elisha—like Elijah before him—was firmly focused on the presence of God. With the double portion of the Spirit, Elisha was prepared to go out and boldly bring the people to repentance, revival, and reformation through the preaching of God's Word.

It should be clear that this event is a precursor to Pentecost. Let me note seven ways in which it is so:

First, just as Elisha followed his master Elijah, knowing that God would take him up, the disciples followed Christ, having been told that He would be lifted up from the earth (Luke 9:51). Elisha refused to turn back, though implored to do so. He would suffer greatly, but he would behold the glory of Elijah's ascension. So, too, the disciples would endure hardships and suffering, but they would yet see Christ ascend in His glory to the right hand of the majesty on high.

Second, just as Elijah went through the Jordan and Elisha with him, Christ passed through His Jordan. Elijah led Elisha down through the midst of the Jordan River. The biblical symbolism of the Jordan, at such a low point of the earth, and marking the boundary into the Promised Land, suggests the reality of death. Not far from Jericho, the Jordan actually flows into the Dead Sea. In the New Testament, Christ, going to the cross, paved a way through the Jordan of death, through which all His disciples, in union with Him, must pass as well (Matt. 20:22). Just as this disciple of Elijah was assured of safe passage, so are the disciples of Christ.

Third, just as Elisha beheld his master ascend to heaven in a whirlwind, leaving him behind to carry on the work of a prophet, Jesus' disciples saw Him taken to heaven and a cloud remove Him from their sight. They, too, were commissioned to carry on the work of the heavenly Prophet.

Fourth, just as Elijah dropped the mantle to clothe Elisha, Christ sent down the Spirit, which had clothed Him in His ministry. When Elisha received Elijah's mantle, it was confirmation that God was sending him to proclaim the word of repentance to the people of Israel and Judah. Elisha was to be clothed from on high, symbolized in his reception of Elijah's mantle. So, too, the disciples received Christ's mantle, going forth and preaching the repentance of sins and salvation in the name of Jesus.

Fifth, just as Elisha, subsequent to Elijah's ascension, parted the Jordan River upon his word and the mantle of Elijah, the disciples, upon receiving the mantle of Christ, saw the success of this mantle. When Elisha parted the waters of the Jordan, any doubt he had concerning his succession of Elijah vanished. This miraculous event was the beginning of Elisha's greater work in the ministry of the Word. So, too, as the disciples stood up, Peter preaching on the day of Pentecost, hearts were rent open, vanishing any doubts of the disciples' succession of Jesus, and they went forth performing greater works than Christ (cf. John 14:12).

Sixth, just as Elisha cried out for the God of Elijah to prosper his ministry, the disciples persevered in prayer to receive the promise of the Father. Elisha knew his only hope was to have Elijah's God as his God. In the same way, the disciples knew they needed the God of Jesus. Peter, opening his first epistle, says, "Blessed be the God and Father of our Lord Jesus Christ" (1 Peter 1:3a). Without the coming of the Spirit, the disciples would have been left as orphans (John 14:18). But the Father gave them a foretaste of the inheritance of glory in Christ through the Spirit.

Lastly, just as Elisha received the Spirit upon the ascension of Elijah, the disciples received the Spirit upon the ascension of Christ. The grand vision that Elisha beheld confirmed that his plea to Elijah had been answered—Elisha received a double portion of Elijah's Spirit. As the disciples were gathered in Jerusalem and the heavens were opened with the Spirit of God descending upon them, Christ gave them of His Spirit.

It is worth noticing how Christ's ascension yielded more fruit for the disciples than Elijah's did for Elisha. First, though Elijah could not promise Elisha that he would receive the double portion of the Spirit, Christ not only made the promise but secured it through His life, death, resurrection, and ascension. Elijah could only point Elisha to God to answer his plea. Christ, the Mediator of a better covenant, promised, breathed, and poured out His Spirit on His own people (John 16:7; 20:22; Acts 2:17).

Second, the Lord answered the disciples' prayers, not just with a whirlwind going up to heaven and then vanishing, but with divided tongues coming down from heaven that "sat upon each of them" (Acts 2:3). While fifty of the sons of the prophets stood afar off and watched Elijah's ascension and the descent of the Spirit, those who heard the apostles' preaching were cut to the heart. The time of types and shadows had passed, the dawn was arising, the fullness of the times had come. To verify the Spirit's coming without measure, Pentecost was echoed as God's Word spread from "Jerusalem, and in all Judea, and in Samaria, and unto the uttermost part of the earth" (Acts 1:8). The God of Elijah and the God of our Lord Jesus Christ had come, and was present, effectually turning the hearts of Israel back to Himself as He had done that day on Mount Carmel hundreds of years earlier.

Conclusion

It is not a coincidence that the two narratives in the Old Testament that specifically mention the Spirit falling upon people—the seventy with Moses, and Elisha as Elijah's successor—both involve the men who mediated between God and Israel in their covenant relationship. Moses and Elijah were the two main mediators of the old covenant, while Jesus was the Mediator of the new covenant. After all, the covenant serves the glory of God through Jesus Christ, and the ascension and outpouring of Christ exhibit this covenant gloriously.

Neither is it a coincidence that after Christ was on the Mount of Transfiguration and spoke there with Moses and Elijah (Luke 9:28–36), the time came "that he should be received up" (Luke 9:51), and He assured His disciples that their "heavenly Father [would] give the Holy Spirit to them that ask him" (Luke 11:13). Christ's ascension assures believers of the earnest of the inheritance that awaits them, bound up in the ascended Christ.

Neither, finally, is it a coincidence that upon the ascension of Christ into heaven, the order of ascension and outpouring was reversed, as we see in Revelation 11:11–12. There we read how two witnesses, reminiscent of Moses and Elijah, will minister God's Word against great hostility and despite severe persecution; nevertheless, when killed, they will receive the Spirit of life again, and ultimately ascend in the sight of their enemies. How exactly this should be interpreted is beyond the scope of this chapter. However, even the reversal of the order of ascension and outpouring proves that Pentecost serves the greater glory of God in Jesus Christ. Pentecost is not the end point of the scheme of redemption; the glory of God upon Christ's return is. Rather, Pentecost affords the church by faith the earnest of what indeed is in Christ already now, and therefore secure for the unending future. By the Spirit, for Christ's sake, believers possess all the blessings of the fullness of God.

CHAPTER 6

The Outpouring of the Spirit: Anticipated, Attained, Available

Michael Barrett

Something happened on the day of Pentecost that marked a new epoch in the progression of God's redemptive program. Pentecost changed things, but the question of what changed has generated more than one theological debate. The most cursory of readings of Acts 2 connects the change to the outpouring of the Holy Spirit on those who were waiting in the Upper Room for power in obedience to Christ's last command before His ascension. That expected power was to be given in the context of advancing the kingdom of Christ from the immediate environs of Jerusalem ultimately to the ends of the earth. Notwithstanding the clear connection between power and the outpouring of the Spirit, the questions and disagreements persist as to what happened at Pentecost that changed things—then and now.

The disagreements concern how the work and ministry of the Holy Spirit differ between the Old and the New Testaments—before and after the Incarnation. The Holy Spirit's work is manifold, but the question regarding the outpouring of the Spirit focuses specifically on the Spirit's work relating to believers in Christ, who were promised power subsequent to the Holy Spirit's coming upon them (Acts 1:8). The New Testament reveals much about the benefits believers enjoy through the Holy Spirit, but it is possible to summarize the Spirit's work regarding Christians under four broad heads. First is regeneration. This is the gracious act of the Holy Spirit that creates spiritual life in the spiritually dead; it is the new birth. This creative act of the Holy Spirit enables the previously dead sinner to repent and believe the gospel. Second is indwelling. This is the constant, unceasing, abiding presence of the Holy Spirit within the believer to give assurance of spiritual life and to comfort the believer with all the benefits of grace. The indwelling Spirit is God's gift to every believer and is the earnest or down-payment guarantee of the full inheritance earned, purchased, and shared by Christ. Third is empowering. This refers to the recurring help the Holy Spirit gives to enable the servant of the Lord to perform and accomplish the work of the ministry assigned to him. The Spirit's empowerment is always service oriented and is needed for every task in the work of the kingdom. Fourth is the influence of the Spirit. I take this head from Paul's imperative that believers should be filled with the Spirit rather than drunk with wine (Eph. 5:18). Being drunk under the influence of wine affects walking, talking, and thinking. Similarly, being under the influence of the Spirit governs actions, conversation, and thoughts. Believers are commanded to submit to the Spirit's leading, convicting, and teaching. Submitting to the Spirit's influence is the way of sanctification.

Unquestionably, every New Testament saint enjoys these benefits. The question remains as to how much they applied to Old Testament saints. I submit that each of these four categories was operating in the Old Testament—yes, even the indwelling of the Spirit as God's constantly abiding presence with individual saints.

That being the case, what happened at Pentecost and what exactly changed? The answer depends on a significant presupposition.

As Protestants in the Reformed tradition, we owe much to our forefathers, who, in confessions of faith and catechisms, expressed the truths of Scripture in ways that frame our knowledge of the Bible. As interpreters of Scripture, we utilize the analogy of faith to ensure consistency and orthodoxy in our consideration of individual texts, themes, and theology. Employing the analogy of faith in biblical interpretation is like looking at the puzzle box when trying to fit together the individual pieces of the puzzle. The box shows the finished picture—how all the pieces fit to form the whole. Similarly, our theological grid provides the frame into which all the individual passages, verses, and doctrines fit together.

Covenant theology is the grid or framework that, I believe, best safeguards the divinely intended message of Scripture. It is a framework that sheds some light on the theme before us: the outpouring of the Holy Spirit. Joel prophesied about a day when God would pour out His Spirit. Peter identified Pentecost as that day. That day of Pentecost changed something about how the Holy Spirit operates. Our question is, what changed? Answering that question is part of a larger issue: the degree of continuity or discontinuity between the Old and New Testaments. This is where our grid can help.

One tenet of covenant theology is that all of history since the Fall has been redemptive in its purpose, focus, and progress. All of history moved unfailingly to the fullness of time when God sent His Son to redeem His people from the curse (Gal. 4:4). Likewise, all of time since has been moving with the same divinely determined certainty to the "second fullness," when Christ will return apart from sin unto salvation (Heb. 9:28). The entire history of the world before the Incarnation was moving steadily toward that stupendous event of the condescension of Christ at His first coming, just as the history of the world since the Ascension of Christ is moving steadily toward the stupendous event of the Second Coming. Recognizing Christ and redemption as the unifying themes in Scripture, covenant theology maintains a high level of continuity between the testaments.

Genesis 3:15, the first declaration of the gospel, is a synopsis of redemptive history. God announced His plan and purpose in sending His Son in the likeness of sinful flesh, the Seed of the woman, to reverse the curse of sin. He also previewed and overviewed the hostility between the two seeds—the woman's and the Serpent's—that would be resolved with the final, fatal crushing of the tempter's head. But until that time, the road of redemption is an obstacle course cluttered with real but doomed opposition. Nothing can frustrate God's purpose, and that is most certainly the case regarding His purpose in Christ. Christ and His kingdom will prevail. In Scripture, the record of God's redemptive plan, instances of this hostility and opposition are often highlighted to underscore the inviolable truth of the certain success and advance of Christ's kingdom, the church. God uses different means to accomplish His purpose, demonstrating the manifold operations of His providence. Significantly, the Holy Spirit is revealed as the divine Agent responsible for victory. He is linked with power. Isaiah states the general principle: "When the enemy shall come in like a flood, the Spirit of the LORD shall lift up a standard against him" (Isa. 59:19). Nothing is more uncontrollable or unstoppable than a rushing flood of water; it destroys everything in its path. But as powerful as a flood of hostile opposition may be, the Spirit drives forward against the foe, stopping any advance with infinite power. One of the key ways in which the Holy Spirit defeats the enemy and fosters the advance of Christ's kingdom is by enabling God's servants to engage the enemy and to assist in the work of the kingdom.

Here is the proposition: advancing the kingdom requires the ministry of the Spirit of God. The Holy Spirit is essential in the progress of redemption. Throughout the course of pre-Incarnation history, the Holy Spirit operated through God's servants to insure that all would be in place for the fullness of time, when God would send His Son. Since the Incarnation, the Spirit is operating through the church at large to achieve its success. The outpouring of the Spirit at Pentecost insures that Christ will build His church; Pentecost inaugurated the season of spiritual power to advance the church to the ends of the earth. The difference in the Spirit's work after Pentecost in contrast to His work before concerns the work of empowering. It is a matter of degree and not essence.

Power Antecedent to Pentecost

Most of the data in the Old Testament regarding the work of the Holy Spirit is about His empowering for service, the very aspect of the Spirit's work that expanded on the day of Pentecost. Although the extent of the empowering of the Spirit heightened after Pentecost, the Old Testament revelation is perhaps more illustrative of the nature and implications of being empowered than the New Testament. A synopsis of Old Testament teaching reveals what it means to be empowered by the Spirit and leads to an answer to the question of what changed on the day of Pentecost.

Before the Incarnation, the Spirit's empowering was limited. That limitation was not in terms of the amount of power He gave but rather in terms of the number of people receiving the power. Apart from a few notable exceptions (such as Bezaleel's empowerment as a craftsman for the construction of the tabernacle, Ex. 31:2), the Holy Spirit's special enabling was focused primarily on the civil and religious leaders of the people. The period of the judges provides multiple examples of God empowering chosen leaders with His Spirit. God raised up judge after judge, put His Spirit upon them, and through them subdued foreign powers whose domination threatened the existence of the covenant nation. These threats to Israel also represented threats to the progression and fulfillment of God's redemptive purpose. There had to be an Israel if there was going to be the Christ. So, to insure the advance of His redemptive plan, God's Spirit came upon unlikely saviors, enabling them to deliver and preserve the nation, seemingly against all odds. Nothing can thwart God's purpose, and the empowering work of the Holy Spirit was a chief means of insuring its success.

Most common before Pentecost was the Spirit's empowering of men in the anointed or messianic offices of prophet, priest, and king. When the Lord anointed a man for one of these offices, He did not abandon him to his own ingenuity or abilities. The Lord supplied the power for service, with the ultimate agent of power being the Holy Spirit. Sometimes this empowering was symbolized in anointing ceremonies in which oil was used as a picture of the Holy Spirit. As the olive oil was poured and smeared on the head of the appointed "messiah," so the Holy Spirit came upon him to enable him to perform the ministry for which he was being consecrated and set apart. Prophets were enabled to prophesy; priests were sanctified for service; kings were authorized to rule. The Old Testament is replete with examples, from Moses the prophet, Aaron the priest, and Saul the king onward, to illustrate the point. These offices were integral to redemptive history and prophetic of the ideal Messiah whose ministry would be so intimately linked with the Holy Spirit.

Although the empowering work of the Spirit was restricted to leadership prior to Pentecost, the magnitude of the Spirit's power was not limited. Perhaps there is no text that better explains the necessity and significance of the Spirit's power in kingdom work than Zechariah 4. This chapter records Zechariah's vision of the candlestick and two olive trees that he applied specifically to Zerubbabel. Zerubbabel, the civil leader after the Babylonian exile, had been called and commissioned to oversee the rebuilding of the temple, which had been razed to the ground by the armies of Nebuchadnezzar. The rebuilding of the temple was a crucial component in the progression of God's redemptive plan leading to the fullness of time. There had to be a temple in place when the Messiah came. But in God's providence, opposition from the outside and discouragement from the inside caused the reconstruction work to cease. Zechariah used a vision of a lampstand and olive trees with multiple pipes dripping oil directly from the trees to the lamps to encourage and motivate Zerubbabel to continue in his essential kingdom work regardless of the hindrances.

The object lesson was clear. Just as the oil supplied the fuel for the lamps to function, so the Holy Spirit would provide the energy Zerubbabel needed to serve the Lord. Zechariah wrote: "This is the word of the LORD unto Zerubbabel, saying, Not by might, nor by power, but by my spirit, saith the LORD of hosts" (4:6). The text highlights the absolute necessity of the Spirit's involvement. The word *might* has the idea of collective strength; the word *power* implies individual ability or charisma. Sadly, we too often rely on or seek after these things in doing the work of the Lord, but without the aid of the Holy Spirit, the work will falter. On the contrary, no obstacle can stand against the operation of the Spirit.

The application to Zerubbabel was threefold. First, Spirit-empowered service would be successful. The mountain that hindered Zerubbabel would be flattened to a plain, and the headstone marking the completion of the temple work would be set in place (4:7). Second, Spirit-empowered service should engender encouragement. Even if the work seems small and insignificant, like holding a plumb line, it pleases the Lord when it is done in the power of His Spirit. Third, the Spirit's empowering is available whenever needed. As the pipes going directly from the olive trees to the lamps picture an inexhaustible supply of oil, so there is never any depletion in the Spirit's power. This kind of service-oriented, kingdom-working power would be evident on the day of Pentecost. Yet, something was going to be wonderfully and remarkably different.

It is significant that the Holy Spirit's empowering for service reached it pre-Pentecost climax in the Lord Jesus Christ. As mysterious as it sounds, the Son of God was empowered by the Holy Spirit for His work as the Savior. This was a matter of Old Testament prophecy (see, for instance, Isa. 42:1; 61:1) as well as New Testament history.

Though the record of Jesus' earthly ministry does not reveal extensive direct evidence of spiritual empowering, the Spirit clearly exerted a vital influence in His ministry. So significant was the Holy Spirit's anointing and empowering of Christ at His baptism, the beginning of His public ministry, that each of the four Gospel narratives records the event (Matt. 3:16; Mark 1:10; Luke 3:22; John 1:32). John's account is perhaps the most instructive for our purpose. In it, we read not only that John the Baptist witnessed the Spirit descending on Jesus at His baptism, but also that "the Baptist" was told beforehand that this would be the unmistakable sign of the Son of God: "Upon whom thou shalt see the Spirit descending, and remaining on him, the same is he which baptizeth with the Holy Ghost" (John 1:33). The Spirit's anointing was messianic evidence. But John the Baptist, the transition prophet between the Old and the New Testaments, was told something and witnessed something that marked Jesus as unique.

As we have seen, all the lesser messiahs experienced the enabling of the Holy Spirit for their service. However, the nature of spiritual empowering in the Old Testament dispensation tended to be temporary and repetitive. Whenever there was a specific task to be performed, there was a special empowering by the Spirit. However, the Lord told John that the Holy Spirit would remain with the ideal Messiah, and that is exactly what John saw happen (John 1:32–33). The simple fact that the Holy Spirit never left the Lord Jesus explains why we never read of the Spirit coming on Him again. His entire ministry was conducted in the power of the Holy Spirit. Although admittedly difficult to understand, at the very least this truth highlights the cooperation of the Godhead in the work of salvation. The Father elected the Mediator; the Son executed the mediation; the Spirit empowered the Mediator. The Westminster Confession of Faith summarizes well the evidence of Scripture:

> It pleased God, in His eternal purpose, to choose and ordain the Lord Jesus, His only begotten Son, to be the Mediator between God and man; the Prophet, Priest, and King.... The Lord Jesus, in His human nature thus united to the divine, was sanctified, and anointed with the Holy Spirit above measure…to the end that…He might be thoroughly furnished to execute the office of a Mediator and Surety. Which office he took not unto himself, but was thereunto called by His Father; who put all power and judgment into his hand, and gave Him commandment to execute the same (8.1–3).

Because Christ successfully accomplished His redemptive work, the outpouring of the Spirit on the day of Pentecost was possible. So, the victorious Christ told His few disciples to wait for power (Acts 1:4, 8). Things were about to change.

Power Anticipated for Pentecost

Whereas the Spirit's empowering for service in the pre-Pentecost era was principally restricted to the leadership, Pentecost lifted that restriction. As early as the ministry of Moses, the Old Testament hinted about the advantages of a more inclusive operation of the Spirit. Although some expressed concern regarding the Spirit-induced prophesying of Eldad and Medad, Moses averred: "Would God that all the LORD's people were prophets, and that the LORD would put his spirit upon them" (Num. 11:29). What Moses desired, Joel prophesied hundreds of years later.

Although Joel did not directly date his prophecy, the circumstantial evidence points to the ninth century B.C.—either during the renegade rule of Queen Athaliah or the early days of the boy king Joash, grandson of Athaliah, who had providentially escaped her deadly plot against the royal seed, which was ultimately against the coming Seed. The days were dark, both politically and spiritually; once again it seemed that God's redemptive purpose leading to Christ was in jeopardy. But not even the wicked queen could frustrate God's purpose and plan. The Lord inspired the prophet Joel to provide the theological interpretation of all the tragic events of the day and to announce details of God's fixed plans for the future.

Judgment for sin was part of his message. Joel made it clear that what seemed to be a natural disaster was in reality God's direct, supernatural intervention into human affairs to accomplish His judgment against the nation's sin. The locust plague was a day of the Lord, and if the nation did not repent, an even worse judgment would come. But repentance opened the way for blessing. What Joel revealed concerning blessing had immediate significance to the nation devastated by the locust invasion—for the Lord would restore the years that the locusts had eaten—and spiritual significance to a future people who would witness the beginning of a new era of God's plan for all nations. Indeed, at the heart of the predicted blessing is what Peter declared fulfilled at Pentecost.

Joel 2:21–32 includes prophecies of blessing that extend from the time immediately following the locust devastation to the days of

Pentecost to days yet distant. Verses 28–32 are particularly relevant. Although this section constitutes a single predictive unit, there are indications that it contains three distinct prophecies. First, verses 28, 30, and 32 each begin with a future tense (*waw perfect*) that may suggest the beginning of a new paragraph or thought unit. Second, the units beginning with verses 28 and 32 each contain an *inclusio* that helps mark the unit divisions. *Inclusio*, a common literary device in the Old Testament, is a verbal parenthesis that sets off discourse units. The first unit (vv. 28–29) begins and ends with the statement "I will pour out my spirit." The last unit (v. 32) begins and ends with the key word "call." The middle section (vv. 30–31) does not use an *inclusio*, but it follows that if the first and last units are so set apart, what is in between is itself a separate unit. That verse 30 begins with the future tense, just like verses 28 and 32, substantiates the conclusion. Each of the predictions Joel makes in this section would be fulfilled sometime after the restoration from the locust plague, but not necessarily at the same time. From the perspective of the New Testament, it is clear that aspects of this prophecy were fulfilled on the day of Pentecost and others wait to be fulfilled when the Lord returns at the end of the age. Without specifying the time intervals, Joel prophesied concerning spiritual power, supernatural signs, and guarantees of salvation.

Spiritual power
The first prediction is the promise of the outpouring of God's Spirit (2:28–29). This outpouring refers to the Spirit's ministry of empowering for service. The verb "pour out" has many different objects in the Old Testament, ranging from literal liquids, such as water or blood, to figurative notions or non-liquids, such as wrath, heart, soul, and spirit. In each instance, the idea is the complete or generous emptying out of whatever the object may be. It is certainly an appropriate word to describe the Lord's provision of inexhaustible power for His people to serve with ability beyond their own.

More than the image of outpouring, the consequences of the outpouring point to the empowering work of the Holy Spirit. In these verses, the recipients of the Spirit engage in kingdom work—activities that are representative of His ministry. The point is not so much that they prophesy, dream dreams, or see visions, but that they are able to do what is normally regarded as "prophet" work as a result of the Spirit's empowerment. The Spirit is poured out on them, and they do something. What is unique about Joel's prophecy is not the fact of the empowering but the objects who are empowered. Joel pointed to a time when the Spirit's power would no longer be restricted to the leadership, when that "exclusive" work would become "inclusive." All classes of people—male and female, young and old—would experience the reality of spiritual power. The reference to "all flesh" even goes beyond the population of Israel to include Gentiles. Indeed, although the expression may designate humanity in general, it can and does refer to Gentiles specifically (see Deut. 5:26; Jer. 25:31, etc.). If Joel had in mind the instructions of Leviticus 25:44–46, which allowed Israelites to make servants of the heathen but prohibited them from so owning their fellow Israelites, it may be that verse 29 intentionally refers to Gentiles as well when it declares that servants and handmaids will also receive this spiritual outpouring. Although the Old Testament era witnessed great demonstrations of spiritual power, Joel told of a coming day when there would be a grand, widespread effusion of spiritual power that was hardly comprehensible. Joel anticipated a remarkable change ahead.

Supernatural signs
The second predictive unit describes celestial and terrestrial signs commonly associated with judgment aspects of the final manifestation of the day of the Lord. It is vain to speculate concerning the essence or mechanics of such signs since they are obviously supernatural. Their function, however, is clear: they are warnings of judgment. Blessing always has its counterpart in curse. To miss the blessing means the judgment is inescapable.

That the prophetic units are not to be fulfilled simultaneously does not diminish the application. The certain fact of judgment more than the time of it is the major incentive to repentance. Although this unit is not specifically fulfilled on the day of Pentecost and does not, therefore, address our question regarding the change in the Spirit's function, Peter includes it in his quotation of Joel with the same relevant application as the Old Testament prophet. To miss the blessing of Pentecost is to experience an aspect of the curse of ultimate judgment.

Salvation guarantees

The third unit includes a timeless prophetic declaration of spiritual salvation. It gives the assurance of salvation to all who call on the name of the Lord. Calling on the Lord is tantamount to approaching Him in saving faith. The apostle Paul understood the calling this way when he quoted this portion of Joel's prophecy in his exposition of saving faith in Romans 10:9–13. Joel confidently linked the calling with being delivered. Calling was the condition; being delivered was the guaranteed consequence.

The verb phrase "shall be delivered," like its New Testament counterpart, has the sense of getting to safety. Although both the Hebrew and Greek words can refer to nothing more than physical rescues, both vividly portray the rescue of the soul from the wrath and condemnation of God's judgment of sinners. This idea of rescue from judgment is a fitting image for salvation in view of the preceding prediction of the coming of the "terrible day of the LORD." This expresses the gracious irony of the gospel. Sinners escape God's wrath not by fleeing from it but by approaching in faith the source of the wrath to find the God of mercy. This has always been true, whether before or after Pentecost.

Whereas at the beginning of the verse those who call on the Lord are saved, at the end of the verse those whom the Lord calls are saved. Notwithstanding any eschatological significance to the text, the message is unmistakably clear. What is true about God's future people is true about His past and present people as well. The means of salvation has always been and will always be the same. There is an inseparable link between God's calling of sinners and sinners' calling on God. Many sinners were saved on the day of Pentecost, but that was not unique to that day.

Power Attained on Pentecost

The risen Christ instructed His one hundred and twenty followers, both men and women, to wait for the promise of the Father (Acts 1:4), and He assured them that when the Holy Spirit would come upon them, they would receive power enabling them to take the gospel "unto the uttermost part of the earth" (v. 8). Secluded in the upper room, they "all continued with one accord in prayer and supplication" (v. 14). Then it happened: "And when the day of Pentecost was fully come, they were all with one accord in one place.... And they were all filled with the Holy Ghost" (2:1, 4). In the power of the Spirit, they left the upper room and made their way through the streets of Jerusalem, speaking "the wonderful works of God" (v. 11). As a result of the Spirit's empowering, each member of that first and little New Testament church—every individual—gave evidence of that power with acts of service and ministry. It was not just the apostles or leaders of the church who preached the gospel in tongues for all to understand. It was the whole church.

What Jerusalem witnessed that day was incomprehensible; there had never been anything like it before. Peter recognized the events to be that extensive effusion of spiritual power that Joel had prophesied. When the actions of the collective church were questioned (vv. 12–13), Peter stood up and declared, "This is that which was spoken by the prophet Joel" (v. 16). Interestingly, Peter departed from both the Hebrew text ("after thus") and the Septuagint ("and it will be after these things") in identifying the time of fulfillment as being "in the last days" (v. 17). So unmistakable were the evidences of the Spirit's work that Peter had no doubt that this was what Joel had predicted. In the New Testament, the expression "the last days" marked the beginning of the new era that commenced with the coming of Jesus Christ in the flesh (Heb. 1:2). The first Pentecost after Christ's resurrection started something remarkable. It was not long after that initial outpouring of the Spirit on the "regular" believers that Gentiles received the same power, just as Joel anticipated (Acts 10:44–45; 15:8).

That Peter quoted the entirety of Joel's three predictive units does not imply that he claimed it was all fulfilled at the one moment; it reflects his understanding of the passage. Peter had certainly heard Christ's Olivet Discourse, describing the supernatural signs, and he himself would write about the final day of the Lord, in which heaven and earth will be cataclysmically dissolved (2 Peter 3:10–11). This coming judgment was a warning not to reject the blessing. In the context of Acts, Peter was addressing those who had mockingly questioned the evidences of the Spirit's blessing and power. They had witnessed the blessing firsthand, but they were in danger of judgment if they rejected the gospel they heard being preached by the Spirit-empowered witnesses. Just as certain as the part of Joel's prophecy being fulfilled before their eyes was the part of the prophecy that would be fulfilled sometime later. Peter applied the predictive unit exactly as Joel did, and that application continues. The fact that about three thousand souls were added to the church that day (Acts 2:41) is all the evidence necessary to see the fulfillment of Joel's third unit (Joel 2:32).

Power Available Because of Pentecost

Pentecost indeed changed something. No longer is the power of the Spirit restricted to those in leadership roles; it is available to every believer. Every Christian who seeks to serve the Lord in any capacity can have the assurance of God-given power in the Person of the Holy Spirit to enable him to serve with boldness and confidence. The leaders in the church, just like their pre-Pentecost predecessors, still need the power of the Spirit to effectively perfect the saints for the work of the ministry God has for them (Eph. 4:11–12). Every Christian, in one way or another, must be engaged in the work of advancing the kingdom of Christ. Some of that work is public; some is behind the scenes. But all work done in the name of Christ and for His glory can be done in the power of Pentecost. Pentecost ushered in a massive effusion of spiritual power that is accessible to every believer; the supply of power is inexhaustible. Not only did Pentecost change things, it marked the start of something that continues today. There is an obvious sense in which the day of Pentecost is past, but there is a very real sense in which it is still present. What Pentecost started has never stopped.

The question remains as to how we can avail ourselves of the available power. The example of the early church provides the pattern. The believers continued in prayer and supplication until they were filled with the Holy Spirit. Significantly, the Lord Jesus, in one of His expositions about prayer, assures us that our heavenly Father will "give the Holy Spirit to them that ask him" (Luke 11:13). Seeing that regeneration by the Spirit is a sovereign act of God, that the indwelling of the Spirit is an unconditional gift, and that living under the influence of the Spirit is a command to obey, it must be that the Spirit given in answer to prayer is for empowering for service. The power of Pentecost is available for the asking. A consciousness of our need should generate a consistent prayer for power, remembering that it is "not by might, nor by power, but by my spirit, saith the LORD of hosts" (Zech. 4:6).

Advancing the kingdom requires the ministry of the Holy Spirit, and in the power of the Spirit the kingdom will advance. Being empowered by the Spirit, the first generation of Pentecost believers advanced the church in Jerusalem to Judea, to Samaria, and even to Rome. It remains for us to continue its advance to the uttermost parts of the earth in the same power the disciples received when the Holy Spirit came upon them. May the Lord pour out His Spirit on us all.

CHAPTER 7

The Cessation of the Extraordinary Spiritual Gifts

George W. Knight III

As Reformed believers seek to face the challenge of the charismatic movement, we must first identify that which we are facing and the movement with which we are dealing, specifying the differences between that movement and the Reformed faith.[1] The challenge we face is the assertion of the charismatics that they have the presence and power of the Holy Spirit. It is implied, if not asserted, that we might think that we have sound doctrine, but what is that compared to the presence and power of the Holy Spirit?

The charismatics hold that the extraordinary spiritual gifts of the Spirit continue, and that they should be sought and utilized by Christians today.[2] The extraordinary spiritual gifts are: the calling of some to be apostles and prophets; speaking in tongues; and direct healing. Thus, the charismatics do not hold that these special gifts have ceased, as do the Reformed,[3] but rather that they continue. Among the charismatics, there are differences on various points, but

---

1. This paper was originally published as "The Vitality of the Reformed Faith: Facing the Challenge of the Charismatic Movement," in *Proceedings of the International Conference of Reformed Churches, October 10–22, 2009* (Christchurch, New Zealand: Inheritance Publications, 2010), 133–53. It is now being republished in a revised edition.

2. Wayne Grudem, ed., *Are Miraculous Gifts for Today? Four Views* (Grand Rapids: Zondervan, and Leicester: IVP, 1996), 11–15. Of the four writers for this book, three hold that the miraculous gifts continue and one does not.

3. See the Westminster Confession of Faith, 1.1: "…to commit the same wholly unto writing: which maketh the Holy Scripture to be most necessary; those former ways of God's revealing his will unto his people being now ceased." For a fine study of this statement, see the doctoral dissertation of G. H. Milne, *The Westminster Confession of Faith and the Cessation of Special Revelation: The Majority Puritan Viewpoint on Whether Extra-biblical Prophecy is Still Possible* (Eugene, Ore.: Wipf & Stock, 2008).

on the continuation of the special gifts they are virtually agreed. As we consider them in this chapter, we will recognize that the book *Are Miraculous Gifts for Today? Four Views* categorizes those who hold that these gifts continue into at least four groupings: Pentecostals, charismatics, Third Wave, and a newer category called "open but cautious." Wayne Grudem, who edited the volume, puts himself in the last category, but he has proposed a new way to understand New Testament prophecy that is not held by the representative of that category.[4] This rather recent book contains essays by competent proponents of each view[5] and an excellent interaction among the four writers. Furthermore, each writer summarizes in some detail, with biblical arguments adduced, the various views held by the group he represents. This work is the basic source for our study, with some attention also being paid to Grudem's view of New Testament prophecy.

The Four Episodes in Acts

One of the most important differences between the Reformed, the Pentecostals, and some charismatics is the belief of the latter two that the book of Acts is our guide for the special gifts and that the baptism of the Holy Spirit, as it appears in Acts, occurs as a special act subsequent to regeneration by the Spirit.[6] Thus, they cite the outpourings of the Holy Spirit on the apostles at Pentecost (Acts 2:1–41), on the Samaritans (Acts 8:5–25), on Cornelius's household (Acts 10:1–11:18), and on John's disciples in Ephesus (Acts 19:1–7). Pentecostals and charismatics say that these passages show that those who were already regarded as disciples were then baptized by the Holy Spirit, and this, they say, is the model for Christians today. An

---

4. See the doctoral dissertation of Wayne Grudem, *The Gift of Prophecy in 1 Corinthians* (Lanham, Md.: University Press of America, 1982), and his more thorough, albeit popular, discussion and interaction with others over the entire New Testament, *The Gift of Prophecy in the New Testament and Today* (Wheaton, Ill.: Crossway Books, 1988).

5. A cessationist view is represented by Richard B. Gaffin Jr., an open but cautious view by Robert L. Saucy, a Third Wave view by C. Samuel Storms, and a Pentecostal view and a charismatic view are both represented in one article by Douglas A. Oss; they are fully identified on pp. 14–15 of Grudem, *Are Miraculous Gifts for Today?*

6. Grudem, *Are Miraculous Gifts for Today?*, 11. For a further clarification of these views, see especially p. 242 for the Pentecostals and p. 257 for the charismatics.

examination of these passages shows, however, that each displays a specific reason for the timing of the baptism by the Holy Spirit, and that reason is unique to each situation and therefore is not intended to be a model for others.[7]

Pentecost: the apostles (Acts 2:1–41)
The Pentecost experience fulfilled Jesus' words to His disciples that they would receive "the promise of the Father" in being "baptized with the Holy Ghost" (Acts 1:4, 5). He said, "But ye shall receive power, after that the Holy Ghost is come upon you: and ye shall be witnesses…unto the uttermost part of the earth" (v. 8). When that power came upon them, "a sound from heaven as of a rushing mighty wind" filled the house and "there appeared unto them cloven tongues like as of fire, and it sat upon each of them," and then "they were all filled with the Holy Ghost, and began to speak with other tongues, as the Spirit gave them utterance" (2:2–4). This was the filling with the Holy Spirit and endowment with power that could come only from the ascended Jesus Christ, who was giving the promise of the Father, and His own promise, to His disciples. This was their experience because they had lived both before and after the resurrection and ascension, and had become believers before the promise was given. These spectacular phenomena of wind and fire were not, however, given again, and even the speaking in tongues, when repeated, seems not to have been as significant as when each person was able to hear the disciples in his own language.

What did Peter, standing with the eleven, say to those who were listening? He gave them the gospel and then said to them: "Repent, and be baptized every one of you in the name of Jesus Christ for the remission of sins, and ye shall receive the gift of the Holy Ghost. For the promise is unto you, and to your children, and to all that are afar off, even as many as the Lord our God shall call" (2:38–39). Peter offered the hearers that which the apostles had received in two stages (forgiveness of sins and the gift of the Holy Spirit) as one

---

7. I first learned of the significance of these passages and how they should function in the life of the church from N. B. Stonehouse, in his article "Repentance, Baptism and the Gift of the Holy Spirit," in his publication of collected articles, *Paul Before the Areopagus and Other New Testament Studies* (Grand Rapids: Eerdmans, 1957), 70–87. This significance has grown with me as well as becoming commonplace to those dealing with this question.

complete gift to be received simultaneously. This is the model for today, not the unique experience of the apostles. Also notice that the hearers were not asked to wait, as the apostles had been asked to do (Acts 1:4), but they responded immediately (2:41). Neither is it recorded that they received the spectacular signs that the apostles had received, nor that they spoke so that those who were fluent in different languages could hear and understand. The passage goes on to say only that these believers "continued stedfastly in the apostles' doctrine and fellowship, and in breaking of bread, and in prayers" (v. 42). The Acts account singles out the apostles, saying, "many wonders and signs were done through the apostles" (v. 43b).

The Samaritans (Acts 8:5–25)
The second account begins by recounting that "Philip went down to the city of Samaria, and preached Christ unto them" (8:5). The response is given in these words: "And the people with one accord gave heed unto those things which Philip spake, hearing and seeing the *miracles* which he did" (v. 6, emphasis added). The result is in verse 12: "But when they believed Philip preaching the things concerning the kingdom of God, and the name of Jesus Christ, they were baptized, both men and women."

The apostles at Jerusalem heard that "Samaria had received the word of God," but when Peter and John went down, they found that the Holy Spirit "was fallen upon none of them: only they were baptized in the name of the Lord Jesus." So, they "laid their hands on them, and they received the Holy Ghost" (vv. 14–17).

This episode has its own uniqueness. The Samaritans became believers and were baptized, but they did not receive the Holy Spirit until the apostles laid hands on them. One may deduce from the text that this order of events was determined by the Lord for a similar reason as in Cornelius's case, when he and his household received the Holy Spirit first and then were baptized (see immediately below in Acts 10 and 11). In Cornelius's case, this sequence of events was to convince the circumcised believers, along with Peter and those back in Jerusalem, that they should receive and welcome Gentiles as fellow believers. In this case, it was to unite the Samaritans and Jews, with the Samaritans realizing they were dependent on the laying on of the hands of the Jewish apostles, and the Jews, represented by the apostles, recognizing that they had to receive into one body with the one Holy Spirit their believing brothers, the Samaritans. Peter and John continued to testify and speak "the word of the Lord" to these believers in Samaria, and as they "returned to Jerusalem," they "preached the gospel in many villages of the Samaritans" (v. 25).

Cornelius's household (Acts 10:1–11:18)
In this account, we read of God persuading Peter that he should take the gospel to Cornelius and his household at Caesarea. Cornelius was a "centurion of the band called the Italian band, a devout man, and one that feared God with all his house…and prayed to God alway" (10:1–2). Peter, after presenting the gospel, concluded his remarks to Cornelius and those with him with these words: "To him give all the prophets witness, that through his name whosoever believeth in him shall receive remission of sins" (v. 43). Luke then writes: "While Peter yet spake these words, the Holy Ghost fell on all them which heard the word. And they of the circumcision which believed were astonished, as many as came with Peter, because that on the Gentiles also was poured out the gift of the Holy Ghost. For they heard them speak with tongues, and magnify God" (vv. 44–46). The speaking in tongues was a sign for all to be aware of the salvation and baptism of the Spirit that had happened to these, the first Gentile believers.

Here again, as in Acts 2, the gospel message and the reception of the Holy Spirit are tied together, but this time the baptism with the Holy Spirit came on the Gentiles before their water baptism in order to convince circumcised believers that Gentiles had really been saved and admitted to the people of God. Peter argued for them to be baptized because they had "received the Holy Ghost as well as we" (v. 47). This action of the Spirit convinced not only those with Peter but also the circumcised believers in Jerusalem, as 11:15–18 indicates:

> And as I began to speak, the Holy Ghost fell on them, as on us at the beginning. Then remembered I the word of the Lord, how that he said, John indeed baptized with water; but ye shall be baptized with the Holy Ghost. Forasmuch then as God gave them the like gift as he did unto us, who believed on the Lord Jesus Christ; what was I, that I could withstand God? When they heard these things, they held their peace, and glorified God, saying, Then hath God also to the Gentiles granted repentance unto life.

Several things need to be noted about this episode. Even though Cornelius was a God-fearing man (10:2), it is clear that he was not a believer, for the angel told Cornelius that Peter would "tell thee words, whereby thou and all thy house shall be saved" (11:14). Peter equated their receiving of the Holy Spirit with what the apostles had experienced when they "believed on the Lord Jesus Christ" (v. 17). It is interesting that Peter relates the gift of the Spirit to the apostles' belief in Jesus and to nothing else, even though the gift came some time after their belief in Him, after Jesus' ascension. But this perspective is exactly the way Jesus had presented the promise of the Spirit in John 7:39: "But this spake he of the Spirit, which they that believe on him should receive: for the Holy Ghost was not yet given; because that Jesus was not yet glorified." Thus, the baptism of the Holy Spirit came upon Cornelius and his household (except for preceding their water baptism) just as Peter had proclaimed and promised to the Pentecost crowd (Acts 2:38–39).

John's disciples in Ephesus (Acts 19:1–7)
Paul came to Ephesus and found some disciples. Luke tells us:

> He said unto them, Have ye received the Holy Ghost since ye believed? And they said unto him, We have not so much as heard whether there be any Holy Ghost. And he said unto them, Unto what then were ye baptized? And they said, Unto John's baptism. Then said Paul, John verily baptized with the baptism of repentance, saying unto the people, that they should believe on him which should come after him, that is, Jesus Christ. When they heard this, they were baptized in the name of the Lord Jesus. (19:2–5)

The Ephesians were believers as surely as John the Baptist was, but ones who had not heard, even though they had received John's baptism, the declaration that Messiah had come. Hearing this good news, they were baptized into the name of the Lord Jesus Christ, "and when Paul had laid his hands on them [aorist participle], the Holy Ghost came on them" (v. 6). This was another unique experience. These men had believingly responded to a message that someone had presented from John the Baptist, and being convicted of their sin, they had repented and been baptized into John's baptism. That is, they had received "John's baptism," but not baptism in the name of Jesus.

Hearing from Paul that John had called men not only to repentance for their sins, but also to "believe in the one to come," namely, Jesus, they believed in Him and received baptism in His name. Whether while baptizing them or thereafter, Paul laid his hands on them and the Holy Spirit came on them. This baptism of the Spirit and its attendant salvation in Jesus was signified to them and to Paul as these disciples "spake with tongues, and prophesied" (v. 6).

What should we learn from these episodes?
We learn from these episodes what the baptism with the Holy Spirit is. Take the apostles and the Samaritans as those from whom we may learn this lesson: both of these groups were regenerated by the Holy Spirit before they were baptized by the Holy Spirit, just as Old Testament believers were regenerated even though they were not baptized by the Holy Spirit. So, the baptism with the Holy Spirit is the empowerment by the Holy Spirit for every New Testament believer, and it is given to everyone who believes in Jesus Christ as Lord (cf. Acts 11:17).

We also learn from these four episodes that they are not models for the Christian church to follow with regard to a delay in the baptism of the Spirit because they have no consistent and uniform pattern. The first (Pentecost, Acts 2) and the fourth (the Ephesians, Acts 19) are most similar, but there is a difference. The apostles heard John the Baptist's message pointing to Jesus, turned to Jesus in true faith as believers, and then waited for the ascended Lord to send God's promise of the Holy Spirit. The disciples of John in Ephesus had heard and responded only to the initial part of John the Baptist's message, that is, repentance, but they had not heard the part about believing in the One who was to come after John the Baptist. But none of us, and none of those whom we reach with the gospel, find ourselves in that situation, and none of us ever will. Neither are we like the Samaritans, disliked by the Jews and equally disliking them, who, having heard the gospel and responded to it, need to recognize that only through the hands of Jewish apostles will we receive the empowering, energizing, and uniting work of the Holy Spirit.

As we shall see below from Paul, we received the Spirit when we believed; we did not need to wait for the apostles, or anyone else, to lay on hands. Yes, we are Gentiles, like Cornelius and his household (Acts 10, 11), but we should not expect that we should speak in tongues to convince circumcised believers that we are really Christians. All of us are in the same position as those to whom Peter proclaimed the gospel right after the Pentecost episode: "Repent, and be baptized every one of you in the name of Jesus Christ for the remission of sins, and ye shall receive the gift of the Holy Ghost" (Acts 2:38).

To this truth Paul also testified, as in 1 Corinthians 12:13, where he states, "For by one Spirit are we all baptized into one body, whether we be Jews or Gentiles, whether we be bond or free; and have been all made to drink into one Spirit." Paul's double use of "all," buttressed by the reference to Jews, Gentiles, slaves, and free men, and underlined by his triple use of "one" (Spirit, body, Spirit), makes clear that "all" believers have been brought into the one body of Christ by the regenerating work of the Holy Spirit, and are being nurtured by that one Spirit. His use of the word "baptized" with the Holy Spirit indicates that the same activity of that Spirit has worked in us "all" that worked in different ways for specific purposes in the book of Acts.

In several verses in Romans 8, Paul reminds Christians how dependent they are on the Holy Spirit, and that without His presence in their lives they are not Christians. He emphatically asserts in verse 9, "if any man have not the Spirit of Christ, he is none of his," and he also asserts in verse 14, "For as many as are led by the Spirit of God, they are the sons of God." Finally, he reminds the Romans, and us, "For ye have not received the spirit of bondage again to fear; but ye have received the Spirit of adoption, whereby we cry, 'Abba, Father.' The Spirit itself beareth witness with our spirit, that we are the children of God" (8:15–16; cf. Gal. 4:6–7). Notice that this work of the Spirit is not only that of regeneration and conversion, but also that of leading believers now (8:14), of causing us to know that we are God's children and that He is our Father (8:15–16), and that having "believed, [we] were sealed with that holy Spirit of promise, which is the earnest of our inheritance until the redemption of the purchased possession, unto the praise of his glory" (Eph. 1:13–14). Indeed, it is the entire work of sanctification.

The Filling of the Spirit

This brings us back to the book of Acts, where we see Jesus' promise to the apostles that they would "receive power when the Holy Spirit has come upon you," and that Holy Spirit-given power would enable them to "be my witnesses" (Acts 1:8). It is this aspect to which we should give further attention as it occurs in Acts, particularly with the use of two verbs for "fill" and a cognate noun of one of the verbs that means "full of."[8]

First we look at πιμπλημι (pimplēmi). The power of the Holy Spirit enabled the apostles' preaching to be powerful and effective, and through that power they were rightly esteemed by others as having "boldness" (Acts 4:8, 13). These two elements are tightly tied together in Acts 4:23–31. Peter, John, and the Christian community asked the Lord to "grant unto thy servants, that with all boldness they may speak thy word" (v. 29), and their prayers were answered, so that "they were all filled with the Holy Ghost, and they spake the word of God with boldness" (v. 31). Thus, "filling" came upon Peter, as an example, one who had already been baptized with the Holy Spirit (2:4; the word actually used is "filled") and who had already been said to be "filled with the Holy Ghost" (4:8). Likewise, Paul was promised that he would "be filled with the Holy Ghost" when he regained his sight (9:17), and 13:8 attests that he was so filled.

Next consider the noun πλήρης (plērēs). The church at Jerusalem was instructed to select men "full of the Holy Ghost and wisdom" (6:3). The church chose such, and about Stephen in particular is it said that he was "a man full of faith and of the Holy Ghost" (v. 5); this description is repeated in 7:55. Likewise, a similar description is given of Barnabas: "he was a good man, full of the Holy Ghost and of faith" (11:24).

The last of the three words is the verb πληρόω. This verb is used in concert with the other verb, πιμπλημι, in Acts 2. The wind "filled all the house where they were sitting" (πληρόω, Acts 2:2) and "they were all filled with the Holy Ghost" (πιμπλημι, Acts 2:4). Also, it is

---

8. One Greek verb is πιμπλμι, and it is used of the filling of the Holy Spirit in Acts 2:4; 4:8, 31; 9:17; and 13:9. Related to this verb is the verb πληροω, which is also used with the filling of the Holy Spirit in Acts in 2:2; 13:52; and Ephesians 5:18, and its cognate noun πλήρης, which is also used with the filling of the Holy Spirit in Acts in 6:3, 5; 7:55; and 11:24.

written that "the disciples [of Antioch] were filled with joy and with the Holy Ghost" (πληρόω, Acts 13:52).

The teaching of Ephesians 5:18

The significance of the interconnected usage of these words in Acts is that Paul addresses Christians in his letter to the Ephesians and exhorts them to "be filled with the Spirit" using one of the same verbs as is used in Acts (Eph. 5:18, πληρουσθε, present passive imperative of πληρόω). Paul explicitly recognizes that they have been "sealed with that holy Spirit of promise" and that they should not "grieve...the holy Spirit of God" who already has indwelt them (1:13; 2:22; 4:30).

He is not asking Christians to seek the Spirit or have Him baptize them or fall on them, because his other letters show that he knows this already has happened. But he does ask Christians to seek to be filled with the Spirit. No matter how we understand the preposition[9] used before the Spirit in the phrase "be filled with the Spirit," this statement correlates the verb "be filled" and "the Spirit." "Be filled with the Spirit" is an imperative, which, by definition, is a command. It is in the passive voice: "be filled." Christians are to seek the "filling" that happens to them by the action of God.[10]

The Lord's teaching in Luke 11:13 is helpful in giving us a proper understanding of the Ephesians 5:18 teaching. In the second half of that passage, Jesus said, "how much more will the heavenly Father give the Holy Spirit to them that ask him!" Since the regenerating work of the Father is not a result of us asking for the Holy Spirit, and neither is the baptism or sealing work of the Holy Spirit dependent upon us asking for the Spirit, what is Jesus teaching with reference to the Spirit? I think that the Lucan passage is speaking about the same phenomenon of the Holy Spirit as the Ephesians passage, namely,

---

9. The English translation usually used is "with." The Greek statement is πληρουσθε ἐν πνευματι. Some render the Greek ἐν, with the word "with" to indicate the sphere in which they are filled, and others render it with the word "by," indicating the instrument that does the filling. See H. W. Hoehner, *Ephesians* (Grand Rapids: Baker, 2002), 703–5, and P. T. O'Brien, *The Letter to the Ephesians* (Grand Rapids: Eerdmans, 1999), 391–93; both opt for the instrumental usage and would render the Greek preposition with the word "by." See also A. J. Köstenberger, "What Does It Mean to Be Filled with the Spirit? A Biblical Investigation," *Journal of the Evangelical Theological Society* 40 (June 1997): 229–40.

10. This understanding accords with the parallel passage in Colossians: "Let the word of Christ dwell in you richly..." (Col. 3:16).

the filling or empowering of the Spirit for the work of serving the Lord. We see an illustration of this aspect in Acts 4:29–31: The disciples prayed, "grant unto thy servants, that with all boldness they may speak thy word.... And when they had prayed...they were all filled with the Holy Ghost, and they spake the word of God with boldness." Those who so prayed had already been regenerated by the Spirit and had received the Spirit. But they prayed for His filling and asked God to use them, enabled by His Spirit.

What should we learn from these passages?
This combination of passages in Acts, Ephesians, and Luke shows that Christians should still be seeking and praying for the filling of the Holy Spirit for empowerment in their Christian service. Yes, it may seem a little strange to speak about the command to be filled with the Holy Spirit, but this is the language of the apostle Paul. Paul prays that God will "grant you, according to the riches of his glory, to be strengthened with might by his Spirit in the inner man; that Christ may dwell in your hearts by faith; that ye, being rooted and grounded in love, may be able to comprehend with all saints what is the breadth, and length, and depth, and height; and to know the love of Christ, which passeth knowledge, that ye might be filled with all the fullness of God" (Eph. 3:16–19). So, we should pray for ourselves and our fellow Christians to be strengthened by "being filled with the Spirit."

But what about the extraordinary displays of the Spirit's presence and work, such as the gift of healing and other signs and wonders, which we read about in Acts 4:29–31, for example? Those must await our consideration of signs and wonders, and the gift of healing.

Prophecy in the New Testament
The noun "prophecy" and its related words, the noun "prophet" and the verb "prophesy," are used in the New Testament, as in the Old, of the revelation given by God to the prophets to be proclaimed.[11] This is evident in the first usage of this concept found in the New Testament church in Acts 2:14 and following, especially in verses 17

---

11. For a brief but rather thorough study of this question of prophecy and its related terms, see my booklet, *Prophecy in the New Testament* (Concerned Presbyterians, 2nd printing, 1996).

and 18, where the verb "prophesy" is used once each in both verses, and where Joel 2:28–32 is cited as being fulfilled.

Paul deals at length with the concept of prophecy in the New Testament in 1 Corinthians 11–14, especially in chapter 14. There he tersely refers to prophecy with the word "revelation" in verse 26, and in verse 30 he writes about "a revelation" being given to one of the "prophets," who should by this act of God be allowed to "prophesy" forthwith, while the other who is speaking should "be silent" so that his brother may do so.

Grudem's view of New Testament prophecy
The Reformed community and most of the charismatics have agreed on this understanding of New Testament prophecy.[12] However, Wayne Grudem, and those who follow him, distinguish New Testament prophecy from Old Testament prophecy. He has asserted that New Testament prophecy does not "possess a divine authority of actual words."[13] Grudem regards New Testament prophecy as "speaking merely human words to report something God brings to mind," or, "as something which God can use to bring things to our attention, but as something which nevertheless can contain human interpretation and mistakes."[14]

He seeks to support this view by appealing to various prophecies in Acts,[15] especially the prophecy of Agabus in Acts 21:10–11. He maintains that "using OT standards, Agabus would have been condemned as a false prophet, because in Acts 21:27–35 neither of his

---

12. Sometimes the word *prophecy* is used to indicate preaching in its popular usage, so that one may hear of a preacher being seen as prophetic in his proclamation, but this is only by extension of its meaning. Usually, as the New Testament does, preaching and teaching on the one hand and prophesying on the other are recognized as distinct and different activities. The prophet communicates directly the message given to him by God. The preacher or teacher communicates the message already given by God.

13. Wayne Grudem, *The Gift of Prophecy in I Corinthians* (Lanham, Md.: University Press of America, 1982), 78; also in Wayne Grudem, *The Gift of Prophecy in the New Testament and Today* (Wheaton, Ill.: Crossway Books, 1988), 83.

14. The first quotation is in the table of contents, 7–8, and in chapter subheadings, on pp. 67 and 89, and the second is found in Grudem, *Prophecy in the New Testament*, 114.

15. For the interaction with Grudem on Acts 21:4, "And through the Spirit they were telling Paul not to go on to Jerusalem," see *Prophecy in the New Testament*, 6–7, note 1.

predictions are fulfilled" (i.e., Paul was not bound by the Jews and he had to be delivered *from* the Jews).[16] Agabus had said, "Thus saith the Holy Ghost, So shall the Jews at Jerusalem bind the man that owneth this girdle, and shall deliver him into the hands of the Gentiles" (Acts 21:11). However, notice that, contrary to Grudem, Paul used very similar words to those in this prophecy to describe to the Jews why he was imprisoned in Rome: "Men and brethren, though I have committed nothing against the people, or customs of our fathers, yet was I delivered prisoner from Jerusalem into the hands of the Romans" (Acts 28:17). Agabus's word "bind," if understood in its metaphorical sense of the ones responsible for Paul's being bound and brought to Rome, certainly had the Jews in view, according to Paul. Paul wrote that after the Romans "had examined me, [they] would have let me go, because there was no cause of death in me. But when the Jews spake against it, I was constrained to appeal unto Caesar" (Acts 28:18–19; cf. also the testimony of Felix, who, "willing to shew the Jews a pleasure, left Paul bound" [Acts 24:27]; note also the numerous times where it is indicated that the Jews were prosecuting the case against Paul, Acts 21:27; 22:30; 24:1–2; 25:2, 15, 24). So, not only is this case of prophecy, and others in Acts, inadequate to make Grudem's case, the thesis itself on its face is not compelling.[17]

Scripture's Teaching on the Extraordinary Gifts

This leads to the question that separates, in general, the Reformed perspective from that of the charismatic—whether or not the extraordinary spiritual gifts continued after the apostolic age. This question, like related matters (Do the apostles continue? Is the canon of Scripture closed?), cannot be solved by citing one or more Scripture passages, but only by "good and necessary consequence may be deduced from Scripture."[18]

---

16. Grudem, *The Gift of Prophecy in I Corinthians*, 79.

17. I am indebted to Victor Budgen, *The Charismatics and the Word of God* (Darlington, England: Evangelical Press, 2001), 270–72, for the arguments used in the text. For further refutation of this erroneous view, see R. B. Gaffin, Jr., *Perspectives on Pentecost* (Phillipsburg, N.J.: Presbyterian and Reformed, 1979), 65–67.

18. Westminster Confession of Faith, 1.6. The sentence as a whole reads as follows: "The whole counsel of God concerning all things necessary for his own glory, man's salvation, faith and life, is either expressly set down in Scripture, or by good and necessary consequence may be deduced from Scripture: unto which nothing at any time is to be added, whether by new revelations of the Spirit, or traditions of men."

The cessation of the apostolic and prophetical offices

First, consider the cessation of the apostolic and prophetical offices and their gifts. The word "apostle," as it appears in the New Testament, designates the Twelve, Paul, and perhaps a few others (Acts 14:14), and it refers to those eyewitnesses of the resurrection who were appointed by Christ to be first in leadership and authority in His church, to communicate His revelation, and to be the foundation for His church.[19] The word "prophet" in the New Testament, when joined with the word "apostle," designates a New Testament person and not an Old Testament figure. This is deduced from the fact that Paul affirms that the apostles and prophets had been "appointed in the church" by "God" respectively "first" and "second"; that is, they were the first and second most necessary gifts for the church (to which teachers were then added as the third most necessary [1 Cor. 12:28]). These two, apostles and prophets, are among the gifts God has given to the church (vv. 28–31). Compare also verses 4–11, which speak of the "diversities of gifts" given by the Spirit for the common good, including "prophecy."

Paul's letter to the Ephesians mentions "apostles and prophets" in three very important situations (Eph. 2:20; 3:5; 4:11). In 4:11, these extraordinary gifts, as well as ordinary gifts that continue, are said to be given by the ascended Christ. In 3:5, apostles and prophets are said to be the receivers and bearers of "the mystery of Christ," which has been "revealed to his holy apostles and prophets by the Spirit." In 2:19–20, they are identified as "the foundation" on which "the household of God" is "built," with "Christ Jesus Himself being the cornerstone." These apostles and prophets are clearly distinguished from each other in 4:11, as they are in 1 Corinthians 12:28, and thus also in Ephesians 2:20 and 3:5.[20]

---

19. See George W. Knight III, *The Pastoral Epistles* (Grand Rapids: Eerdmans, 1992), 58, for the biblical references for each of the items mentioned above. In addition to this predominant New Testament usage, in a couple of places the word designates the "messenger" or "delegate" sent by the church, for example, 2 Corinthians 8:23 and Philippians 2:25, and the word for "apostle" is also used sometimes to designate "false" apostles (2 Cor. 11:13; cf. 11:5; 12:11).

20. In Ephesians 4:11, both apostles and prophets have their distinguishing definite article in the Greek, and also a distinguishing μεν and δε. Grudem's assertion that the references in Ephesians 2:20 and 3:5 should be understood to mean "the apostles who are also prophets" (*The Gift of Prophecy in I Corinthians*, 105) must candidly be said to be a case of special pleading for his argument that New Testament

The foundation of the apostles and prophets
Paul refers to apostles and prophets as "the foundation" in Ephesians 2:19–20, meaning that the church is built out and up from the revelation given by Christ, with the apostles and prophets elaborating and explaining the mystery, which has been made known to them by the Holy Spirit (3:4–11, especially v. 5).[21] The data in the New Testament show that once Judas (the betrayer) was replaced, there were no more replacements for the other apostles, and the same evaluation is implied for the prophets joined so closely with the apostles. The non-replacement of the apostles is evident in the reference in the book of Revelation that the wall of the Jerusalem to come has "twelve foundations, and in them the names of the twelve apostles of the Lamb" (Rev. 21:14). From the reference in Ephesians 2:19–20 to the apostles and prophets being the foundation, it should be clear that these offices are not perpetual in the life of the church, but they served rather as the once-laid foundation for the church. The implication is that neither the apostles nor the prophets (given by Christ as one of the primary spiritual gifts) continued beyond the foundational stage of the church, except in the book of Revelation.

Thus, the instruction in 1 Thessalonians 5:20 and 1 Corinthians 12–14 with reference to prophets and prophecy was relevant in the apostolic age, as was the instruction for replacing Judas in Acts 1:23–26, but when that gift was no longer given, that instruction was mute. This fact has further implications, namely, that not all of the spiritual gifts continue in the life of the post-apostolic church.

The use of "signs," "wonders," and "miracles"
When the gospel was being proclaimed in the early church, it was accompanied by "signs" (σημεια), often by "wonders" (τερατα), and at least four times by "miracles" (δυναμεις), and these were often (but not always) brought about by the apostles.[22] The actions that

---

prophecy continues. He appropriately recognizes that Ephesians 2:20 indicates the foundational and non-repetitive character of the "apostles," and therefore from his perspective (that "prophecy" continues) the passage must not be understood as referring to "prophets" themselves.

21. Peter T. O'Brien, *The Letter to the Ephesians* (Grand Rapids: Eerdmans, 1999), 218.

22. Σημεια are aptly rendered by the English word "signs," as they point to the message they accompany and signify its truthfulness and reality. Τερατα are used in the New Testament only in the plural and only with σημεια. Those who experienced this phenomenon were amazed at what they were seeing, and thus the

were usually in view when these signs were in evidence were those of healing. Acts 4:22 says it explicitly with these words: "on whom this miracle of healing was shewed" (cf. 4:16 and the context). Similarly, in Acts 4:30, we read that the church prayed to God that He would enable them to speak the gospel boldly "by stretching forth thine hand to heal; and that signs and wonders may be done by the name of thy holy child Jesus." The case with Philip, however, makes it clear that healing was not the only sign they performed, for Luke relates that the people heard and saw "the miracles" which he did: "unclean spirits, crying with loud voice, came out of many that were possessed with them: and many…were healed" (Acts 8:6–7).

The most significant thing to learn from these signs is how they signify the reality of the gospel of Christ. Immediately after Peter cites the passage from Joel with its reference to wonders and signs (Acts 2:19), he spells out the significance of these signs with reference to Jesus: "Jesus of Nazareth, a man approved of God among you by miracles and wonders and signs, which God did by him in the midst of you" (Acts 2:22), by the use of the verb "approved." This result of the signs is repeated throughout Acts: "fear came upon every soul" when these signs "were done by the apostles" (Acts 2:43); "And by the hands of the apostles were many signs and wonders wrought among the people…. And believers were the more added to the Lord, multitudes both of men and women" (Acts 5:12, 14). It is specifically said that "the people with one accord gave heed unto those things which Philip spake, hearing and seeing the miracles which he did" (Acts 8:6). Likewise, Paul and Barnabas were encouraged to speak boldly for the Lord when He "gave testimony unto the word of his grace, and granted signs and wonders to be done by their hands" (Acts 14:3).

---

translation "wonders" is appropriate. Notice as an example of this phenomenon Acts 8:13, where τερατα is not used with the other two, but the verb used indicates "he was amazed." δυναμεις generally means power or capability, but in the four or so times that it occurs with these other two words, it is usually rendered "miracles." The apostles are in view in the majority of usages in the book of Acts (cf., e.g., Acts 5:12), but Stephen and Philip are also involved with these "signs" (Acts 6:8 and 8:6, respectively). Σημεια is used thirteen times in Acts; twice each in four Pauline letters, but not always with the same significance; once in Hebrews, seven times in Revelation; and forty-eight times in the four Gospels. Τερατα is used nine times in Acts; once each in three Pauline letters; once in Hebrews; and once each in Matthew, Mark, and John. δυναμεις, which occurs 119 times in the New Testament, is used four times in Acts accompanying the other two words.

The words of the apostle Paul give a similar report. He summarizes his ministry to the Gentiles in these words: "For I will not dare to speak of any of those things which Christ hath not wrought by me, to make the Gentiles obedient, by word and deed, through mighty signs and wonders, by the power of the Spirit of God; so that from Jerusalem, and round about unto Illyricum, I have fully preached the gospel of Christ" (Rom. 15:18–19). Thus, he writes to the Corinthians, saying, "Truly the signs of an apostle were wrought among you in all patience, in signs, and wonders, and mighty deeds" (2 Cor. 12:12).

Finally, the writer to the Hebrews summarizes the gospel message he had received from those before him with these words: "God also bearing them witness, both with signs and wonders, and with divers miracles, and gifts of the Holy Ghost, according to his own will" (Heb. 2:4). The key statement is, "God also bearing them witness" by signs.[23]

Leaving aside the references to our Lord in the Gospels and again in Revelation, only in Acts and in these words in these three epistles, which look back to previous experiences, are there these tremendous teachings about signs, wonders, and miracles. Do not these facts themselves indicate that they refer only to the foundational stages of the church? Are these not the corroborative works that God gave to the apostles and those who labored with them as they laid the foundation for the church (Eph. 2:20), and did they not cease when the apostles died and the apostolic era itself came to an end?

The Waning or Cessation of Other Extraordinary Gifts
Speaking in tongues
Consider also some of the other special gifts and their apparent waning within the New Testament itself. Take the phenomenon of speaking in tongues and the associated events. In its first occurrence with the apostles (Acts 2:1–13), the phenomenon was accompanied by "a sound from heaven as of a rushing mighty wind" and "cloven tongues like as of fire [that] sat upon each of them" (vv. 2–3). The most striking aspect of this event is that the apostles "began to speak with other tongues as the Spirit gave them utterance" (v. 4).

---

23. Συνεπιμαρτυρεω is the Greek verb used here. It means to "testify at the same time" (BDAG), with the dative words in the Greek "signs and wonders and various miracles" signifying the means used to give that testimony.

The result was that each one in the crowd could hear them speak the mighty works of God "in his own language" (vv. 6, 7–11).

But in the other episodes in the book of Acts when speaking in tongues is reported (10:46; 19:6), the wind and fire are not mentioned, nor is the ability of others to understand in their own languages. When the speaking of tongues is mentioned in 1 Corinthians 12–14, an interpreter is required if one is to speak in public (1 Cor. 14:27–28). In the Corinthians reference, the one speaking in tongues no longer speaks to the hearers "in his own language," but someone has to interpret what he says for them to understand.

It is noteworthy that aside from the three special occasions in Acts (2:1–13, Pentecost [the apostles]; 10:44–48, Peter and Cornelius [the Gentiles]; and 19:1–7 [Paul and John's disciples in Ephesus]) and Paul's lengthy instruction about these and other gifts in 1 Corinthians 12–14, the phenomenon of speaking in tongues is not mentioned, either as a characteristic of a believer or as a necessity for an officer in Christ's church. Was this one of the signs given in the foundational period of the building of Christ's church that not only faded, changed, and became less spectacular, but faded away altogether as a sign?[24] If this be so, then the words of instruction for it, like those for prophecy, also became moot when it was no longer given as a "sign" (which both tongues-speaking and prophecy are called in 1 Cor. 14:22).[25]

The gift of healing

The gift of healing, one aspect of the "signs," manifests the same waning in the New Testament. During Christ's ministry and that of the apostles, the gift of healing was in full display, as in the extensive

---

24. Compare the language of the apostle Paul in 1 Cor. 13:8, where he writes, "as for tongues, they will cease." The voice of the Greek verb is middle, whereas the other two verbs concerning prophecy and knowledge are passive. Daniel B. Wallace suggests for this middle the understanding of "they will cease [on their own]," or more fully in his text, "cease of their own accord, i.e., 'die out' without an intervening agent (indirect middle)." See Wallace, *Greek Grammar Beyond the Basics* (Grand Rapids: Zondervan, 1996), 422ff., not only for his treatment of this verb and its understanding, but also for his defense of that understanding over against the dominant opinion among New Testament scholars that the verb is future deponent and therefore active in meaning. See also footnote 26.

25. Σημειον, the same word as was used in the Acts accounts when they spoke of signs, wonders, and miracles.

healing of Peter and the other apostles in Acts 5:12–16, where the people even "brought forth the sick into the streets, and laid them on beds and couches," and people "out of the cities round about unto Jerusalem [brought] sick folks...and they were healed every one" (vv. 15–16). Think not only of them "all" being healed, but also consider the spectacular phenomenon that people put their sick in the streets, "that at the least the shadow of Peter passing by might overshadow some of them" (v. 15).

During the ministry of Paul, recorded in Acts, "God wrought special miracles by the hands of Paul: so that from his body were brought unto the sick handkerchiefs or aprons, and the diseases departed from them, and the evil spirits went out of them" (Acts 19:11–12). Here was one of those "signs," designated by the third item in that threefold list, i.e., "miracles" (*terata*, translated by the English Standard Version as "extraordinary miracles"), with the result that "fear fell on them all, and the name of the Lord Jesus was magnified" and "so mightily grew the word of God and prevailed" (Acts 19:17, 20).

However, except for the examples in the Gospels and Acts, and the three references to the "gifts of healing" in 1 Corinthians 12 (9, 28, 30), the rest of the New Testament does not characterize Christians or officers in the church as possessing this special gift. Even Paul, through whom God had done many miracles with the handkerchiefs and aprons that had touched his skin (Acts 19:11–12), later in his ministry prayed that God would take away "a thorn...given me in the flesh" (2 Cor. 12:7), only to learn that the thorn would stay and that God's grace was sufficient for him (2 Cor. 12:8–9). Furthermore, and even more telling, Paul "left Trophimus, who was ill, at Miletus" (2 Tim. 4:20) rather than personally healing him! Finally, note Paul's statement about Epaphroditus in Philippians 2:25–27. Paul writes that he had been ill, and underlines his statement with these words: "Indeed he was sick nigh unto death" (2:27a). After this vivid description, he writes thankfully of God's mercy in raising Epaphroditus from his illness and out of the near-death situation. We read that "God had mercy on him; and not on him only, but on me also, lest I should have sorrow upon sorrow" (2:27b). This statement most likely implies that God did the healing.

What conclusion can be drawn from these situations? Is it not appropriate to deduce that the extraordinary sign of healing had done its work in undergirding the laying of the foundation of the gospel, and that it had ceased as a sign gift? Indeed, God still does heal in answer to prayer, but not by means of one who has the gift of healing, and not always, as the two examples from Paul make evident. The Christian should indeed ask God to heal, if it is God's will, and be willing to accept the verdict, whatever it may be, as the expression of God's will. On the matter of public prayer for the one who requests it, James writes these instructions for the elders, as well as the one requesting their prayers: "Is any sick among you? Let him call for the elders of the church; and let them pray over him, anointing him with oil in the name of the Lord: and the prayer of faith shall save the sick, and the Lord shall raise him up; and if he have committed sins, they shall be forgiven him" (5:14–15).

Conclusions

We can deduce from this survey of the evidence that God laid the foundation for His church in the apostles and prophets, and that He gave to them and those with them certain signs, wonders, and miracles to corroborate the gospel proclaimed and the foundation being laid. With the cessation of their task, the ministry of the apostles and prophets ceased, and so did the signs given to them, the beginning of which cessation we see within the New Testament itself.[26] Thus, we can deduce that the extraordinary gifts of the Spirit are no longer being given to the church. At the same time, we must still gladly say that the ordinary spiritual gifts are still given and are still needful for the church and for Christians.

How can we arrive at such a deduction? Not because we are wiser or more perceptive than the charismatics, but only because we have searched out God's Word and want to be obedient and resigned to it.

What has this search produced that is beneficial to the soul and life of believers, as well as edifying to their minds? It is that in Christ they have all that they need, and they do not need to seek something better or higher, such as a follow-up baptism of the Holy

---

26. In this argument, we are not appealing to "the perfect" as meaning the close of the canon in 1 Corinthians 13:8–12, as some others have done, because we think that Paul is writing about something else there and not about the subject we are addressing (for my fuller treatment of this passage see *Prophecy in the New Testament*, 21–22, footnote 12). See also footnote 24.

Spirit. Except for those few instances in the New Testament when God was especially instructing His church that the Samaritans and the Gentiles were one with the Jewish believers and apostles, the New Testament repeatedly affirms that when people are united to Christ by faith they thereby receive the Holy Spirit.[27] Thus, all Christians have the vitality of being united to Christ and indwelt by His Holy Spirit. As with so many other gifts and graces of God, they are continually urged by the apostle Paul to be filled with the Spirit and to walk by the Spirit, and not just rest content that they have once believed, once repented, and once been baptized by the Spirit.

How, then, are we to interact with our charismatic fellow Christians? When the opportunity is appropriate, we should talk with them in an understanding way and try to show them why we think that the supernatural special gifts have ceased because they have done the tasks God assigned for them. When they point to their own lives as proof positive of their charismatic thinking, we should try to point out to them other ways of understanding their lives. Were they only nominal Christians who have now come to really trust in God, and therefore, like the Ephesian disciples, have of course received the baptism of the Holy Spirit as they trusted in Christ? Or were they really believers who turned from a lackadaisical walk as God heard their prayer and filled them with His Holy Spirit, in which they were already baptized? In our eagerness to protect the Christian flock from the error of the charismatics, we must at the same time seek to lead those who are involved in that error to the truth.

The vitality of the Reformed faith is evidenced in the regenerating work of God immediately leading to the baptism of the Holy Spirit and the ongoing filling of that Spirit in God's people. This work of God enables His people to understand that God sovereignly founded His church in the apostolic age on the apostles and prophets with a

---

27. The Holy Spirit is the One who makes us alive in our deadness in sins and brings us to embrace Christ offered in the gospel by saving faith. God in adoption gives us the Holy Spirit; i.e., He baptizes us in Him. Thus, the Spirit first makes us alive, and then when we are united to Christ by faith, God pours His Spirit within us. The Westminster Larger Catechism puts it quite well in answer 74: "Adoption is an act of the free grace of God, in and for his only Son Jesus Christ, whereby all those that are justified are received into the number of his children, have his name put upon them, the Spirit of his Son given to them, are under his fatherly care and dispensations."

display of extraordinary gifts, and also to understand that God continues to build His church on that foundation without those apostles and prophets by the ordinary, not extraordinary, spiritual gifts He still gives His church. This vitality and understanding enables those who embrace the Reformed faith to meet the challenge of the charismatic movement.

CHAPTER 8

The Supply of the Spirit of Jesus Christ

John P. Thackway

For I know that this shall turn to my salvation through your prayer, and the supply of the Spirit of Jesus Christ.
—Philippians 1:19

The apostle Paul wrote the above words from his prison in Rome. "The supply of the Spirit" is an interesting phrase, and we find it only here. There are similar expressions in the New Testament, for example: "filled with the Spirit" (Eph. 5:18); "an unction from the Holy One" (1 John 2:20); "the love of the Spirit" (Rom. 15:30); "led by the Spirit of God" (Rom. 8:14); and "the comfort of the Holy Ghost" (Acts 9:31). However, the way Paul put it here is unique, and it is full of instruction for us. How did he come to be in Rome, and what did he mean when writing these words?

The apostle had wanted to visit Rome for a long time. However, it was not his goal to plant a church there, because one already existed. On the day of Pentecost, when Jews from Rome were in Jerusalem and heard Peter's sermon (Acts 2:10), they may have returned home and started a church in the heart of the empire.

Paul instead wanted to visit the church there for its *edification*. At Corinth, halfway round his third missionary journey, he wrote his epistle to the Romans and told them he was praying for this: "Making request, if by any means now at length I might have a prosperous journey by the will of God to come unto you. For I long to see you, that I may impart unto you some spiritual gift, to the end ye may be established…. So, as much as in me is, I am ready to preach the gospel to you that are at Rome also" (Rom. 1:10, 11, 15).

Paul had tried to come earlier, but the Lord had prevented him: "Now I would not have you ignorant, brethren, that oftentimes I purposed to come unto you, (but was let hitherto,) that I might have some fruit among you also, even as among other Gentiles" (v. 13).

Paul evidently accepted the providence that denied his visit to Rome, and this has something to teach us. Even a worthy ambition must acknowledge a higher hand and bow to it. Our concern must always be whether *the Lord* would have us do something or not. Though it may seem good to us, it is not necessarily good in *His* eyes. This is why Paul has the proviso in verse 10, "by the will of God."

About three years later, the Lord gave Paul his desire to minister in Rome. However, it was not by means of an extra missionary journey for that purpose. It began one day in Jerusalem, when a lynch mob falsely accused him of desecrating the temple (Acts 21:27ff.). Roman soldiers intervened, but still accused by the Jews, Paul was arraigned before local Roman governors. With no hope of justice from Felix, Festus, and Agrippa, he exercised his right of Roman citizenship and appealed to Caesar. So, after a perilous voyage and shipwreck, the apostle eventually arrived in Rome in chains and under house arrest (28:16, 30, 31) to await his appeal.

He was finally in Rome, but not as a free man. The great preacher to the Roman world was limited to receiving visitors and ministering to them privately. How different this was from what he imagined, and how disappointing for him! The Lord's ways are past finding out.

However, Paul's attitude was clearly one of submission to his Master, because in another epistle from Rome he calls himself "the prisoner of Jesus Christ" (Eph. 3:1). He could have said he was the prisoner of Nero, but Nero was not the one who really put him there: he saw the Lord's hand in it, and to that he bowed. Paul could recognize that the Lord had placed him in a Roman prison for a purpose. Through grace, he was enabled to have a humble spirit, beautifully expressed in these lines,

> I ask Thee for the daily strength
> To none that asks denied:
> A mind to blend with outward life,
> While keeping at Thy side;

> Content to fill a little space,
> If Thou be glorified.[1]

It is not so much our situation that matters—it is how we act in that situation that counts. What an example Paul is!

Remember, too, that Paul had written to the Romans, "If *by any means*...I...might come unto you" (1:10). The means the Lord chose were false accusation, arrest, judicial hearings, voyage and shipwreck, and remanded in custody! This teaches us to be careful of what we say in prayer. Our words may well come back to us—not to haunt us, but as the Lord reminding us of what we professed. He does not want us merely to state things; He wants us really to mean them. May we have grace to be taken at our word and be proved sincere in all that we say, for we may be tested sooner than we realize.

Coming to our text in Philippians 1:19, Paul writes from prison to the Philippians. He says his confinement will be made profitable to him through their prayers and as "the supply of the Spirit of Jesus Christ" is given him. These words are his testimony.

Paul does not ask them to pray for his release, for his appeal to be successful, or that he might escape death. What he wants most is their prayers for such a supply of the Spirit as will sanctify the experience to him. He knows he has only as much grace as the Holy Spirit has worked in him, and he will have only as much help in trial as that same Spirit is pleased to give him. If this was so for Paul, how much more so for us.

With this in mind, let us consider this unique expression, "the supply of the Spirit of Jesus Christ." What did it mean for Paul and what can it mean for us?

The Spirit Himself

When he writes, "the Spirit of Jesus Christ," Paul describes Him with reference to our Lord in two ways: His saving name, "Jesus," and His messianic title, "Christ."

Paul expresses it like this because He is the Spirit whom the Father promised to Jesus Christ. In the everlasting covenant between the Father and the Son, the Spirit was the third party in the plan of salvation. The Father gave the Spirit to serve our Lord and to equip

---

1. From the hymn "Father, I Know That All My Life" in *Hymns and Meditations*, ed. Anna Laetitia Waring (New York: E. P. Dutton, 1873), #1.

Him to fulfill His work of redeeming us. Any loving father would do this for a loved son who was to undertake a great task. Think of it: the third Person of the Godhead ministering to the second Person of the Godhead in the days of His flesh! Coming into the world to save us, our Lord would be wonderfully helped by the Spirit, as we shall see. By Him, "The LORD [would be]…the saving strength of his anointed" (Ps. 28:8). We can trace how this was fulfilled.

We know of it first in prophecy. The Spirit in the Old Testament prophets (1 Peter 1:11) inspired them to predict this promised help. One example among many is Isaiah 42:1: "Behold my servant, whom I uphold; mine elect, in whom my soul delighteth; I have put my spirit upon him." Here, Isaiah foreshadows the Spirit-empowered Messiah.

We know of it in our Lord's incarnation. In Hebrews 10:5, Paul, quoting Psalm 40, writes, "Wherefore when he cometh into the world, he saith, Sacrifice and offering thou wouldest not, but a body hast thou prepared me." The One who formed that body for God's Son was the Holy Spirit, as the angel said to Joseph: "that which is conceived in [Mary] is of the Holy Ghost" (Matt. 1:20).

Earlier, when Gabriel announced this to Mary herself, he said, "the Holy Ghost shall come upon thee, and the power of the Highest shall overshadow thee: therefore also that holy thing which shall be born of thee shall be called the Son of God" (Luke 1:35). This reminds us of the beginning, when the Holy Spirit "moved upon the face of the waters" (Gen. 1:2)—literally, "brooded, hovered over"—to create all things. So here, the Spirit formed our Lord's manhood in Mary's womb and united it with His deity.

It was a heavenly provision and enduement. In Matthew 3:17, we read that the Spirit descended on Christ at His baptism, and the Father said (echoing the words of Isaiah 42:1, "mine elect, in whom my soul delighteth"), "this is my beloved Son, in whom I am well pleased." The Spirit came to supply and service the Son of man for the great work of redemption. Jesus did not need this as God, but as God's Servant He accepted it, and this showed His subordination to the Father. This is confirmed in Isaiah 48:16, where the Messiah says, "the Lord GOD, *and his Spirit*, hath sent me" (emphasis added). As the nineteenth-century Scots divine George Smeaton wrote, "The task assigned to the Spirit, and carried out by Him in all respects, was to anoint and equip the Mediator for all the duties of that servant's place which He was abased to fill."[2]

This was all our incarnate Redeemer needed: "The Spirit of Jesus Christ." The Father did not send His Son on this colossal mission to save us without the Spirit's enabling to fulfill the work. He was the supply of heaven for heaven's Beloved One.

It is true, the Father gave the Redeemer other help. Angels ministered to Him.

As Jonathan Edwards wrote, "The angels…were committed to him, to be subject to him in his mediatorial office, to be ministering spirits to him in this affair."[3] We see this as our Lord underwent His temptations in the wilderness (Mark 1:13); His agony in Gethsemane (Luke 22:43); His resurrection (Matt. 28:2–7; John 20:12, 13); and His ascension (Acts 1:9–11). Truly, He was "seen of angels" (1 Tim. 3:16) and was wonderfully helped by them.

The disciples also ministered to His needs. How much their love and support meant to Him! There was the hospitality at Bethany (Luke 10:38–42). There were the women "which ministered unto him of their substance" (Luke 8:3). It is true that the disciples were not always consistent. Our Lord had to ask: "Where is your faith?… Could ye not watch with me one hour?" (Luke 8:25; Matt. 26:40). We detect a note of disappointment in these words, for our Lord appreciated the company and trust of His own while in the world. He loved them unto the end and treasured *their* love.

However, the greatest ministry was that of the Spirit. We can see this throughout the Gospels, for example in Luke 4:1, 14, where we read: "And Jesus being full of the Holy Ghost returned from Jordan, and was led by the spirit into the wilderness…. And Jesus returned in the power of the spirit into Galilee: and there went out a fame of him through all the region round about." And Peter could preach in Acts 10:38, "God anointed Jesus of Nazareth with the Holy Ghost and with power…for God was with him."

Clearly, this wonderful provision supplied our Lord right up to the climax of His work: His death on the cross. In one of his

---

2. George Smeaton, *The Doctrine of the Holy Spirit* (Edinburgh: Banner of Truth, 1974), 122.

3. Jonathan Edwards, *History of Redemption* (Mulberry, Ind.: Sovereign Grace Publishers, 2000), 30.

sermons, Robert Murray M'Cheyne expressed it beautifully, quoting Hebrews 9:14:

> Never did the Holy Ghost find such a rest as in the bosom of Emmanuel—never did He find such a home as *that*.... And when He hung on the Cross, the Holy Spirit seemed *still* to be within Him. God the Father hid His face from Him; for He cried out, *My God, My God, etc.* As if He had said, "I thought that thou wouldst have been the last in the world to have forsaken me." *Even then* the Spirit was dwelling within Him; for it is written, He, through the eternal Spirit offered himself without spot to God.[4]

Likewise, the Spirit's might was present to bring about the resurrection. In addition to the Father's power and our Lord's own power, the Holy Spirit raised up our Lord. He was "declared to be the Son of God with power, according to the spirit of holiness, by the resurrection from the dead" (Rom. 1:4).

All of this gives our Lord His messianic title. "Christ" is a translation of the Greek *christos*, which literally means "anointed." It comes from the metaphor of oil, the biblical symbol of the Holy Spirit. We find this used of the Messiah in Isaiah 61:1: "The Spirit of the LORD God is upon me; because the LORD hath anointed me to preach good tidings." In Hebrews 1:9, Paul quotes Psalm 45:7, referring to Christ: "God, even thy God, hath anointed thee with the oil of gladness above thy fellows."

The phrase "above thy fellows" in this verse is saying that Christ has more of the Spirit than anyone else. Who are His "fellows"? We are—His people—and we also have the Spirit. This reminds us that the Spirit given to Christ is also given to us. It happened like this. His resurrection was the beginning of His exaltation, concerning which Peter declared, "being by the right hand of God exalted, and having received of the Father the promise of the Holy Ghost, he hath shed forth this, which ye now see and hear" (Acts 2:33). In other words, He has shed the Spirit upon us. Christ's anointing is *our* anointing also. John Gill comments:

---

4. Robert Murray M'Cheyne, "The Ministry of Jesus and of His Servants," *Banner of Truth* no. 571 (April 2011): 13–14. This sermon does not appear in M'Cheyne's published writings; it was taken from a listener's notes published in *The Sword and the Trowel* (Oct. 1867).

Now Christ was anointed as Mediator from all eternity;...but he was declared to be Lord and Christ, the anointed one; and received gifts for men, the fullness of the Spirit without measure, and with which he was anointed above his "fellows"; by whom are meant, not the angels, nor the kings and princes of the earth; but the saints, who are so called, because they are of the same nature, and are of the same family, and are partakers of the same spirit, and grace; and having received the unction from him, are also kings, priests, and prophets, and will be companions with him to all eternity.[5]

This is very wonderful. Christ has made you and me partakers of the same Holy Spirit that He has! Remember the description of the anointing of Aaron in Psalm 133:2. There, it is said that the oil went over his head, down his beard, and onto the skirts of his garments—a picture of the Spirit upon Christ, and upon His members, the church, also. Union with Jesus Christ means we partake of His Spirit. We are anointed ones, too, who have "an unction from the Holy One" (1 John 2:20) and are "Christ-ians" (see Acts 11:26). What has been supplied to Christ is supplied also to us: without measure to Him, and in large measure to us.

The Spirit Supplied

Going back to our verse, what does Paul mean when he mentions "the supply of the Spirit"? He means that the Spirit that was supplied to his Master can be supplied to him also. And this is so for every believer in Christ! This is why Paul is led to say these things. What, then, does this mean for us experientially and practically?

First, we can say that we share in this wonderful supply. The Spirit who ministered to the incarnate Son of God, and was everything He needed, ministers to us also. What an encouraging precedent this is! Did He fail our Lord? Neither does He fail us.

Second, it means that the Spirit can be all we need. "Supply" (*epichoregia*) is an interesting word. It was used of a payment to a chorus master to defray the expenses of a chorus or dance. In our passage, it is in its strengthened form, and therefore means a very generous

---

5. John Gill, *Exposition of the Old and New Testaments* (1809; repr., Paris, Ark.: Baptist Standard Bearer, 1989), 9:378 [on Heb. 1:9].

payment to ensure a lavish production. The Spirit therefore is not barely enough for us: He is *abundantly* supplied.

That supply is always in proportion to what we need. The greater the need, the greater the supply: "He giveth more grace" (James 4:6). Have you noticed the "As...so's" in Scripture? For instance, Deuteronomy 33:25, where God promises, "*as* thy days, *so* shall thy strength be." And 2 Corinthians 1:5, "*as* the sufferings of Christ abound in us, *so* our consolation also aboundeth by Christ." This proportionality encourages us to believe that when our need comes, the supply of the Spirit comes also. We should let it also check our tendency to worry about future needs: "How will I make out if I lose my job, if my husband is taken from me, if this or that trial comes," etc.? The answer is that we do not get tomorrow's grace today. The supply of the Spirit is there for us when the need is there, and not before. Therefore, "Take no thought for the morrow..." (Matt. 6:34).

An interesting question arises at this point: Is the supply something the Spirit provides or the Spirit Himself? Putting it another way, is the Spirit the Giver or the Gift? J. B. Lightfoot says that the Greek will bear either interpretation, and we should take it as being both.[6] In my view, this is correct. Suppose a lady becomes married to a wealthy and devoted husband. Are her needs met by what he gives to her or by what he is to her? Both are true—they are simply two ways of looking at the same thing. And both are wonderfully true for us concerning the supply of the Spirit: He gives us what we need, and He gives us Himself.

Let us now apply these truths to ourselves more fully.

Are you a minister of the gospel?
"Who is sufficient for these things?" is the heartfelt cry of ministers, and rightly so. What help we need! Here is our help—in full supply. What was true of the Messiah can be true for us: "The Spirit of the LORD God is upon me; because the LORD hath anointed me to preach good tidings." The Spirit is supplied to us to enlighten, enliven, enlarge, empower, and enable us to be "the LORD's messenger in the LORD's message unto the people" (Hag. 1:13). This is how

---

6. J. B. Lightfoot, *Saint Paul's Epistle to the Philippians: A Revised Text with Introduction, Notes, and Dissertations* (Grand Rapids: Zondervan, 1953), 91.

our sufficiency is of God. Let us venture forth and trust to this promised supply. As one old divine put it: "I go, He comes."

There is, of course, sovereignty in the Spirit's working. Sometimes
we feel marvellously helped in preaching. Other times we feel anything but helped—and yet those are often the times when the Lord
gives the blessing. God hides pride from man and uses "earthen vessels" for His glory alone. The Scottish Free Church minister Kenneth
MacRae once wrote in his diary: "I had no sense of liberty and felt
very disappointed. On my return home, however, a remark of Matthew Henry comforted me: 'When God's servants are bound, yet His
word and Spirit are not bound; spiritual children may then be born
to them.' May it be so."[7]

Are you being persecuted?
Paul was persecuted by Jews and by Romans. Evidently, the supply
of the Spirit was such that he could "rejoice" (Phil. 1:18). This is like
our Lord in this world, who, though He was the man of sorrows, yet
could "rejoice in spirit," literally "in the Spirit" (Luke 10:21). Joy is
one of the Spirit's fruits (Gal. 5:22), and the new Christians at Thes-
salonica experienced this. They had "received the word in much
affliction, *with joy of the Holy Ghost*" (1 Thess. 1:6, emphasis added)—
the joy was more powerful than the affliction!

The account of a girl in a Muslim country illustrates this remarkably. She was converted through a broadcast ministry, and when
questioned by her uncle, she confessed she had become a Christian.
Upon hearing this, he "picked up a chair, broke it over her back, then
took a leg and began beating her." She was rescued by her father
and sent out of the country. A fellow Christian asked what she was
thinking while her uncle was beating her to death. She replied, "I
was thinking that this man has a religion that he would kill for, but
I have a Savior that I would die for."[8] Was that not something more
powerful than affliction: "joy of the Holy Ghost"?

Sometimes, however, persecution comes in the form of our being
savagely criticized by others—not gracious, constructive criticism

---

7. *The Diary of Kenneth A. MacRae: A Record of Fifty Years in the Christian Ministry*,
ed. Iain H. Murray (Edinburgh: Banner of Truth, 1980), 281.

8. J. Ligon Duncan III, "The Resurgence of Calvinism in America," in *Calvin
for Today*, ed. Joel R. Beeke (Grand Rapids: Reformation Heritage Books, 2009), 231.

that, if received in a humble, teachable spirit, does us good (Ps. 141:5), but the withering, destructive kind. This is hard to bear, and can tempt us with vengeful feelings, self-justification, arguing with the person in our heads, and much more. It is a comfort to know that the Lord Jesus knew what it was to be attacked this way; He identifies with us in our sufferings. And the Spirit who was upon our Lord is upon us also, and will give us grace to do as He did, for "when he was reviled, [He] reviled not again; when he suffered, he threatened not; but committed himself to him that judgeth righteously" (1 Peter 2:23). We can leave our cause and reputation in our Father's hands, too, and say like Jeremiah: "O LORD, thou hast seen my wrong: judge thou my cause" (Lam. 3:59).

Are you being tempted?
Doubtless, we will be tempted, because remaining sin never weakens: it often unexpectedly revives in renewed strength. This is why "we…through the Spirit [must] mortify the deeds of the body" (Rom. 8:13)—we cannot do it ourselves. Although our Lord had no carnal lusts to mortify, yet He had a devil to resist and temptation to reject. The Spirit was upon Him for this, too (Luke 4:1, 14). He is given to us that we might resist temptation and be strengthened against sinning. B. H. Carroll once said: "The Holy Spirit is greater than total depravity. [He] can overcome total depravity, because total depravity is of the first birth; but this being born again by the power of the Holy Spirit makes one of another seed, of the word of God, that liveth and abideth forever."[9]

This means the Spirit helps us overcome sin by quickening in us a loathing of it and strengthening us against it. He raises thankfulness to the Lord for grace, inflames our hearts with love to Christ, and produces hunger for holiness (Matt. 5:6). In all this, He enables us to resist temptation from the highest motive, gospel gratitude, and keeps us close to our Beloved.

In addition, maybe He will lovingly convict us of what caused the temptation in the first place: that second look, the permitted thought that led on to other ones, dipping a toe into forbidden territory, the unwise association, and a host of other subtle invitations

---

9. B. H. Carroll, *An Interpretation of the English Bible: James, 1 and 2 Thessalonians, 1 and 2 Corinthians*, ed. J. B. Cranfill (1948; repr., Grand Rapids: Baker, 1986), 176.

to the tempter. We should keep the greatest distance not only from sin but also the greatest distance from temptation, and pray as our Savior taught us, "Lead us not into temptation, but deliver us from evil" (Matt. 6:13a).

Do you need wisdom?
If we know anything of our hearts, we feel our lack of wisdom very much (James 1:5). However, the Spirit that was upon our Redeemer is "the Spirit of wisdom and understanding" (Isa. 11:2), granting Him all its "treasures" (Col. 2:3). That same Spirit is with us to work in us that heavenly wisdom (James 3:17). Let us pray, as foolish sinners, for this every day. And let us heed the lessons the Holy Spirit teaches us through Scripture (Col. 3:16), through experiences in life, through the example of others (Prov. 13:20)—even through our sinful failures—that we might be "wise as serpents, and harmless as doves" (Matt. 10:16).

Do you struggle with a mysterious providence?
From time to time, the Lord does things in our lives we cannot understand or see the reason for. The supply of the Spirit helps us look at things spiritually. Paul is our example here. He assures the Philippians that "the things which happened unto me have fallen out rather unto the furtherance of the gospel" (1:12). The phrase "fallen out" means literally "to come," that is, "to come about, come into being." There is purpose in it. It has not just happened but "fallen out" from the lap of God's providence (cf. Prov. 16:33).

This is true of every event in the life of the Christian. Nothing happens of itself, by chance, or merely by human agency—God is the great First Cause. He rules and overrules all things for our highest blessing. Mysterious providences are not mysterious to Him. Be encouraged by this. He says, "For I know the thoughts that I think toward you...thoughts of peace, and not of evil, to give you an expected end" (Jer. 29:11).

Do you feel afraid and weak?
The Spirit supplies the strength we need when we feel fearful and weak. Again, Paul could say, "I can do all things through Christ which strengtheneth me" (Phil. 4:13). The word is literally

"in-strengthened." Though we are weak, by His comfort we are strong. However, the Spirit does not give us a lump sum of grace to live upon, which would almost encourage us to look to ourselves. He grants us a continual supply as pensioners who must always ask for more. In this way, we are kept dependent, but kept blessed. It is a supply always as great as our need. Trust Him and go forward.

Are you troubled about dying?
Many Christians fear to die, and they echo the words, "Such a worm as I,/Who sometimes am afraid to die."[10] We need divine assurance for this ultimate experience, for we "have not passed this way heretofore" (Josh. 3:4). The Holy Spirit can supply this in great measure, for in Romans 15:13 we read, "Now the God of hope fill you with all joy and peace in believing, that ye may abound in hope, through the power of the Holy Ghost." This assurance can be so strong that we can be like the apostle in custody, indifferent as to whether he died or lived (Phil. 1:20–24). However, we must remember that we will have dying grace when we *are* dying, and not before.

Conclusion
Let us notice Paul's assurance: "I know." The supply of the Spirit is no uncertain thing. Paul knows that it will help his Christian progress. It "shall turn to my salvation." He expects prison will be sanctified to him, so that he will be more consecrated to God.

Paul knows that this sanctification will transpire as others remember him: "Through your prayer." He assumes he has their prayers—he does not need to ask for them. What a privilege to be prayed for! Compared with the material gifts the Philippians sent Paul, this is the best gift of all.

What a great thing we do when we pray for others! Let us never underestimate it. We commend them by name to the God of all grace for the supply of the Spirit. They may not be literally in prison, but there is the "prison" of discouragement, Satan's oppression, an "impossible" situation, depression, fear, etc. We can ask for the supply of the Spirit for them. We can ask for our family members, for

10. From the hymn "When Thou, My Righteous Judge, Shalt Come," in *Revival Hymns*, comp. A. B. Earle, rev. ed. (Boston: James H. Earle, 1874), #80. The hymn is sometimes attributed to Selina Hastings, countess of Huntingdon.

our ministers and office-bearers, for the church, for missionaries, for fellow-believers—as well as for ourselves—so that we all might know the supply of the Spirit of Jesus Christ.

To whom do we pray in asking for this? Pray to the Father, who supplied the Spirit to His Son. Pray to the Son, who has proved how efficacious the Spirit is, and makes Him over to us. Pray to the Spirit Himself, who came upon our Lord as He prayed. He is ours as heaven's supply and the token of heaven's love to us. He is ours, so we might prove Paul's words in Philippians 4:19: "My God shall supply all your need according to his riches in glory by Christ Jesus."

DOCTRINAL STUDIES

CHAPTER 9

The Person of the Holy Spirit

Morton H. Smith

The Person of the Holy Spirit is the most basic of all the subjects we are considering in this book, for it deals with the nature of the One whose work we are examining. George Smeaton (1857–1889), professor of exegetical theology at New College, Edinburgh, said in speaking of the personality of the Holy Spirit, "it must not be passed over. Nor must attention be so absorbed with the work of the Spirit so as to forget *Himself*.... The divine dignity of the Spirit demands... that no obscuring influence shall come between the soul and the agency of the living person."[1]

The Bible nowhere explicitly says that the Holy Spirit is a person. For that matter, neither does it say that the Father or the Son is a person. It does not give metaphysical definitions of this sort. The term *person*, in reference to the Holy Spirit, has come down to us from the ancient church in its formulation of the doctrine of the Trinity.

John Calvin argued that if we do not use words like *essence* and *person*, we cannot affirm the faith "universally received, that the Father, Son, and Holy Spirit are the one God; and that nevertheless the Son is not the Father, nor the Spirit the Son, but that they are distinguished from each other by some peculiar property."[2] Calvin then gave his understanding of the term *person* as used in discussions of the Trinity: "What I denominate a Person, is a subsistence in the Divine essence, which is related to the others, and yet distinguished

---

1. George Smeaton, *The Doctrine of the Holy Spirit* (Edinburgh: Banner of Truth, 1980), 100.

2. John Calvin, *Institutes of the Christian Religion*, trans. John Allen (Grand Rapids: Eerdmans, 1949), 1.13.5.

from them by an incommunicable property. By the word *subsistence* we mean something different from the word *essence*."[3]

Calvin contributed to the better understanding of the doctrine of the Trinity by correcting what some have inferred from the writings of some of the Nicene fathers, namely, that God the Father is the fountain and source of all being, and therefore is to be considered the source of the being of the Son. Calvin correctly insisted that the Father is God of Himself, the Son is God of Himself, and the Spirit is God of Himself. In other words, each of the Persons in His essence is God. Only the personal qualities of Sonship and of procession can be said to be derived from the Father. The Nicene fathers, recognizing that generation and procession might suggest a subordination of the second and third Persons, ascribed the terms *eternal generation* and *eternal procession* to indicate that each of these Persons is just as eternal as the Father.

Philip Schaff discussed the word *person*, indicating that in the Latin it could refer to the mask that an actor puts on, but suggesting with W. G. T. Shedd that this is not the best word, for it could be understood in a Sabellian sense. Sabellianism, otherwise known as Modalism, held to the idea of one God who took on different modes at different times. This was one of the heresies that Nicea refuted. To hold such a view was to deny the three separate Persons of the Trinity. The opposite danger is Tritheism—taking each Person as a separate individual. Nicea steered a course between these two tendencies, holding to only one God, but within that one God three Persons, each with His own personal property: "To the first person fatherhood, or the being unbegotten, is ascribed as his property; to the second, sonship, or the being begotten; to the Holy Ghost, procession. In other words, the Father is unbegotten, but begetting; the Son is uncreated, but begotten; the Holy Ghost proceeds from the Father (and according to the Latin doctrine, also from the Son)."[4] The Nicene fathers distinguished between the essence of deity (*homoousios*) and the individual Persons (*hypostasis*) in the Godhead.

The Westminster Shorter Catechism has beautifully summarized the doctrine of the Trinity in three questions: "What is God?" "God

---

3. Calvin, *Institutes*, 1.13.6.
4. Philip Schaff, *History of the Christian Church* (New York: Charles Scribner, 1895), 3:679.

is a spirit, infinite, eternal and unchangeable in his being, wisdom, power, holiness, justice, goodness and truth." In this question, the catechism defines the essence of deity. It then asks how many gods there are: "There is but one only, the living and true God." Then the question is raised as to how many Persons there are in the Godhead: "There are three persons in the Godhead, the Father, the Son and the Holy Ghost, and these three are one God, the same in substance, equal in power and glory."[5]

It has sometimes been said that if one could demonstrate the deity of Christ and the personality of the Holy Spirit, one could prove the Trinity. It is obvious that Jesus is a Person, speaking to the Father as a separate Person. The question concerning Him is whether He is more than just a man. Is He God? The Spirit of God is obviously divine, but is He more than just a power of God? Is He a Person?

One could easily get bogged down if one were to try to give a technical definition of the term *person* as defined by modern psychology. It is obvious that the church fathers were not using the term in any such technical sense. Essentially, what they found in their study of the Bible regarding the Trinity was that there were different centers of self-consciousness that could be expressed by the "I-thou" relation.

What is a person? Professor John Murray suggested that, as used in defining the Persons of the Trinity, the basic idea was a separate seat of self-consciousness. *Webster's Encyclopedic Unabridged Dictionary* defines *person* thus: "a self conscious or rational being."[6] The dictionary adds the character of rationality or intelligence. Thus, as we study the scriptural references to the Spirit to see whether it is proper to speak of the Spirit as a Person, we are looking for a self-conscious being and/or a rational being. If one can think for himself, make decisions for himself, act for himself, and speak for himself, then he can be described as a person.

Accepting this simple understanding of the idea of person, it must be asked whether there is biblical warrant for describing the Holy Spirit as a Person. We shall seek to survey both the Old and New Testaments regarding this question. For my overview of the teaching of the Old Testament, I have found B. B. Warfield's essay

---

5. Westminster Shorter Catechism, Q. 4–6.
6. *Webster's Encylcopedic Unabridged Dictionary* (New York: Portland House, 1989).

entitled "The Spirit of God in the Old Testament"[7] to be most helpful, and I commend it to all for further study of this subject. As a basis for my survey of the New Testament passages, I am particularly indebted to the excellent work by Henry Barclay Swete, *The Holy Spirit in the New Testament*.[8] Swete served as professor of divinity at Cambridge University during the last half of the nineteenth century.

Smeaton asserted "that it is as clear as noon-day that Scripture speaks of a Person or a subsistence, not of a divine influence or energy; and the Christian Church from the beginning, notwithstanding the deflections of individuals, may be said to have asserted the Spirit's personality, and to have based it on the Scriptures."[9]

He placed the arguments for the personality of the Spirit under the following heads: the personal actions ascribed to Him abundantly prove it (John 14:26; 1 Cor. 12:11); His distinction from the Father and the Son, and His mission from both, prove it (John 15:26); the co-ordinate rank and power that belong to Him equally with the Father and the Son prove it (Matt. 28:19; 2 Cor. 13, 14); His appearance under a visible form at the baptism of Christ and on the day of Pentecost proves it; the sin against the Holy Ghost, implying a Person, proves it; and the way in which He is distinguished from His gifts proves it (1 Cor. 12:11).[10]

Warfield grouped the texts of the Old Testament referring to the Spirit of God under four basic categories. First, the Spirit as related to creation and providence. Second, the Spirit as related to the establishment of the theocracy of Israel. Third, the Spirit as related to the Messiah. Fourth, the Spirit as related to the individual believer. I shall examine selected texts in each of these categories to discover what is either explicitly or implicitly taught regarding the Person of the Holy Spirit.

Warfield taught that the basic biblical doctrine regarding the Holy Spirit is to be found in both the Old and New Testaments, but that the Old Testament does not have as much about this as the New

---

7. B. B. Warfield, "The Spirit of God in the Old Testament," in *Biblical Doctrines* (New York: Oxford University Press, 1929), 101–29, and in *Biblical and Theological Studies* (Philadelphia: Presbyterian and Reformed, 1952), 127–56.

8. Henry Barclay Swete, *The Holy Spirit in the New Testament* (1910; repr., Grand Rapids: Baker, 1964).

9. Smeaton, *Doctrine of the Holy Spirit*, 108.

10. Smeaton, *Doctrine of the Holy Spirit*, 109.

does. He pointed out that the term "Spirit of God" is found in the opening verses of Genesis. After briefly surveying the teaching of both the Old and New Testaments, he came to the conclusion: "There can be no doubt that the New Testament writers identify the Holy Ghost of the New Testament with the Spirit of God of the Old."[11] Again, "In both Testaments the Spirit of God appears distinctly as *the executive of the Godhead.*"[12]

Old Testament
Creation
"In the beginning God created the heaven and the earth. And the earth was without form, and void; and darkness was upon the face of the deep. And the Spirit of God moved upon the face of the waters" (Gen. 1:1–2). H. C. Leupold, in his commentary on Genesis, answered the question of whether this One in Genesis 1:2 is a Person:

> We must guard against overstatement in the case, but we maintain very definitely: the Spirit of God is the Holy Spirit, the third person in the Trinity. For all the attributes ascribed to this divine person in the Old Testament agree fully with what is revealed in the New Testament concerning his person and his work. Absolutely none other than the Holy Spirit is here under consideration.[13]

Again he wrote:

> We could never believe that this hovering over the face of the waters was idle and purposeless. From all other activities that are elsewhere ascribed to the Holy Spirit we conclude that his work in this case must have been anticipatory of the creative work that followed, a kind of impregnation with divine potentialities. The germs of all that is created were placed into dead matter by Him. His was the preparatory work for leading over from the inorganic to the organic.[14]

In a very suggestive passage dealing with the mention of the Holy Spirit in Genesis 1:2, Leupold wrote:

---

11. Smeaton, *Doctrine of the Holy Spirit*, 130.

12. Smeaton, *Doctrine of the Holy Spirit*, 131.

13. H. C. Leupold, *Exposition of Genesis* (Grand Rapids: Baker Book House, 1950), 49.

14. Leupold, *Exposition of Genesis*, 50.

In the beginning, we are told, God created the heavens and the earth. And then the process is detailed by which the created earth, at first waste and void, with darkness resting upon the face of the deep, was transformed by successive fiats into the ordered and populous world in which we live. As the ground of the whole process, we are informed that again "the spirit of God was brooding upon the face of the waters," as much as to say that the obedience, and the precedent power of obedience, of the waste of waters to the successive creative words—as God said, Let there be light; Let there be a firmament; Let the waters be gathered together; Let the waters and the earth bring forth— depended upon the fact that the Spirit of God was already brooding upon the formless void. To the voice of God in heaven saying let there be light the energy of this brooding upon the face of the waters responded and lo! there was light. Over against the transcendent God above creation there seems to be postulated here God brooding upon creation, and this suggestion seems to be that it is only by virtue of God brooding upon creation that the created thing moves and acts and works out the will of God. The Spirit of God, in a word, appears at the very opening of the Bible as God immanent; and, as such, is set over against God transcendent.... The Spirit of God thus appears from the outset of the Old Testament as the principle of the very existence and persistence of all things, and as the source and originating cause of all movement and order and life. God's thought and will and word take effect in the world, because God is not only over the world, thinking and willing and commanding, but also in the world as the principle of all activity *executing*: this seems the thought of the author of the biblical cosmogony.[15]

Many other passages refer to the Spirit's work in creation: "By his spirit he hath garnished the heavens" (Job 26:13a); "The Spirit of God hath made me, and the breath of the Almighty hath given me life" (Job 33:4); "By the word of the LORD were the heavens made; and all the host of them by the breath of his mouth" (Ps. 33:6). Elihu declared that the Spirit is the source of man's understanding: "But there is a spirit in man: and the inspiration of the Almighty giveth them understanding" (Job 32:8).

---

15. Leupold, *Exposition of Genesis*, 133–34.

From these passages, we see the Spirit not only as Creator of the heavens, but also of the individual human, and even as the source of human intelligence. We may infer from these passages that the Spirit is the source of human personality and human intelligence, and thus that the Spirit must be a personal Spirit.

In Psalm 139, David demonstrates that the Spirit is a Person. He speaks of the Spirit as creating him in his mother's womb (v. 15). He also indicates that the Spirit is with him wherever he goes (vv. 7–9). Thus, he holds to the presence of the Spirit with him everywhere. Another interesting point in this psalm is the fact that David addresses the Spirit as a Person, as he addresses Him with "thou" and "thee." For David, then, the Spirit is not just a power or a principle, but He is personal and to be addressed as such.

The prophets also spoke of the Spirit as the Creator of heaven and the earth: "Who hath measured the waters in the hollow of his hand, and meted out heaven with the span, and comprehended the dust of the earth in a measure, and weighed the mountains in scales, and the hills in a balance? Who hath directed the Spirit of the LORD, or being his counsellor hath taught him?" (Isa. 40:12–13).

Theocracy

The Holy Spirit was a gift of governance. The Spirit of God is set forth as the One who established men in office in Israel. Thus, He lay behind the erection of the kingdom of God on earth as seen in the theocratic nation of Israel. He gave Moses the gifts to govern the people. This is not explicitly stated with the establishment of Moses, but is taught when He broadens the governance to the seventy elders: "And the LORD said unto Moses, Gather unto me seventy men of the elders of Israel, whom thou knowest to be the elders of the people, and officers over them; and bring them unto the tabernacle of the congregation, that they may stand there with thee. And I will come down and talk with thee there: and I will take of the spirit which is upon thee, and will put it upon them; and they shall bear the burden of the people with thee, that thou bear it not thyself alone" (Num. 11:16–17).

It is clear from this passage that Moses had been endowed by the Spirit of God to govern the people, and that same Spirit equipped the seventy elders to bear the burden of the governance of the people with Moses. If the Spirit equips men with the ability to govern, it must be because He Himself is a personal being, who governs the universe.

As Moses came to the end of his life, he was instructed to designate Joshua as his successor, and the Spirit came upon him also: "And the LORD said unto Moses, Take thee Joshua the son of Nun, a man in whom is the spirit, and lay thine hand upon him" (Num. 27:18).

The book of Judges repeatedly speaks of the Spirit of God coming upon individuals to set them apart as judges or rulers of the people: "And when the children of Israel cried unto the LORD, the LORD raised up a deliverer to the children of Israel, who delivered them, even Othniel the son of Kenaz, Caleb's younger brother" (Judg. 3:9); "And the Spirit of the LORD came upon him, and he judged Israel" (3:10); "But the Spirit of the LORD came upon Gideon" (6:34); "Then the Spirit of the LORD came upon Jephthah" (11:29); "And the Spirit of the LORD began to move him [Samson]" (13:25; cf. 14:6, 19). We see the same in the first book of Samuel: "And the Spirit of God came upon Saul when he heard those tidings, and his anger was kindled greatly" (1 Sam. 11:6); "Then Samuel took the horn of oil, and anointed him in the midst of his brethren: and the Spirit of the LORD came upon David from that day forward" (16:13).

In addition to the gift of authority to govern, the Spirit of God gave the gift of wisdom, understanding, and workmanship for the building of the tabernacle: "And the LORD spake unto Moses, saying, See, I have called by name Bezaleel the son of Uri, the son of Hur, of the tribe of Judah: and I have filled him with the spirit of God, in wisdom, and in understanding, and in knowledge, and in all manner of workmanship" (Ex. 31:1–3).

It is clear from the following citations that the prophets understood that the Spirit of God gave them their message. They did not view the Spirit just as a force but as a Person instructing them regarding their messages: "And the LORD came down in a cloud, and spake unto him, and took of the spirit that was upon him, and gave it unto the seventy elders: and it came to pass, that, when the spirit rested upon them, they prophesied, and did not cease" (Num. 11:25); "Now these be the last words of David.... The Spirit of the LORD spake by me, and his word was in my tongue" (2 Sam. 23:1–2); "But truly I am full of power by the spirit of the LORD, and of judgment, and of might, to declare unto Jacob his transgression, and to Israel his sin"

(Mic. 3:8); "Yet many years didst thou forbear them, and testifiedst against them by thy spirit in thy prophets" (Neh. 9:30).

The Messiah

We also see in the theocratic period talk of the Spirit and Messiah. Isaiah 11:1–2 says: "And there shall come forth a rod out of the stem of Jesse, and a Branch shall grow out of his roots: and the spirit of the LORD shall rest upon him, the spirit of wisdom and understanding, the spirit of counsel and might, the spirit of knowledge and of the fear of the LORD." This is one of the most explicit of the Old Testament texts regarding the doctrine of the Trinity, for it contains references to all three Persons. The Messiah, of course, is the shoot out of the stock of Jesse. Though He is not identified as divine in this passage, He had been so identified in Isaiah 9:6, where He is called "Wonderful, Counselor, the Mighty God, the everlasting Father, the Prince of Peace." Reference to the Father is found in the phrase "Spirit of the LORD." The Spirit is explicitly referred to, and the description of His relation to the Messiah as "the spirit of wisdom and understanding" certainly speaks of personal qualities.

The prophet Isaiah refers to the three Persons: "Behold my servant, whom I uphold; mine elect, in whom my soul delighteth; I have put my spirit upon him: he shall bring forth judgment to the Gentiles" (Isa. 42:1).

Jesus saw the Spirit of Jehovah as the one who commissioned Him as the Messiah; hence, He taught that the Holy Spirit is a Person of the Godhead. The Messiah, speaking prophetically, says that both the Father and the Spirit sent Him: "Come ye near unto me, hear ye this; I have not spoken in secret from the beginning; from the time that it was, there am I: and now the Lord GOD, and his Spirit, hath sent me" (Isa. 48:16); "The Spirit of the Lord GOD is upon me; because the LORD hath anointed me to preach good tidings unto the meek; he hath sent me to bind up the brokenhearted, to proclaim liberty to the captives, and the opening of the prison to them that are bound; to proclaim the acceptable year of the LORD, and the day of vengeance of our God; to comfort all that mourn" (Isa. 61:1–2).

Individuals

The Old Testament also depicts the Holy Spirit acting in individuals. The Holy Spirit strives with us: "And the LORD said, My spirit shall not always strive with man, for that he also is flesh: yet his days shall be an hundred and twenty years" (Gen. 6:3). In Psalm 51, David expresses his concern lest the Spirit be removed from him. Warfield indicates that this may have to do with the abiding operation of the Spirit on all believers, or it may have to do with the gift of the Spirit in establishing him as king.

One of the clearest indications that the Spirit of God in the Old Testament was considered to be personal is found in Isaiah 63:9–10: "In all their affliction he was afflicted, and the angel of his presence saved them: in his love and in his pity he redeemed them; and he bare them, and carried them all the days of old. But they rebelled, and vexed [grieved] his holy Spirit: therefore he was turned to be their enemy, and he fought against them."

The idea that the rebellion of Israel grieved the Holy Spirit indicates that the Spirit was viewed as a personal being, who could and did have personal responses to the activities of human beings. Only a personal being could so respond. This note is carried over to the New Testament.

Finally, we see that the Holy Spirit instructs His people: "Thou gavest also thy good spirit to instruct them, and withheldest not thy manna from their mouth, and gavest them water for their thirst" (Neh. 9:20).

New Testament
The names for the Holy Spirit in the Old Testament are "the Spirit of God [Elohim]" or "of the LORD [Jehovah]." "The Holy Spirit" and "the Spirit" are given Greek terms in the Septuagint and thus prepared for use in the New Testament. The use of "Holy Spirit" is rare in the Old Testament, but it appears eighty-eight times in the New Testament. The simple title "Spirit" is used forty-six times, and "Spirit of God" or "of the Lord" occurs twenty-five times. The New Testament has more frequent references to the Spirit than the Old because all Christian life and thought is more frequently emphasized as being under the influence of the Spirit.

Swete wrote: "The question of the Spirit's relation to God is never formally raised, and receives only a partial answer. It is clear indeed that in the New Testament as in the Old the Holy Spirit belongs to the sphere of the Divine and the uncreated. The Spirit of God which searches the depths and knows the heart of God is Divine, as the spirit of man is human."[16] There is nothing in the Bible regarding the Spirit comparable to what is said of Jesus—"the Word was with God and the Word was God"—or His existence in the form-essence of God. Nevertheless, the statements we have assume the same for the Spirit as for the Word.

Our task is to examine a number of the New Testament passages that speak of the Spirit to determine whether the basic elements of the doctrine of the Trinity are present; namely, affirmations of the deity of the Spirit, as well as assertions distinguishing the Spirit from the other Persons of the Trinity. Also, we shall look for characteristics of personality: traits of a self-conscious rational being and actual personal functions.

Gospels

First, as we come to the New Testament, we find that both of the Gospels that give us accounts of the birth of Jesus teach the same thing regarding the Holy Spirit and the birth of Jesus. Luke writes: "Then said Mary unto the angel, How shall this be, seeing I know not a man? And the angel answered and said unto her, The Holy Ghost shall come upon thee, and the power of the Highest shall overshadow thee: therefore also that holy thing which shall be born of thee shall be called the Son of God" (Luke 1:34–35).

When Joseph hears of her pregnancy, he is given the same message by an angel—that the miraculous conception of Jesus is the result of the Holy Spirit implanting Him in the womb of the virgin: "Then Joseph…was minded to put her away privily. But while he thought on these things, behold, the angel of the Lord appeared unto him in a dream, saying, Joseph, thou son of David, fear not to take unto thee Mary thy wife: for that which is conceived in her is of the Holy Ghost" (Matt. 1:19–20).

These references to the Spirit as the Holy Spirit presuppose His divinity. Only God is good and holy; thus, only a spirit who is divine may rightly be called the Holy Spirit.

Second, the baptism of Jesus is one of the most remarkable events in the Bible as a revelation of the Trinity:

---

16. Swete, *The Holy Spirit in the New Testament*, 288.

And Jesus, when he was baptized, went up straightway out of the water: and, lo, the heavens were opened unto him, and he saw the Spirit of God descending like a dove, and lighting upon him (Matt. 3:16).

Now when all the people were baptized, it came to pass, that Jesus also being baptized, and praying, the heaven was opened, and the Holy Ghost descended in a bodily shape like a dove upon him, and a voice came from heaven, which said, Thou art my beloved Son; in thee I am well pleased (Luke 3:21–22).

In this event, all three of the Persons of the Godhead are represented. The Father speaks from heaven, the Son has just been baptized, and the Spirit comes upon Him in a visible form to anoint Him for office as the Messiah. The three Persons had all been represented in messianic passages of Isaiah, but not in such an open way. The deity of each of the Persons is assumed. The Father, who speaks from heaven, is certainly God. The declaration that Jesus is His Son suggests an equality of essence, and the Spirit of God descending from heaven also suggests that He is divine.

Third, we see the Spirit in Jesus' ministry. Upon being anointed to office, Jesus was led and equipped by the Spirit throughout His ministry as the Messiah. He was led by the Spirit to face Satan in the temptation and then led by the Spirit into His ministry: "Then was Jesus led up of the Spirit into the wilderness to be tempted of the devil" (Matt. 4:1); "And Jesus returned in the power of the Spirit into Galilee: and there went out a fame of him through all the region round about" (Luke 4:14); "And when he had opened the book, he found the place where it was written, The Spirit of the Lord is upon me, because he hath anointed me to preach the gospel to the poor; he hath sent me to heal the brokenhearted, to preach deliverance to the captives, and recovering of sight to the blind, to set at liberty them that are bruised, to preach the acceptable year of the Lord. And he closed the book, and he gave it again to the minister, and sat down. And the eyes of all them that were in the synagogue were fastened on him. And he began to say unto them, This day is this scripture fulfilled in your ears" (Luke 4:17b–21).

As we have already observed, this messianic prophecy actually involves all three persons of the Trinity. The Spirit is from the Lord, God the Father. The Messiah is anointed by the Spirit, and thus equipped to carry out His functions as Messiah. Each of the messianic functions is that of a Person: to preach, to proclaim release and recovery of sight, to set at liberty the bruised, and to proclaim the acceptable year of the Lord. Thus, the Spirit who both commissioned and enabled Him to act must have been a Person, not just a dynamic force.

Paraclete
The promise of the Paraclete, Comforter, or Advocate by Jesus is the promise of a Person other than Himself: "And I will pray the Father, and he shall give you another Comforter, that he may abide with you for ever; even the Spirit of truth; whom the world cannot receive, because it seeth him not, neither knoweth him: but ye know him; for he dwelleth with you, and shall be in you. I will not leave you comfortless: I will come to you" (John 14:16–18); "But the Comforter, which is the Holy Ghost, whom the Father will send in my name, he shall teach you all things, and bring all things to your remembrance, whatsoever I have said unto you" (John 14:26); "But when the Comforter is come, whom I will send unto you from the Father, even the Spirit of truth, which proceedeth from the Father, he shall testify of me" (John 15:26).

The Great Commission and trinitarian benediction
Trinitarian formulas were in use from the beginning of the New Testament church: "And Jesus came and spake unto them, saying, All power is given unto me in heaven and in earth. Go ye therefore, and teach all nations, baptizing them in the name of the Father, and of the Son, and of the Holy Ghost" (Matt. 28:18–19); "The grace of the Lord Jesus Christ, and the love of God, and the communion of the Holy Ghost, be with you all" (2 Cor. 13:14).

Both of these passages coordinate the three Persons of the Godhead together as one God, and each of the three Persons as of equal importance with the others. Baptism is in the singular name of the Father, the Son, and the Holy Spirit. The benediction speaks a particular blessing from each of the three Persons. With these formulas before her, it is no wonder that the church, in refuting various errors over the first four centuries, ended up with the Nicene Creed, which gives the basic doctrine of the Person of Christ and of the Trinity.

Ministry of the Holy Spirit

The New Testament highlights the ministry of the Holy Spirit. Jesus said to His disciples:

> Nevertheless I tell you the truth; it is expedient for you that I go away: for if I go not away, the Comforter will not come unto you; but if I depart, I will send him unto you. And when he is come, he will reprove the world of sin, and of righteousness, and of judgment: of sin, because they believe not on me; of righteousness, because I go to my Father, and ye see me no more; of judgment, because the prince of this world is judged. I have yet many things to say unto you, but ye cannot bear them now. Howbeit when he, the Spirit of truth, is come, he will guide you into all truth: for he shall not speak of himself; but whatsoever he shall hear, that shall he speak: and he will shew you things to come. He shall glorify me: for he shall receive of mine, and shall shew it unto you. All things that the Father hath are mine: therefore said I, that he shall take of mine, and shall shew it unto you. A little while, and ye shall not see me: and again, a little while, and ye shall see me, because I go to the Father (John 16:7–16).

It is not my task to describe the various works of the Spirit but to point out how He is active in each of His works as a Person, not just a force. He convicts of sin, righteousness, and judgment, which are certainly the actions of a rational being, not of an abstract force. He teaches us in all truth, certainly a function of a rational being. He glorifies Christ and declares His gospel, activities of a rational, personal being.

The Holy Spirit and the Church

Baptism of the church

In His last words before His ascension, Jesus spoke of the Holy Spirit coming on the church and empowering it for its upcoming mission to the world: "For John truly baptized with water; but ye shall be baptized with the Holy Ghost not many days hence. When they therefore were come together, they asked of him, saying, Lord, wilt thou at this time restore again the kingdom to Israel? And he said unto them, It is not for you to know the times or the seasons, which the Father hath put in his own power. But ye shall receive power, after that the Holy Ghost is come upon you: and ye shall be witnesses unto me both in Jerusalem, and in all Judaea, and in Samaria, and unto the uttermost part of the earth" (Acts 1:5–8).

He fulfilled this promise on the day of Pentecost:

> And when the day of Pentecost was fully come, they were all with one accord in one place. And suddenly there came a sound from heaven as of a rushing mighty wind, and it filled all the house where they were sitting. And there appeared unto them cloven tongues like as of fire, and it sat upon each of them. And they were all filled with the Holy Ghost, and began to speak with other tongues, as the Spirit gave them utterance (Acts 2:1–4).

> And it shall come to pass in the last days, saith God, I will pour out of my Spirit upon all flesh: and your sons and your daughters shall prophesy, and your young men shall see visions, and your old men shall dream dreams: and on my servants and on my handmaidens I will pour out in those days of my Spirit; and they shall prophesy (vv. 17–18).

> This Jesus hath God raised up, whereof we all are witnesses. Therefore being by the right hand of God exalted, and having received of the Father the promise of the Holy Ghost, he hath shed forth this, which ye now see and hear (vv. 32–33).

In these passages, we have the record and explanation of Pentecost, namely, the gift of the Spirit. This event was the baptism of the church of Christ with the Holy Spirit, and the gift of the Spirit to all believers. In this, we again see references to all three of the Persons. The Father is understood to have rewarded the Son with the gift of the Spirit, which He then pours forth on His church.

Various activities of the Spirit that imply personality

One of the passages in Scripture that most clearly shows the Spirit acting as a Person is in His calling and sending forth of men in the mission of the church: "As they ministered to the Lord, and fasted, the Holy Ghost said, Separate me Barnabas and Saul for the work whereunto I have called them. And when they had fasted and prayed, and laid their hands on them, they sent them away. So they, being sent forth by the Holy Ghost, departed unto Seleucia; and from thence they sailed to Cyprus" (Acts 13:2–4).

Note here several personal actions: First, the Spirit is represented as speaking to the church: "the Holy Ghost said." He describes His authoritative action: "I have called them." The church obeyed this command of the Spirit, and Barnabas and Saul are described as "being sent forth by the Holy Ghost." The church certainly understood that the Holy Spirit was a Person as described in these actions.

Later, the Spirit is seen directly guiding His servants as to where He wanted them to minister. We see the Holy Spirit acting as a Person, forbidding some from going to preach in certain places: "Now when they had gone throughout Phrygia and the region of Galatia, and were forbidden of the Holy Ghost to preach the word in Asia, after they were come to Mysia, they assayed to go into Bithynia: but the Spirit suffered them not" (Acts 16:6–7).

James's statement at the Jerusalem Council presupposes the idea that the Holy Spirit is a Person: "For it seemed good to the Holy Ghost, and to us, to lay upon you no greater burden than these necessary things" (Acts 15:28).

The Holy Spirit helps us in our infirmities: "Likewise the Spirit also helpeth our infirmities: for we know not what we should pray for as we ought: but the Spirit itself maketh intercession for us with groanings which cannot be uttered. And he that searcheth the hearts knoweth what is the mind of the Spirit, because he maketh intercession for the saints according to the will of God" (Rom. 8:26–27). In particular, He assists us in our praying, since He makes intercession for us. He is the searcher of hearts, and He makes intercessions for us that are according to the will of God.

In 1 Corinthians 2:11–16, Paul teaches that He shares in the knowledge of God:

> For what man knoweth the things of a man, save the spirit of man which is in him? Even so the things of God knoweth no man, but the Spirit of God. Now we have received, not the spirit of the world, but the spirit which is of God; that we might know the things that are freely given to us of God. Which things also we speak, not in the words which man's wisdom teacheth, but which the Holy Ghost teacheth; comparing spiritual things with spiritual. But the natural man receiveth not the things of the Spirit of God: for they are foolishness unto him: neither can he know them, because they are spiritually discerned. But he that is spiritual judgeth all things, yet he himself is judged of no man. For who hath known the mind of the Lord, that he may instruct him? But we have the mind of Christ.

This passage is a strong assertion of the deity of the Spirit, based on His knowledge of the things of God. In addition, we find Him to be given to the church, that we, too, may be taught by the Spirit to know the things of God. In this we are said to have the mind of Christ, thus indicating that the will of the Spirit and of Christ are united. Though They are separate Persons, They are one God, and thus the will of each Person is in accord with the will of the other Persons.

In 1 Corinthians 12:4–13, the Spirit is depicted as the sovereign author of gifts:

> Now there are diversities of gifts, but the same Spirit. And there are differences of administrations, but the same Lord. And there are diversities of operations, but it is the same God which worketh all in all. But the manifestation of the Spirit is given to every man to profit withal. For to one is given by the Spirit the word of wisdom; to another the word of knowledge by the same Spirit; to another faith by the same Spirit; to another the gifts of healing by the same Spirit; to another the working of miracles; to another prophecy; to another discerning of spirits; to another divers kinds of tongues; to another the interpretation of tongues: but all these worketh that one and the selfsame Spirit, dividing to every man severally as he will. For as the body is one, and hath many members, and all the members of that one body, being many, are one body: so also is Christ. For by one Spirit are we all baptized into one body, whether we be Jews or Gentiles, whether we be bond or free; and have been all made to drink into one Spirit.

In this passage, Paul speaks of the diverse gifts that exist in the church, and indicates that they have all come from one God. The Spirit is represented as acting on His own as a Person in distributing the gifts according to His good pleasure. Despite the wide diversity of the gifts, they are all from the one Spirit, and we are part of one body despite our wide differences in background.

As we saw in the Old Testament, the Spirit is the source of prophecy: "For the prophecy came not in old time by the will of man: but holy men of God spake as they were moved by the Holy Ghost" (2 Peter 1:21). This verse speaks of the way in which the Spirit led the prophets. Since the Spirit inspired the writing of the Scriptures, we may take this as a description of how He guided those who actually wrote the Bible.

Because He is a Person and not just an abstract force, the Holy Spirit can be tempted and lied to:

> But Peter said, Ananias, why hath Satan filled thine heart to lie to the Holy Ghost, and to keep back part of the price of the land?... Then Peter said unto her, How is it that ye have agreed together to tempt the Spirit of the Lord? behold, the feet of them which have buried thy husband are at the door, and shall carry thee out (Acts 5:3, 9).

Because the Holy Spirit is Personal, He can be blasphemed and sinned against: "And whosoever shall speak a word against the Son of man, it shall be forgiven him: but unto him that blasphemeth against the Holy Ghost it shall not be forgiven. And when they bring you unto the synagogues, and unto magistrates, and powers, take ye no thought how or what thing ye shall answer, or what ye shall say: for the Holy Ghost shall teach you in the same hour what ye ought to say" (Luke 12:10–12; cf. Mark 3:28–29).

Conclusions

As we conclude this brief survey of selected passages concerning the Spirit, it should be clear that the Bible gives warrant for the church's doctrine of the Trinity, first formulated in the Nicene Creed and confessed ever since. First, the Bible clearly affirms that there is only one living and true God. Second, the Bible also, from its opening, affirms the distinction of different Persons in the Godhead. Third, the Spirit of God, or the Holy Spirit, is one of those three Persons, not just some abstract idea or a force. This we have seen in our survey of the Old Testament, and especially in the revelation of the New Testament.

With the death, resurrection, and ascension of the Lord Jesus, the church has received the baptism of the Holy Spirit, and every true believer has the Spirit of God dwelling in his body. Also, the church universal is seen as the temple of God. We thus have a special incentive to take care of our bodies, because they are the temple of the Holy Spirit. In addition, we should be concerned about the spiritual health of the church universal, since she is also the temple of the Holy Spirit, who dwells within her.

Of particular significance to us who name the name of Christ are the words of the apostle Paul, warning us not to grieve or quench the Person of the Holy Spirit: "And grieve not the holy Spirit of God, whereby ye are sealed unto the day of redemption" (Eph. 4:30); "Quench not the Spirit" (1 Thess. 5:19). May the Lord assist us all to recognize the Person and personality of the Holy Spirit, who dwells within us, and to guard against grieving or quenching Him in His work of sanctifying us.

CHAPTER 10

The Love of the Holy Spirit

Geoffrey Thomas

Ye adulterers and adulteresses, know ye not that the friendship of the world is enmity with God? Whosoever therefore will be a friend of the world is the enemy of God. Do ye think that the scripture saith in vain, The spirit that dwelleth in us lusteth to envy? But he giveth more grace. Wherefore he saith, God resisteth the proud, but giveth grace unto the humble. Submit yourselves therefore to God.

—James 4:4–7a

The fifth verse of James 4 is the only verse in the letter to contain a reference to the Holy Spirit, although that is disputed. The sentence can be translated in a number of ways. Is this verse referring to our spirits or to God the Holy Spirit? Is the jealousy a sinful attitude or the yearning of God for His people, longing for their whole undivided affection?

The New International Version translators judged that a possible translation is "the spirit he caused to live in us envies intensely." In other words, they thought the reference to the spirit is to our inward spirits. But if we look down at the textual footnotes of this verse in the NIV, we see that there are two other suggested translations. All are possible correct translations, but I believe that the second footnote gives the best translation: "the Spirit he caused to live in us longs jealously." This is B. B. Warfield's preference,[1] which is supported by Thomas M'Crie's *The Love of the Spirit*, based on Romans

---

1. B. B. Warfield, "The Love of the Holy Spirit," in *The Person and Work of the Holy Spirit* (Amityville, N.Y.: Calvary Press, 1997), 97.

15:30: "Now I beseech you, brethren, for the love of the Spirit...."[2] So let us consider these words in their context.

Love for God of Some Christians in the Early Church Was Growing Cold

There were people in those congregations who were leaving their first love and taking lingering glances at the world. James is extraordinarily straight when he speaks to these New Testament Christians. He said to them earlier: "Ye lust, and have not: ye kill, and desire to have...ye fight and war.... Ye ask amiss" (vv. 2–3). Then he addresses them as "Ye adulterers and adulteresses" (v. 4). They must have loved and respected this man who was the half-brother of our Lord very much to have accepted so meekly what he preached to them. I have to remember that I, as a preacher, am as much under this apostolic word as anyone else. I do not choose to come to a church and be addressed in this way: "You adulterous person." But we find in this portion of Scripture issues that God wants to raise with His people. Let us all love and respect the same apostolic word and say to our Lord, "Is it I?"

"[K]now ye not that the friendship of the world is enmity with God?" he asks them. The "world" in the Bible is a theological world. It is first of all the creation of God, owned and ruled by Him. The "cosmos" is the world order, to be subdued by man and enjoyed. But it is now also a fallen world, disordered, rebellious, and aloof through our father Adam's broken relationship with God. The world is organized sinful mankind in the mass, under the power of the god of this world, solidly given over to unrighteousness, hostile to the truth and to the people of God. Bad people organized into a bad system—that is our enemy, the world. It is dominated by "the lust of the flesh, and the lust of the eyes, and the pride of life" (1 John 2:16); its motives are pleasure, profit, power, and promotion. So, the world in the Scriptures is a subtle organization of mankind, operating in terms of laws, goals, and gods that are not those of the God and Father of our Lord Jesus Christ. It was the world that crucified Christ. In its most important languages, the world once declared its cynical enmity toward God, writing on a placard, a crude notice above Jesus'

---

2. Thomas M'Crie, *The Love of the Spirit* (Grand Rapids: Inheritance Publishers, 2006).

head on the cross—"This is the king of the Jews." The words were written in the languages of the leading nations of the world. The world was a friend of a murderer named Barabbas and an enemy of the blameless Son of God. It still is. The world will choose a rogue before a righteous man every day. More than seventeen hundred years ago, the great historian Cyprian wrote to Donatus, "It is a bad world, an incredibly bad world."[3] Certainly it is so in its philosophy of materialism and force, determination and moral despair.

The poet Elias Lieberman has given us a rather shocking picture of the world:

> Man's mind reaches past the stars,
> Probes the atom,
> Measures waves of ether in the infinite spaces…
> But he still lives in an old house,
> An old house full of echoes!
>
> Tear down the rotted boards;
> Scrap the bat-haunted chambers;
> Stop the babbling of simian tongues
> Pretending to blabber wisdom!
>
> I am tired of echoes…echoes…echoes
> In the old house.[4]

Man can take photographs of the depths of space, but he lives in an old house full of echoes. When I was a boy, my friends and I passed a derelict mansion on our way to Thomastown Park in Merthyr. Occasionally we would climb over the wall, go through a window, and stand in the vast hall of this empty house. We were afraid to climb the stairs with their rotten boards, or enter any of the dark rooms. We would smell the damp and look at the fungus. It was all too silent and menacing. Those who live in a world without the living God are like children walking around a very old condemned house. There are still some features that remind them of its former glory, and occasionally there are bursts of creative energy and flashes of brilliance that excite all the residents, and they cheer one another

3. Cited in George Hodges, *Saints and Heroes to the End of the Middle Ages* (New York: Henry Holt and Co., 1911), 6.

4. Elias Lieberman, "It Is Time to Build," #1123 in *Masterpieces of Religious Verse,* ed. James Dalton Morrison (New York: Harper & Brothers, 1905), 357.

up at political party conferences and conventions, saying, "It's going to get wonderful." The opening ceremony of the Olympic games, the sight of two athletes running for the line, a speech, a piece of writing, or a great song sung well can produce something to lift the spirits temporarily, but then the overwhelmingly destructive spirit of our age can take over again.

Within the New Testament congregations, there were those taking many a lingering look at the world. There was a professing Christian named Demas who is mentioned three times in the New Testament. The first time is in Paul's letter to Philemon, verse 24, where the apostle lists his fellow workers: "Mark, Aristarchus, Demas, Lucas." What a grand brotherhood! In the second case, in Colossians 4:14, we read, "Luke, the beloved physician, and Demas, greet you." There is no description of Demas being a fellow worker in that verse, but he is still keeping in good company. The last occasion when Demas is mentioned is 2 Timothy 4:10, where Paul writes chillingly, "Demas hath forsaken me, having loved this present world." Demas had fallen in love with the decaying house and deserted God.

Do you feel that as a danger? Are there people who once worshiped with us, professed they believed what we believed, and began to live in a Christian way, but today they are not in any place of worship? What happened to some of the teenagers we baptized? They fell in love once again with the ideas and values of the world. They got their sense of humor from the world, their thrills, and their purpose in living, and that is where they found their boyfriends. Today they are ice-cold toward Jesus Christ. They live as if He never existed.

How is it with you? Which way are you heading? How does your mind turn when it is empty? In idle moments, what does it naturally think about? What absorbs your interests and affections? Are you falling in love with the world? Or does the love and service of the Lord Jesus mean more and more to you? Friendship with the world is hatred toward God.

Love for the World Is Spiritual Adultery

James gets even bolder: "Ye adulterers and adulteresses." Christians are God's bride, so longing, loving looks at the world are the beginnings of unfaithfulness. There cannot be two loves in this relationship. Princess Diana once said that "there were three of us in this marriage, so it was a bit crowded." In the wedding ceremony, her husband had vowed, "To have thee only unto me until death us do part." To love a world system that scorns the Lord Jesus is a breach of our betrothal to our Husband, God. That is why James addresses them as "adulterers and adulteresses." The lover of the world is God's unfaithful bride.

B. B. Warfield, in his mighty sermon on these verses says: "We cannot have two husbands; to the one husband to whom our vows are plighted, all our love is due. To dally with the thought of another lover is already unfaithfulness."[5] We sing of Christ:

> From heaven He came and sought her
> To be His holy bride.
> With His own blood He bought her,
> And for her life He died.[6]

The Son of God was desperately in love with His people. They had been given to Him by His Father, and He came from heaven for His bride, taking all her liabilities and going to the cross for her, there discharging every debt she owed. Now, with sympathy for all her feelings of infirmity, He prays for her without ceasing. He loves her as His own body. Are there those in the professing church who will love the Lamb of God and yet also love a world system that hates Him?

This divine affection for His people is the teaching of Scripture. James asks in verse 5, "Do ye think that the scripture saith in vain..." anything? It is a rhetorical question. James is asserting as strongly as he can that no saying of Scripture is empty. He appeals to the extraordinary authority of the Bible to support his ideas about the special relationship between God and His people, and his point that loving the world is adulterous. There are numerous Old Testament passages in which the Lord expresses His love for His people in terms of a groom's love for his chosen bride. He is a jealous God. He announces this in the Ten Commandments. He has the burning jealousy of a loving husband toward the tenderly cherished wife who has wandered from the path of fidelity. The prophets take up this theme, especially in the third chapter of Jeremiah: "Turn, O backsliding children, saith the LORD; for I am married unto you" (v. 14).

---

5. B. B. Warfield, *Person and Work of the Holy Spirit*, 97–98.
6. From the hymn "The Church's One Foundation" by Samuel J. Stone, 1866.

James is challenging us: Do we think the prophets are speaking of these things without some great reason? We are the bride of Christ, and He is our loving Husband. He died for us in order for us to live for Him, and He is taking us to a place He has prepared for us, because He delights in us. This is the wonder of our relationship with the Lord. As we walk through life, we must remember that the Lord is walking alongside us with His arm around us. Francis Schaeffer, who also picked up this theme in contrasting Christianity with Eastern religions that are increasingly popular in the West, said: "Shiva came out of his ice-filled cave in the Himalayas and saw a mortal woman and loved her. When he put his arms around her, she disappeared, and he became neuter. There is nothing like this in the Scriptures. When we accept Christ as our Saviour, we do not lose our personality. For all eternity our personality stands in oneness with Christ."[7]

So, the Bible shows how serious is this great sin of adultery, then calls those who are guilty of falling in love with the world (turning away from God) "adulterers and adulteresses." The prophet cries, "How is the faithful city become an harlot!" (Isa. 1:21), speaking about the city where God's house is set. Jerusalem the golden has become a prostitute. In Ezekiel 6:9, the Lord cries, "I am broken with their whorish heart." It is not a matter of indifference to God how we live day by day. "God is not just a theological term; He is not a 'philosophical other.' He is a personal God, and we should glory in the fact that He is a personal God. But we must understand that since He is a personal God, he can be grieved. When His people turn away from Him, there is sadness on the part of the omnipotent God."[8] There is also jealousy: in Zechariah 8:2, we read, "Thus saith the LORD of hosts; I was jealous for Zion with great jealousy, and I was jealous for her with great fury."

The Holy Spirit Jealously Longs for God's People

All this is the background to the reference to the Spirit in our text—church members who love the world are guilty of spiritual unfaithfulness, and God feels a holy jealousy when this occurs. James

---

7. Francis Schaeffer, "The Church before the Watching World," in *The Complete Works of Francis Schaeffer: A Christian Worldview* (Wheaton: Crossway Books, 1985), 4:136.

8. Schaeffer, "The Church Before the Watching World," in *Works*, 4:142.

says, "The spirit that dwelleth in us lusteth to envy" (4:5).[9] The language is of intensity, full of the hungry ache of love. God's Spirit longs for us, James says. As I write, my grandson's fiancée is in Vietnam for some months teaching English as a second language; meanwhile, he is in London. They are longing intensely for one another, knowing they are planning to get married at the end of the summer. This word "longs" is the same verb the Greek translators of Psalm 42 employed: "As the hart panteth after the water brooks, so panteth my soul after thee, O God." But James turns that feeling around, so that what we have here is not our panting in longing for the Lord but God panting after His people. It is a term of deep jealousy; in fact, it is used by Greek classical writers. But this particular phrase "jealous longs" is found just in this verse in the entire Bible; it applies to the passionate love of God the Holy Ghost for us. It describes that envious agony of heart that tears a person apart; the Spirit contemplates a rival taking away from Him the affection of someone He loves. She is turning away from Him and loving His rival; she is giving her love to the one who despises Him—she loves *him* of all people! The church is loving the world system that has nothing but contempt for Christ, and the Spirit longs jealously. This is the response in God, how He views us when we dally with the world and its fashions, fads, rewards, and glittering prizes. God is jealous when our ardor for Him wanes and we begin to love the world. Did the world die for us, rise for us, or ever live to intercede for us? Was it the world that forgave us our sins? Why, then, have we taken our love to the world? Our love should be pledged to Him, but now the Spirit looks as we abandon our first love, withdrawing from Jesus and taking our love to town. James portrays the Spirit as deeply unhappy at this, so that He pants after us with jealous envy. Warfield says:

> Let us not, however, refuse the blessed assurance that is given us. It is no doubt hard to believe that God loves us. It is doubtless harder to believe that He loves us with so ardent a love as is here described. But He says that He does. He declares that when we

---

9. The interpretation of this verse is hotly debated. A recent and comprehensive defense of the divine jealousy view can be found in K. Erik Thoennes, *Godly Jealousy: A Theology of Intolerant Love* (Fearn, Ross-shire: Christian Focus, 2005), 123–33. See further Alexander Ross, *Commentary on the Epistles of James and John* (Grand Rapids, Eerdmans, 1954), 77–79; and Joseph Mayor, *The Epistle of St. James* (repr., Grand Rapids: Zondervan, 1954), 140–42.

wander from Him and our duty towards Him, He yearns after us and earnestly longs for our return; that He envies the world our love and would fain have it turned back to Himself. What can we do but admiringly cry, "Oh, the breadth and length and height and depth of the love of God which passes knowledge!" There is no language in use among men which is strong enough to portray it. Strain the capacity of words to the uttermost and still they fall short of expressing the jealous envy with which He contemplates the love of His people for the world, the yearning desire which possesses Him to turn them back to their duty to Him. It is this inexpressibly precious assurance which the text gives us; let us, without doubting, embrace it with hearty faith.[10]

The Holy Spirit Passionately Loves Us

James is emphasizing here that the Holy Spirit loves us. Of course, God is love, and Father, Son, and Holy Spirit all share the same substance or being. All are equally powerful, merciful, knowledgeable, longsuffering, and so on. All are equally loving; the Spirit loves us just as the Father or Son loves us, but how far have we lived in our Christian lives without being conscious that we are the objects of the love of the Spirit? We are more aware that God the Father so loved the world that He gave His only begotten Son. "Behold, what manner of love the Father hath bestowed upon us, that we should be called the sons of God," cries the apostle John (1 John 3:1). There are many such references to the Father's love, and also to the Son's love for us: "the love of Christ, which passeth knowledge" (Eph. 3:19); "Hereby perceive we the love of God, because he laid down his life for us" (1 John 3:16); "Who shall separate us from the love of Christ?" (Rom. 8:35); "[Who] loved me and gave himself for me" (Gal. 2:20). What encouragement we find in such truths, so that the youngest Christian child can lisp, "Jesus loves me this I know, for the Bible tells me so." In the darkest days these truths are our comfort. When the telephone rings and the news is the very worst, this is the bedrock of our peace, the immeasurable love of Father and Son for us.

Yet there is this third Person who is equally loving, God the Holy Spirit, our blessed Advocate and Counselor.

---

10. Warfield, *Person and Work of the Holy Spirit*, 101.

The Spirit's love is everlasting

It is without a break from eternity to eternity. As it is infinite, we cannot get at the beginning of it, and we shall never see the end of it. It is from everlasting to everlasting, like God Himself. From the past in eternity it has run on and on without a break in time, and it will continue to all eternity. The love of the Spirit cannot be broken. Did not the sin of man break it? If anything could break the love of the Spirit, sin would do it. We know that the Holy Spirit can be grieved, but sin did not break it. The Spirit still loves the people of God notwithstanding their sin. Sin did not break the love of the Spirit, but it did grieve Him, and for a short time it quenched His flowing forth. Before it could flow again, a new way had to be opened up, and that was by way of the blood of Christ. As soon as that blood flowed, the Spirit came flowing down from heaven. He has flowed abundantly on all He loves ever since Golgotha, and He shall continue to love them forever and ever.

The Spirit's love is unchangeable

Clearly from the context of this passage, with its warnings about not loving the world, we learn how changeable is our love for the Spirit. We are like the sea that ebbs and flows, but the love of the Spirit is not like that. The Spirit is the Lord; He changes not, and neither does His love. Did He not love His people with an unchangeable love when they were unconverted? Yes. His love gripped them in their darkness. He brought Christians into their lives, led them to come to church, and, perhaps, made them read a booklet. His influence in them caused that booklet to make an impact on them. He illuminated their minds; He gave them life; He gave them conviction of their sin and need; He sealed them. He did all this to them when they were yet unconverted because He loved them. That love of the Spirit was the reason for their salvation. He could see nothing in them worthy of salvation, but He loved them nonetheless.

The Spirit loves freely

In other words, there is nothing we can pay Him to love us like that. There is nothing we can do to merit that love. We must always remember that Christ's death did not buy God's love. No, the death of Christ was not the cause of God's love. It was the effect of His love. As the Savior said, "God so loved the world that he gave his only begotten Son" (John 3:16). So, we can say: "God so loved the world that He sent the Holy Spirit to give life, faith, and holy desires to all His people." Christ did not buy God's love, the Spirit did not buy God's love, and we cannot buy God's love. But what Christ did opened the way for the Spirit to love us.

The Spirit's love is sovereign

The Lord Jesus insists on this: "The wind bloweth where it listeth… so is every one that is born of the Spirit" (John 3:8). Why should He love Jacob, the cheat and liar? Why should He love Saul of Tarsus, the proud persecutor? Why should He love you or me? We were all equally ungodly, and He was under no obligation to love any of the human race, yet what love the Spirit showed to a company of people more than any man could number. He might have left them all to perish, but He breathed in them and gave them life and new hearts.

It is of the Spirit's love that James is speaking here, saying that He longs jealously, that He yearns over us. Do you think Scripture says that without reason? Is it utterly inconsequential for us to learn that the Holy Spirit loves us? Is it an irrelevance? Of course, there are not as many references to God the Holy Spirit in the New Testament as there are to God the Son. For example, in Matthew's Gospel there are only five or six references to the Holy Spirit. The Gospel is full of our blessed Lord. The Father planned our salvation, the Son accomplished it, and the Spirit applies that accomplished redemption to our souls. Each step was necessary, and each action of all the Persons was the purest expression of divine love. But think again of the wonder of the Spirit of Holiness loving you and coming to indwell you. Imagine someone in London having problems with his drains and phoning Buckingham Palace to ask that some of the members of the royal family come with rods and clear the blocked sewer! He would get other men to do that necessary work, would he not? But consider the reality of the Holy Spirit coming into our desperately deceitful hearts and cleaning up our lives, the holiest being that has ever been or ever will be, coming into intimate contact with such depravity. Warfield wrote: "The Spirit of all holiness is willing to visit such polluted hearts as ours, and even to dwell in them, to make them His home, to work ceaselessly and patiently with them,

gradually wooing them—through many groanings and many trials—to slow and tentative efforts toward good; and never leaving
them until, through His constant grace, they have been won entirely
to put off the old man and put on the new man and to stand new
creatures before the face of their Father God and their Redeemer
Christ. Surely herein is love!"[11]

Let me put it like this. Imagine God had once summoned all
the spirits into His presence and had said: "Now we've got a new
Christian in mind. He'll never be very special. He'll spend his entire
life in the middle of nowhere in central Wales. Who would like to
live in him and keep an eye on him for the next sixty years?" There
might have been a long silence as the assembled spirits thought of all
the people they would rather be with for the next decades—mighty
preachers, heads of Christian organizations, doctors, politicians,
revivalists, evangelists, or Christian athletes. Finally, a very junior
spirit, with the greatest reluctance, said, "Go on then…I'll have a
go," and every other spirit was very relieved that it did not have to
be him. Of course, that is not how it was. It was not left to volunteers.
James says that God has caused the Spirit to live in us. The God who
planned redemption and sent His own Son now sends the Spirit to
throb with love in our very hearts.

Would you not tremble for your salvation if you knew that there
was some reluctant agent helping you, constantly wishing he was
within someone else? We know how cold we are. "Prone to wander—
Lord, I feel it—prone to leave the God I love,"[12] we confess in song.
Where would we be without the help of the Holy Spirit? The world
is constant in the temptations it brings before us. Our own falls are
many. We often cry, "O wretched man that I am! who shall deliver
me from the body of this death?" (Rom. 7:24). We are so neglectful
of God. Hours go by each day in which we never think of the Lord
or speak to Him. What if we treated our spouses like that? How can
the Spirit bear us? It is because of His immense love—patient, kind,
always protecting, always trusting, always hoping, always persevering, never failing. He longs jealously for us amid all the incredible
stumbling blocks we put in front of Him.

---

11. Warfield, *Person and Work of the Holy Spirit*, 105.
12. From the hymn "Come, Thou Fount of Every Blessing" by Robert Robinson, 1758.

He "dwelleth" in us, James says. He does not make an occasional school inspection. He does not pop in from time to time as we might call on our friends. He does not come on approval like a lodger putting the landlord on probation, so that if he does not like the surroundings he will move on. These lives of ours are the home of the Holy Spirit, to settle, to stay, to make His permanent dwelling place. We are touched thinking of the brother of the American pilot, shot down over Vietnam and missing, who gave up his job and spent months looking for him, following every lead. He was known over a huge area of that country as the "pilot's brother." His love for him took him into village after village, talking to criminals, warlords, and corrupt officials, giving his hard-earned money away for any information, continuing with unwearied patience, not put off by many a dead end so that he might find and rescue his brother.

So, too, the love of the Spirit constrains Him to keep in step with us throughout our lives. We fall into the gutter—He lies with us there. We end up with broken marriages, broken lives, and broken hearts—He is still there. We go to prison—He enters the cells with us and also spends those years behind bars. We cannot conceive of the foulness of sin as seen by God. Who can imagine the energy of the Spirit in shrinking from the polluting touch of sin? Yet He comes into the desperately wicked human heart and dwells there, not for Himself or for any good to accrue to Himself, but that He might cleanse us and fit us to be what He made us to be—the bride, the Lamb's wife. His love for us is so strong, mighty, and constant that it can never fail. When He sees us rushing headlong to destruction, He does not get off the runaway bus. He still longs jealously over us. When our hearts despise themselves, the Spirit still labors with us in pitying love. His love burns all the stronger because we so deeply need His help.

By the Loving Spirit We Are Given More Grace

The Spirit loves us passionately, understands the pressures and temptations we are meeting, knows our infirmities, and helps us. In one of her newsletters, Elisabeth Elliot talks of a husband and wife named Bill and Debbie Rettew of Greer, South Carolina, who have adopted nineteen children, ten of whom are seriously handicapped. Three more little boys have recently joined them, so that there are now twenty-eight in the family, living in a well-ordered, peaceful home "spilling over with sacrificial love, filled with joys and sorrows."[13] They began with one handicapped child, then the number grew as God sent others into their home. They lavish on these children all their touching care, washing and drying, dressing and undressing, helping them to eat and go to the bathroom, and they do it in the name of the Lord Jesus Christ and with the strength that the loving Spirit provides. We see there a reflection of the Spirit's care for us—we who have been handicapped by sin.

How can people such as Bill and Debbie do what they do? James tells us here—"He giveth more grace" (v. 6). The family increases, and the grace to care for them increases, too. The sufferings increase, and the grace of strength increases, too. We are afraid of what might happen—an accident, a stroke, some physical calamity that will make us helpless, pain-torn creatures whose eyes are tortured with fright and desperation. We may not measure our ability to cope by our own limited resources. The Holy Spirit gives us more grace. Annie Johnson Flint has written a beloved hymn on these words:

> He giveth more grace when the burdens grow greater,
> He sendeth more strength when the labours increase;
> To added affliction He addeth His mercy,
> To multiplied trials He multiplies peace.
>
> His love has no limit, His grace has no measure,
> His power no boundary known unto men;
> For out of His infinite riches in Jesus
> He giveth, and giveth, and giveth again!
>
> When we have exhausted our store of endurance,
> When our strength has failed ere the day is half done,
> When we reach the end of our hoarded resources,
> Our Father's full giving is only begun.
>
> His love has no limit, His grace has no measure,
> His power no boundary known unto men;
> For out of His infinite riches in Jesus
> He giveth and giveth, and giveth again!

---

13. Elisabeth Elliot, "Count Your Blessings," *The Elisabeth Elliot Newsletter* (November/December 1998): 2.

CHAPTER 11

Regeneration and Sanctification

Ian Hamilton

The Father's great purpose and passion is to honor His Son. This is His number one priority: "For whom he did foreknow, he also did predestinate to be conformed to the image of his Son, that he might be the firstborn among many brethren" (Rom. 8:29). But how is the Father to make His Son the "firstborn among many brethren"? How are sinners, who are by nature "children of wrath" (Eph. 2:3), to become "brothers" of God's Son? This is the background to the biblical doctrine of regeneration.

It is not my intention to discuss whether God's effectual call or regeneration is prior in the application of Christ's redemption to sinners. If I had to choose, I would say that God's effectual, saving call is prior. It is by God's sovereign, wholly gracious call that we are actually united to Christ (cf. 1 Cor. 1:9; Rom. 8:28–30). Moreover, it is in union with Christ that we are united "to the inwardly operative grace of God,"[1] and regeneration is the beginning of inwardly operative grace. So, the new birth provides the link between God's call and our response to His call.

Neither is it my intention to examine the doctrine of regeneration through the lens of historical theology. If I were to do this, we would see that for the Reformers (John Calvin in particular[2]), regeneration had more to do with the lifelong transformation of the believer than the initial intrusion of new life in the sinner, enabling him to

---

1. John Murray, *Redemption Accomplished and Applied* (Edinburgh: Banner of Truth, 1961), 93.

2. John Calvin, *Institutes of the Christian Religion*, The Library of Christian Classics, Vol. 20 (Philadelphia: Westminster Press, 1960), ed. John T. McNeill, trans. F. L. Battles, 3.3.1, 9.

repent and believe the gospel. My concern is simply to focus on the narrower, biblical understanding of regeneration and its inevitable fruit: conversion.

When our Lord Jesus Christ began His public ministry, He said, "The time is fulfilled, and the kingdom of God is at hand: repent ye and believe the gospel" (Mark 1:15). He later said, "Verily I say unto you, Except ye be converted, and become as little children, ye shall not enter into the kingdom of heaven" (Matt. 18:3). But how can any of us do this? Sin has not merely disabled and defiled us, it has spiritually killed us (see Eph. 2:1; Jer. 17:9), and dead men and women cannot do anything. How, then, can any of us be saved? This is why the third chapter in John's Gospel is so critical to our understanding of the gospel.

Our Lord Jesus teaches us here the "logical link" between the Bible's teaching on the pollution and depravity of the human heart on the one hand and the demands and requirements of membership of God's kingdom and family on the other. Here Jesus explains to Nicodemus the crucial doctrine of regeneration, the new birth, the birth from above, which alone enables us to turn from our sin to God's Son; to believe and embrace the great salvation in His Son that God offers to all of us; and so to be converted!

What Is Regeneration?
To be regenerate is to share in the risen life and power of Jesus Christ and to enter into vital fellowship with Him. To be regenerate is to be a "new creation," to share in the life of the world to come, here and now. This is precisely Paul's teaching in 2 Corinthians 5:17: "Therefore if any man be in Christ, he is a new creation: old things are passed away; behold, all things are become new." Paul's language is actually starker: "If any man is in Christ, new creation." Regeneration is nothing less than "the life of God in the soul of man."[3]

In the New Testament, the term for "regeneration" ($\pi\alpha\lambda\iota\nu\gamma\epsilon\nu\epsilon\sigma\iota\alpha$, *palingenesia*) occurs only twice. In Matthew 19:28, it refers to the renewal of all things—the final rebirth of the universe (cf. 2 Peter 3:18)—and is cosmic in its effects. The only other occurrence

---

3. The quoted material refers to the title of Henry Scougal's (1650–1678) classic, *The Life of God in the Soul of Man, or the Nature and Excellency of the Christian Religion* (repr., Harrisonburg, Va.: Sprinkle, 2005).

of *palingenesia* is in Titus 3:5, where Paul speaks of the "washing of regeneration, and renewing of the Holy Spirit." So, whenever we think about the individual's regeneration, we should think of it within or pointing toward the cosmic regeneration.

This cosmic regeneration, however, is not something that is future. It has already begun in the resurrection of our Lord Jesus Christ; His resurrection initiated the new age of the Spirit. First Peter 1:3 causally relates regeneration to Christ's resurrection: "Blessed be the God and Father of our Lord Jesus Christ, which according to his abundant mercy hath begotten us again unto a lively hope by the resurrection of Jesus Christ from the dead." The point I am making is this: God's ultimate purpose is not your or my regeneration or new birth, but the renewal of all things under the headship of His Son Jesus Christ (cf. Eph. 1:9–10).

So, while the word "regeneration" (*palingenesia*) does not occur in John 3:3, the words "born again" (or, perhaps better, "born from above") convey the identical meaning. Regeneration is a completely new beginning, one that only God can effect.

Why Is Regeneration Necessary?

Jesus tells Nicodemus plainly how regeneration or the new birth is necessary (cf. 3:3, 5). He tells Nicodemus three things.

First, regeneration is an indispensable necessity. Without the new birth, we cannot "see the kingdom of God" (John 3:3) or "enter into the kingdom of God" (v. 5). A person may enter the kingdom of God without ever being baptized or coming to the Lord's Supper, though this would be both irregular and wholly unusual. The sacraments are vitally important, but not indispensably important. The dying thief entered the glory of God's nearer presence never having been baptized or having partaken of the Lord's Supper. But no one ever has and no one ever will enter the kingdom of God without being regenerated by the Holy Spirit. Everyone in God's kingdom has been born again; God has given them new hearts. He has made them what they could never make themselves, "new creations." If you are not a new creation, you have no hope of heaven!

Second, regeneration is a universal necessity. What Jesus says to Nicodemus, He says to everyone everywhere. Why is regeneration a universal necessity? For this one reason: by nature every human heart is defiled and corrupted by sin. This is what Jesus is referring to in verse 6: "That which is born of the flesh is flesh." "Flesh" here means human nature as it is dominated and polluted by sin. Un-renewed human nature can only reproduce itself. So, regeneration is a universal necessity because by our own efforts we can only reproduce more of what we are, more of the same. No amount of education will produce regeneration. No amount of religion will do anything to change what we are at heart. The new birth is a universal necessity because the disabling, defiling power of sin is universal.

Third, regeneration is an unchangeable necessity. It is unchangeable because of the issues with which it deals. Jesus' teaching here shows us that regeneration does not deal with passing, changing things, but with the unchanging laws of God's kingdom (cf. vv. 3–5). The necessity of regeneration does not lessen with the passing of time. Society is as dead in trespasses and sins at this moment as it was in 1900, 1600, 800, or at any time in the past. Time has not made us better. Anyone except the willfully blind can see that.

Regeneration is a once-for-all, irreversible spiritual transformation. Everything else flows from this Spirit-wrought inward transformation. We will see later the marks or evidences of the new birth, because it is a birth that cannot be hidden—it is a "new creation"! In regeneration, God changes what we are, not temporarily but eternally. This is why the gospel comes first to persuade us of our bankruptcy before God and our absolute need of the birth from above. Until that happens, we must remain outside God's kingdom. Only when we come to an end of ourselves will we cry out, "God be merciful to me [the] sinner" (Luke 18:13).

How Does God Regenerate Sinners?

First, in regeneration, God the Holy Spirit works sovereignly: "The wind [Spirit] bloweth where it listeth [wills]" (John 3:8a). With these words, Jesus is highlighting the sovereignty of the Spirit's renewing work in our hearts. He comes to whom He wills, where He wills, and when He wills! The great Dutch theologian Herman Bavinck made the point well: "For God no door is locked, no creature unapproachable, no heart inaccessible. With His Spirit He can enter the innermost being of every human, with or without the Word, by way of or apart from all consciousness, in old age or from the moment of conception."[4] Just as children share in Adam's sin without their knowledge, so they can share in Christ's grace without their knowledge. John the Baptist was "filled with the Holy Spirit, even from his mother's womb" (Luke 1:15).

Second, in regeneration, God the Holy Spirit works inscrutably: "but [thou] canst not tell whence it cometh, and whither it goeth: so is every one that is born of the Spirit" (John 3:8b). The Spirit's work in the new birth is mysterious, inscrutable. It is hidden from view. However, while it is mysterious, it is not invisible. In every Spirit-renewed life, the Spirit leaves His "fingerprints." Just as the wind is unseen but leaves its mark wherever it blows, so it is with the Spirit. Above all, perhaps, by the Spirit we cry, "Abba, Father" (Gal. 4:6).

In all of this, we are totally passive; if we were not passive, there would be no gospel at all. Unless God by His sovereign grace turns our hearts from unbelief to faith and from enmity to love, we never give Him the faith and love the gospel calls from us. If we were not wholly passive, we would be able to claim a particle of the glory for ourselves. Salvation would no longer be "of the Lord"; it would be, at least partially, the prerogative of the "spiritually inclined." The biblical doctrine of the new or heavenly birth safeguards the gospel as gospel and the alone glory of God.

But this raises a question: If we are passive in regeneration, what is the role of the Bible, of preaching and witnessing, and of evangelists and evangelism in spreading the gospel? Do our Christian witness and the preaching of God's Word only "kick in" after God brings a person to the new birth? No! God's great "instrument" in bringing sinners to new beginnings is the "word of truth" (cf. James 1:18). The word "instrument" is vital here. God can bring sinners to the new birth without any means; He is the sovereign Lord! But His normal way of working is to use "means." This is what we see here in Jesus' encounter with Nicodemus.

Here is Nicodemus, "a man of the Pharisees...a ruler of the Jews." He is a man with an impressive religious pedigree (cf. v. 10: "a master of Israel" is literally "the teacher of Israel"). But all is not well with his soul. So, he "came to Jesus by night" (John 3:2). He has

---

4. Herman Bavinck, *Reformed Dogmatics* (Grand Rapids: Baker Academic, 2008), 4:123.

been unsettled in some way; he senses all is not right between him and God. Now, here is the significant thing: How does Jesus respond to this searching, as-yet-unhumbled religious leader? Jesus knows that he lacks a new heart (2:25); that he is still, with all his orthodox religion, dead in trespasses and sins. So, what does Jesus say to him? Does He say, "Nicodemus, you need a new heart; but only God can give you a new heart, so, go to God"? No. Jesus evangelizes Nicodemus! Jesus seeks to distress his conscience. So long as Nicodemus, or anyone else for that matter, thinks he is okay spiritually, he will never "go to God." So, Jesus tells Nicodemus the sorry truth about himself: "That which is born of the flesh is flesh" (v. 6). Our fallen human nature can do many things: we can educate ourselves, make ourselves more religious, even intellectually embrace evangelical and Reformed truth. But we cannot give ourselves new hearts that trust Christ, repent of sin, and love God. Sin has utterly disabled us. This is the greatest of all disabilities. We are spiritually unable to do the one thing we need to be done for us; flesh gives birth to flesh.

Do you see what Jesus is doing? He is seeking to bring conviction of sin to Nicodemus. Only when you are convicted and convinced of your sin and its seriousness will you "go to God." Nicodemus needs to see and feel his need of a new heart, a new beginning with God.

So, the first responsibility of an evangelist—and every Christian is an evangelist—is to press home to consciences the bad news that flesh only gives birth to flesh, and God uses His truth to pierce well-guarded consciences. This is one reason why the Scriptures are called "the sword of the Spirit" (Eph. 6:17). God's Word and God's Spirit must never be separated. The Spirit uses the Word He inspired as a "sword" (Heb. 4:12–13). Let me say again, it is the Spirit who gives us new hearts, not the Word. But the Spirit ordinarily uses the Word to effect His work of regeneration.

This in no sense undermines divine sovereignty. The Word is the instrumental cause of regeneration, while the Spirit is the efficient cause. This is signalled in the New Testament by the use of the preposition εκ (*ek*, "out of") to indicate the divine originating cause (e.g., John 3:5; 1 John 3:9; 5:1) and δια (*dia*, "through") to express the instrumental cause (e.g., John 15:3; 1 Cor. 4:15; 1 Peter 1:23). John Owen put this memorably: "He that would utterly separate the Spirit from the word had as good burn his Bible. The bare letter of the New Testament will no more ingenerate faith and obedience in the souls of men…than the letter of the Old Testament."[5] Word and Spirit belong together. They are inseparable.

How Does Regeneration Evidence Itself?

The renewing, new-creation work of the Holy Spirit in our lives necessarily makes itself known. The Spirit leaves His "fingerprints" unmistakably on every life He indwells. It is the Spirit in us that causes us to cry, "Abba, Father" (Gal. 4:6). It is the Spirit in us who produces all-around likeness to Jesus Christ in our lives (cf. Gal. 5:22–23). It is the Spirit who helps us to "mortify the deeds of the body" so that we might "live" (cf. Rom. 8:13). It is the Spirit who helps us in "our infirmities," especially in prayer (cf. Rom. 8:26). We could go on. There are, however, two evidences of the Spirit's renewing presence in our lives that are not often considered.

First, the Spirit's new life within leaves us looking forward to the final "regeneration" at the end of the age (Matt. 19:28). By His resurrection, our Lord Jesus Christ became the "firstborn among many brethren." In the new birth, we are born into the family of God, and the new light of the world to come begins to irradiate our lives. We yet live in "this present evil world" (Gal. 1:4), but we live the life of the world to come because it has already come in the indwelling presence of God's Spirit, the Spirit of God's new and proper Man, Jesus Christ. The Spirit's indwelling, renewing presence imparts a new direction, even trajectory, to our lives.

Second, the Holy Spirit's regenerating presence and power create and inspire within us godly self-examination. A converted life is, at heart, a deeply penitent life: a "broken spirit and a contrite heart are the abiding marks of the believing soul."[6] Where there is no broken spirit and contrite heart, there is, and can be, no regeneration, and therefore no conversion. This is a missing note in evangelicalism today. My point is not that we should constantly be examining ourselves. The Puritans often said that for every one look you take at yourself, you should take ten looks to Christ. However, it is right that we lay our lives alongside that of our Savior and see, however

---

5. John Owen, *Pneumatologia, or, A Discourse Concerning the Holy Spirit*, in *The Works of John Owen* (London: Banner of Truth, 1965), 3:192.

6. Murray, *Redemption*, 116.

dimly, the renewing work of the Spirit in us (cf. 2 Cor. 13:5). This work is not assurance by self-examination. It is noting the gracious work of God's Spirit in our hearts, perhaps especially in creating in us "a broken spirit and a contrite heart." The Spirit is the "Holy" Spirit. He cannot but give us both a heart-hatred of sin and a heart-desire after holiness.

The regenerate life cannot be a hidden life; by its very nature it is a converted life. It is a life that is modelled on the life of the spiritual Man, our Lord Jesus Christ, whose life we share. It is no wonder that the writer to the Hebrews says, "Follow peace with all men, and holiness, without which no man shall see the Lord" (Heb. 12:14).

It can hardly be doubted that evangelical Christianity in the past century has not been characterized by "new creation." We have been strong on rhetoric but weak on Spirit-wrought, transformed, Christ-like living. We need to be reminded afresh that "the kingdom of God is not meat and drink; but righteousness, and peace, and joy in the Holy Ghost" (Rom. 14:17). We need to understand that where there is no "new creation" there is no saving religion, no matter how eloquently, passionately, and evangelically men and women profess the faith. "Therefore if any man be in Christ, he is a new creature: old things are passed away; behold, all things are become new" (2 Cor. 5:17). The Scriptures could not be clearer. Are you clear on this vital matter?

What Follows Regeneration?

If God's great purpose and passion is to honor His Son (Rom. 8:29), His second great priority is the sanctification of His people. Conformity to Christ means, in some measure, reflecting His moral grace and glory in all we are, do, and say. The New Testament is adamant that "without [holiness]…no man shall see the Lord" (Heb. 12:14). Holiness of life is not an optional extra for the Christian. We cannot be united to Jesus Christ and not in some way reflect that union in our lives. In union with Jesus Christ, we receive Him not only as our wisdom, righteousness, and redemption, but also as our sanctification (1 Cor. 1:30). In other words, an unsanctified Christian is not a Christian at all.

In the language of the Bible, to be sanctified means to be "set apart for God," to be "a peculiar people," a people for His own possession

(1 Peter 2:9). This truth lies behind God's summons to His "old and new covenant" people: "Be ye holy; for I am holy" (1 Peter 1:15; cf. Lev. 11:44). The sanctification of God's regenerate people embraces a number of striking features.

What Is Sanctification?

First, sanctification is the agreed purpose of God the Trinity (1 Peter 1:2). It is the specific purpose of God the Father (cf. Eph. 1:3–4; Rom. 8:29; 1 Thess. 4:8). Next, it is the purchased goal of Christ's redemption (cf. Eph. 5:25ff.). Jesus Christ Himself is our sanctification (1 Cor. 1:30). Sanctification, as with all spiritual graces and blessings, is found in Christ (cf. John 15:4–5). In this respect, the cross of Christ is as vital to our sanctification as to our salvation. By His cross, our Lord Jesus cleansed us from sin's guilt, enabling us to begin to be holy. He has removed God's wrath from us (Rom. 3:25), enabling us to pursue holiness without fear. He has rescued us from sin's dominating power (Rom. 6), enabling us to grow in the grace of our Lord Jesus within the clear air of God's kingdom, not in the contaminating and controlling atmosphere of the kingdom of darkness (cf. Col. 1:13). Moreover, sanctification is the all-absorbing focus of the Spirit's present ministry. The Holy Spirit is "the Spirit of holiness" (Rom. 1:4). It should be a fixed conviction in every Christian's heart and mind that what the Spirit first produced in Christ, He comes to reproduce in His people. This is the Spirit's ministry of replication. He is the "Spirit of Christ" (Rom. 8:9).

Second, sanctification is an act of God's grace before it is a work of God's grace. Theologians refer to this aspect of sanctification as "definitive sanctification" (1 Peter 1:2; 1 Cor. 1:2; 6:11).[7] In union with Christ, Christian believers have experienced a definitive, absolute, irreversible separation from sin, from its prevailing power as well as from its condemning guilt (cf. Rom. 6:1–10).

Third, sanctification is rooted in the grammar of the gospel (cf. Rom. 12:1). The Bible has a theological grammar. Before we are ever commanded to do anything, we are confronted with God's prevenient grace. We see this dramatically in the preface to God's Ten Words in Exodus 20:2: "I am the LORD thy God, which have brought thee out of the land of Egypt, out of the house of bondage. Thou

---

7. See the chapter on sanctification in Murray, *Redemption*, 141ff.

shalt have no other gods before me." In the language of grammar, gospel imperatives are always preceded by gospel indicatives. What God commands is always rooted in and flows out of what God has done. This great truth keeps Christian sanctification from becoming pompous, priggish, clinical, and metallic. "By the grace of God I am what I am" (1 Cor. 15:10a). For this reason, grace is the mark of the sanctified man or woman; the sanctified Man was "full of grace and truth" (John 1:14)!

Fourth, sanctification is "horticultural," not "mechanical." The Christian grows in holiness in a variable manner. Most of the time, the growth is erratic and irregular, not even and predictable. It is horticultural rather than mechanical. Owen writes that, just as "the growth of plants is not by a constant insensible progress...but... by sudden gusts and motions...[so] the growth of believers consists principally in some intense vigorous actings of grace on great occasions."[8] It has pleased the Lord not to give us steady, uninterrupted growth in grace; rather, He is pleased to have us cry to Him, wait on Him, and seek His face, often in the midst of trials, before He grants us to grow in likeness to the Savior. He does this, if for no other reason, to humble us and keep us dependent on Him.

In this connection, Owen proceeded to answer a pressing pastoral question: "I do not see much, if any, growth in grace in my life. Am I therefore devoid of the root of holiness?" Owen's response was measured, searching, and pastorally reassuring. First, he said, "every one in whom is a principle of spiritual life, who is born of God, in whom the work of sanctification is begun, if it be not gradually carried on in him, if he thrive not in grace and holiness, if he go not from strength to strength, it is ordinarily from his own sinful negligence."[9] Owen urged us then to search our hearts if we appear to be regressing in holiness, and to cast off the sin that so easily besets us. Second, Owen proceeded quickly to balance what he had just said. It is one thing for holiness to be present and another for the believer to be conscious of it. Indeed, continued Owen, "there may be seasons wherein sincere, humble believers may be obliged

---

8. Owen, *Pneumatologia, or, A Discourse Concerning the Holy Spirit*, in *Works*, 3:397.
9. Owen, *Pneumatologia, or, A Discourse Concerning the Holy Spirit*, in *Works*, 3:400.

to believe the increase and growth of [holiness] in them when they perceive it not, so as to be sensible of it."[10]

Owen never forgot he was a pastor, writing for Christ's lambs. He was quick to reassure struggling saints: "What shall we say, then? Is there no sincere holiness where…decays are found? God forbid."[11]

Fifth, sanctification flourishes in the soil of the fellowship of the church (cf. Eph. 3:18; 4:15–16). Likeness to Christ is nourished within the fellowship of the saints and under the ordained ministry of God's appointed servants. I do not mean in any way that we should neglect personal or private devotions, or family worship. However, the church (with all its weaknesses and sins) is the supreme context for growth in grace. Prize the assembling together of the saints. Cherish every opportunity to meet with God's people. David Clarkson, Owen's assistant and successor, wrote a famous treatise with the biblical title, "Public worship is to be preferred before private."[12]

Sixth, sanctification is essentially likeness to Jesus. Let me finish where I began: the Father's great purpose is that we be "conformed to the image of his Son, that he might be the firstborn among many brethren" (Rom. 8:29). God's ultimate purpose is not your or my holiness, but that His Son be "the firstborn among many brethren." Where there is no likeness to Jesus, there is no holiness! You may be an eloquent, passionate, insightful preacher, but if you are not like Jesus, you are not holy, and Scripture makes plain that without holiness, no one shall enter heaven (Heb. 12:14). You may profess to be Reformed from the top of your head to the soles of your feet, but

---

10. Owen, *Pneumatologia, or, A Discourse Concerning the Holy Spirit*, in *Works*, 3:401.

11. Owen, *Pneumatologia, or, A Discourse Concerning the Holy Spirit*, in *Works*, 3:404.

12. David Clarkson, *Works*, vol. 3 (Edinburgh: James Nichols, 1864), 190ff. Clarkson was entirely typical of the Puritan mainstream when, preaching on Psalm 87:2 under the title "Public worship to be preferred before private," he argued from Scripture that "the Lord is more glorified by public worship," "there is more of the Lord's presence in public worship," "here are the clearest manifestations of God," "there is more spiritual advantage to be got in the use of public ordinances," and "public worship is more edifying." He proceeds to remind us that public worship is "the nearest resemblance of heaven that earth knows: for in heaven, so far as the Scripture describes it to us…all the worship of that glorious company is public…. They make one glorious congregation and so jointly together sing the praises of him that sits on the throne, and the praises of the Lamb, and continue employed in this public worship to eternity" (194). I fear that this instinctive corporate and covenantal understanding of the Christian life is not as imbedded within the life of the Reformed church today as it once was.

if you are not like Jesus, you are not holy (nor are you Reformed). Do you, do I, remind people of Jesus? Every Christian is destined to "bear the image of the man of heaven" (1 Cor. 15:49). "But we all, with open face beholding as in a glass the glory of the Lord, are changed into the same image from glory to glory, even as by the Spirit of the Lord" (2 Cor. 3:18).

But what will this "image" look like? It will look like Jesus Christ. In Colossians 3:12–14, Paul shows us what likeness to Christ will look like in the life of God's people: "Put on therefore, as the elect of God, holy and beloved, bowels of mercies, kindness, humbleness of mind, meekness, longsuffering, forbearing one another, and forgiving one another.... And above all these things put on love, which is the bond of perfectness." This is what God's elect look like in their sanctification. Is this what you and your church look like?

Conclusion
We live today in an era of marked spiritual declension. Of course there are glorious exceptions, thanks be to God. But generally the church of Christ has drifted far from the experiential and transforming religion we read about in the Bible and throughout the history of the church. It is not mere antiquarianism or a passion for some non-existent past "golden age" that leads me, in the light of this declension, to plead for a return to "the ancient paths" (Jer. 6:16). The reason for my plea is simple: it is in these "ancient paths" that we find "where the good way is" (Jer. 6:16). This ancient way is the good way, not because it is ancient (to think that would be ridiculous in the extreme), but because it is God's revealed way, the way of His awesome holiness and superabundant grace. It is as we walk in this ancient way that we "find rest for [our] souls" (Jer. 6:16). More than ever God's people need to go back and relearn the Lord's ways. As the church seeks to have a voice in an increasingly secular, Christ-defying world, it needs to hear again the words of Isaiah to God's wayward people: "To the law and to the testimony: if they speak not according to this word, it is because there is no light in them" (Isa. 8:20).

CHAPTER 12

The Sealing and Witnessing Work of the Holy Spirit

William Shishko

Reformed luminary Professor John Murray stated: "This is the era of the Holy Spirit. I must bring this indictment against the church that we have dishonored the Holy Spirit by failing to lay hold of the plenitude of grace and resource which he imparts."[1] Sometimes this neglect of what is truly the *sine qua non* of effective gospel ministry comes from hesitation to draw attention to the One whose ministry is like a spotlight that does not draw attention to itself, but rather illumines an object to be seen by others. The Lord Jesus said of the work of the Holy Spirit, "When he, the Spirit of truth, is come...He shall glorify me: for he shall receive of mine, and shall shew it unto you" (John 16:13ff.). Yet we must not, as Sinclair Ferguson says, understand this to mean that we should avoid dealing distinctively with the Holy Spirit and His work:

> To draw the conclusion from this that we should not focus our attention on the Spirit at all, or grow in personal knowledge of him is a mistake. The fact that within the economy of the divine activity he does not draw attention to himself but to the Son and the Father is actually a reason for us to seek to know him better, to experience communion with him more intimately, not the reverse. He is to be glorified together with the Father and the Son.[2]

---

1. John Murray, *The Collected Writings of John Murray* (Edinburgh: Banner of Truth, 1982), 3:211.

2. Sinclair B. Ferguson, *The Holy Spirit* (Downers Grove, Ill.: InterVarsity Press, 1996), 186.

In our responses to the so-called charismatic movement,[3] we seriously err if we do not emphasize the person and work of the Holy Spirit. Rather, we should boldly and heartily give the robust biblical and theological development of that theme, particularly since we do, indeed, live in "the era of the Holy Spirit." Our response to the errors of Arminianism must be a full presentation of the biblical teaching regarding human responsibility as well as the biblical teaching on divine sovereignty. Our response to charismatic excesses in worship must be a full presentation and outworking of the regulation and animation of worship by the Word and Spirit of God. Similarly, our response to the errors of Pentecostalism must be a full presentation of what the Scriptures teach regarding the person and work of the Holy Spirit, together with the immense practical outworking of that teaching. Even if the Reformed community has made strides in the former, we still lack much in the latter. I trust that this chapter will contribute positively in both areas.

Historical Developments

While the language of "seal," "sealing," "witness," and verbal equivalents is found dozens of times in the New Testament, the passages most relevant to our consideration are as follows:[4] "The Spirit Himself *bears witness* with our spirit that we are children of God" (Rom. 8:16); "And the one who establishes us with you into Christ, and anointed us is God, who also *sealed us* and gave the down payment of the Spirit in our hearts" (2 Cor. 1:21ff.); "In whom [i.e., in Christ], also, you, having heard the word of truth—the gospel of your salvation—in whom also, having believed, you *were sealed* with the promised Holy Spirit, who is the down payment of our inheritance unto the redemption of the [purchased] possession, unto the praise of his glory" (Eph. 1:13ff.); "And do not grieve the Holy Spirit of God, by whom you were sealed unto the day of redemption" (Eph. 4:30).

---

3. A proper understanding of the theology of the New Testament should prompt us to re-claim this phrase by boldly stating that our Lord's entire work in this age is the true charismatic movement. Among the many excellent developments of this theme, note particularly Donald Macleod's *The Spirit of Promise* (Fearn, U.K.: Christian Focus Publications, 1986), especially chapter 5, "Is the Church Today Charismatic?", 39–48.

4. The translations of the passages that follow are my own.

As one might expect, these vivid and dynamic descriptions of the Holy Spirit's work in the believer have been developed in intriguing ways throughout the history of the Christian church. By the second century, the "sealing" of the Spirit began to be identified with baptism and/or the laying on of hands that often accompanied baptismal ceremonies. Building on the pattern of the Hellenistic world,[5] in which seals (i.e., the production of a stamp or seal on a suitable object by means of an instrument, usually a signet or ring) marked ownership and served as proofs of identity or as guarantees against violence,[6] baptism was naturally understood as a sign that the baptized one was owned by the triune God, was identified with Him, and would, from that point, be protected by God Himself. Also, because seals (which often bore the images of gods[7]) had public and private functions expressing royal authorization,[8] baptism as a seal indicated that the baptized one had publicly and officially become part of a new kingdom. This view of baptism as the meaning of the seal or sealing work of the Spirit predominated through the Middle Ages. It has its modern defenders and proponents in the work of the Anglican G. W. H. Lampe[9] and, more recently, in G. R. Beasley-Murray's *Baptism in the New Testament*.[10]

At the time of the Protestant Reformation, John Calvin revived the biblical emphasis on faith in connection with the sealing work of the Holy Spirit (cf. Eph. 1:13ff.). He focused on the various aspects of the believer's personal assurance and the genuineness of his faith as the meaning of the Spirit's work in sealing the believer.[11]

Calvin rightly noted that the Holy Spirit Himself, not baptism or the laying on of hands, is the seal;[12] he regarded the "confirming," "anointing," and "sealing" as presented in 2 Corinthians 1:21

---

5. For a helpful development of the term "seal" and its use in the surrounding culture as well as in the Old and New Testaments, see the article by Gottfried Fitzer in *Theological Dictionary of the New Testament* (Grand Rapids: Eerdmans, 1971), 7:939–53.

6. Fitzer, *Theological Dictionary*, 940ff.

7. Fitzer, *Theological Dictionary*, 940.

8. Fitzer, *Theological Dictionary*, 942.

9. G. W. H. Lampe, *The Seal of the Spirit* (London: Longmans, Green, and Co., 1951).

10. G. R. Beasley-Murray, *Baptism in the New Testament* (Grand Rapids: Eerdmans, 1962), see especially 171–77.

11. John Calvin, *Commentaries on the Epistles of Paul to the Galatians and the Ephesians* (Grand Rapids: Baker, 1979), 208.

12. Calvin, *Epistle to the Galatians and Ephesians*, 301.

and following as, essentially, synonyms for the work of the Spirit in "[sealing] upon our hearts the certainty of his own word."[13] This is also the emphasis in Calvin's *Institutes of the Christian Religion*,[14] although it is significant that Calvin (in referring to Ephesians 1:13ff. among other texts) also observed that the Spirit's sealing work is connected with our actual hope and proleptic enjoyment of eternity: "Surely the gospel does not confine men's hearts to delight in the present life, but lifts them to the hope of immortality. It does not fasten them to earthly pleasures, but by announcing a hope that rests in heaven it, so to speak, transports them hither."[15] Here Calvin anticipated what would later be developed more fully by Geerhardus Vos, Herman Ridderbos, and others. It is likewise significant that, unlike what became the established teaching of the early and medieval church, nowhere did Calvin link the sealing work of the Spirit with baptism. For Calvin, as for Paul, the Holy Spirit anoints, seals, and bears witness in the souls of believers in Jesus Christ.

We would expect that during the Puritan period, with its emphasis especially on the internal aspects and outworking of true faith, attention would be given to the various terms for the Holy Spirit's work in believers. This was certainly the case with the sealing work of the Holy Spirit. John Flavel (1628–1691)[16] continued Calvin's emphasis on assurance as of the essence of both the sealing and witnessing work the Holy Spirit in Christians. Yet Flavel (with other Puritan writers) shifted the emphasis from the Spirit Himself as the seal to the supposed effects of that sealing. He also introduced distinctions in the sealing work of the Spirit.[17] One may possess the "objective seal," he says, but "may not be formally sealed, i.e. his sanctification may be very doubtful to himself, and he may labor under great fears about it."[18] For Flavel, there are various "seasons" of the Spirit's sealing work in a genuine Christian, and there are also various "ways

---

13. John Calvin, *Commentary on the Epistle of Paul to the Corinthians* (Grand Rapids: Baker, 1979), 2:140.

14. For example, see John Calvin, *Institutes of the Christian Religion*, ed. John T. McNeill, trans F. L. Battles (Philadelphia: Westminster Press, 1960), 3.2.36.

15. Calvin, *Institutes*, 2.10.3.

16. John Flavel, *The Works of John Flavel* (Edinburgh: Banner of Truth, 1968), 6:401–10.

17. Flavel, *Works*, 6:404.

18. Flavel, *Works*, 6:405.

and manners of sealing."[19] In so explaining the Spirit's sealing work, he established a pattern that others would later follow. In that pattern, the sealing work of the Spirit is something of a title for what, practically speaking, becomes an aspect of the entire work of sanctification in a believer.[20]

In true Puritan fashion, Flavel also gave various directions, including ones to those who have not yet been sealed, to those who have been sealed but have lost the comfort of that work, and to those who presently enjoy the comforts of sealing.[21] Clearly, this was a departure from the assumption that all believers are recipients of the sealing work of the Holy Spirit. Flavel may have taken this approach to the subject because of the influence of the translation of the Authorized Version (1611), in which Ephesians 1:13 is infelicitously translated "in whom also *after that ye believed*, ye were sealed with that holy Spirit of promise" (emphasis mine). This pattern of interpretation was also followed by Richard Baxter (1615–1691),[22] Thomas Brooks (1608–1680),[23] and Richard Sibbes (1577–1635), who gave the subject its fullest development from a Puritan perspective.[24]

It is of great interest that the Puritan John Owen (1616–1683) gradually grew to reject the approach taken by his fellow Puritans.

---

19. Flavel, *Works*, 6:405ff.

20. This approach to the subject, with variations, would be followed by Octavius Winslow, "The Sealing of the Spirit," in *The Work of the Holy Spirit* (Edinburgh: Banner of Truth, 1961), 137–51; C. R. Vaughan, *The Gifts of the Holy Spirit* (Edinburgh: Banner of Truth, 1975), 259–75; and, to a lesser extent, by Benjamin Warfield, in his article "The Sealing of the Holy Spirit," in *Faith and Life* (Edinburgh: Banner of Truth, 1974), 289–97. However, Warfield, in correctly noting that "the seal is the Holy Spirit" and that He is also "the earnest, i.e. down payment of our inheritance," suggestively adds, "He is both the pledge that the inheritance shall be ours, and a foretaste of that inheritance itself" (293). This, too, anticipates the emphasis of Vos, Ridderbos, and others in the twentieth century. John Owen, too, states that the sealing of the Spirit is "materially the same with our sanctification." See *The Works of John Owen* (repr., Edinburgh: Banner of Truth, 1965), 4:400.

21. Flavel, *Works*, 6:409f.

22. Richard Baxter, *The Practical Works of Richard Baxter* (Ligonier, Pa.: Soli Deo Gloria, 1990–91), 1:4.

23. Thomas Brooks, *The Complete Works of Thomas Brooks* (Edinburgh: Banner of Truth, 1980), 2:229ff.

24. See Richard Sibbes, *Works of Richard Sibbes* (Edinburgh: Banner of Truth, 1981), 3:452–64 (exposition of 2 Cor. 1:22); 5:409–506 (exposition of Eph. 4:30); 6:374–77 (in which Sibbes draws lessons from the sealing of Christ and relates them to the sealing of believers).

While, in 1657, he wrote, "I am not very clear in the certain particular intendment of this metaphor" (i.e., the seal of the Spirit),[25] he followed the historic train of previous Reformed interpretation in understanding the nature of the sealing as "imparting of the image or character of the seal to the thing sealed.... The Spirit in believers really communicating the image of God, in righteousness and true holiness, unto the soul, sealeth us."[26] While, with Calvin, fully granting that the end of the sealing work includes "assuring our hearts of [the promises of God] and their stability,"[27] Owen also noted that it is not the promise that is sealed to believers, but that believers themselves are sealed.[28]

By the end of his life, Owen had come to clearer and firmer views of the meaning of the sealing of the Holy Spirit. In his posthumously published *Two Discourses Concerning the Holy Spirit and His Work* (1693),[29] Owen devoted an entire chapter[30] to "The Spirit: A Seal, and How." In commenting specifically on 2 Corinthians 1:21 and following, and Ephesians 1:13 and 4:30, Owen affirmed (over against most of his contemporaries) that the Spirit Himself is the seal.[31]

Determinative for the thinking of this later Owen was his observation that the sealing work of the Spirit in Jesus Christ the Mediator (cf. John 6:27) is the pattern and source for the sealing work done in those in union with Jesus Christ by faith.[32] After giving a number of qualifying remarks, Owen drew this conclusion regarding the actual meaning of the sealing work of the Holy Spirit in the great original, Jesus Christ:

> This sealing of the Son is the communication of the Holy Spirit in all fullness unto him, authorizing him unto and acting his divine power in, all the acts and duties of his office, so as to evidence the presence of God with him, and his approbation of him, as the only person that was to distribute the spiritual food of their souls unto men: for the Holy Spirit, by his powerful

---

25. Owen, *Works*, 2:242.
26. Owen, *Works*, 2:242.
27. Owen, *Works*, 2:243
28. Owen, *Works*, 2:243.
29. Owen, *Works*, 4:351–520.
30. Owen, *Works*, 4:399–406.
31. Owen, *Works*, 4:400.
32. Owen, *Works*, 4:401.

operations in him and by him, did evince and manifest that he was called and appointed of God to this work, owned by him, and accepted with him; which was God's sealing of him.[33]

With this pattern in view, Owen drew inferences regarding the meaning of the sealing work of the Spirit in those in union with Christ by faith. While agreeing with his Puritan predecessors and contemporaries that "our conformity unto [Christ] is the design of all gracious communications unto us,"[34] he placed in the forefront that this work is necessarily connected with every aspect of new creation (cf. 2 Cor. 5:17).[35] Hence, Owen linked the sealing and witnessing work in the believer and brought them both clearly under the specific category of assurance rather than under the general rubric of sanctification. At the same time, the sealing work of the Spirit necessarily produces, from the believer, a testimony to the world that the sealed one is truly owned by God and marked with the stamp of the world to come.

We should add that Owen also rightly connected the doctrine to union with Christ, and also introduced (as did particularly Calvin and Sibbes before him) what we might call a proto-eschatological emphasis that would anticipate developments in twentieth-century New Testament theology.

Lloyd-Jones's Perspective

Before exploring those more recent theological developments and their implications for the understanding of the sealing and witnessing work of the Holy Spirit, it is necessary to address what can only be regarded as an unfortunate setback within the Reformed community as it sought both to respond to the rise of Pentecostalism and to provide positive, biblically formed views of the subject of the Holy Spirit and the various aspects of His work.[36]

---

33. Owen, *Works*, 4:403.

34. Owen, *Works*, 4:403ff.

35. Owen, *Works*, 4:404.

36. Among the earlier contributions were John R. W. Stott's *Baptism and Fullness* (Downers Grove, Ill.: InterVarsity Press, 1979) and J. I. Packer's *Keep in Step with the Spirit* (Old Tappan, N.J.: Fleming H. Revell, 1984). On a less popular and more scholarly level, see Frederick Dale Bruner's *A Theology of the Holy Spirit* (Grand Rapids: Eerdmans, 1970) and J. D. G. Dunn's *Baptism in the Holy Spirit* (London: Society for

In 1978, the fifth volume in Dr. D. Martyn Lloyd-Jones's series of expositions on the book of Ephesians was published in the United Kingdom. A year later, it was released in the United States.[37] In that volume, Lloyd-Jones devoted five chapters to Ephesians 1:13, successively dealing with the meaning of being sealed with the Spirit, the nature of that sealing, true and counterfeit experiences, and "problems and difficulties concerning the sealing."[38] It is hardly an oversimplification to say that Lloyd-Jones's development of the subject was, in most respects, like common Pentecostal views.

Aligning himself with many of the previously cited Puritan writers (and very questionably including Charles Hodge in this number) and marshalling the Authorized Version's translation of Ephesians 1:13 into his cause, Lloyd-Jones revived the view that the sealing work of the Spirit may come (or usually does come) as a subsequent experience following one's faith in Christ: "I assert that this 'sealing with the Spirit' is something subsequent to believing, something additional to believing."[39] Using examples from John and Acts, he labored to show that faith and the distinctive new covenant expressions of the work of the Holy Spirit are frequently separated in the experience of Christians. He further used Old Testament examples, as well as examples of the extraordinary experiences of Christians in the past, in order to illustrate his understanding of the sealing work of the Spirit. Strikingly, in only one of those examples did the writer whom Lloyd-Jones used as an illustration personally equate his experience with the Holy Spirit's sealing work.

Clearly, Lloyd-Jones imported into the sealing work of the Spirit his own conceptions of elevated Christian experience. While rightly re-affirming the standard elements of authentication, ownership, and security[40] as inherent in the concept of sealing, and while also rightly distinguishing the sealing work from regeneration, sanctification, and other aspects of the Spirit's work, Lloyd-Jones nevertheless concluded that sealing is a "direct, immediate, overwhelming experience

---

Christian Missions, 1970), as well as Richard. B. Gaffin, Jr.'s *Perspectives on Pentecost* (Phillipsburg, N.J.: Presbyterian and Reformed Publishing, 1979).

37. D. Martyn Lloyd-Jones, *God's Ultimate Purpose* (Grand Rapids: Baker, 1979).

38. Lloyd-Jones, *God's Ultimate Purpose*, 243–300.

39. Lloyd-Jones, *God's Ultimate Purpose*, 250.

40. Lloyd-Jones, *God's Ultimate Purpose*, 245.

and testimony by the Spirit."[41] It brings "the immediate, direct, blessed assurance that we are the children of God, 'heirs of God and joint-heirs with Christ.'"[42] Lloyd-Jones, again in line with Pentecostalism, hinted that the sealing work brings something beyond what a believer receives from the inscripturated Word of God: "Without the sealing of the Spirit you can know that your sins are forgiven; *but not in this special and certain manner*"[43] (emphasis mine). Also in line with Pentecostal calls to "seek" subsequent experiences of the Spirit's work, Lloyd-Jones urged believers to seek the sealing work of the Spirit.[44] While Lloyd-Jones could find precedent for this in some of the Puritan applicatory sections treating this doctrine, there is no precedent for it in Scripture.

While Lloyd-Jones's approach to the subject captivated some and confused others, it met with some effective rebuttals.[45] It is sufficient at this point to note that, for whatever reasons, Lloyd-Jones's interpretation of Ephesians 1:13 does not adequately take into account the unique redemptive-historical significance of the Gospels and Pentecost.

Twentieth-Century Advances

On a much brighter note, the development of conservative biblical theology in the twentieth century brought many helpful advances in understanding the work of the Holy Spirit since Pentecost. With the seminal yet magisterial works of Vos[46] and Ridderbos,[47] many theological concepts that may have been implicit in the best of the Reformed and Puritan tradition of exegesis became clearer and stood out in sharper focus as soteriological categories came to be understood against the backdrop of New Testament eschatology. In short, the "not yet" of the eternal kingdom to be ushered in at the return of Christ has "already" entered history with the coming of the Messiah,

---

41. Lloyd-Jones, *God's Ultimate Purpose*, 278.

42. Lloyd-Jones, *God's Ultimate Purpose*, 279.

43. Lloyd-Jones, *God's Ultimate Purpose*, 284.

44. Lloyd-Jones, *God's Ultimate Purpose*, 294, 295.

45. One of the best succinct responses to Lloyd-Jones's material is found in Macleod, *The Spirit of Promise*, chapter 6, "The Sealing of the Spirit."

46. Especially Geerhardus Vos, *The Pauline Eschatology* (Phillipsburg, N.J.: Presbyterian and Reformed Publishing, 1991).

47. Especially Herman Ridderbos, *Paul: An Outline of His Theology* (Grand Rapids: Eerdmans, 1975).

His defeat of Satan, the world, and the powers of sin by the cross, His ushering in of a new mode of existence in His resurrection from the dead, and His kingly work of bringing that work into history with the application of redemption by the Holy Spirit.

The bud of Owen's introduction of new-creation motifs as he treated the effects of the sealing work of the Spirit[48] blossomed with Vos and Ridderbos, among others:

> [We] turn to another train of thought, which clearly starts from the eschatological end of the line, and from that looks backwards into the present life. This is the case in 2 Cor. 1:22; 5:5; Eph. 1:14.... The "earnest" consists in the Spirit.... Now the Spirit possesses this significance of "pledge" for no other reason than that He constitutes a provisional installment of what in its fullness will be received hereafter.... [The] Spirit is viewed as pertaining specifically to the future life, nay as constituting the substantial make-up of this life, and the present possession of the Spirit is regarded in the light of an anticipation. The Spirit's proper sphere is the future aeon; from thence He projects Himself into the present, and becomes a prophecy of Himself in His eschatological operations.[49]

This cosmic and aeonic eschatological emphasis opened up not only the language of sealing but also those terms that consistently accompany it in the New Testament. This, in turn, provided a window to understand these concepts—a window that delivers our understanding from the realm of the purely experiential and brings it into a realm of experience actually suggested by the terms themselves as they are defined redemptive-historically. In this age, believers are, by the Spirit, stamped with the mark of eternity as a down payment of its fullness in the new heaven and the new earth. For the believer, that eternity is nothing less than an eternity lived in a body totally transformed by the Spirit into the glorious image of Christ (cf. 1 Cor. 15:42–49; 2 Cor. 3:17ff.).

Exegetical and Theological Conclusions
With this rich background of the history of interpretation before us, we can now draw some exegetical and theological conclusions

---

48. Owen, *Works*, 4:404.
49. Vos, *Pauline Eschatology*, 164ff.

regarding the New Testament data on the sealing and witnessing work of the Holy Spirit. The schools of interpretation that have addressed these concepts are not, in each case, mutually exclusive. One helps to inform and refine the other.

First, water baptism or the laying on of hands is the sealing work of the Spirit, but the Spirit Himself *is* the seal and *does* the sealing work: "Ye were sealed *with that Holy Spirit of promise...*" (Eph. 1:13, emphasis mine); "[t]he Holy Spirit of God, *whereby ye are sealed* unto the day of redemption" (Eph. 4:30, emphasis mine). The Spirit Himself is the content of the Old Testament promise (cf. Acts 2:33; Gal. 3:14), and He is likewise that promised Spirit by which believers are sealed. According to Sinclair Ferguson, "The usage of the New Testament...implies that it is the Spirit himself who is the seal of the believer, just as the sealing of Christ (John 6:27) is best understood not as His water baptism as such, but as the coming on Him of the Spirit at this baptism."[50] There is, in fact, no reference to baptism in 2 Corinthians 1:22 or Ephesians 1:13 or 4:30. While water baptism is a seal, and particularly a seal of the Spirit's work in baptizing us into one body (1 Cor. 12:13), and while it is also true that "there is, in every sacrament, a spiritual relation, or sacramental union, between the sign and the thing signified: whence it comes to pass, that the names and effects of the one are attributed to the other,"[51] it is incorrect to confuse water baptism with the Spirit in His sealing work.[52]

Second, while, as a general meaning, the sealing of the Spirit should be understood as an impress of the Spirit on the soul of the believer, the often-repeated specific aspects of "sealing," both in Scripture and in the surrounding cultures, all certainly apply to the sealing work of the Holy Spirit. These are well stated by Hodge:

> A seal is used, 1. To indicate proprietorship [ownership]. 2. To authenticate or prove to be genuine. 3. To preserve safe or inviolate. The Holy Spirit, which in one view is unction, in another view is a seal. He marks them in whom he dwells as belonging to God. They bear the seal of God upon them, cf. Rev. 7:2, 2:19.... He also bears witness in the hearts of believers that they are the

---

50. Ferguson, *The Holy Spirit*, 180. Cf. Gordon Fee, *God's Empowering Presence* (Peabody, Mass.: Hendrickson, 1994), 669, 671, 294–96.

51. Westminster Confession of Faith, 27.2.

52. Ridderbos, *Paul*, 400.

children of God. He authenticates them to themselves and others as genuine believers. And he effectually secures them from apostasy and perdition, cf. Eph. 1:3, 4:30.... The indwelling of the Spirit, therefore renders the believer secure and steadfast; it is his anointing; it is the seal of God impressed upon the soul, and therefore the pledge of redemption.[53]

At the same time, these aspects of sealing should be more fully informed by the terms that are closely linked with the sealing of the Spirit. The Spirit who seals is the Spirit who is also a down payment (Greek, *arrabōn*; cf. 2 Cor. 1:22; Eph. 1:14) of our eternal redemption. To be "sealed with the Holy Spirit" and to be given the Spirit as a "down payment of our eternal inheritance" are explanatory of one another.[54] All commentators rightly note that the down payment (or "earnest") is both a pledge that the eternal inheritance will be given and the first installment of the inheritance itself. Peter T. O'Brien wrote:

> In giving [the Spirit] to us God is not simply promising us our final inheritance, but actually providing us with a foretaste of it, even if it "is only a small fraction of the future endowment."... Because of the ministry of the Spirit to their hearts and lives, they can begin to enjoy this everlasting possession *now*. The Spirit received is the first installment and guarantee of the inheritance in the age to come that awaits God's sons and daughters.[55]

Third, sound exegesis strongly favors the view that the sealing work of the Spirit does not take place subsequent to the act of believing in Christ. The act of believing that brings union with Jesus Christ brings every benefit of Christ with it, including the sealing work of the Holy Spirit, though subjectively believers often only realize this gradually over time. The aorist participles in Ephesians 1:13 (i.e.

---

53. Charles Hodge, *A Commentary on I & II Corinthians* (Edinburgh: Banner of Truth, 1974), 400, 401.

54. Charles Hodge, *Princeton Sermons* (Edinburgh: Banner of Truth, 1958), 85.

55. Peter T. O'Brien, *The Letter to the Ephesians* (Grand Rapids: Eerdmans, 1999), 121. Charles Hodge also rightly relates this to the agricultural metaphor, "the first-fruits of the Spirit" (Rom. 8:23), as a synonym of the Spirit as a "down-payment": "Those influences of the Spirit which believers now enjoy are at once a prelibation or antepast of future blessedness, the same in kind though immeasurably less in degree, and a pledge of the certain enjoyment of that blessedness; just as the first-fruits were a part of the harvest, and an earnest of its ingathering." *A Commentary on Ephesians* (Edinburgh: Banner of Truth, 1991), 35.

akousantes, pisteusantes) may denote actions that precede the action of the main verb (i.e., the aorist passive indicative form of *sphragizō*), but they may also indicate coincident or following action. In fact, Greek tenses do not primarily indicate the time of an action (past, present, or future) so much as they indicate the state of an action (complete, incomplete, or indefinite). Donald Macleod, in challenging the views of Lloyd-Jones regarding the sealing work of the Spirit as subsequent to the act of believing, made these important observations:

> The unwisdom of deducing from the aorist participle in Ephesians 1:13 that there is a clear interval between believing and being sealed is well illustrated in a very familiar clause from the gospels: "Jesus answered and said (*apokritheis eipen*)." *Apokritheis* is an aorist participle exactly similar to *pisteusantes* (believing) in Eph. 1:13. Yet it would be absurd to say that the Lord's *saying* was subsequent to the Lord's answering; and even more absurd to hold that it was possible to have answered without having said. In fact, the relation between believing and being sealed is exactly the same as that between believing and being justified. Faith is logically prior to justification, but this does not mean there is an interval between them or that it is possible to be a believer and yet not be justified. Similarly, faith comes before sealing, but this does not necessitate any interval between them.[56]

Indeed, other texts show conclusively that each believer not only possesses the Spirit, but also all of the blessings that flow from Him. The very nature of the Christian life is to live in, with, and by the Holy Spirit who indwells the believer: "Hope maketh not ashamed; because the love of God is shed abroad in our hearts by the Holy Ghost which is given unto us" (i.e., without exception; Rom. 5:5); "Now if any man have not the Spirit of Christ, he is none of his" (Rom. 8:9). The apostle Paul, in the immediate context of Ephesians 1:13, notes that all the saints have "every spiritual blessing [i.e., blessing that comes from and by the Holy Spirit] in the heavenly places" in Christ (Eph. 1:3). Further, when Paul states in Ephesians 4:30, "And grieve not the holy Spirit of God, whereby ye are sealed unto the day of redemption," there is no indication that this sealing work applies only to some. Indeed, the universality of the command assumes the universality of the gift in view.

---

56. Macleod, *The Spirit of Promise*, 50.

Fourth, because the sealing of the Spirit is an aspect of the believer's union with Christ, it is quite proper to consider Christ's sealing with the Spirit (John 6:27) as the great original from which the believer's seal derives its meaning. The import of Christ's affirmation, "Labour not for the meat which perisheth, but for that meat which endureth unto everlasting life, which the Son of man shall give unto you: *for him hath God the Father sealed*" (emphasis mine), is somewhat cryptic. At least our Lord is referring to a seal that authenticates His messianic work as the promised Son of Man (cf. Dan. 7:13).

Regardless of how one understands the time or way in which the Father set His seal on the Son, it is highly significant that both the use of "Son of Man" and the context of the messianic work of giving the things—food, pertaining to eternal life—are richly eschatological in nature. In John's Gospel, "Son of Man" is "increasingly laden…with associations of revelation brought from heaven to earth" (cf. John 1:51; 3:13; 5:27).[57] In the ultimate "sealed One," the impress of everything pertaining to the glory of heaven and of the age to come manifests itself. The Holy Spirit not only descended from heaven, but He also remained upon Christ following His baptism (John 1:32). He is the beloved Son whom the Father uniquely claims and authenticated as the One to be heard (cf. Matt. 3:17; 17:5; Mark 1:11; 9:7; Luke 3:21ff.; 9:35). This sealing work in Christ undergirded His self-offering (Heb. 9:14), preserved Him through death, secured His resurrection (Rom. 8:11), and, from the time of Christ's resurrection, is now bound up with the exalted Son's power as the last Adam, the messianic Man from heaven (cf. Rom. 1:4; 1 Cor. 15:45, 47). All of this must inform our understanding of the weightiness of the sealing work of the Spirit done by the exalted Christ in those in union with Him by faith.

Fifth, while it is incorrect to say that believers must "seek" the sealing work of the Spirit, it is basic to the theology of the New Testament that believers should live out of that sealing work as an aspect of their union with Christ, the pre-eminent sealed One. Just as Christians live out of and enjoy the practical implications of their justification (Rom. 5:1ff.), adoption (Rom. 8:12ff.), and union with Christ in His death and resurrection (Rom. 6:1ff.), so we are meant to live out of and enjoy the down payment of the Holy Spirit as that

---

57. D. A. Carson, *The Gospel According to John* (Grand Rapids: Eerdmans, 1991).

which seals us. Given the strongly eschatological thrust of the sealing work as explained by both a down payment (Eph. 1:14; 2 Cor.
1:22) and firstfruits/guarantee (2 Cor. 5:5), it would seem to be most
appropriate that those things connected with a believer's "heavenly
mindedness" be placed under the rubric of the sealing work of the
Spirit. Indeed, rather than seeking the sealing, one might say that
because of the sealing of the Spirit the believer is called to seek the
things inherent in the Spirit as a down payment of eternity. Here the
language of Colossians 3:1–4 is most fitting: "If ye then be risen with
Christ, seek those things which are above, where Christ sitteth on the
right hand of God. Set your affection on things above, not on things
on the earth. For ye are dead, and your life is hid with Christ in God.
When Christ, who is our life, shall appear, then shall ye also appear
with him in glory."

Sixth, over against the extra-biblical mysticism to which this
subject can fall prey, we must emphasize far more than we do that
our understanding of the sealing work of the Spirit, like our understanding of every other work of the Spirit, must be governed by the
authority of Christ speaking in and by His inscripturated word. The
Holy Spirit works by the Word (John 14:17; 16:13), and the works
of the Holy Spirit must be understood by that Word. Likewise, the
Holy Spirit uses the Scriptures to form in believers everything that
truly flows from His sealing work (cf. John 17:17).

Lines of Application

This brings us to briefly consider some lines of application that flow
from a correct understanding of the sealing work of the Holy Spirit.
A few of the Puritans who rightly sought to "improve" (that is, make
practical use of) the doctrine, went, at times, beyond what the Scriptures actually say.

First, it is right and best to put the meaning of the Holy Spirit's
sealing work under the broader category of assurance. While it is
impossible for us to gain access to God's decree of election, the sealing work of the Spirit is a primary source of the evidence that one
is truly an object of God's sovereign saving grace. This is because of
the close connection of the sealing of the Spirit and the Spirit as both
down payment and firstfruits/guarantee of the full realization of the
believer's redemption at the day of Christ's return (cf. Eph. 1:13; 4:30).

It is also under the category of assurance growing out of the sealing work of the Holy Spirit that we are to understand the accompanying witnessing work of the Holy Spirit: "The Spirit itself beareth witness with our spirit that we are children of God" (Rom. 8:16). Thus, the Westminster Confession of Faith is right to refer to the seal of the Spirit in its section "Of the Assurance of Grace and Salvation":

> This certainty is not a bare conjectural and probable persua-
> sion grounded upon a fallible hope; but an infallible assurance
> of faith founded upon the divine truth of the promises of sal-
> vation, the inward evidence of those graces unto which these
> promises are made, the testimony of the Spirit of adoption wit-
> nessing with our spirits that we are children of God, *which Spirit
> is the earnest of our inheritance, whereby we are sealed to the day of
> redemption* (emphasis mine).[58]

Second, there is necessarily a profound Christ-centeredness to the believer's experience of the sealing work of the Holy Spirit. This is not only because the Spirit's work in this "age of the Spirit" is to serve economically as the presence of Christ in His people (John 14:16–18), but also because it is the Spirit's distinctive work to take the things of Christ and declare them (John 15:26; 16:14). Even as seals in the world of the Old and New Testaments often bore the image of a king or a god[59] and impressed that image on that which received the seal, so the seal of the Spirit bears the likeness of Christ.[60] Whatever else this means, by virtue of this sealing work the believer begins to "glory in the Lord" (1 Cor. 1:31) as a foretaste of the praise of Christ's glory that will come with the full payment that will follow the down payment (cf. Eph. 1:14).

Third, the sealing of the Spirit is worked out in no small measure in the spirit of adoption in the believer (Rom. 8:14–17). As the great prototype, the sealed One, is declared to be the beloved Son, so those sealed in union with Him are impressed with a sense of sonship such that they naturally cry out "Abba, Father!" (Rom. 8:15). This is the nucleus of the witnessing work of the Spirit in the believer. Hodge wrote, "In testifying to our being the children of God, the Spirit

---

58. Westminster Confession of Faith, 18.2.
59. Fitzer, *Theological Dictionary*, 942.
60. Hodge, *Princeton Sermons*, 86.

testifies that we are born of God, that we are objects of his paternal love, and that we are heirs of the inheritance of the saints in life."[61]

Fourth, the sealing of the Spirit is inseparably connected with the variegated meaning of the work of the Holy Spirit as the "Paraclete" (cf. John 14:16, 26; 15:26; 16:7). Whether this pregnant term is understood as "Comforter," "Helper," "Encourager," or anything else in its broad semantic range, the Spirit is closely tied to assistance in the battle contexts of the believer's life as he remains in a world inveterately hostile to the kingdom of God (John 15:18–25; 16:2ff., 8–11). This assistance ought to be seen in connection with the sealing work as, in part, a securing of the believer in the midst of danger and as preservation from apostasy. This perspective is especially prominent in the book of Revelation. This book, which was given particularly to encourage saints who were undergoing or who were about to undergo faith-challenging persecution, frequently mentions the comfort of the seal (Rev. 7:3–8; 9:4).

Fifth, each of these experimental aspects of the seal of the Spirit, including the desire for holiness, which is the preeminent mark of the new heaven and the new earth (Ezek. 36:26ff.; cf. Zech. 14:20ff.; Rev. 21:27; 22:3; 22:14ff.), and the fruit of the Spirit (Gal. 5:22ff., which, quite literally, are firstfruits of the full harvest of these things in the new heaven and new earth), must always be informed and conditioned by the eschatological character of the gift as both down payment and firstfruits/guarantee. This is the consistent pattern in all of the relevant biblical references (cf. Rom. 8:23; 2 Cor. 1:21ff.; Eph. 1:13ff.). This particularly is in the forefront of Paul's affirmation of the believer's longing for the mortal to be swallowed up by life: "Now he that hath wrought us for the selfsame thing is God, who also hath given unto us the earnest of the Spirit," i.e., firstfruits (2 Cor. 5:5). It is significant that this is the climax of Paul's lengthy argument (2 Cor. 4:1–5:10) as to why he and his fellow ministers did not "faint" (4:1, 16). In the midst of the most severe opposition, "the eternal weight of glory" is felt and seen by faith (4:16; 5:7) as that which far outweighs "this light affliction, which is but for a moment" (4:17).

---

61. Hodge, *Princeton Sermons*, 83ff.

No doubt that sense of the eschatological weight of glory came by virtue of the Spirit's seal of that glory in them.[62]

Sixth, more consideration must be given not only to the meaning of the sealing of the Spirit on individual believers, but also to the meaning of that work for the church corporate. That field is beyond the scope of this chapter. Nevertheless, the self-evidently corporate character of the glorified spiritual church triumphant in the "not yet" cannot but challenge us to give more attention to how, by the seal of the Spirit, this is demonstrated in the Spirit-indwelt church militant in the "already." The observation of Gordon Fee is appropriate at this point:

> This essential framework (i.e. the "already" and "not yet") likewise conditions Paul's understanding that the church is an eschatological community whose members live in the present as those stamped with eternity. We live as expatriates on earth; our true citizenship is in heaven (Phil. 3:20).[63]

Conclusion

At the risk of over-simplification, the seal of the Spirit (the meaning of which is developed by the related term "earnest"—in Greek, *arrabōn*; cf. 2 Cor. 1:22; Eph. 1:14) may be likened to an engagement ring.[64] An engagement ring hardly possesses the inherent power of God the Holy Spirit; nevertheless, its significance gives an earthly analogy to the heavenly gift of the sealing of the Holy Spirit as a down payment.

One who wears an engagement ring shows that she is already owned or claimed by another. The engagement ring, when taken seriously, shows with authority that the one wearing the ring is linked to another. It is a means of protecting the person from the advances of another. It witnesses to the bearer and to others a certain truth about

---

62. We should not miss the point that this extended argument follows an equally lengthy description of the ministry of the new covenant (2 Cor. 3) in an economy in which "the Lord is that Spirit" (v. 17), and in which those who turn to the Lord and behold His glory in the gospel "are changed into the same image from glory to glory, even as by the Spirit of the Lord" (vv. 18ff). One cannot help but see that in back of this, too, is the seal of the Spirit as the image of Christ Himself.

63. Fee, *God's Empowering Presence*, 804.

64. It is interesting that the modern Greek meaning of *arrabōn* is "engagement ring"; cf. W. E. Vine, ed. *Vine's Expository Dictionary of Biblical Words* (Nashville: Thomas Nelson, 1985), 2:190.

the relationship she has. It impresses the bearer constantly with thoughts of the estate of marriage to come. Indeed, it is an anticipation or a foretaste of that estate in which the engagement ring will be surpassed by a wedding ring, and anticipation will be replaced with realization. The down payment of the engagement ring will be fully paid with entrance into the state of marriage.

With all of its limitations, this is a helpful analogy as, from now on, we read, "Ye were sealed with that holy Spirit of promise, which is the earnest of our inheritance until the redemption of the purchased possession, unto the praise of his glory" (Eph. 1:13b–14).

CHAPTER 13

The Ordinary and Extraordinary Witness of the Spirit

Malcolm H. Watts

The earlier part of Paul's epistle to the Romans deals with the doctrine of universal sin and then proceeds to the Lord Jesus Christ's work for us and in us. Chapter 8 is a very definite climax, and Charles Hodge is undoubtedly correct when he states concerning it: "His theme here is *the security of believers*.... The whole chapter is a series of arguments, most beautifully arranged, in support of this one point."[1] We should take account of this sequence of truths in order rightly to understand the apostle's teaching in Romans 8:16.

Believers are secure because (1) they are "in Christ," and therefore one with Him, possessing all His saving benefits (v. 1; cf. 1 Cor. 1:30); (2) through His redemptive work, there is for them now "no condemnation," they being delivered from the condemning power of the law, which binds "sin" and "death" upon them (vv. 2, 4; cf. Gal. 3:13); (3) the gospel, coming to them in the power of the Holy Spirit, has brought to them spiritual and eternal "life" (v. 2; cf. John 5:24, 25); (4) as a result of this, they are in the constant care and keeping of the Holy Spirit (v. 4; cf. Gal. 5:18); (5) furthermore, the Spirit indwells them, and we know His presence is perpetual and abiding (v. 9; cf. John 14:16, 17); (6) a consequence of this is that, by virtue of the Spirit's indwelling, their bodies one day will be rescued from the power of death and the grave (v. 11; cf. Phil. 3:20, 21); and (7) they presently enjoy the status of "sons," and as the apostle subsequently writes, "sons" are "heirs" destined to share their Father's estate and wealth (vv. 14, 15; cf. Heb. 6:17).

---

1. Charles Hodge, *Commentary on the Epistle to the Romans* (Edinburgh: Andrew Elliot and James Thin, 1875), 245.

As Samuel Gilfillan of Comrie writes in his treatise on *The Dignity, Grace, and Operations of the Holy Spirit*, "The salvation of a saint is certain, but his knowledge of this is not always the same."[2] So, Paul logically continues, moving on to the important subject of *Christian assurance*.

Several features of Christian assurance are worth noting. To begin with, it is true that God's children, at the first, may be in some real uncertainty about their present state and future prospects, "as an infant," observes Thomas Doolittle, "may be born to a great estate, and have a certain title to it; but yet he might not know it, or make it out to himself or others."[3] Do not misunderstand me at this point. Spiritual infants *are* savingly blessed, but they may well be lacking in knowledge and experience, and therefore subject to *weakness*, along with various doubts and fears (Matt. 14:31; Mark 9:24; 1 Peter 2:2). Precisely for this reason, the youngest and the most *un*certain should seek an *assured confidence*. Hence we find such exhortations as, "show the same diligence to the full assurance of hope unto the end" and "give diligence to make your calling and election sure" (Heb. 6:11; 2 Peter 1:10).

Edward Leigh, a Puritan, writes in his *Body of Divinity*: "Every wise man will labour to get a good thing as sure as he can.... When this is once got, the soul is possessed of the most invaluable treasure of the world."[4]

Although "growth in grace"—receiving further measures of grace, with stronger exercise of particular graces, such as faith—should therefore always be in evidence (Prov. 4:18; Hos. 14:7; 2 Peter 3:18), as is the case with physical growth, *all believers do not grow spiritually at the same rate*. As a result, some are commended for the quality of their faith while others are told that their faith leaves much to be desired (1 Thess. 1:3; 3:10), and so it is that some are more assured of God's love than others are (Ps. 63:3; Isa. 49:14–16; 1 Cor. 3:1).

---

2. Samuel Gilfillan, *Practical Views of the Dignity, Grace and Operations of the Holy Spirit* (Edinburgh: William Oliphant, 1826), 175.

3. Thomas Doolittle, "If we must aim at assurance, what should they do, that are not able to discern their own spiritual condition?", in *Puritan Sermons 1659–1689* (repr., Wheaton: Richard Owen Roberts, 1981), 1:253.

4. Edward Leigh, *A Systeme or Body of Divinity* (London: Printed for A.M. for William Lee, 1654), 526.

Furthermore, it must be acknowledged that assurance can *ebb and flow*. God may sovereignly withdraw it at times, as in Psalm 30:6, 7 and Isaiah 54:8, but it is more likely that we may be responsible for the loss of it. We may forfeit it in a number of ways: by sin, spiritual complacency, grieving or quenching of the Spirit, unbecoming pride, or, as is fairly common, strong and stubborn unbelief. We may be deprived of it, too, by our failure to discern God's gracious dealings with us, by overmuch trust in our feelings and not enough trust in His promises, and by our tendency to be pessimistic and depressed over our spiritual state (see such passages as Job 15:11; Pss. 30:6, 7; 42:5; Prov. 18:26; Song 5:2–6; Isa. 54:8; 59:2; Hos. 11:3; Eph. 1:18, 19; 4:30; 1 Thess. 5:19; 1 Peter 5:5).

Affliction and temptation can also be involved (Luke 22:31, 32; 1 Peter 1:6). But the good news is that, if lost, assurance may be recovered by several means; for example, by recalling the grand truths of the gospel (1 John 4:16), by praying for divine favor (Pss. 35:3; 106:4), and by continuing in godliness and holiness (Isa. 32:17; 2 Peter 1:5–8).

Assurance is wonderful and wonderfully beneficial. It quickens us in our spiritual lives (Luke 1:46, 47), preserves us from evil (2 Cor. 7:1), removes our fears (Ps. 4:7, 8), sweetens the bitterness of sorrow (Rom. 8:38, 39), draws us near to God (Heb. 4:14–16), and weans us from this world, drawing us to heaven above (Luke 2:29, 30; Phil. 1:21–23). Asks Arthur Hildersham, a Puritan: "Canst thou prove by the Word of God, that thou art in the state of salvation? Then art thou a happy man."

No doubt assurance is desirable, but is it attainable? In His promises, God declares that it is, saying, "Thou shalt know, that I the LORD am thy Saviour and thy Redeemer" (Isa. 60:16). Certainly this has been the experience of His people from earliest times, as the following passages clearly show: "I know that my Redeemer liveth" (Job 19:25); "O God, thou art my God" (Ps. 63:1); "My beloved is mine, and I am his" (Song 2:16); "The Son of God...loved me, and gave himself for me" (Gal. 2:20); "Unto him that loved us, and washed us from our sins in his own blood...be glory and dominion for ever and ever" (Rev. 1:5, 6). This should surely encourage us to seek for assurance with all our hearts. William Bridge, a minister of the seventeenth century, delivered the following exhortation: "O, therefore, you that have gone doubting up and down, and had no assurance of your condition all this while, assurance of your union with Jesus Christ; for the love of God get it now, as you desire to have the comfort of this truth that now I have been upon, get it now. You see, beloved, those times we have fallen upon are dying times; and truly I may say, dying times and doubting hearts cannot stand together.... Labour to get assurance of your union with Christ, and maintain your confidence and assurance."[5]

These introductory matters considered, we are now in a position to examine the *nature* of Christian assurance.

Assurance of Faith

There is in saving faith a certain and definite assurance, an assurance grounded on the infallible testimony of God's holy Word:

1. The "God of truth," the God "that cannot lie," has "inspired" or "breathed out" His words in "Scripture," so that the written Word, including the gospel's promise, is "settled" and "faithful" (Ps. 119:89, 138). When it says that everyone who has truly believed and repented shall certainly be saved, the penitent believer may rest assured that this will indeed be the case (Ezek. 18:21; John 3:36).

2. Faith rests wholly and altogether upon God's Word, as may be gathered from what David wrote: "I trust in thy word" (Ps. 119:42). For this very reason, the apostle calls it "the word of faith" (Rom. 10:8), because faith not only receives it but also relies upon it with the firmest confidence. David again, this time in a prayer, refers to "the word...upon which thou hast caused me to hope" (Ps. 119:49).

3. Christ in the promise is the principal object of faith. This Paul made clear to the jailor when he told him, "Believe on the Lord Jesus Christ, and thou shalt be saved, and thy house" (Acts 16:31). Thus, Thomas Brooks eloquently writes, "The promise is but the shell, Christ is the kernel; the promise is but the casket, Christ is the jewel in it; the promise is but the field, Christ is the treasure that is hid in that field; the promise is a ring of gold, and Christ is the pearl in that ring; and upon this sparkling, shining pearl, faith delights most to look."[6] The gospel reveals that the Son of God is given to be the Savior of sinners and that He is able, willing, and ready to save them

---

5. William Bridge, *The Works of William Bridge* (London: Printed for Thomas Tegg, 1845), 1:222.

6. Thomas Brooks, *The Works of Thomas Brooks* (Edinburgh: James Nichol, 1866), 1:446.

(Neh. 9:17; Isa. 38:20; Matt. 23:37; Luke 1:69; John 3:16; 6:37; 2 Cor. 9:15; Heb. 7:25). *There* is the sinner's assurance.

4. More particularly, assurance springs from the free offer of the gospel. Christ, along with His righteousness and salvation, is made over to lost sinners in a "deed of gift or grant," that whoever shall receive Him shall be saved unto life everlasting (Prov. 8:4; Luke 2:10, 11; John 3:14, 15; 6:32). In His gospel presentation of Christ to needy sinners, God is perfectly sincere, tendering what He is fully prepared to give. In fact, He confirms, to our greater assurance, His goodwill and His genuine desire when with a most solemn oath He says, "As I live, saith the Lord GOD, I have no pleasure in the death of the wicked; but that the wicked turn from his way and live" (Ezek. 33:11).

5. In the Word, there is given to sinners a legal warrant for believing. A poor sinner may accept all that is written concerning Christ, but still he may hesitate to venture and to claim for himself this wonderful Savior. Why is this? Well, the problem may be that the sinner is not at all sure that he has any certain entitlement to Him. Let him consider, however, the words of the apostle John: "We testify, that the Father sent the Son to be *the Saviour of the world*" (1 John 4:14, emphasis added). That surely must mean that if you are in the world, He is there for you, so that you have the authority or right to exercise appropriating faith and to take Him as your own personal Savior. John, a little later in the same epistle, explains more fully and makes it so plain: "This is the record, that God hath given us eternal life, and this life is in his Son. He that hath the Son hath life" (5:11, 12). The "record" or "testimony" of God surpasses all others. God declares that, in His free mercy, He has provided, in Jesus Christ, nothing less than eternal life, and this life is *lawfully obtainable* by receiving the Savior and all fullness in Him. John Ryland of Northampton, in his farewell sermon to the church there, spoke these words: "There is not a sinner in this congregation but has as fair a warrant to apply to the Saviour as any of the saints now in glory had previous to their first application. Whoever inquires, 'May I come to Christ, and will he receive me if I do?' I reply boldly, 'Yes, you may, and he will undoubtedly save you with an everlasting salvation.'"[7]

---

7. Quoted in *Memoirs of the Life and Character of the Late James Hervey*, by John Brown of Whitburn (London: Printed for Ogle Duncan, & Co, William Whyte & Co, and Oliver & Boyd, 1822), 481.

6. What is exercised toward Christ is "faith," *not* doubt; and that "faith" is, as Thomas Boston defines it, "an appropriating persuasion,"[8] since convinced of the divine mercy and promise, we lay hold upon Christ Jesus and apply to ourselves His saving merits. The Scots Confession of 1560, in Article 3, states that "regeneration is wrought by the power of the Holy Ghost (Rom. 5:6) working in the hearts of the elect of God, an assured faith in the promises of God revealed to us in His Word, by which faith they apprehend Christ Jesus with the graces and benefits promised in Him."[9] John Rogers of Dedham, in his "Doctrine of Faith," defines faith as, "A particular *persuasion of my heart*, that *Christ Jesus is mine* [by virtue of the gospel's grant of Him to sinners], and that I shall have life and salvation by his means."[10] This accords with such passages as, "If thou believest with all thine heart, thou mayest [be baptized]" (Acts 8:38) and "We believe that by the grace of the Lord Jesus Christ we shall be saved, even as they" (Acts 15:11). What of *doubting* then? In "Fisher's Catechism," the question is asked, "Is doubting then in the nature of faith, because it is incident to the believer?" In the answer, it is accurately stated that, "Doubting can no more be said to be in the nature of faith, because through the prevalence of unbelief and corruption, it sometimes takes place in the believer, than darkness can be said to be in the nature of the sun, because it is sometimes eclipsed; for faith and doubting are in their own nature opposite, Matth. xxi. 21—*If ye have faith, and doubt not.*"[11]

7. This "assurance of faith" rests entirely on what God has said to us in His Word, *not* on what He has done to us in our hearts. In other words, there is in faith some assurance that Christ is ours, ours in the sense that the gospel says He certainly may be ours; but, upon believing, He becomes actually and savingly ours. Let me put it another way. In the gospel, "Jesus Christ" is "evidently set forth"

---

8. Thomas Boston, *The Whole Works of the late Reverend Thomas Boston* (Aberdeen: George and Robert King, 1850), 7:255.

9. *Reformed Confessions of the 16th and 17th Centuries*, ed. James T. Dennison, Jr. (Grand Rapids: Reformation Heritage Books, 2010), 2:189, 190. Also, *The Scots Confession, 1560 and Negative Confession, 1581*, ed. G. D. Henderson (Edinburgh: Church of Scotland Committee on Publications, 1937), 45.

10. Quoted in *Gospel Truth Accurately Stated and Illustrated*, ed. John Brown, Whitburn (Glasgow: Blackie, Fullarton, & Co., 1831), 216.

11. *The Assembly's Shorter Catechism Explained*, by some Ministers of the Gospel (Edinburgh: Printed by and for John Gray, 1774), Part Second, 185.

(Gal. 3:1) as a "gift" for sinners, and so for us (Isa. 9:6; John 3:16; 2 Cor. 9:15), and we have good ground and the strongest reason to "receive" Him as our very own Savior (John 1:12; Col. 2:6). There is, then, in the nature of faith a real confidence or assurance, although it is perfectly true that, subsequent to our believing, we may have the assurance of interest and possession, enabling us to say, "My beloved is mine [i.e., mine in *possession*], and I am his" (Song 2:16).

Assurance of Sense

It is now time to consider this assurance: namely, the assurance that we have believed, and that therefore Christ, favor, and heaven are ours. Romans 8:16 makes mention of what Thomas Manton describes as a "double testimony" or "witness."[12] Before proceeding, we should give a little attention to the word used in this verse: *summartureo*, which really means an "affirmation," a "declaration," or the delivery of a "report." The prefix, *sun*, translated in Romans 8:16 as "with," suggests some kind of "joint" witness:

1. This solemn witness is to the nature of *our standing and state before God* (Col. 1:6).

2. It is required of such witnesses that they be both *truthful and faithful* in what they affirm (cf. Deut. 19:6–18).

3. The purpose of their affirmations is to establish what is *reality*, in order to avoid deception (Jer. 17:9; 2 Cor. 13:5).

4. *Two witnesses*, at least, are required, which is the general rule of law, so that there is a safeguard against false witness (Deut. 17:6; 19:15; John 8:17).

5. There is *nothing more important* than this, because without it we cannot confidently draw near to God (Heb. 10:19–22).

6. One beneficial effect of these testimonies is the *removal of disturbing doubts and fears* (Ps. 23:4; John 6:69).

7. The confirmation relates to *many truths and experiences*: justification, adoption, and sanctification, as well as God's amazing love, the Holy Spirit's indwelling (with all attendant benefits), and the hope of a place in the everlasting kingdom (Rom. 5:5; 8:33; 1 Cor. 3:16; Gal. 4:6; Titus 2:14; 2 Peter 1:10, 11).

---

12. Thomas Manton, *The Works of Thomas Manton* (London: James Nisbet & Co, 1873) 12:125.

There is indeed a "double testimony" in Romans 8:16—"the Spirit itself beareth witness *with* our spirit...." In the previous verse, the reference is to *our spirit*, which cries, "Abba, Father," but in verse 16, *the Holy Spirit* Himself concurs. John Murray observes that "this latter witness is conceived of as working conjointly with the witness borne by the believer's own consciousness."[13]

Our Spirit

This is the soul, as regenerated and renewed, which is able both to ascertain and to confirm the truth of grace, which accords with Solomon's words, "The spirit of man is the candle of the LORD, searching all the inward parts of the belly [i.e., the very depths of a man's being]" (Prov. 20:27), and also with John's, "Beloved, if our heart [i.e., our soul] condemn us not, then have we confidence toward God" (1 John 3:21).

Isaac Watts comments as follows: "God has given each of our spirits a power of reflecting on our own hearts, and lives, whereby we may become witnesses and judges for or against ourselves; and by this power we pass a judgment both concerning our particular actions, concerning the temper of our spirits, and concerning our state toward God.... But when we compare the habitual frame and temper of our spirits, as well as the transactions and conduct of our lives, with the plain description and characters of the children of God, that are given us in his word; hereby we judge of our own state, whether it be a state of sin, or a state of grace."[14]

On account of this, there are passages that exhort us to "prove our own selves" and to "examine ourselves" (1 Cor. 11:28; 2 Cor. 13:5). This is sometimes called "the reflex act of faith," and it is a necessary duty if we are to reach a sure conclusion about how it is with us before God.

What must "our spirit" discover in order that we may be truly assured?

1. Our spirit, on searching, may find that a great change has taken place. This is true of anyone who has become a real Christian,

---

13. John Murray, *Epistle to the Romans* (London: Marshall, Morgan & Scott, 1967), 297.

14. Isaac Watts, *The Works of the Rev. Isaac Watts* (Leeds: Printed by Edward Baines, 1800), 2:94.

for Scripture states quite clearly, "If any man be in Christ, he is *a new creature*: old things are passed away; behold all things are become new" (2 Cor. 5:17, emphasis added); and again, "In Christ Jesus neither circumcision availeth anything, nor uncircumcision, but *a new creature*" (Gal. 6:15, emphasis added).

2. There may be within us no awareness of our being in any way righteous, but rather a deep sense of our sin's filthiness and odiousness. This is a definite mark of saving grace, for, in one of our Lord's parables, grace so moved a man that he "smote upon his breast, saying, God be merciful to me *a sinner*" (Luke 18:13, emphasis added). Similarly, the apostle Paul in referring to "sinners," added those significant words, "of whom I am *chief*" (1 Tim. 1:15, emphasis added).

3. It may also be most apparent that self-dependence no longer exists: instead, there is within a total reliance upon Christ and His redeeming work. This shows that conversion has taken place, for converted people are addressed like this: "*In whom [i.e., in Christ] ye also trusted*, after that ye heard the word of truth, the gospel of your salvation" (Eph. 1:13, emphasis added; cf. John 6:47). Also, "Being justified freely by his grace through the redemption that is in Christ Jesus: whom God hath set forth to be a propitiation [the means of turning away the wrath of God] through *faith in his blood*" (Rom. 3:24, 25, emphasis added).

4. Whereas before there was nothing but antipathy toward God, now, it may be, there is clear evidence of the character and disposition of a child of God, which includes a genuine, tender, and respectful love for Him as our heavenly Father. This is ever the case with true believers, who are His "*sons and daughters*" (2 Cor. 6:18, emphasis added), who love Him and, in loving Him, seek to obey and serve Him: "[They] that *love* God" are "the called according to his purpose" (Rom. 8:28, emphasis added), and they prove "*obedient* children" (1 Peter 1:14, emphasis added), determined to "*serve* the living God" (1 Thess. 1:9, emphasis added).

5. On further search, it may appear that there is no trace of the old disposition of wanting little or no experience of God, but there is a new desire for experiential knowledge of him, born of communion and fellowship. This is a sure indication that there is real religion with a man. The godly man is ever saying, "my heart and my flesh *crieth out for the living God*" (Ps. 84:2, emphasis added). For him, there could

be no sweeter hour than that spent in the presence of His God. Therefore, he glories in the fact that, through Christ Jesus and by the Holy Spirit, he has *"access…*unto the Father" (Eph. 2:18, emphasis added).

6. Perhaps more self-examination will bring yet another revealing characteristic to light. Where once there was no interest in the means of grace, there is now a deep interest in the Word of God and prayer. It is surely the converted man who confesses that God's Word is *"better unto me than thousands of gold and silver"* (Ps. 119:72, emphasis added), and, *"I bow my knees* unto the Father of our Lord Jesus Christ" (Eph. 3:14, emphasis added).

7. It may be that the old spiritual carelessness is gone and that another very different feature has taken its place, namely, the aim and actual endeavor to please God in the pursuit of gospel holiness and service. That singular man of God, Enoch, left a testimony behind him, "that he *pleased God"* (Heb. 11:5, emphasis added), and New Testament believers are addressed as *"holy* and beloved" (Col. 3:12, emphasis added) and described as *"lights* in the world; *holding forth the word of life"* (Phil. 2:15, 16, emphasis added).

8. Believers were once very worldly in heart and life, but now, through grace, this world neither attracts them nor squeezes them into its wretched mold. As our beloved Savior did "overcome the world," its ambitions, pleasures and various temptations, so in the heart of every true saint there is a faith determined to gain the victory over this present evil world: "Whatsoever is born of God *overcometh the world"* (1 John 5:4, emphasis added).

9. Formerly the believer, in a state of nature, was both unhappy and restless, but, in a state of grace, the divine consolation brings him inward peace and joy. Blessed indeed is the man who knows that. The believing psalmist testifies, "thy *comforts* delight my soul" (Ps. 94:19, emphasis added), and all believers know the God "who *comforteth* in all our tribulation" (2 Cor. 1:4, emphasis added).

10. Truly fearful is it to be, as the unconverted are, "without hope," but the great change has surely taken place if there is in the soul "the *hope* of glory" (Col. 1:27, emphasis added; cf. 1 Peter 3:15; 1 John 3:3), even a *"hope* of eternal life" (Titus 1:2, emphasis added).

This is by no means an exhaustive list of the marks and evidences, but they are some of the important and distinguishing ones by which a true believer can be certainly recognized. Our spirit, reflecting within, can look at itself and judge if there are definite indications of a true, saving work of grace. If it concludes that there are, it may rejoice in a wonderful assurance of the love of God.

His Spirit

The verse presently being considered says, "The Spirit itself beareth witness with our spirit," teaching us that the Holy Spirit bears witness *jointly* with our spirit, assisting and concurring in this matter of attaining to blessed assurance.

Here, I believe, we need to distinguish between what theologians have called the "ordinary" and the "extraordinary" witness of the Spirit.

The ordinary witness

When reference is made to any witness of the Spirit, it is not to be thought that, in confirming the believer's pardon and acceptance, he communicates through some supernatural vision or voice. By entertaining such a notion, some have been led to despair, not experiencing such a thing; while others have been led to presumption, fancying that they have indeed experienced it.

Nevertheless, this particular passage *does* say, "the Spirit itself [or Himself]," that is, in His very own person, by His very presence, some impression, or a spiritual activity, bears a unique and precious testimony to the fact that a person is truly the Lord's.

At this point, we must consider the more general and common ways in which the Spirit witnesses:

1. The Holy Spirit bears His testimony by *attending God's Word* read, heard, or preached, blessing it to our souls and, in particular, blessing the divine promises that are shown to belong to us. The apostle reminds the Corinthians that his preaching among them was "in demonstration of the Spirit and of power," that is, the Holy Spirit powerfully proved that the gospel was indeed true, "that [their] faith should not stand in the wisdom of men, but in the power of God," meaning that, with such an experience, their faith might appear produced by God's efficacious power (1 Cor. 2:3, 4).

Similarly, Paul reminds the Thessalonians that when he first preached the gospel among them, it came "in power" and "in the

Holy Ghost," with the result that they received an unshaken "assurance" (1 Thess. 1:5).

2. Under the ministry of the Spirit, *Jesus Christ, the Redeemer, is revealed to us* in a very special manner. Christ, in His Upper Room Discourse, said concerning the Spirit, "he shall testify of me," and again, "he shall glorify me: for he shall receive of mine and show it unto you" (John 15:26; 16:14), meaning that, in His office and by His work, He would work through the Word to make Christ known to His people (cf. 2 Cor. 3:18; Eph. 1:17).

This discovery of Christ is not outward, as through the gospel only, but inward, as by the Spirit's influence. The result is an apprehension of Christ in the soul, which is what Paul means when he writes, "it pleased God, who…called me by his grace, to reveal his Son *in me*," a knowledge that clearly came with assurance, for he goes on to say that he was immediately ready and prepared to proclaim the good news about the Savior: "that I might preach him among the heathen" (Gal. 1:15, 16, emphasis added).

3. *Our hearts are touched* and *our affections stirred* by the Spirit. The Lord Jesus taught that the Spirit works *in us* by means of the Word. "It is the spirit that quickeneth," He said, and then He spoke of His words as "spirit" and *"life"* (John 6:63, emphasis added). We know that where there is spiritual *life* there will be both *sense* and *feeling*; and therefore we may suppose that it was the Spirit, "the spirit of burning" (Isa. 4:4), who was responsible for the impressions felt by the two disciples on the way to Emmaus, causing them to say, "Did not *our heart burn within us*, while he talked with us by the way, and while he opened to us the Scriptures?" (Luke 24:32, emphasis added) It was certainly an experience that brought assurance, for when they came to "the eleven," they said, "The Lord is risen *indeed*" (v. 34, emphasis added).

A vital part of the Spirit's work in the heart, of course, is to stir and *draw forth our graces*, graces such as faith, hope, and love, and all the graces that are within our souls. When mention is made of graces, what exactly is intended? We know what *grace* is: it is the free and undeserved love of God. What, then, are *graces*? If grace (unmerited kindness) is the fountain, graces are the streams that flow from that fountain, the qualities the Holy Spirit imparts.

The Spirit produces the principles and, at times, calls them into action. Some verses in the Song of Solomon prove helpful in our understanding of this. For example, in 4:12–15, the Lord is represented as contemplating His people, who are likened to a "garden" and replete with many graces, "camphire, with spikenard," etc. In verse 16, He calls for the Spirit, likened to the "wind" (Ezek. 37:9, 14; John 3:8), to move over the plants, to "blow upon [the] garden," that those precious graces within may be drawn forth into lively exercise, "that the spices thereof may flow out." When the Spirit brings this to pass, and our graces, peculiar to the Lord's people, are very much in evidence, it is a witness of testimony that we are believers indeed.

4. The Spirit, "the spirit of wisdom and revelation" (granting further capacity to understand and making fresh discoveries of spiritual things), enables us to possess *greater "knowledge,"* and that which is above all other, the knowledge of God (Eph. 1:17, emphasis added). That knowledge includes perception, appreciation, and real enjoyment, and a believer, by this experience of God and His favor, is *convinced* that it is "better than life" (Ps. 63:3), and the beginning of the soul's blessedness and of heaven's happiness, even "life eternal" (John 17:3). Thus it is that we receive the Holy Spirit's "witness" to the fact that our religion is true and vital.

5. Another relevant truth is that of the Spirit's *inhabitation or indwelling.* Our Lord, in conversation with the woman of Samaria, compared the Spirit to water, and in developing this, He affirmed that the Spirit will be *in* the believer as the water is in the well. His actual words were, "The water that I shall give him shall be *in him* a well of water springing up into everlasting life" (John 4:14, emphasis added). Much later in His ministry, addressing people at the Feast of Tabernacles, He returned to this theme and said of the believer that "out of his belly [i.e., his inner man] shall flow rivers of living water" (John 7:38). The apostle John adds a note that reads, "this spake he of the Spirit" (v. 39). The image was clear enough, and the envisaged experience and blessing most important.

In the Upper Room, at the end of His life and ministry, He referred yet again to the Spirit's special residence in His people, saying, "he dwelleth with you, and shall be *in* you" (John 14:17, emphasis added). The apostle wrote further on this in the epistles, teaching that "the Spirit of God [dwells] in you" (Rom. 8:9; cf. v. 11; 1 Cor. 3:16; 2 Cor. 6:16).

At times we can *feel* His presence within. For example, when we are cast down, the Spirit is there to grant a gracious reviving. When we are weak or faint, He is there to impart strength and lift us up. When we are in a state of apparent desertion, He is there to instigate us to fervent prayer. When we are deeply distressed, He is there to minister in our hearts the divine consolation (see such passages as Isa. 57:15; John 14:16, 17; Rom. 8:26; Eph. 3:14–16). In these and other ways, the Spirit *testifies* to the fact that He resides in us for one very good reason—we belong to God. This is compelling testimony.

6. The fact that the Spirit is in us, engaged in *a sanctifying work*, is also a witness. At regeneration, the divine image, in some measure, is stamped upon our souls, but in sanctification, that image is formed more fully and more clearly. As stated in the Westminster Shorter Catechism, "Sanctification is the work of God's free grace, whereby we are renewed in the whole man after the image of God" (Q. 35).[15] This definition faithfully represents Scripture's teaching that, in the souls of the Lord's people, a work of renewal is being progressively done, as taught in Philippians 2:12 and Hebrews 13:20, 21, that, as the apostle writes to his converts, "Christ be formed in you" (Gal. 4:19; cf. Eph. 4:23, 24; Col. 3:10). We become acutely aware of this work because it produces a growing abhorrence of sin and an intense longing after purity. Paul speaks for true believers when he refers to "sin" as "the evil that I *hate*" (Rom. 7:15, emphasis added; cf. 12:9), and Proverbs 11:23 correctly observes that "the *desire* of the righteous is only good" (emphasis added).

Do such feelings exist in men generally? No, they certainly do not. What, then, does their presence indicate? It indicates that the person is evidently in a state of grace. Because these are very strong and powerful feelings, they constitute a compelling, experimental testimony concerning our salvation.

7. The Spirit facilitates communion and the soul's *enjoyment of God*, and thereby He attests that we have true religion and no vain delusion. "Communion" (Greek: *koinonia*) means "having in

---

15. *The Confession of Faith; the Large and Shorter Catechisms, together with the Sum of Saving Knowledge* (Edinburgh: Printed by Sir D. Hunter Blair and M. S. Tyndall Bruce, 1841), 412, 413.

common": God grants to us influences and impressions, particularly of His goodness, mercy, and grace, and we make our returns to Him, in causing our thoughts, desires, and delights to go out and center in Him. Thus, we are able to enjoy God; that is, to discover Him as our chief good and to experience great happiness in His presence, not only in this life but also for the life to come: "I sat down under his shadow with great delight, and his fruit was sweet unto my taste" (Song 2:3); "In thy presence is fulness of joy; at thy right hand there are pleasures for evermore" (Ps. 16:11).

The Holy Spirit brings all this about; hence, we read of "the communion of the Holy Ghost" (2 Cor. 13:14) and also of "joy in [or by the power and grace of] the Holy Ghost" (Rom. 14:17). The Spirit, by elevating our souls, both enables and directs them into the presence of God, our exceeding joy.

This is a further witness of the Spirit—and a most powerful one—that God is our blessed and everlasting portion.

8. Yet another example of the Spirit's witnessing work is the *peace and quietness* imparted to our souls. As we have already seen, in his epistle to the Romans, Paul expresses his desire for them, that God, he says, would "fill you with all joy and peace," not "joy" only but "joy and peace." Elsewhere, this "peace" is expressly said to be imparted through the power of the Spirit: it is called "the fruit of the Spirit (Gal. 5:22).

Previously our souls may have known disturbing griefs, cares, and fears, but then, quite wonderfully, "he giveth quietness"; there is an inward and delightful calm. The Spirit thus bears testimony to the fact that there are grounds for peace in everlasting love, the covenant of grace, and Christ's blood and righteousness.

9. At a critical moment, perhaps, the Spirit can witness by *stirring our memories* to recall a particular Scripture passage or even some past experience. As to the former, we know that is possible, for did not our Lord say, "the Comforter…shall…bring all things to your remembrance, whatsoever I have said unto you" (John 14:26)? As to the latter, we have examples of Spirit-filled men doing this, such as David, "the LORD that delivered me out of the paw of the lion, and out of the paw of the bear, he will deliver me out of the hand of this Philistine" (1 Sam. 17:17; cf. Gen. 32:10, 11; 2 Cor. 1:10; 2 Tim. 4:17, 18).

God is faithful. What He has said, He will surely honor and maintain. What He has done, He is well able to perform, again and again. He does care for us as His beloved people. The Spirit, testifying out of the storehouse of our memories, persuades us that this is indeed so.

10. One final testimony of the Spirit (to be mentioned) is to the fact that, as God's children, we belong to heaven and therefore we long to be there. The Holy Spirit is *such a blessing in our souls* that sometimes we feel as if we are in the very suburbs of heaven, experiencing the beginnings of heavenly blessedness ("the firstfruits," or the first portion of the harvest; the "earnest" or the deposit of what is to come, i.e., the full settlement, Rom. 8:23; 2 Cor. 1:22; 5:5). These foretastes of final salvation move us to long for the glory that is yet to be revealed: "Make haste, my beloved…" (Song 8:14); "earnestly desiring to be clothed upon with our house which is from heaven" (2 Cor. 5:2); "having a desire to depart, and to be with Christ" (Phil. 1:23).

Why is the Spirit giving us these anticipations of heaven's glory? Why does He make us so homesick that we find ourselves looking forward to an entrance into God's everlasting kingdom? He is hereby witnessing to the certain truth that heaven belongs to us and that we belong to heaven.

The Extraordinary Witness

In preparing this chapter, I came across in my study a book of sermons by Jonathan Dickinson, onetime president of Princeton College, New Jersey, and I noticed that among his sermons was one entitled "The Witness of the Spirit." I turned immediately to it, eager to read what Dickinson had written on the Spirit's *extraordinary witness.* Sure enough, he referred to it, noting that "the Spirit of God doth sometimes bear witness in a more IMMEDIATE and EXTRAORDINARY way, to the adoption of his children." I read on most eagerly, only to be met with these words: "But here, I must confess, I am at once non-plussed…." This was followed by a few sentences of a very general nature, and then he intimated it was time to "dismiss this head."[16]

---

16. Jonathan Dickinson, *The Witness of the Spirit,* in *Sermons and Tracts* (Edinburgh: Printed for M. Gray, 1793), 314.

That we are touching now on a most profound subject, no one, I think, will be prepared to deny. There are several preliminary points to be stated and noted:

1. When mention is made in this context of something "*immediate,*" what is intended is something "not reliant on other testimony" and, perhaps, "sudden" and "unexpected." Thomas Goodwin is quick to explain, "it is always in and with the Word, and according to it, and therefore they are said to be 'sealed with the Spirit of promise.'"[17] The other word, "extraordinary," suggests it is "not common," that not all the Lord's people receive this testimony.

2. It should not be doubted that God is able, through the Spirit, to communicate after the manner of Psalm 35:3: "Say unto my soul, I am thy salvation." Did not our Lord speak of the Spirit's ministry in similar terms, saying: "I will pray the Father, and he shall give you another Comforter.... At that day ye shall know that I am in the Father, and ye in me, and I in you" (John 14:16, 20; cf. Dan. 9:23; 10:19)?

3. In the New Testament, reference is made to a "sealing" of the Spirit (2 Cor. 1:22; Eph. 1:13; 4:30). Paul Bayne, a Puritan, helpfully writes, "The sealing...doth figuratively signify a singular confirmation given to faithful ones touching their redemption."[18] After we believe, the Spirit may—and sometimes does—"attest the reality" of our state by grace and "make certain" to us that we now belong to the Lord (cf. John 3:33; Rom. 15:28), and what is now before us is a singular experience of this assuring work. Without doubt there can be a very powerful impression upon our hearts of the Holy Spirit, whereby we are comfortably certified of our saving interest in Christ.

4. A mystery surrounds this. Scripture declares, in general, "thou knowest not what is the way of the spirit" (Eccl. 11:5). In John's Gospel, our Lord is recorded as likening the "Spirit" to the "wind" (in Hebrew and Greek the same word can be translated in both these ways), and He says we cannot discern the manner of their movements (John 3:8). In both cases, the manner of their working is unknown and unknowable.

---

17. Thomas Goodwin, *The Works of Thomas Goodwin* (Edinburgh: James Nichol, 1864), 8:367.

18. Paul Bayne, *An Entire Commentary upon the Whole Epistle of St. Paul to the Ephesians* (Edinburgh: James Nichol, 1866), 80.

5. This particular work of the Spirit is very much a secret, private matter. Our Lord promises, besides the gift of "the hidden manna" (a personal experience of Christ) and "a white stone" (possibly some token of acquittal and acceptance), "a new name written [on the stone] which no man knoweth saving he that receiveth it [that is, a special and intimate token of our relationship to the Lord]" (Rev. 2:17). Henry Cowles concludes that all this "naturally refers to those personal testimonies of his approval which are currently known as 'the witness of the Spirit.'"[19]

6. In a sense, this is the greatest and most effective of all the witnesses. Confirming other testimony, it is not dependent upon them, but it enables the heart to know for sure its own state before God. As John teaches, there are the witnesses of "water" and "blood" (sanctification and justification), but over and above them is the witness of "the Spirit," which, Goodwin observes, "is not a testimony fetched out of a man's self, or the work of the Spirit in man, as the others were; for the Spirit speaks not by effects, but speaks from himself."[20]

7. So powerful is this unusual witness that it relieves all the darkness produced by doubt and fear; and it enables us to walk in wonderful light, even the light of an assured assurance. It is said that the early believers were "walking…in the comfort of the Holy Ghost" (Acts 9:31).

As the Lord enables, we shall now briefly consider the precise nature of the Spirit's "extraordinary witness":

1. There were promises in the Old Testament to the effect that in "the last days"—and, therefore, throughout this present Christian age—there would be numerous *visitations of the Spirit*. Passages such as the following immediately come to mind: "I will pour my Spirit upon thy seed, and my blessing upon thine offspring" (Isa. 44:3; cf. 35:6, 7; 41:17–19; Ezek. 34:26; Joel 2:28, 29).

Although the Spirit came to the church in a formal way on the day of Pentecost to begin His new-covenant ministry of glorifying the triumphant Christ (John 7:39; Acts 2:1, 2), yet there were, according to the book of Acts, subsequent "comings" when He evidently

19. Henry Cowles, *The Revelation of John* (New York: D. Appleton and Company, 1884), 72.
20. Goodwin, *Works*, 8:366.

revisited His people. One example is with respect to the Jerusalem church, when, some time after Pentecost, "the place was shaken where they were assembled together; and they were all filled with the Holy Ghost" (Acts 4:31).

We do not doubt that the Holy Spirit still comes to churches in mighty and unusual ways. We do not doubt either that He comes to individuals similarly. Does not David refer to this very experience when he says, "Make no tarrying, O my God," and, "O when wilt thou come to me?" (Pss. 40:17; 101:2; cf. 70:5)? The Lord Jesus taught that to those who seek, God will "give the Holy Spirit" (Luke 11:13), and He was certainly given at significant times to Peter and Paul, who were suddenly "filled with the Holy Ghost," an experience that clearly brought strength and confidence (Acts 4:8; 13:9). It is possible, then, for the Holy Spirit to make His presence felt in an exceptional way, granting an undeniable impression and a definite assurance "when he is come" (John 16:8).

2. The Spirit is able *remarkably to illuminate the written Word*. In that Word, there are revelations of divine mercy and grace, discoveries of covenant privilege, exhibitions of redemption's benefits, discoveries of unfailing consolation, and descriptions of the heavenly glory. But while it is an unspeakable blessing to know *anything* of such things, it is ever true that, sadly, so many of them are as hidden treasures on account of our inability to perceive and to understand them.

We have cause to pray with David, "Open thou mine eyes, that I may behold wondrous things out of thy law" (Ps. 119:18). In answer to that prayer, the Spirit is given, "the spirit of wisdom and revelation" (Eph. 1:17). The "anointing" or "unction" is the Holy Spirit; His illuminating grace is "the eyesalve that thou mayest see" (Rev. 3:18).

This special witness of the Spirit is to establish and confirm the reality of our state by grace, granting to us such an "understanding" that there is supernaturally produced in our hearts "full assurance" or unassailable conviction (Col. 2:2).

3. While all Scripture is intended for us, there are times when *one particular passage or verse comes to us with great force* as if directed and, in some strange way, actually spoken to us (Ps. 107:20; Song 2:8). It is as if some word, so applicable to our condition, is being specially highlighted or emphasized. It may be something like, "The eternal God is thy refuge"; "The LORD is thy keeper"; "Fear thou

not; for I am with thee"; "Though he cause grief, yet will he have compassion"; "Be of good cheer; it is I; be not afraid"; "What I do thou knowest not now; but thou shalt know hereafter" (Deut. 33:27; Ps. 121:5; Isa. 41:10; Lam. 3:22; Matt. 14:27; John 13:7); or, of course, it may be a word far less familiar to us but one peculiarly suited to our personal problem or distress. This was something David longed for when he said, "Say unto my soul, I am thy salvation" (Ps. 35:3).

But whence comes this voice? The answer must be, by the ministry of the Spirit. When the prophet Ezekiel fell exhausted to the earth (Ezek. 1:28), "the spirit" of life and grace "entered" into him while Christ "spake" unto him; and then, not only was he raised up, but he was also enabled to hear the divine voice: "I heard him that spake unto me" (2:2). As William Greenhill observes, "It is the Spirit of God that enables us to discern the things of God, and *assures* our spirits of the truth and reality of them."[21]

4. The Spirit's special testimony is known and *felt in the heart*. In the prophecy of Hosea, there is a beautiful passage in which God promises to bring His unfaithful people back to Himself. He says that He will "allure" (entice or persuade) them, lead them into "the wilderness" (the place of solitude and humbling), and that there He will "speak comfortably" (literally "to" or "upon her heart") to them (Hos. 2:14). This may mean that He will "speak kindly" to His people, to relieve their grief, as in Isaiah 40:2 (cf. Gen. 34:3; Ruth 2:13; 2 Chron. 30:22). These are marginal readings, though I have little doubt that this idea is included; however, I think it also strongly suggests that God will speak in a way that makes a deep impression, that reaches hidden depths and stirs inmost feelings.

The minister cannot do this; the Word on its own cannot do it; but the Spirit can so apply a passage that the effect is profound. "Who teacheth like him?" (Job 36:22); He brings "the light" of truth and shines it "in our hearts" (2 Cor. 4:6); "the Comforter, the Holy Spirit...he shall teach you" (John 14:26), and shall teach spiritually and inwardly, touching the affections and granting consolation: a powerful witness, relieving the distress of doubt and uncertainty!

5. Noting that Scripture refers to "the love of the Spirit" (Rom. 15:30), we should observe that, by the Spirit's sacred influence, the

---

21. William Greenhill, *An Exposition of the Prophet Ezekiel* (Edinburgh: James Nichol, 1864), 74.

divine "love" is sometimes felt and known. The Spirit secretly communicates to us the lovingkindness of God and, more than that, He wonderfully seals this to us: "the love of God is shed abroad in our hearts by the Holy Ghost" (Rom. 5:5). God has not kept His love to His people pent up, as it were, in His own breast, but, by the Spirit, He makes us experimentally aware of it, so the fact that He loves us becomes a matter of conviction in us and hereby we are assured that the hope we have will never fail; as Paul says, "hope maketh not ashamed" (5:5).

In the beautiful Song of Solomon, which says so much of Christ's love for His people, believers are represented as making two requests: "Set me as a seal upon thine heart; as a seal upon thine arm" (8:6), which may allude to the names of the twelve tribes engraven on the precious stones of the high priest's breastplate and shoulder pieces (Ex. 28:9–12, 15–21, 29). The first request—"Set me as a seal upon thine heart"—seems to be a desire to be stamped upon the Savior's heart or to be granted a place in His affections. Sincere believers do indeed long for this. There is nothing they want more. They seek a share of His heart's love. The second request—"Set me…as a seal upon thine arm"—is a yearning not just to be loved by Him but actually to *see* and therefore to *know* His wonderful love. The seal in His heart is concealed, but the seal on His arm is *revealed*. O to be *convinced* of everlasting love! That is the witness, the extraordinary witness of the Spirit.

6. On occasions, there may be granted to us an *unusual liberty in prayer and a sure confidence that we have been heard.* The Scriptures allude to "power" in prayer, as when the patriarch Jacob "wept, and made supplication" (Hos. 12:4). Similarly, the prophet Elijah is said to have "prayed earnestly": literally, "with prayer, he prayed," indicating the intensity of his soul in this exercise (James 5:17). There can be no doubt that believers may be so led out in prayer that they "cry" or fall to "groanings which cannot be uttered" (Rom. 8:15; cf. v. 26; Gal. 4:6). By this kind of praying, this "boldness," we press through into God's holy presence, discovering "access," and, in our hearts, we are confident of His favor and the acceptance of our persons and our prayers—"full assurance" (Eph. 3:12).

The Spirit is responsible for such prayer. Although reference is made to "the effectual fervent prayer" (James 5:16), the two qualifying words here are actually a translation of one Greek word that can, and perhaps should, be translated "the inwrought prayer." That suggests the internal agency of the Holy Spirit, as in Zechariah 12:10, Romans 8:26, 1 Corinthians 14:15, and Jude 20. This is "the Spirit of adoption," who thus bears witness to the fact that we have the hearts of sons before our heavenly Father (Rom. 8:15; Gal. 4:6).

7. Another way the Spirit can bear special witness is by granting us *some unmistakable sign of the divine favor*. I suppose this is what David desired when he said at the end of one of his psalms, "Show me a token for good" (Ps. 86:17). The word translated "token" really means "sign," some proof of God's interest in us and love toward us.

What might that "token" be? It might be a new knowledge of God (John 17:3; Col. 1:10); a precious insight into His truth (Matt. 11:25; 1 John 2:27); a fresh sense of the sweetness of Christ (Ps. 104:34; Song 1:3); a discovery of His secret will (Ps. 25:14; Eph. 5:17); a wonderful awareness of our pardon (Isa. 43:25; Mic. 7:18); a gracious spiritual reviving (Ps. 112:4; Isa. 57:15); a strong empowerment for service (Luke 4:14; Acts 1:8); or a renewed and enlarged hope for the future (Jer. 14:8; Heb. 6:11).

The Holy Spirit grants these "tokens" as "spiritual blessings," which several of the references above mention or imply. In this connection, after making the request, David asks that the effects may be apparent to others, that they may conclude that "thou, LORD, hast holpen me, and comforted me" (Ps. 86:17). Both of these words ("help" and "comfort") are associated with the work of the Spirit (John 14:26; Rom. 8:26). Therefore, in such "tokens" there is a quite remarkable witness of the Spirit.

8. The Spirit can also work in our hearts *exceptional joy and peace*. It is His prerogative to create within some believers unspeakable joy (Rom. 14:17; Gal. 5:22), as it is His to create the peace that passes understanding (Gen. 8:11; Gal. 5:22). Take one verse as proof of this: "Now the God of hope fill you with *all joy and peace* [in the greatest abundance and in the highest degree] in believing…*through the power of the Holy Ghost*" (Rom. 15:13, emphasis added).

William Janeway, a Puritan, found himself in spiritual darkness in his last illness. Speaking to his son, he said: "Oh that I could say cheerfully, I can die." However, just a little later, his son returned to his bedside to hear: "Oh, son! Now it is come, it is come, it is come. I bless God that I can die: the Spirit of God hath witnessed with my spirit that I am his child. Now I can look upon God as my dear Father, and Christ as my Redeemer: I can now say, This is my Friend and this is my Beloved! My heart is full; it is brim full; I can hold no more. I know what that sentence means, 'The peace of God which passeth understanding.' I know now what that white stone is, whereon a new name is written, which none know but they that have it.... O now I can die! It is nothing; I bless God I can die."[22]

Since only the Lord's people know these things, the Spirit bears striking witness through them to the fact that we have ground for such feelings, in the sure possession of God, His love, the covenant, redemption, and heavenly glory.

9. There is also *an amazing work of sanctification done in the soul*, producing high degrees of godliness and holiness. This can be at various times in a Christian's life, but we observe that it may be especially evident toward the end of his life. The apostle teaches that God is able to prepare us for death, when "mortality" will be "swallowed up of life" (2 Cor. 5:4), by suiting us to the heavenly and eternal world: "Now, he that hath wrought us for the selfsame thing is God" (v. 5; cf. Col. 1:12). Once again, it is the Spirit who is responsible for this, for Paul continues, "who also hath given unto us the earnest [or "foretaste"] of the Spirit." Unsurprisingly, then, God's Word makes mention of "the sanctification of the Spirit" (2 Thess. 2:13; 1 Peter 2:2).

This is an impressive witness, the undoubted truth that we are going home to be "present [literally, 'at home'] with the Lord" and to be "partakers of the inheritance of the saints in light" (2 Cor. 5:8; Col. 1:12).

10. There is one last witness to mention: the Spirit can cause us to know *something of the reality and blessedness of heaven*. This can be extraordinary indeed and quite beyond words to describe. Paul, in one of his letters, wrote of "the first fruits of the Spirit": these are the *beginnings* of the full crop or future perfection of glory (Rom. 8:23). In another letter he mentioned "the earnest of the Spirit" (2 Cor. 5:5; cf. 1:22; Eph. 1:14), by which is intended a *deposit*, the full amount being yet to come.

---

22. F. A. Cox, *Introductory Essay on the Family of the Janeways and the Times in Which They Lived*, in *Heaven upon Earth*, by James Janeway (London: Thomas Nelson, 1847), 6.

What sublime experiences some have had as they approached death! I mention here but one: Edward Payson (1783–1827), an eminent early nineteenth-century American minister. A short while before his death, he wrote to his sister as follows:

> Were I to adopt the figurative language of Bunyan I might date this letter from the land of Beulah, of which I have been for some weeks a happy inhabitant. The celestial city is full in my view. Its glories beam upon me, its breezes fan me, its odours are wafted to me, its sounds strike upon my ears, and its spirit is breathed into my heart. Nothing separates me from it but the river of death, which now appears as an insignificant rill, that may be crossed at a single step, whenever God shall give permission. The Sun of Righteousness has gradually been drawing nearer and nearer, appearing larger and brighter as he approached; and now he fills the whole hemisphere, pouring forth a flood of glory, in which I seem to float…. A single heart, and a single tongue seem altogether inadequate to my wants: I want a whole heart for every separate emotion, and a whole tongue to express that emotion…. O, my sister, my sister! Could you but know what awaits the Christian; could you know only so much as I know, you could not refrain from rejoicing, and even leaping for joy.[23]

Conclusion

In closing, it will be seen at once that there are real similarities between the Spirit's acts of *ordinary* and *extraordinary* witness. The question arises, Is the difference between them simply one of degree? The answer would seem to be: in a way, yes; but in another way, no. The extraordinary witness certainly appears, in one sense, to be just a *more powerful and impressive testimony* to the soul; but, saying that, we have not really said everything, because this witness does belong to *the sphere of unusual, singular, and exceptional experiences*. Perhaps one could say of it that it is as distinguishable from the ordinary witness in much the same way as a true and wonderful revival is distinguishable from the Spirit's ordinary and common blessing. It

---

23. *A Memoir of the Rev. Edward Payson, D.D.* (London: Published by R.B. Seeley and W. Burnside, 1830), 458, 459.

is not therefore altogether the same: it is, as revival, a *unique, striking, and remarkable ministry* of the Holy Ghost, bringing hitherto unknown assurance to us of our adoption as God's children.

If God graciously wills it, may we know something of this extraordinary witness, granting us *days of heaven upon the earth.* Such blessed days will surely serve as wonderful previews and foretastes of eternity!

HISTORICAL THEOLOGICAL
STUDIES

CHAPTER 14

The Holy Spirit in the Early Church

William VanDoodewaard

God's Word reveals to us that the Holy Spirit's work is beautiful, mysterious, and powerful. Throughout the history of the church, significant exegetical, biblical-theological, historical, and systematic study, writing, preaching, and teaching have been poured into the realm of knowing the Person of the Holy Spirit and His work. Yet, far less frequent, at least in the past century, have been attempts to apply or correlate the doctrine of the Holy Spirit's work as revealed in Scripture to the history of the church after the closing of the biblical canon. For those who love church history and historical theology, certainly the study of historical theology on the Person and work of the Holy Spirit is a legitimate, necessary, and valuable pursuit. But what if we were to seek to trace some of the actual work of the Holy Spirit in the early church, using the biblical-theological paradigm given in the New Testament?

Cautions and Limits

Undoubtedly we must proceed with caution. First, we must realize, as Carl Trueman reminds us: "History is not the same as the past. It is rather a re-presentation of the past…with all of the contingency and limitations that such implies."[1] Our vision of what occurred in the past is limited; we are finite beings with access to a limited number of documents and artifacts from the past. While Scripture is inerrant and infallible, extra-canonical historical documents carry a wide range of potential weaknesses, errors, and real limitations.

---

1. Carl Trueman, *Histories and Fallacies: Problems Faced in the Writing of History* (Wheaton, Ill.: Crossway, 2010), 69.

We simply cannot fully know or reconstruct the past. This alone is a significant reason for us to pause and reflect on the need for care and humility in any historical endeavor.

Second, we have a profound biblical caution. Jesus told Nicodemus, as recorded in the Gospel of John, that the work of the Holy Spirit is like the wind: we do not know where it comes from or where it goes (John 3:8). This theme is repeated in Scripture. Sinclair Ferguson, commenting on the work of the Spirit in inspiring the Scriptures, states:

> As to *how* this divine out-breathing and Spirit-bearing influence the production of Scripture, little is said or claimed. God reveals himself in various ways: dreams, visions, individual illumination and research, as well as ordinary and extraordinary divine providences, are involved in the process.... The mode of the operation of the divine Spirit on the human spirit remains as mysterious as his activity in creation and re-creation (cf. Psalm 139:7–6; Luke 1:35; John 3:8–9).... Nowhere is the *modus operandi* of the Spirit's activity fully explained. The words of Ecclesiastes are as true here as elsewhere: "As you do not know the path of the wind, or how the body is formed in the mother's womb, so you cannot understand the work of God, the Maker of all things" (Eccl. 11:15).[2]

In the Holy Spirit's works of creation, inspiration, and regeneration, there is much that we do not know and that God does not reveal to us. God is God and we are not; we need to know and be reminded of this infinite, profound, and rightly humbling difference in regard to our graciously God-given creaturely abilities.

A Brief Biblical Paradigm of the Work of the Holy Spirit

While the work of the Holy Spirit is not fully knowable or wholly traceable, God does desire us to be able to know and trace His work, and to engage in doing so. Psalm 48 calls us "to walk about Zion," to go around the city of God, considering its strength, beauty, and glory. Why? So that we can tell the next generation that "this God is our God forever and ever." The church, even in its present earthly weakness, glimmers with divine glory because it is the work and

---

2. Sinclair Ferguson, *The Holy Spirit* (Downers Grove, Ill.: InterVarsity Press), 27, emphasis in original.

dwelling place of God, in which the person of the Holy Spirit is inti-mately involved.

The Holy Spirit's work is rightly understood only in the context of the personal distinctions and unity of being and essence of the triune God.[3] The Holy Spirit comes from and is given by the Father, sent by the Father and the Son. In His earthly ministry, the Spirit reveals Christ to us, unites us to Christ, and unites us to the body of Christ, the church. He applies to us the redemption accomplished by Christ, and He is the One by whom, in and through Christ, we are adopted as sons and made aware that we are the children of God. When focusing on the work of the Holy Spirit, we want to be careful not to lose sight of the triune harmony of involvement in, and relationship to, the Spirit's work. Ferguson notes that "it is not only *because of Christ* that we come to know the Spirit more fully, but actually *in Christ*. Indeed, it is apparently a principle of the divine Spirit's working that he declines to disclose himself in any other way (John 16:13–15)."[4]

The Old Testament reveals that the Holy Spirit's work includes the giving of gifts, abilities, and wisdom to men, enabling miracles, inspiring prophecies, and actively and effectually carrying out the work of salvation. The Old Testament also contains prophecies of

---

3. While God in His Word reveals much about the work of the Holy Spirit, it is an area that has received less attention than is due by Reformed theologians. Most Reformed systematic theologians briefly summarize these scriptural truths, while a few dedicated volumes on the Holy Spirit, such as John Owen's *The Holy Spirit: His Gifts and Power* (Grand Rapids: Kregel, 1954); Abraham Kuyper's *The Work of the Holy Spirit* (Grand Rapids: Eerdmans, 1946); and, more recently, Sinclair Ferguson's *The Holy Spirit*, deal with the Person and work of the Holy Spirit more extensively. See, for example, Louis Berkhof, *Systematic Theology* (Grand Rapids: Eerdmans, 1996), 98–99; John Calvin, *Institutes of the Christian Religion*, ed. John T. McNeill, trans. F. L. Battles (Philadelphia: Westminster Press, 1960), 1.13.14–15; Charles Hodge, *Systematic Theology* (Grand Rapids: Eerdmans, 1997), 1:522–34; Robert Reymond, *A New Systematic Theology of the Christian Faith* (Nashville: Thomas Nelson, 1998), 312–14.

4. Ferguson, *The Holy Spirit*, 30, emphasis in original. In describing the relation-ship of the work of the Spirit to Christ, Ferguson goes on to say "The Spirit is ideally suited to be the chief witness for Christ because he was the intimate companion of Jesus throughout his ministry…. From womb to tomb to throne, the Spirit was the constant companion of the Son. As a result, when he comes to Christians to indwell them, he comes as the Spirit *of Christ* in such a way that to possess him is to possess Christ himself, just as to lack him is to lack Christ. This relationship is implied by Paul's words in Romans 8:9–10…. [The Spirit] was with Christ 'from the beginning' (John 15:27)." Ferguson, *The Holy Spirit*, 37, emphasis in original.

God's gracious outpouring of His Spirit in the last days, the coming day of the Lord (Joel 2:28–32). Turning to the New Testament, we see in the Gospels of Luke and John and the book of Acts that Jesus promises the Holy Spirit to His disciples, to His church.[5] What does our Lord say that this giving of the Spirit will entail? What will be His activity and work?

In John 14–16, Christ promises the coming of the Holy Spirit, declaring that it is to the advantage of His disciples and the church as a whole that He, Jesus, departs and the Spirit comes (16:7). Jesus also describes the Holy Spirit as the Comforter or Helper, the Spirit of truth. The Holy Spirit's work includes the inspiration and preservation of the Word: teaching the apostolic writers, guiding them into all truth.

The Spirit's activity includes the work of conviction and conversion. Calvin states:

> He [the Holy Spirit] is the author of regeneration…through him we come into communion with God…. Our justification is his work; from him is power, sanctification, truth, grace, and every good thing that can be conceived, since there is but one Spirit from whom flows every sort of gift.[6]

Charles Hodge comments similarly:

> It is the special office of the Holy Spirit to convince the world of sin; to reveal Christ, to regenerate the soul, to lead men to the exercise of faith and repentance; to dwell in those whom he thus renews, as a principle of a divine and new life.[7]

With the completion of Christ's earthly ministry, God by His Spirit brings about the inauguration of "a communion with Christ in which the Spirit who dwelt on Christ now dwells on and in believers."[8] The glorious inauguration of the church's communion with Christ commences with the great outpouring of the Holy Spirit, after the ascension of Christ, at Pentecost. Peter proclaims to the

---

5. This, of course, does not negate the work of the Holy Spirit in the Old Testament. For a good discussion of the distinction between the work of the Spirit prior to and after Pentecost, see Kuyper, *The Work of the Holy Spirit*, 120–28 and Ferguson, *The Holy Spirit*, 79–92.

6. Calvin, *Institutes*, 1.13.14.

7. Hodge, *Systematic Theology*, 1:532.

8. Ferguson, *The Holy Spirit*, 71.

Jerusalem crowds that Christ, being exalted to the right hand of the Father, has received from the Father the promised Holy Spirit and poured out what they see and hear. Abraham Kuyper describes this using the following illustration of Christian existence prior to and after Pentecost:

> The rain descends from heaven and man gathers it to quench his thirst. When householders collect it each in his own cistern, it comes down for every family separately; but when, as in modern city life, every house is supplied from the city reservoir, by means of mains and water pipes, there is no more need of pumps and cisterns. Suppose that a city whose citizens for ages have been drinking water each from his own cistern proposes to construct a reservoir that will supply every home. When the work is completed the water is allowed to run through the system of mains and pipes into every house. It might be said that on that day the water was poured into the city.... [Christ] gathered the full stream of the Holy Spirit for us all, in His own Person. With Him all saints are connected by the channels of faith. And when, after His ascension, this connection with His saints was completed, and He had received the Holy Spirit from His Father, then the last obstacle was removed and the full stream of the Holy Spirit came rushing through the connecting channels into the heart of every believer.[9]

Not only does the outpouring of the Spirit at Pentecost bring organic union and communion to the church in Christ, but Pentecost is also a Babel undone as the epochal moment of the activation of the Great Commission, which "takes place in the power of the Spirit."[10] This is confirmed through the book of Acts and the Epistles as the Spirit works powerfully by the Word, causing the gospel to advance from Jerusalem to Judea, to Samaria, and the ends of the earth. By His Holy Spirit, as Daniel prophesied, God sets up a kingdom that will never be destroyed. His kingdom advances and conquers through the kingdoms of this world, and will stand forever (Dan. 2:44). Acts, the Epistles, and Revelation further confirm and expound on the powerful, beautiful, multifaceted work of the Holy Spirit.

---

9. Kuyper, *The Work of the Holy Spirit*, 123–24.
10. Ferguson, *The Holy Spirit*, 59.

Certainly all Christians, including theologians and historians, agree that the Holy Spirit continues His work beyond the penning of the last books of the New Testament. Having this inspired, inerrant, infallible record of Scripture, we will now consider the post-apostolic age of the early church, aiming to further trace the work of the Holy Spirit beyond the bounds of the canon of Scripture, applying these principles and patterns given in the Word in three case studies: the inspiration and preservation of the New Testament canon; the understanding and defense of scriptural doctrine; and repentance, faith, and new life.

Case Studies of the Work of the Holy Spirit in the Early Church

#1: The inspiration and preservation of the New Testament canon

The Word of God declares to us the work of the Spirit in its formation. Jesus promised this to His disciples: the Holy Spirit, whom the Father would send in Christ's name, would teach them all things, bringing to their minds all the things Jesus had said to them (John 14:26). The Holy Spirit directed the apostolic writers into all truth, speaking to them what He heard and knew in perfect union with the Father and Son, and showing them things to come. Through His work of inspiration, the Spirit displayed and glorified Christ, communicating Him and His words to the apostolic writers, fulfilling His promise that while heaven and earth would pass away, Christ's Word would not (John 16:13–14; Luke 21:33). Peter, as an apostle, confirms these promises of the Spirit's work, reminding us that no prophecy of Scripture came from someone's own interpretation. The Scriptures were not created by human will, but were spoken and written from God, by the power, guidance, inspiration, and illuminating direction of the Holy Spirit. The writers of Scripture spoke "as they were moved" by the Holy Spirit (2 Peter 1:20–21).

The Gospels and Epistles themselves are compelling and enduring evidence of the truth and fulfillment of Jesus' promises regarding the work of the Holy Spirit. Each is written by an apostle of Jesus Christ (cf. 1 John 1:3–4). Each, as a unique part of the Word of God, shows a perfect unity and coherence with the whole of the rest of Scripture.

Part of the Holy Spirit's work was the immediate recognition of these realities during the apostolic period, and the preservation and defense of the inspired Scriptures through the post-apostolic era of the early church. The church was aware of the criteria of apostolicity and coherence with the whole of existing Scripture—the "rule of faith." Yet, there was and continues to be more than that. The Holy Spirit, both then and now, testifies to our spirits that the books of the New Testament are the testimony of God. Why? Because He is the Spirit of truth. The Holy Spirit, as Jesus promised, is working and delights to work to illumine us, guide us to, and make us aware of and receptive to the Word of God.

This is what we see happening in the early church. The apostolic writers, such as Timothy and Peter, cross reference other apostolic writers, such as Paul and Luke, testifying that their epistles are the Scriptures (cf. 1 Tim. 5:8, 2 Peter 3:15–16). In the late first and early second century, we have men like Clement (ca. 96) referring to and citing the Gospels and Epistles as Scripture. At one point Clement states:

> Look carefully into the Scriptures, which are the true utterances of the Holy Spirit.... Take up the epistle of the blessed apostle Paul. What did he write to you when the Gospel first began to be preached? Truly he wrote to you under the inspiration of the Spirit.[11]

Compared with the paradigm of the work of the Holy Spirit presented to us in Scripture, this statement of Clement appears indicative of the gracious and powerful work of the Spirit in Clement's heart and mind, bringing him to a clarity of awareness of and receptivity to the New Testament as the Word of Christ.

Abundant similar indicators of the Holy Spirit's work in the preservation and proclamation of the New Testament Scriptures exist. Ignatius reveals an understanding of the authority of the apostolic writings of the New Testament canon and self-awareness that his own writing does not bear inherent scriptural authority.[12] Polycarp of Smyrna cites Psalm 4:5 and Ephesians 4:26 as proof of the Spirit's inspiration, prefacing his citation with the words "as it is said in the Scriptures."[13] Many other patristic testimonies and references

---

11. Clement, *Epistle to the Corinthians* in *The Ante-Nicene Fathers* (Edinburgh: T. & T. Clark, 1989), 1:17–18. All following citations from this series will be referred to simply by author, title of work, and then volume and page references.

12. Ignatius, *Epistle to the Philadelphians*, 1:84–85.

13. Polycarp, *Epistle to the Philippians*, 1:35.

exist, including those of Papias, Justin Martyr, and Tatian, as well as later figures such as Irenaeus, Clement of Alexandria, Tertullian, and Origen.[14]

At the same time, there was opposition to the work of the Holy Spirit: men such as Marcion rose, publishing selective revisions of the Gospels and Epistles, prompting others, such as Tertullian, to declare in defense of the New Testament Scriptures, "what Pontic mouse ever had such gnawing powers as he who has gnawed the Gospels to pieces!" Others, such as Origen, noted there were some in the church who were assailed with doubt over the canonicity of New Testament epistles such as 2 Peter and 2 and 3 John. Along with the challenges inside the visible church, there were external pressures that intensified with the spread of the gospel and growth of the church: regional and broader persecutions within the Roman Empire that sought to extinguish Christianity. These intensified in the third century, culminating with Diocletian's efforts to eliminate both Christians and Christian writings—including biblical manuscripts.[15]

Despite doubts, intellectual attacks, and physical persecutions, not only were the biblical manuscripts received and preserved, but the Holy Spirit also moved the church to wide recognition of them in the councils of Laodicea (363), Hippo (393), and the third and fourth councils of Carthage in 397 and 419. These further certified the reality of New Testament canonicity that Christians already acknowledged. Modern critical studies of the various New Testament manuscripts (some 5,686 in Greek, with a total New Testament supporting base of more than 24,000) from the early church period reveal an incredible harmony of precise content, with the few copyist divergences not affecting any point of doctrine.[16] This, despite the attempt of some

---

14. See, for example, Irenaeus, *Against Heresies*, 1:414; Clement of Alexandria, *Stromata*, 2:409, 551; Tertullian, *Apology*, 3:32–33; Origen, *De Principiis*, 4:252.

15. Diocletian's first "Edict Against the Christians" was published February 24, 303, ordering the destruction of Christian Scriptures, liturgical books, and places of worship across the empire. By his fourth edict in 304, Diocletian ordered public sacrifices with mandatory attendance; those who refused were to be executed. Timothy D. Barnes, *Constantine and Eusebius* (Cambridge, Mass.: Harvard University Press, 2006), 22–24. See also Eusebius, *Ecclesiastical History* (Peabody, Mass.: Hendrickson, 1998), 281; Lactantius, *On the Manner in Which the Persecutors Died*, 7:303–17.

16. For an excellent summary of the attestation to the reliability of the New Testament canon and its manuscripts, see F. F. Bruce, *The New Testament Documents: Are They Reliable?* (Grand Rapids: Eerdmans, 1994).

scholars to use text criticism to undermine the authority of Scripture, again reflects the gracious, powerful, and beautiful work of the Holy Spirit in the preservation of the inspired text of the New Testament in the early church and beyond.

#2: Understanding and defense of scriptural doctrines
A second area in which we can trace the Holy Spirit's work is the understanding and defense of scriptural doctrines in the early church. In certain respects, the acceptance of the New Testament canon reflects this. Christ's promise that the Holy Spirit would guide His disciples into all truth certainly finds a primary fulfillment in the formation of the New Testament text and canon. The triune God graciously reveals Himself to us in Scripture, giving us everything we need to know for salvation (2 Tim. 3:15). The early church's recognition of the New Testament as the Word of God, through the work of the Holy Spirit, also reflected the Spirit's illumination of hearts and minds in the early church to a biblical doctrine of Scripture. Clement of Alexandria (ca. 195) spoke of the "omnipotent authority" of Scripture and declared that "we have the Lord as the source of teaching—both by the Prophets, the Gospel, and the blessed apostles."[17] He added, "In the Scriptures there is given from God…the gift of God-given knowledge."[18] Hippolytus (ca. 205) states:

> Brethren, there is one God, the knowledge of whom we gain from the Holy Scriptures and from no other source…. Even as He has chosen to teach them by the Holy Scriptures, so let us discern them.[19]

Along with the work of the Holy Spirit to transform, teach, and guide early Christians in understanding the doctrine of Scripture as revealed in the Word, other scriptural doctrine was also promoted and defended. This was true both in terms of teaching within the church and active witness to the surrounding world. Clement of Rome proclaimed the riches of justification by faith in Christ:

> All the Old Testament saints were honoured and glorified, not through themselves, not through their own works or righteous

---

17. Clement of Alexandria, *Stromata*, 2:551.
18. Clement of Alexandria, *Stromata*, 2:558.
19. Hippolytus, *Against the Heresy of One Noetus*, 5:227.

behaviour, but through the will of God. And we too, who have been called through God's will in Christ Jesus, are not justified through ourselves, or through our own wisdom or understanding or godliness, or through our own deeds done in holiness of heart; no, we are justified through faith. For it is through faith that Almighty God has justified all people that have ever lived from the beginning of time. To Him be glory for ever and ever! Amen.[20]

Justin Martyr exalted Christ in his *Apologies* and *Dialogue with Trypho*, contrasting the one true God and His gracious Word with the religious and philosophical systems of Roman paganism and Judaism. Irenaeus defended the doctrine of Christ against the heresies of the Gnostics. Alexander, Athanasius, the Cappadocian fathers (Gregory of Nyssa, Gregory of Nazianzus, and Basil of Caesarea), and the gathered leadership of the church at Nicaea, Constantinople, and Chalcedon defended and proclaimed both the doctrine of the Trinity and the doctrine of Christ in His Person and natures. Again, examples abound in the life of the early church. In light of their harmony with scriptural teaching, and in comparison with a biblical paradigm of the work of the Holy Spirit, they stand as indicators of the Spirit's gracious work. The fact of remaining, and at times abundant, evidences of human weakness, difficulty, and even error in understanding and formulating Christian doctrine in the life of the early church is not a negation of the Holy Spirit's work. Rather, it shows us the contrast between human knowledge, ability, and sin, even in believers, and the fullness of divine truth taught by Word and Spirit.

#3: Repentance, faith, and new life in Christ
The early church father Irenaeus states that "without the Spirit of God we cannot be saved."[21] Part of the Holy Spirit's work is to reveal Christ to us, bring us to repentance and faith in Christ, unite us to Christ, and unite us to the body of Christ, the church. He powerfully and personally applies the redemption accomplished by Christ through the proclamation and reading of the Word. As such, another indication of the gracious work of the Holy Spirit in the early church,

---

20. Clement of Rome, *Epistle to the Corinthians*, 1:13.
21. Irenaeus, *Against Heresies*, 1:535.

and one in harmony with those already mentioned, is found in evidences of spiritual transformation to life in Christ.

One beautiful testimony to this Christ-centered, life-transforming work of the Holy Spirit is found in the *Letter to Diognetes*. The authorship of this second-century writing is uncertain. The writer gives himself the title "Mathetes," meaning "a disciple," but he is otherwise unknown.[22] Despite the lack of clarity of authorship, scholars agree that this work was penned sometime between AD 125 and 200. "Mathetes" writes:

> When our wickedness had reached its height, and its wages—punishment and death—were clearly hanging over us, the time arrived which God had appointed beforehand, for Him to manifest His own kindness and power. He revealed how His love had such an overwhelming regard for the human race, and that He did not hate us or thrust us away or remember our sins against us, but showed great longsuffering and patience with us. He Himself took upon Himself the burden of our transgressions; He gave His own Son as a ransom for us, the Holy One for sinners, the Blameless One for the wicked, the Righteous One for the unrighteous, the Incorruptible One for the corruptible, the Immortal One for mortals. For what else could cover our sins except His righteousness? Who else could justify wicked and ungodly people like us, except the only Son of God? O sweet exchange! O unsearchable work! O blessings that surpass all expectation! The wickedness of the many has been swallowed up in a single Righteous One; the righteousness of One has justified a multitude of transgressors! Even before Christ came, God showed us that our nature was incapable of achieving life. Now, having revealed the Savior, Who is able to save what could not previously be saved, God has willed by these truths to persuade us to trust in His kindness, and to reckon Him as our Nourisher, Father, Teacher, Counsellor and Healer, our Wisdom, Light, Honor, Glory, Power and Life, so that we should have no anxiety about mere food and clothing....
>
> I do not speak of things strange to me, nor do I aim at anything inconsistent with right reason, but having been a disciple of the Apostles, I am become a teacher of the Gentiles. I minister

---

22. *The Ante-Nicene Fathers*, 1:23. See also *Early Christian Greek and Latin Literature*, 1:209–10.

the things that are delivered to me.... For who that is rightly taught and begotten by the loving Word, would not seek to learn accurately the things which have been clearly shown by the Word to His disciples.... For whatever things we are moved by the will of the Word commanding us, we communicate to you with pains, and from a love of the things that have been revealed to us.[23]

A second testimony to the gracious work of the Spirit in bringing repentance, faith, and new life in Christ is found in the steady perseverance of the early Christians in the faith. Willingness to suffer hardships, persecution, and even death, when considered in the light of a biblical paradigm of the work of the Holy Spirit, presents us with a glorious aspect of His activity. He is the Comforter, and His mighty work in this role is seen in the perseverance of the saints: their preservation in Christ, by the Spirit, to the finish (Rom. 8). This is displayed in early church records of Christians facing death through persecution in the Roman Empire.

The first organized persecution outside of Jerusalem and Judea took place in Bithynia under the governor Pliny the Younger (ca. 112). Pliny described the spread of "this superstition [Christianity]... like a contagion" to an extent that Greco-Roman paganism was in evident decrease.[24] Subsequent regional and broader persecutions occurred under the emperors Diocletian and Galerius. Polycarp of Smyrna (ca. 167), when called on by a proconsul to recant or face death, declared: "Eighty and six years have I served Him. He never did me any injury. How then can I blaspheme my King and my Savior?" When bound to be burned, he prayed, "Father I bless Thee that Thou hast deemed me worthy of this day and hour, that I might take a portion of the martyrs and the cup of Christ.... Among these may I today be welcome before Thy face as a rich and acceptable sacrifice."[25] The account of the martyrdoms of Ponticus and Blandina (ca. 177) likewise stand as vivid evidences of the comforting work of the Holy Spirit:

23. Mathetes, *Letter to Diognetes*, 1:28–29.
24. Betty Radice, trans., *The Letters of the Younger Pliny* (New York: Penguin, 1963), 293–95.
25. *Epistle Concerning the Martyrdom of Polycarp*, 1:41.

The mob tried again and again to make them swear by the gods, but in vain. Ponticus was encouraged by his sister in Christ, so that the pagans saw she was urging him on and stiffening his resistance, and he bravely endured every punishment till he gave back his spirit to God. Last of all, like a noble mother who had encouraged her children and sent them ahead of her in triumph to the King, blessed Blandina herself passed through all the ordeals of her children and hastened to rejoin them, rejoicing and exulting in her departure as if she had been invited to a wedding supper rather than thrown to wild beasts. After whipping her, giving her to the beasts, and burning her with hot irons, the authorities finally dropped her into a basket and threw her to a bull. The beast gored her again and again, but she was now indifferent to all that happened to her, because of her hope, her firm grip on all that her faith meant, and her communion with Christ. Then she too was sacrificed. The pagans themselves admitted that they had never known a woman suffer so much or so long.[26]

While history documents numerous willing martyrs for the sake of false religions, the substantial evidence of individuals willingly dying for the sake of Christ, His gospel, and a faithful testimony to Him indicates that the perseverance of these early church martyrs is the fruit of the work of the Holy Spirit.

Through raging persecutions and the challenges of false teachings, the Holy Spirit continued His unstoppable transforming and preserving works of grace, resulting in the vast growth of the early church. In the space of three centuries, the church grew from a small number in Jerusalem and surrounding regions at Pentecost to countless numbers turned to Christ across the Mediterranean world and beyond.[27] So many were brought to new life in Christ by the Spirit that kingdoms extraneous to the Roman Empire, such as Armenia,

---

26. Eusebius, *Ecclesiastical History*, 156.

27. Moderate historical estimates quantify the numerical growth being from a tiny fraction of one percent of the population at Pentecost to ten percent of the population of the Roman Empire; a numeric growth likely from several thousand to six million Christians out of a population of 60 million prior to the end of persecution. Others estimate the latter statistic should be nearer a quarter, or 15 million of the population of the Roman Empire.

and the empire itself abandoned persecution, in time not only sanctioning but also adopting Christianity.[28]

Conclusion

The history of the early church, when considered in light of a biblical paradigm of the work of the Holy Spirit, reveals glorious evidence for His ongoing ministry. The brief elements and patterns considered here are only a tiny sampling of His vast, gracious, and powerful works accompanying the Word as it is proclaimed to the ends of the earth. Our exercise of theologically examining history has brought us to walk around a few, small corners of Zion, the city of God, tracing just a few, partial aspects of the glorious, beautiful, and continuing work of the Holy Spirit. As you reflect on the history of the church in faith, tracing the grace of the living God at work through the ages to our own, and in your own life, echo the prayer of the early church:

> Eternal God, Father of our Lord Jesus Christ, Creator of man and of woman...look down [on us] Thy [servants], and [fill us with] the Holy Spirit.... Cleans[e] [us] from all filthiness of flesh and spirit, that [we] may worthily carry out the work committed to [us], to Thy glory, and the praise of Thy Christ, with whom be glory and adoration to Thee and the Holy Spirit forever. Amen.[29]

Worship God for the work of His Spirit. Join the psalmist in proclaiming with awe, love, and wonder: this God is our God forever and ever! He will guide us forever.

---

28. The adoption of Christianity brought with it a new series of threats and challenges to the existence and witness of the church.

29. A revised form of the prayer found in the *Constitutions of the Holy Apostles*, 7:492.

CHAPTER 15

Richard Sibbes on Entertaining the Holy Spirit

Joel R. Beeke

I shall never cease to be grateful to...Richard Sibbes, who was balm to my soul at a period in my life when I was overworked and badly overtired, and therefore subject in an unusual manner to the onslaughts of the devil.... I found at that time that Richard Sibbes...was an unfailing remedy. His books The Bruised Reed *and* The Soul's Conflict *quietened, soothed, comforted, encouraged and healed me.*

—D. Martyn Lloyd-Jones[1]

Richard Sibbes (1577–1635) was one of the greatest Puritans of his age. He greatly influenced the direction and content of Puritan preaching, theology, and writing in England and America.[2] His theology of the

---

1. D. Martyn Lloyd-Jones, *Preaching and Preachers* (Grand Rapids: Zondervan, 1971), 175.

2. For further sources on Sibbes, see Frank E. Farrell, "Richard Sibbes: A Study in Early Seventeenth Century English Puritanism" (PhD diss., University of Edinburgh, 1955); Sidney H. Rooy, "Richard Sibbes: The Theological Foundation of the Mission," in *The Theology of Missions in the Puritan Tradition: A Study of Representative Puritans: Richard Sibbes, Richard Baxter, John Eliot, Cotton Mather, and Jonathan Edwards* (Grand Rapids: Eerdmans, 1965), 15–65; Bert Affleck, Jr., "The Theology of Richard Sibbes, 1577–1635" (PhD diss., Drew University, 1969); Harold P. Shelly, "Richard Sibbes: Early Stuart Preacher of Piety" (PhD diss., Temple University, 1972); Beth E. Tumbleson, "The Bride and Bridegroom in the Work of Richard Sibbes, English Puritan" (MA thesis, Trinity Evangelical Divinity School, 1984); Cary N. Weisiger, "The Doctrine of the Holy Spirit in the Preaching of Richard Sibbes" (PhD diss., Fuller Theological Seminary, 1984); Maurice Roberts, "Richard Sibbes: The Heavenly Doctor," in *The Office and Work of the Minister* (London: Westminster Conference Papers, 1986), 96–113; J. William Black, "Richard Sibbes and *The Bruised Reed*," *Banner of Truth*, no. 299–300 (Aug.–Sept. 1988): 49–58; Mark E. Dever, *Richard Sibbes: Puritanism and Calvinism in Late Elizabethan and Early Stuart England* (Macon, Ga.: Mercer University Press, 2000); Paul Oliver, "Richard Sibbes and the Returning Backslider,"

Holy Spirit was especially important because of its emphasis on how the Spirit operates in the daily life of the Christian. Sibbes winsomely referred to that process as "entertaining the Spirit" in the soul. For Sibbes, that entertaining meant welcoming with hospitality and nurturing our friendship with the indwelling Spirit. "There is nothing in the world so great and sweet a friend that will do us so much good as the Spirit, if we give him entertainment," Sibbes wrote.[3]

Sibbes's teaching on entertaining the Holy Spirit can be divided into the following four categories: (1) the indwelling of the Spirit, (2) the sealing of the Spirit, (3) the comfort of the Spirit, and (4) grieving the Spirit. After a brief look at who Sibbes was, we will explore these categories in Sibbes's work on the Spirit.

Synopsis of Sibbes's Life

Sibbes was a native of Suffolk, the Puritan county of old England that furnished numerous illustrious emigrants to New England.[4] He was born a few miles from Bury St. Edmonds in 1577, the year the Lutherans drafted their Formula of Concord. He was baptized in the parish church in Thurston, where he grew up and went to school. He was the oldest of six children.

As a young child, Sibbes loved books. However, his father, Paul Sibbes, who was a hardworking wheelwright and (according to Zachary Catlin, a contemporary biographer of Sibbes) "a good, sound-hearted Christian," became irritated with his son's book expenses.[5] The father tried to cure his son of book-buying by offering him wheelwright tools. But the boy was not dissuaded. With the support of others, Sibbes was admitted to St. John's College in Cambridge at the age of eighteen. He earned a bachelor of arts degree in 1599, a fellowship in 1601, and a master of arts degree in 1602. In 1603, he was converted under the preaching of Paul Baynes. Baynes, who is

---

in *Puritans and Spiritual Life* (London: Westminster Conference papers, 2001), 41–56; Ronald N. Frost, "The Bruised Reed by Richard Sibbes (1577–1635)," in *The Devoted Life: An Invitation to the Puritan Classics*, ed. Kelly M. Kapic and Randall C. Gleason (Downers Grove, Ill.: InterVarsity, 2004), 79–91.

3. Richard Sibbes, "A Fountain Sealed," in *The Works of Richard Sibbes*, ed. Alexander B. Grosart (1862–1864; repr., Edinburgh: Banner of Truth Trust, 2001), 5:431.

4. Portions of this section are adapted from Joel R. Beeke and Randall J. Pederson, *Meet the Puritans* (Grand Rapids: Reformation Heritage Books, 2003), 534–37.

5. "Appendix to Memoir," in Sibbes, *Works*, 1:cxxxv.

remembered most for his commentary on Ephesians, succeeded William Perkins (1558–1602) at the Church of St. Andrews in Cambridge.

Sibbes was ordained to the ministry of the Church of England in Norwich in 1607, was chosen as one of the college preachers in 1609, and received a bachelor of divinity degree in 1610. From 1611 to 1616, he served as lecturer at Holy Trinity Church, Cambridge. His preaching awakened Cambridge from the spiritual indifference into which it had fallen after the death of Perkins, and a gallery had to be built to accommodate the visitors. John Cotton and Hugh Peters were converted under Sibbes's preaching. During his years at Holy Trinity, Sibbes also helped turn Thomas Goodwin from Arminianism, and moved John Preston from witty preaching to plain, spiritual preaching.

Sibbes came to London in 1617 as a lecturer for Gray's Inn, the largest of the four great Inns of Court, which still remains one of the most important centers in England for the study and practice of law. In 1626, Sibbes complemented this lectureship by becoming master of Catharine Hall (now St. Catharine's College) at Cambridge. Under his leadership, the college returned to its former prestige. It graduated several men who would serve prominently at the Westminster Assembly, including John Arrowsmith, William Spurstowe, and William Strong. Soon after his appointment, Sibbes earned the doctor of divinity degree at Cambridge. He soon became known as "the heavenly Doctor" due to his godly preaching and heavenly conversation. Izaac Walton wrote of Sibbes:

> *Of this blest man, let this just praise be given,*
> *Heaven was in him, before he was in heaven.*[6]

In 1633, King Charles I offered Sibbes the vicarage of Holy Trinity, Cambridge, his last major new appointment. Sibbes continued to serve as lecturer at Gray's Inn, master of Catharine Hall, and vicar of Holy Trinity until his death in 1635.

Sibbes never married, but he established an astonishing network of friendships that included a variety of godly ministers, illustrious lawyers, and parliamentary leaders of the early Stuart era. Mark Dever observes that Sibbes believed, "Godly friends are walking

---

6. Walton wrote this in his copy of Sibbes's *The Returning Backslider*. Stapleton Martin, *Izaak Walton and His Friends* (London: Chapman & Hall, 1903), 174.

sermons."[7] On thirteen occasions he wrote introductions to the writings of his Puritan colleagues.

Sibbes was a gentle and warm man who avoided the controversies of his day as much as possible. "Fractions breed factions," he insisted.[8] His battles with Archbishop Laud, Roman Catholics, and Arminians were exceptions rather than the rule for him. He remained close friends with many pastors and leaders who espoused more radical reform than he did for the Church of England.

Sibbes was an inspiration to many of his brethren. He influenced Anglicanism, Presbyterianism, and Independency, the three dominant parties of the church in England at that time. He was a pastor of pastors, who lived a life of moderation. "Where most holiness is, there is most moderation, where it may be without prejudice of piety to God and the good of others," he wrote.[9]

The historian Daniel Neal described Sibbes as a celebrated preacher, an educated divine, and a charitable and humble man who repeatedly underestimated his gifts.[10] Yet Puritans everywhere recognized Sibbes as a great Christ-centered, experiential preacher. Both learned and unlearned in upper and lower classes profited greatly from Sibbes, who was an alluring preacher.

Sibbes meant to woo: "To preach is to woo," he wrote.[11] He said, "The main scope of all [preaching] is, to allure us to the entertainment of Christ's mild, safe, wise, victorious government."[12] Sibbes brought truth home, as Robert Burns would say, "to men's business and bosoms." Catlin wrote of Sibbes, "No man that ever I was acquainted with got so far into my heart or lay so close therein." Maurice Roberts adds, "His theology is thoroughly orthodox, of course, but it is like the fuel of some great combustion engine, always passing into flame and so being converted into energy thereby to serve God and, even more, to enjoy and relish God with the soul."[13]

---

7. Dever, *Richard Sibbes*, 50.

8. Quoted by Alexander B. Grosart, "Memoir," in Sibbes, *Works*, 1:lxi.

9. Sibbes, "The Bruised Reed and Smoking Flax," in *Works*, 1:57.

10. Daniel Neal, *The History of the Puritans* (New York: Harper & Bros., 1843), 1:323.

11. Sibbes, "The Fountain Opened," in *Works*, 5:505.

12. Sibbes, "The Bruised Reed and Smoking Flax," in *Works*, 1:40.

13. Roberts, "Richard Sibbes," 104.

David Masson, known for his biography of John Milton, wrote, "From the year 1630, onwards for twenty years or so, no writings in practical theology seem to have been so much read among the pious English middle classes as those of Sibbes."[14] The twentieth-century historian William Haller judged Sibbes's sermons to be "among the most brilliant and popular of all the utterances of the Puritan church militant."[15]

Sibbes's last sermons, preached one week before his death, were expositions of John 14:2, "In my Father's house are many mansions.... I go to prepare a place for you." When asked in his final days how his soul was faring, Sibbes replied, "I should do God much wrong if I should not say, very well."[16] Sibbes's will and testament, dictated on July 4, 1635, the day before his death, commences, "I commend and bequeath my soul into the hands of my gracious Savior, who hath redeemed it with his most precious blood, and appears now in heaven to receive it."[17]

The Complete Works of Richard Sibbes, meticulously edited with a 110-page memoir by Alexander Grosart, was published by James Nichol of Edinburgh in the 1860s and reprinted by the Banner of Truth Trust.[18] Sibbes's most famous work, *The Bruised Reed*, which has done so much good in healing troubled souls, is now available in paperback from Banner of Truth Trust.[19]

Let us turn now to Sibbes's teaching on the entertainment of the Spirit.

The Indwelling Spirit

The Spirit's indwelling is requisite to entertaining Him, Sibbes said. He taught that when the Spirit of God enters the heart of a sinner, regenerating him and persuading him of the truth of the gospel, the

---

14. David Masson, *The Life of John Milton* (Boston: Gould and Lincoln, 1859), 1:406.

15. William Haller, *The Rise of Puritanism* (New York: Columbia University Press, 1938), 152.

16. Dever, *Richard Sibbes*, 94.

17. Grosart, "Memoir," in Sibbes, *Works*, 1:cxxviii.

18. Cited throughout this chapter as Sibbes, *Works*. For an English translation of the concluding Latin sermon in volume 7, see Richard Sibbes, "Antidote against the Shipwreck of Faith and a Good Conscience," *Banner of Truth*, no. 433 (Oct. 1999): 11–22, and no. 434 (Nov. 1999): 11–22.

19. Richard Sibbes, *The Bruised Reed* (1630; repr., Edinburgh: Banner of Truth Trust, 1998).

Spirit immediately begins to live within that person.[20] The Spirit does not draw attention to Himself, however. Rather, the Spirit works to knit our hearts to God and to Jesus Christ. Sibbes wrote:

> He [the Spirit] sanctifieth and purifieth, and doth all from the Father and the Son, and knits us to the Father and the Son; to the Son first, and then to the Father...because all the communion we have with God is by the Holy Ghost. All the communion that Christ as man had with God was by the Holy Ghost; and all the communion that God hath with us, and we with God is by the Holy Ghost. For the Spirit is the bond of union between Christ and us, and between God and us.[21]

While the Father and Son perform no work without the Spirit, the Spirit also does no work apart from the Father and the Son. Sibbes explained: "As the Spirit comes from God the Father and the Son, so it carries us back again to the Father and the Son. As it comes from heaven, so it carries us to heaven back again."[22] The role of the Spirit is to introduce and intimately acquaint us with the Father and the Son.

Thus, if we are believers, the Spirit establishes communion between us and the other two Persons of the Trinity. It is as if He captures us and lifts us up to know the Father and the Son's love for us. The Holy Spirit lifts us to see by faith the crucified and resurrected Jesus seated in glory. That is why the Spirit comes, and that is how He functions in our lives. Therefore, we may say that while, in one sense, fellowship between us and God is reestablished once and for all, yet in another sense the Spirit maintains and increases that fellowship during our entire lives.

Sibbes said that as the Spirit draws us to the Father and the Son, He confirms His government in our hearts. This government is not at odds with the Spirit's purpose of revealing the things of Christ to us; rather, His internal governing reveals Jesus Christ seated on the throne of grace. Indeed, the Spirit helps us conform to the character and behavior of Christ. The Spirit lives in us to restore and transform our souls, and ripens us for glory. Submitting to the Spirit is thus critical, Sibbes said. In *A Fountain Sealed*, he wrote:

---

20. Sibbes, "A Fountain Sealed," in *Works*, 5:413–14; "Divine Meditations and Holy Contemplations," in *Works*, 7:199–200.

21. Sibbes, "A Description of Christ," in *Works*, 1:17.

22. Sibbes, "The Church's Echo," in *Works*, 7:545.

Let us give up the government of our souls to the Spirit. It is for our safety so to do, as being wiser than ourselves who are unable to direct our own way. It is our liberty to be under a wisdom and goodness larger than our own. Let the Spirit think in us, desire in us, pray in us, live in us, do all in us; labor ever to be in such a frame as we may be fit for the Spirit to work upon.[23]

The believer is like a "musical instrument," tuned and played by the Spirit. Therefore, Sibbes wrote, "Let us lay ourselves open to the Spirit's touch."[24] When the Spirit has ruling sway in our lives, He fine-tunes our souls much like a musical instrument, and then He plays our lives as a piano concerto before God.

Sibbes described this process of tuning and the touch of the Holy Spirit: "He must rule. He will have the keys delivered to him; we must submit to his government. And when he is in the heart, he will subdue by little and little all high thoughts, rebellious risings, and despairing fears."[25]

How may we know that we have this blessed, indwelling, governing Spirit? Sibbes said, "By living and moving, by actions vital, etc. even so may a man know he hath the Spirit of God by those actions that come only from the Spirit, which is to the soul, as the soul is to the body...every saving grace is a sign that the Spirit is in us."[26] Wherever the indwelling Spirit is, He gradually transforms the soul to be holy and gracious like Himself. The government of the Spirit is not realized immediately. The revolution and overthrow of our old nature comes upon regeneration, while the government of the Spirit is established only in a process so that we may learn more of and abide more to the constitution of our new life in Jesus Christ.

Restored communion with God the Father and the Son by means of the government of the Spirit cannot but produce spiritual warfare. The transformation that the Holy Spirit effects in the believer is accompanied by external and internal struggle. Externally, we face the powers of darkness, even the prince of darkness himself, Sibbes warned, because the devil is profoundly envious of the man who

---

23. Sibbes, "A Fountain Sealed," in *Works*, 5:426.
24. Sibbes, "A Fountain Sealed," in *Works*, 5:426.
25. Sibbes, "A Fountain Sealed," in *Works*, 5:431.
26. Sibbes, "Exposition of 2 Corinthians Chapter 1," in *Works*, 3:478.

walks in the Spirit.[27] Satan will do all within his power to destroy the comfort of that man.

Indeed, all spiritual graces meet with conflict, Sibbes said, "for what is true, is met with a great deal of resistance of that which is counterfeit."[28] What is of the Spirit is always in conflict with what is not of the Spirit. Internally, our fleshly desires are continually at war with the Spirit, for when the Spirit comes to a person, He pulls down all strongholds. He carves out a path for Himself in the thick of battle.

Our souls are the battlefield upon which the Spirit marches, and He will have the final victory, Sibbes said. For wherever the Spirit dwells, He also rules, for He will not be an underling to lusts. He repairs the breaches of the soul. In this battle, we must submit to the Spirit in all things, however, for only then will we experience the victorious life that is the inheritance of believers in Jesus Christ. To be sure, the greatest battles were won on Calvary and in our hearts when we were brought to new birth, but we must also fight daily battles in our lives of sanctification. Our ever-present foes—our flesh, the world, and the devil—unceasingly strive to tear up the foundation upon which we stand as children of the Most High.

Sibbes said that we must show that we treasure the indwelling power of the Spirit. We cannot value God's love and holiness granted to us in the Spirit without exercising self-denial. Life in the Spirit, while beginning at regeneration, must continue to bear fruit for the rest of the believer's life. As Sibbes wrote, "As we may know who dwells in a house by observing who goes in and them that come out, so we may know that the Spirit dwells in us by observing what sanctified speeches he sends forth, and what delight he hath wrought in us to things that are special, and what price we set upon them."[29]

The believer's greatest encouragement in spiritual warfare is the *abiding presence of the Spirit.* The Spirit is the leader and enabler of our souls. Sibbes wrote, "If we be sound Christians, the Spirit of God will enable us to do all things, evangelically, that we are called unto."[30] He said, "Therefore let us have an high esteem of the Holy Spirit, of

---

27. Sibbes, "Exposition of 2 Corinthians Chapter 1," in *Works*, 3:478.
28. Sibbes, "Exposition of 2 Corinthians Chapter 1," in *Works*, 3:478.
29. Sibbes, "Divine Meditations and Holy Contemplations," in *Works*, 7:199.
30. Sibbes, "The Soul's Conflict with Itself," in *Works*, 1:188.

the motions of it, and out of an high esteem in our hearts beg of God the guidance of the Spirit, that he would lead us by his Spirit, and subdue our corruptions, that we may not be led by our own lusts."[31] It is through what Sibbes termed "the motions," or "holy stirrings of the Spirit," that the Spirit enables us to overcome the sin that attacks us internally and the forces of darkness set against us externally.[32] The Spirit of Christ is powerful and strong. Through His indwelling, we are able "to perform duties above nature, to overcome ourselves and injuries," Sibbes said.[33] The Spirit, he added, will "make us to be able to live and die, as it enabled Christ to do things that another man could not do."[34]

Sibbes's conclusion was inevitable: "Where there is no conflict, there is no Spirit of Christ at all."[35] In this he echoed the apostle Paul's teaching that if we mortify the deeds of the flesh by the Spirit, we are led by the Spirit (Rom. 8:13). We, then, by grace, entertain the Spirit. We befriend and show hospitality to that Spirit who gives us the victory over all enemies by faith (1 John 5:4).

But the Spirit does more than indwell the believer and give victory in spiritual warfare. He is also the sealer of our souls.

The Sealer of Our Souls

Sibbes often preached on the Spirit's sealing. A series of his sermons transcribed by a noblewoman, Lady Elizabeth Brooke, was published in 1637 as *A Fountain Sealed*.[36] His sermons on 2 Corinthians 1:22–23, published in 1655 in *Exposition of 2 Corinthians Chapter 1*,[37] were about the Spirit's sealing. So was a sermon on Romans 8:15–16, *The Witness of Salvation: or, God's Spirit Witnessing with Our Spirits*, which was published in 1629.[38]

According to Sibbes and many other Puritans, looking at the role of the Spirit in sealing the souls of believers is very much like examining His work in personal assurance of faith and salvation. Sibbes,

---

31. Sibbes, "A Description of Christ," in *Works*, 1:26.
32. Sibbes, "The Ungodly's Misery," in *Works*, 1:392.
33. Sibbes, "A Description of Christ," in *Works*, 1:22.
34. Sibbes, "A Description of Christ," in *Works*, 1:22.
35. Sibbes, "A Description of Christ," in *Works*, 1:22.
36. Sibbes, "A Fountain Sealed," in *Works*, 5:409–56.
37. Sibbes, "Exposition of 2 Corinthians Chapter 1," in *Works*, 3 *passim*.
38. Sibbes, "The Witness of Salvation," in *Works*, 7:367–85.

however, viewed our sealing in the Spirit as two distinct matters. He distinguished between the office or function of the Spirit as a seal given in regeneration to a sinner and the work of the Spirit in applying that seal to the believer's consciousness.

John Owen would later call this distinction unbiblical, for he said we are sealed when we are born again, and the Bible gives no justification for a second kind of sealing. Owen, following the early Reformers, taught a one-to-one correlation between those regenerated by the Spirit and those sealed by the Spirit. John Calvin, for example, said that it is impossible to believe without being sealed by the Spirit. For Calvin, sealing represented the presence rather than the activity of the Spirit. Thus, the sealing work of the Spirit belongs to the essence of faith.[39]

By the time of Perkins, who was often called the father of Puritanism, more attention was devoted to the Spirit's activity in sealing the promises of the gospel to the believer. The focus was no longer on the Spirit Himself as the indwelling seal but on His activity in sealing or attesting the promises. Perkins's successor, Baynes, attempted to reconcile the thoughts of Calvin and Perkins on the sealing of the Spirit. Baynes taught that the sealing could be applied both to the Spirit as indweller and to the consequences of that sealing in the regenerate life. He wrote, "The Holy Spirit *and* the graces of the Spirit are the seal assuring our redemption."[40] Thus, Baynes distinguished between being sealed by the Spirit, which all believers possess, and being made conscious of such sealing, which only those who are conscious of the graces of the Spirit possess.

Sibbes agreed with his predecessor at St. Andrews, Baynes, though he emphasized the sealing of the Spirit as a "superadded work" and "confirmation" of the believer's faith.[41] In so doing, Sibbes turned the doctrine of the sealing of the Spirit in a direction that would gain prominence among the Puritans for several decades.

39. See Joel R. Beeke, *The Quest for Full Assurance: The Legacy of Calvin and His Successors* (Edinburgh: Banner of Truth Trust, 1999), 201–208.

40. Paul Bayne [Baynes], *Commentary upon the Whole Epistle of St. Paul to the Ephesians* (repr., Stoke-on-Trent, England: Tentmaker Publications, 2001), 81.

41. Sibbes, "Exposition of 2 Corinthians Chapter 1," in *Works*, 3:455–56.

As I have already implied, Sibbes thought of the Spirit's sealing in two ways: (1) a one-time sealing, and (2) a sealing that comes later as one matures in the Christian life.

The once-and-for-all sealing of salvation is granted when a person first believes in Christ and God's promises. Sibbes taught that as a king's image is stamped upon wax, so the Spirit stamps believers' souls with the image of Christ from the very moment of belief.[42] Such sealing produces in every believer a lifelong desire to be transformed fully into the image of Christ.

This seal, which every believer possesses, consciously or unconsciously, serves as a mark of authenticity. It distinguishes the believer from the world. As merchants mark their wares and herdsmen brand their sheep, so God seals His people to declare that they are His rightful property and that He has authority over them, Sibbes said.[43]

The second aspect of Sibbes's doctrine of sealing is more elusive. Owen argued that Sibbes said sealing had to occur twice in the life of the believer. But Sibbes was not arguing for a second measure of *positional assurance*, as if to imply that God was not altogether sure of our stance with Him or His stance toward us upon conversion. Sibbes plainly stated: "Sealing of us by the Spirit is not in regard of God but ourselves. God knoweth who are His, but we know not that we are His but by sealing."[44] The sealing then is *for our benefit exclusively*, not for God.

So, the second kind of sealing Sibbes wrote about is a process. It is the kind of assurance that can increase gradually throughout our lives by means of singular experiences and by daily, spiritual growth. This sealing has degrees; it can grow with spiritual maturity. Sibbes wrote: "The Spirit sealeth by degrees. As our care of pleasing the Spirit increaseth so our comfort increaseth. Our light will increase as the morning light unto the perfect day. Yielding to the Spirit in one holy motion will cause him to lead us to another, and so on forwards, until we be more deeply acquainted with the whole counsel of God concerning our salvation."[45]

---

42. Sibbes, "Exposition of 2 Corinthians Chapter 1," in *Works*, 3:453.
43. Sibbes, "Exposition of 2 Corinthians Chapter 1," in *Works*, 3:454.
44. Sibbes, "A Fountain Sealed," in *Works*, 5:446–47.
45. Sibbes, "A Fountain Sealed," in *Works*, 5:452.

Sibbes learned through pastoral experience that many believers are content with the measure of faith and assurance they receive upon their conversion and do not labor for further growth. That prompted Sibbes to suggest that there are three kinds of Christians.[46]

First, there are those who have saving faith but live under a spirit of bondage. They are filled with doubts and fears. They lack the reflex act of faith that ascertains marks and evidences of the Spirit's saving work in their lives. Sibbes said that they ought to pray for more faith and light to discern the Spirit's work within them.

Second, some Christians are under the Spirit of adoption but still have fears. They are sealed with evidences of faith, but are often still beset with perplexity and doubt. Their degree of assurance is usually highest when their trials are greatest. Sibbes wrote, "For those who have been sealed by the Spirit and yet not so fully as to silence all doubts about their estate: those should, out of that beginning of comfort which they feel, study to be pliable to the Spirit for further increase."[47]

Third, Sibbes said that some believers are "carried with large spirits to obey their Father" as the fruit of the superadded, direct seal of the Spirit that persuades them of their sonship to God.[48] Those who experience the freedom of a "large spirit" receive a private seal—an unmistakable witness of the Spirit to their souls. The Spirit's private seal is a "stablishing, confirming grace," Sibbes said.[49] He identified this sealing with the immediate testimony of the Holy Spirit, by which the Father's love is pronounced upon the believer in particular, usually through the application of such texts as "I am thy salvation" or "thy sins are pardoned."[50] According to Sibbes, this establishing seal grants believers freedom to appropriate full assurance through the work of each Person in the Trinity, though the emphasis is on the Spirit in His saving activity. Sibbes wrote:

> Every person in the blessed Trinity hath their several work. The Father chooseth us and passeth a decree upon the whole groundwork of our salvation. The Son executeth it to the full.

---

46. Sibbes, "A Fountain Sealed," in *Works*, 5:447–48.
47. Sibbes, "A Fountain Sealed," in *Works*, 5:440.
48. Sibbes, "A Fountain Sealed," in *Works*, 5:448.
49. Sibbes, "Exposition of 2 Corinthians Chapter 1," in *Works*, 3:422.
50. Sibbes, "A Fountain Sealed," in *Works*, 5:440.

The Spirit applieth it, and witnesseth our interest in it by leading our souls to lay hold upon him, and by raising up our souls in the assurance of it, and by breeding and cherishing sweet communion with Father and Son, who both of them seal us likewise by the Spirit. This joy and comfort is so appropriated to the Spirit, as it carrieth the very name of the Spirit.[51]

Sibbes sounds mystical at times in describing this special sealing, particularly in statements such as "the Holy Ghost slides and insinuates and infuseth himself into our souls."[52] But Sibbes warded off mysticism in two ways. First, he maintained that this special sealing must never be divorced from the Word of God.[53] By speaking of sealing in degrees, Sibbes linked all advancement in grace to the Spirit and Word, for any consciousness of sealing by the Spirit is always through the applied Word.

Second, Sibbes said that the genuineness of such sealing may be readily examined. One may know the voice of the Spirit of God by inquiring what followed "this ravishing joy" of experimental sealing, Sibbes wrote.[54] Fruits of sanctification, such as peace of conscience, the spirit of adoption whereby we cry, "Abba, Father," prayers of fervent supplication, conformity with the heavenly image of Christ, and applying ourselves to holy duties rather than old lusts inevitably result from such "a secret whispering and intimation to the soul."[55] Sibbes thus emphasized both the intuitive testimony of the Spirit and the sanctifying fruits of the Spirit. The Spirit's sealing is inward in its essence and outward in its fruit.

Sibbes taught that this special sealing is granted by the Spirit to saints particularly in times of great trial. He said that the Spirit gives such seals "even as parents [who] smile upon their children when they are sick and need comfort: so above all other times God reserves this hidden sealing of his children with a spirit of joy when they need it most."[56] Such sealing is "a sweet kiss vouchsafed to the soul."[57] Paul in the dungeon, Daniel in the lion's den, and his three friends in

---

51. Sibbes, "A Fountain Sealed," in *Works*, 5:439.
52. Sibbes, "A Description of Christ," in *Works*, 1:24.
53. Sibbes, "A Fountain Sealed," in *Works*, 5:441.
54. Sibbes, "A Fountain Sealed," in *Works*, 5:441.
55. Sibbes, "Yea and Amen," in *Works*, 4:134.
56. Sibbes, "Exposition of 2 Corinthians Chapter 1," in *Works*, 3:458.
57. Sibbes, "Yea and Amen," in *Works*, 4:134.

the fiery furnace all experienced that encouragement. It is the hidden manna and the white stone with a written name that none can know but he that has it (Rev. 2:17).[58]

The sealing of the Spirit consoles the believer especially in the hour of death, Sibbes said. Even if the stamp of the Spirit is almost worn away, it is still valid if there are "some evidences, some pulses, some sighs and groans against corruption."[59] The cause of the effacing of the stamp lies in the believer's yielding too much to his corruptions; nevertheless, the stamp abides.

In summary, Sibbes's interest in sealing was more pastoral than academic. He knew that true assurance results in an increased desire for holiness and for more intimate communion with God. Sibbes's argument was clear: When the Holy Spirit puts His holy seal on a believer, that person will bear the fruits of holiness. Sealing prompts assurance, and the more assurance we have, the more love we feel for God and the more we obey Him. Consequently, all Christians ought to pray for "a spirit of revelation that we may be *more* sealed," Sibbes said.[60]

Owen understood why Sibbes and other Puritans in his era proposed the notion of a sealing subsequent to regeneration. He recognized that Sibbes and others were attempting to call believers to a life of *assuredness*. Owen affirmed the call for this kind of assurance, yet he argued against equating full assurance with the sealing of the Spirit. He felt that sound exegesis of Ephesians 1:13 did not support such a view.

Though some of us may also fear that Sibbes went beyond Scripture at times in his doctrine of sealing, we should recognize that Sibbes was discussing a different sort of event than what Owen suggested. Sibbes had a dynamic view of sealing. Sealing is a continuous and progressive activity, Sibbes said. Owen held a more static view of sealing. He viewed the seal "as sealed," whereas Sibbes viewed the seal primarily as "a sealing." Sibbes was talking about an experiential, behavioral, and character-modifying realization of the depth of the love of God—the witness of the Spirit that

---

58. Sibbes, "Exposition of 2 Corinthians Chapter 1," in *Works*, 3:458.
59. Sibbes, "Exposition of 2 Corinthians Chapter 1," in *Works*, 3:461.
60. Sibbes, "A Fountain Sealed," in *Works*, 5:454.

grows through life. Sibbes was saying that this kind of sealing is a great boost to our sanctification.

The Comforter

Sibbes taught that sanctification is not only promoted by the Spirit's indwelling and sealing, but also by the Spirit's activity as comforter. He wrote, "Is it not the greatest comfort to a Christian soul when God, in want of means, comes immediately Himself unto us and comforts us by His Spirit?"[61] By "want of means," Sibbes meant those times when circumstances and earthly comforts fail us.

If you are a Christian, you know that life and its difficulties can be discouraging. Especially when God's promises and providence seem to contradict each other, we are prone to lose our quiet confidence in God and become, like David, cast down and disquieted within (Ps. 43:5). We yield to the discouragements of the flesh. Sibbes said such disquiet and grief is "like lead to the soul, heavy and cold."[62]

At those times especially we need the Holy Spirit to draw close to our souls. In his book *Yea and Amen*, Sibbes wrote, "It must needs be so because no less than the Spirit of God can quiet our perplexed spirits in times of temptation."[63] He went on to say, "Spiritual comforts flow immediately from the Spirit of comfort who hath His office designed for that purpose."[64]

Sibbes excelled in showing why the Spirit alone can comfort our battered souls. He wrote:

> When the soul is distempered, it is like a distempered lock that no key can open. So when the conscience is troubled, what creature can settle the troubled conscience, can open the ambages [the winding passages] of a troubled conscience in such perplexity and confusion? And therefore to settle the troubled conscience aright, it must be somewhat *above* conscience; and that which must quiet the spirit must be such a Spirit as is *above our spirits.*[65]

61. Sibbes, "The Saint's Safety in Evil Times," in *Works*, 1:319.
62. Sibbes, "The Soul's Conflict," in *Works*, 1:142.
63. Sibbes, "Yea and Amen," in *Works*, 4:144.
64. Sibbes, "Yea and Amen," in *Works*, 4:144.
65. Sibbes, "Exposition of 2 Corinthians Chapter 1," in *Works*, 3:477.

Sibbes appreciated the complexity of individuals and understood how that complexity remains even after we become believers. Hardships are part of being a Christian, for a Christian is engaged in the pursuit of holiness. Yet the Spirit is able to give grace to the believer to rise above discouragements, no matter how great they are. Sibbes wrote: "Oh, therefore get this blessed Spirit to enlighten thee, to quicken thee, to support thee, etc., and it will carry thy soul courageously along above all oppositions and discouragements whatsoever in the way to happiness."[66] As surely as the difficulties of life are genuine, so, too, the comfort of the Spirit is genuine and able.

The Spirit is more than just a spiritual bandage. He is *the* Comforter, the healing balm for our hearts. We wholeheartedly agree with Sibbes that the Holy Spirit "is a comforter, bringing to mind useful things at such times when we most need them."[67] What are these useful things if not the profound love of the Lord for us *in spite of our wretched state*—a love that ushers us through suffering and gives purpose to all of life.

Sibbes also taught that the role of the Holy Spirit as comforter is tied to the Word of God. "The Spirit gives no comfort but by the word.... If it be God's comfort, assure thyself God would have his word to make way unto it," Sibbes wrote.[68] He said that in times of discouragement, the believer must question his own soul about the causes of discontent. He must charge himself to trust God and His Word, recognizing that with the Spirit as his indwelling comforter, there is no good reason to be discouraged. He must be "meditating on the promises of God, and wedging them home upon the heart," Sibbes said.[69] By using the promises, he must labor for a calmed spirit by insisting that until the Spirit "meekens" the soul, it is not quiet enough to receive the seed of the Word. As Sibbes wrote, "It is ill sowing in a storm; so a stormy spirit will not suffer the word to take [its] place."[70]

Sibbes taught that in applying the Word to the believer's troubled soul, the Spirit calls forth answering motions in the believer,

66. Sibbes, "The Difficulty of Salvation," in *Works*, 1:399.
67. Sibbes, "Divine Meditations and Holy Contemplations," in *Works*, 7:200.
68. Sibbes, "The Witness of Salvation," in *Works*, 7:383.
69. Sibbes, "The Witness of Salvation," in *Works*, 7:383.
70. Sibbes, "The Soul's Conflict," in *Works*, 1:143.

leading him to find quiet and rest in God. Indeed, the believer must continue to examine his soul by faith until he finds rest in God. Perfect rest in God will be found only in heaven, Sibbes said. Here on earth, however, the believer can find rest by means of "sanctifying and quieting graces."[71]

Quieting the soul helps a believer recover some of the communion with God that was destroyed by the fall. Prior to the fall, man's soul was like "an instrument in tune, fit to be moved to any duty; as a clean, neat glass [or mirror], the soul represented God's image and likeness," Sibbes wrote.[72] Since the fall, the only way to find such harmony of a soul "fitted as a clean glass to receive light from above"[73] is to depend on the Spirit and aim for peace and harmony with God, who is "the God of peace,…the God of order."[74] Sibbes called believers to "the beauty of a well-ordered soul" that is in tune with the Spirit of God.[75] Such a soul is comforted even in great trials, Sibbes said. It receives with meekness the engrafted Word and, by keeping its affections in due proportion, responds to the Holy Spirit's internal motions, which lead the soul to find rest and peace in God. All such motions tend to rest and end in God, "the center and resting-place of the soul," Sibbes wrote. "Then whatsoever times come, we are sure of a hiding-place and sanctuary."[76]

Would you be comforted and quieted in your soul? Labor to entertain the Spirit. Give room to His motions in your soul, remembering, as Sibbes concluded: "The soul without the Spirit is darkness and confusion, full of self-accusing and self-tormenting thoughts. If we let the Spirit come in, [He] will scatter all and settle the soul in a sweet quiet."[77]

Grieving the Spirit

If the Spirit helps us commune with the Father and the Son, governs our spirits, defends us in spiritual conflict, leads us in faith, seals our

---

71. Sibbes, "The Soul's Conflict," in *Works*, 1:279.
72. Sibbes, "The Soul's Conflict," in *Works*, 1:173.
73. Sibbes, "The Soul's Conflict," in *Works*, 1:211.
74. Sibbes, "The Soul's Conflict," in *Works*, 1:168.
75. Sibbes, "The Soul's Conflict," in *Works*, 1:167.
76. Sibbes, "The Soul's Conflict," in *Works*, 1:289.
77. Sibbes, "A Fountain Sealed," in *Works*, 5:452.

souls, and comforts us till death, then what happens when we fail Him and succumb to our own sin and folly?

At such times, we grieve the Spirit, Sibbes said. In *A Fountain Sealed*, Sibbes cried, "What greater indignity can we offer to the Holy Spirit than to prefer base dust before his motions leading us to holiness and happiness? What greater unkindness, yea, treachery to leave directions of a friend to follow the counsel of an enemy; such as when we know God's will, yet will consent with flesh and blood… in leaving a true guide and following the pirate."[78]

Like his fellow Puritans, Sibbes was most critical of people in the established church who did not exhibit the fruits of saving faith. He challenged those who claimed to have walked with God for many years but whose lives showed little effect of their relationship with the Almighty. He warned: "Of all the sins, the sins of professors of religion [those who profess to be Christians] grieve the Spirit most. And of all professors, those that have most means of knowledge, because their obligations are deeper and their engagements greater…. The offense of friends grieves more than the injuries of enemies."[79]

Sibbes did not stop there. He went on to say that as the Holy Ghost is a Spirit, so spiritual sins such as pride, envy, and an evil spirit grieve Him most.[80] Carnal sins grieve the Spirit, too, for they drown the soul in physical delights and defile the Spirit's temple. We need to be changed from the inside out by the Spirit of God. As long as we do not aim for a life of devotion and conformity to Jesus Christ, we grieve the Spirit.

Sibbes offered still more ways in which we grieve the Spirit. He wrote, "We commonly grieve the Spirit of God…when the mind is troubled with a multitude of busyness; when the soul is like a mill where one cannot hear another; the noise is such as takes away all intercourse [communication]."[81] That is to say, when we fill our lives with things other than spiritual concerns, we bring grief to the blessed Spirit. Activity is not synonymous with spirituality, as popular Christian culture would have us believe. Rather, we are called to humble dependence and meditation upon the Spirit. As Sibbes said,

---

78. Sibbes, "A Fountain Sealed," in *Works*, 5:416.
79. Sibbes, "A Fountain Sealed," in *Works*, 5:417.
80. Sibbes, "A Fountain Sealed," in *Works*, 5:419.
81. Sibbes, "A Fountain Sealed," in *Works*, 5:422.

"This grieves the Holy Spirit also when men take the office of the Spirit from him," that is, when we do things in our own strength and by our own light.[82] We all too willingly go about our Christian tasks in our own strength, never realizing that in doing so we become our own end, and our activities become meaningless.

Conclusion: Rely on the Spirit

According to Sibbes, the Spirit must be an integral part of our lives, our churches, and our world. The Spirit must be entertained in every facet of Christian life and experience. We must relish His indwelling, His sealing, and His comforting work, while striving not to grieve Him. Sibbes labored to make biblical theology relevant to the person in the pew. His books challenge us to pursue a biblical understanding of the Holy Spirit and to faithfully communicate that understanding to others in the body of Christ.

Today, the relationship between believers and the Holy Spirit is too often like a bad marriage in which a husband takes advantage of his wife's contributions but fails to appreciate and celebrate his relationship with her. To reverse this situation, Sibbes advised that we should make a daily effort to appreciate the Holy Spirit, and to share our thoughts and plans with Him in prayer as we gaze by faith into the face of God. We should walk in daily communication with the Spirit through the Word, relying upon every office that the Holy Spirit provides, as described in Scripture. As Sibbes wrote, "The Holy Spirit being in us, after he hath prepared us for a house for himself to dwell in and to take up his rest and delight in, he doth also become unto us a counselor in all our doubts, a comforter in all our distresses, a solicitor to all duty, a guide in the whole course of life, until we dwell with him forever in heaven, unto which his dwelling here in us doth tend."[83] Thus, by the Holy Spirit, we, like Sibbes, can have a measure of heaven in us before we are in heaven.

---

82. Sibbes, "A Fountain Sealed," in *Works*, 5:422.
83. Sibbes, "A Fountain Sealed," in *Works*, 5:414.

CHAPTER 16

The Holy Spirit in the Westminster Standards

Joseph Morecraft III

The Westminster Standards are filled with references to the Holy Spirit and with mature and comprehensive teaching about Him. Nine chapters in the Confession deal with Him. He is mentioned by name forty-two times in the Confession (WCF), thirty-eight times in the Larger Catechism (WLC), and ten times in the Shorter Catechism (WSC).

Those three documents explain His deity, His Personhood in the Trinity, His relation to the Word of God, His relation to the Person and work of Christ, His objective work outside the believer, His subjective work in the believer (applying salvation to him), and His work in the unbeliever.

The Standards give the Holy Spirit several names and titles, including "the Spirit of adoption," "the eternal Spirit," "the Holy Ghost," "the free Spirit of God," "God's Spirit," "His Holy Spirit" (referring to the Father), "God the Holy Spirit," and "the Spirit of God."

But the most frequent names given to the Spirit relate Him to Jesus Christ. Referring to Christ, He is called "His Spirit" fourteen times; "His Holy Spirit" three times; "the Spirit of Christ" five times; and "the Spirit of His Son" once. This tells us something about the Standards' emphasis in their teaching on the Spirit: He is the Spirit of Christ. Where Christ is, there He is. Their Persons are distinct, but Their presence is the same. Being in Christ is being in the Spirit. We are in Christ and Christ is in us; we are in the Spirit and the Spirit is in us. As 2 Corinthians 3:17 says, "Now the Lord is the Spirit; and where the Spirit of the Lord is, there is liberty." When Christ is received, the Spirit is received; therefore, he who does not have the Spirit of Christ does not belong to Christ.

The Deity of the Holy Spirit

The Holy Spirit is truly and fully God. Whatever can be said about God can be said about the Spirit. The Father, the Son, and the Holy Spirit are "the same in substance, equal in power and glory" (WLC, Q. 9). We know the Spirit is God because "names, attributes, works and worship as are proper to God only" (WLC, Q. 11) are given Him in the written Word of God.

Because He is God, He never contradicts Himself, He will never confront a problem He cannot solve, He will never find a sinner too wicked and too defiant to convert, He cannot be manipulated by human beings, and He is not dependent on or needful of human beings. He is the sovereign God. He is like the wind that "bloweth where it listeth, and thou hearest the sound thereof, but canst not tell whence it cometh, and whither it goeth: so is every one that is born of the Spirit" (John 3:8).

The Personhood of the Holy Spirit

The Holy Spirit is not an impersonal force, an atmosphere, or a warm feeling that fills a church. He is a living, thinking, loving Person who has a will and a moral character, and who fellowships with people. He is, after all, the third Person in the Holy Trinity. As the Larger Catechism states in question 9, "There be three persons in the Godhead, the Father, the Son, and the Holy Spirit, and these three are one true eternal God."

Although these three Persons are equally God, each has a distinctive feature not applicable to the others: "It is proper to the Father to beget the Son, and to the Son to be begotten of the Father, and to the Holy Spirit to proceed from the Father and the Son from all eternity" (WLC, Q. 10). Two things in this answer should be carefully noted.

First, the distinct feature of the Holy Spirit is that He proceeds from the Father and the Son from all eternity. The Larger Catechism supports its statement with two Scripture texts. In John 15:26, Jesus says, "But when the Comforter is come, whom I will send unto you from the Father, even the Spirit of truth, which proceedeth from the Father, he shall testify of me" In Galatians 4:6, the apostle writes, "And because ye are sons, God hath sent forth the Spirit of His Son into your hearts, crying, Abba, Father."

What is the point of this procession of the Spirit from the Father and the Son? Herman Bavinck answers: "The trinity is not complete apart from the person of the Holy Spirit considered as truly God.... The entire [doctrine] of the trinity, the mystery of Christianity, the heart of religion, stands or falls with the deity of the Spirit."[1]

Second, the words "and the Son" in the phrase "He proceeds from the Father and the Son" have a controversial history. They constitute the famous *filioque* clause that was added to the Nicene Creed by the Council of Toledo in AD 589, completing the patristic doctrine of the Trinity. It is the inevitable implication of orthodox Christology, closing the door to the heresy of the subordination of Persons in the Trinity in the faith of the church.

The *filioque* clause was rejected by the Eastern church, but in the West the clause secured the full equality of the Father, the Son, and the Spirit. The complete doctrine of the *filioque* clause is, first, that the Father and the Son are of the same essence, and, second, that the Holy Spirit is the Spirit of God the Father and the Spirit of Christ. The doctrine that the Spirit proceeds also from the Son links the doctrine of the Trinity with the doctrine of Christ, and the doctrine of Christ with the doctrine of man, "by bringing the Holy Spirit and His work into more immediate connection with Christ, and through Him, with the church and the believer."[2]

Without the *filioque* clause, the Son is subordinated to the Father within the Trinity, and with that comes the depreciation of revelation. And where divine revelation is depreciated, nature and reason are asserted as man's primary order and standard—nature eats up grace. When that happens, the determination of history in human minds passes from the Trinity to the state or the empire.

The Relation of the Holy Spirit to the Word of God

The unity of the Word of God and the Spirit of God is emphatic in the Westminster Standards. This unity is referred to seven times in the Confession (1.5, 6, 10; 8.8; 10.1; 14.1; 27.3), seven times in the Larger Catechism (Q. 2, 4, 43, 67, 72, 76, 155) and once in the Shorter

---

1. Herman Bavinck, *The Doctrine of God*, trans. William Hendricksen (Edinburgh: Banner of Truth, 1977), 311.

2. Philip Schaff, quoted in R. J. Rushdoony, *The Foundation of Social Order* (Phillipsburg, N.J.: Presbyterian and Reformed, 1968), 122.

Catechism (Q. 24). The Confession's summarizing statement is that God's Word and God's Spirit "only do sufficiently and effectually reveal [God] unto men for their salvation" (WLC, Q. 2). We are totally dependent upon the Word and Spirit for a true and saving knowledge of God. Since the Spirit is the author of Scripture, we should follow Him in interpreting Scripture. To understand the Bible, then, we must pray for the enlightenment of the Spirit. As the psalmist prayed, "Open thou mine eyes, that I may behold wondrous things out of thy law" (Ps. 119:18).

The Confession also says, "The supreme judge by which all controversies of religion are to be determined…and in whose sentence we are to rest, can be no other but the Holy Spirit speaking in the Scripture" (1.10). This expression—"the Holy Spirit speaking in the Scripture"—reminds us that "Scripture is not a dead word but the living and abiding speech of the Holy Spirit. The Reformers needed to emphasize this quality of Scripture in order to offset the plea of Rome that a living voice is necessary for the faith and guidance of the church and also to meet the same argument of enthusiasts for the inner voice of the Spirit in the believer."[3]

So, then, it is obvious why the Standards make so much of the unity of the Spirit and the Word. The written Word is powerless to save without the accompanying work of the Spirit. We cannot expect the Spirit to lead us apart from the Word. Desiring the Word without the Spirit leads to empty externalism and cold intellectualism; desiring the Spirit without the Word leads to fanaticism, mysticism, and irrationalism.

The Spirit and the Word are connected in three ways: the Holy Spirit is the divine author of the Bible; the Holy Spirit persuades the believer of the infallible truth and the divine authority of the Bible; and the Holy Spirit guides the believer and the church to a proper understanding of the Bible.

First, the Confession speaks of the sixty-six books of the Bible as "given by the inspiration of God" (1.2). It supports this statement with 2 Peter 1:21, which says concerning the Bible that "holy men of God spake as they were moved by the Holy Ghost," thus making

---

3. John Murray, "The Finality and Sufficiency of Scripture," in *The Collected Writings of John Murray* (Edinburgh: Banner of Truth, 1976), 1:17.

the Holy Spirit the ultimate Author of the Bible, the original Hebrew and Greek manuscripts being "immediately inspired by God" (1.8).

What the Confession means by "inspiration" can be determined by statements it uses elsewhere: "It pleased the Lord to reveal Himself and to declare that His will unto His church, and afterwards...to commit the same wholly to writing" (1.1; see also 1.2, 5, 8); the Bible is of "infallible truth and divine authority" (1.3); and the believer receives as "true whatever is revealed in the word, for the authority of God himself speaking therein" (14.2).

Second, the Confession answers the question, How do believers come to believe that the Bible is the Word of God? It answers, first, that the Bible contains self-authenticating evidence that it is the Word of God, and, second, that our full persuasion of its divine authority comes from the internal witness of the Holy Spirit.

The witness of the Spirit does not bring new revelation; neither is it audible. Rather, it "opens a person's spiritual vision to appreciate the marks of truth which were objectively present in Scripture all along."[4] Without this witness of the Spirit, the sinful human mind would not be persuaded of the infallible truth and divine authority of the Bible. As John Calvin wrote: "Our mind has such an inclination to vanity that it can never cleave fast to the truth of God; and it has such a dullness that it is always blind to the light of God's truth. Accordingly, without the illumination of the Holy Spirit, the word can do nothing."[5]

Because of a false view that teaches that the Spirit's witness is not to Scripture as a whole but only to Scripture's central message of Christ, it must be made clear that the Spirit bears witness to the truth of the gospel and to the Bible as a whole. In the Confession, we read that faith believes the whole of Scripture because it is the Word of God (14.2). Saving faith receives as true whatever is written in the Bible, and its central response is receiving and resting on Christ alone for salvation. As Wayne Spear says: "Spirit-given faith does not grasp the saving message of Scripture apart from the trustworthy

---

4. Wayne Spear, "Word and Spirit in the Westminster Confession," in *The Westminster Confession into the Twenty-First Century,* ed. J. Ligon Duncan (Ross-Shire, U. K.: Christian Focus, 2003), 1:50.

5. John Calvin, *Institutes of the Christian Religion,* ed. John T. McNeill, trans. Ford Lewis Battles (Philadelphia: Westminster Press, 1960), 3.2.33.

Scripture as a whole. Separated from the whole content of revelation the 'saving message' evaporates into thin air and becomes something else than the Bible says it is."[6]

Third, the Holy Spirit guides the believer and the church to a proper and saving understanding of the Bible: "The whole counsel of God, concerning all things necessary for His own glory, man's salvation, faith, and life, is either expressly set down in Scripture, or by good and necessary consequence may be deduced from Scripture.... Nevertheless, we acknowledge the inward illumination of the Spirit of God to be necessary for the saving understanding of such things as are revealed in the Word" (WCF, 1.6).

Because of the darkening effects of sin on our minds, there is an absolute necessity for the work of the Holy Spirit with the Word upon the heart of the believer, enlightening his mind to make him understand and receive the mind of God revealed in the Bible.

However, the Confession makes clear that this illumination of the Spirit does not negate the necessity for diligent study of the Bible. In fact, it accompanies believing, diligent study of Scripture. As the Confession states, "All things in Scripture are not alike plain in themselves, nor alike clear to all; yet those things which are necessary to be known, believed, and observed, for salvation, are so clearly propounded and opened in some place of Scripture or other, that not only the learned, but the unlearned, in a due use of the ordinary means, may attain unto a sufficient understanding of them" (1.7).

The Relation of the Holy Spirit to the Person and Work of Christ

The Confession tells us two central truths about the relation of the Spirit to Jesus: the Spirit caused the sinless conception of Jesus and the Spirit enabled Jesus to accomplish His redemptive work.

First, let us consider the role of the Holy Spirit in the incarnation of Christ. How did it happen? The angel simply told Mary, "the Holy Ghost shall come upon thee, and the power of the Highest shall overshadow thee: therefore also that holy thing which shall be born of thee shall be called the Son of God" (Luke 1:35). This is all we know: the Holy Spirit caused Jesus' conception; He did not do it

---

6. Spear, "Word and Spirit," in *The Westminster Confession into the Twenty-First Century*, 1:55.

from a distance, but came upon Mary; and He worked this miracle by the almighty power of God.

This work of the Spirit in the incarnation resulted in the simultaneous creation of the humanity of Jesus from Mary, His mother, and the immaculate conception of Jesus, that is, the preservation of His humanity from sin. Edwin Palmer wrote: "Thus the Holy Spirit was necessary in Christ's life from its very inception. He was necessary for two reasons: first, in order that Christ might be born; and, second, in order that His human nature might be preserved from the guilt and corruption of Adam's sin so that He could be our Savior."[7] Jesus was "without sin, being conceived by the power of the Holy Ghost in the womb of the virgin Mary, of her substance" (8.2).

Second, consider the role of the Holy Spirit in equipping Jesus for His redemptive work. In the Westminster Confession, we read that the human nature of Jesus "was sanctified and anointed with the Holy Spirit above measure" (8.3) and are told that Jesus offered Himself in sacrifice unto God "through the eternal Spirit" (8.5). The first is a reference to John 3:34—"For He whom God hath sent speaketh the words of God: for God giveth not the Spirit by measure unto Him." The second refers to Hebrews 9:14—"how much more will the blood of Christ, who through the eternal Spirit offered Himself without blemish to God." O. Palmer Robertson writes:

> God's giving of the Holy Spirit to Christ at His baptism was the fulfillment of the Old Testament prophecy of the coming of the Spirit to the messianic King, enabling Him to be the servant of the Lord for our salvation (Isa. 11:1, 2; 42:1): It was in the power of this anointing Holy Spirit that Jesus presented His body as a sacrifice unblemished by sin which therefore could remove sin, Heb. 9:14. The presence of the Spirit in the offering of Christ assures the believer that this sacrifice was acceptable to God and so the conscience of the sinner can be freed to live a life of worshipful service. From the beginning of His ministry at the time of His baptism to the climactic offering of His life-blood in substitution for sinners, the power of the Holy Spirit was at work in Him. According to the testimony of the Confession, Christ offered His perfect obedience and sacrifice of Himself "through

7. Edwin H. Palmer, *The Person and Ministry of the Holy Spirit: The Traditional Calvinistic Perspective* (Grand Rapids: Baker, 1974), 67.

the eternal Spirit" (WCF, 8.5) and without the Spirit's work His obedience and sacrifice would have been impossible.[8]

The Objective Work of the Holy Spirit

The Holy Spirit's work is not entirely subjective, that is, in the soul of the believer. The Bible and the Confession present Him as doing many objective works outside the soul.

First, the Holy Spirit inspired the prophets and apostles to write the Holy Scriptures; they were breathed out by the Holy Spirit (2 Tim. 3:16), so that every word is God's Word. Robertson says: "Not a single bit of information ever at any time, can be added to the perfected words inspired by God's Spirit as found in the Scriptures. But now the finality of revelation through the Son has brought to perfection the previous pieces of the Spirit's work."[9] Second, the Holy Spirit caused the sinless conception of Jesus. Third, as we have seen, the Holy Spirit equipped Jesus to accomplish His redemptive work.

Fourth, the Holy Spirit created the world and all in it. The Confession states: "It pleased God the Father, Son and Holy Ghost, for the manifestation of the glory of His eternal power, wisdom and goodness, in the beginning to create, or make of nothing, the world and all things therein" (4.1). In the beginning, the Spirit hovered over the waters (Gen. 1:2). With the Father and Son, He created everything, including man: "The spirit of God has made me; the breath of the Almighty gives me life" (Job 33:4). He created life and He sustains it. Every second of our lives is sustained by the Holy Spirit. The life of every person on earth depends on the work of the Holy Spirit. Every human being owes his continued existence to Him.

The Subjective Work of the Holy Spirit in the Heart

The most complete teaching on the Holy Spirit in the Westminster Standards concerns the Spirit's role in the application of the benefits and realities of salvation to the hearts, lives, and personal histories of God's chosen people. As we teach our children, God the Father

---

8. O. Palmer Robertson, "The Holy Spirit in the Westminster Confession of Faith," in *The Westminster Confession into the Twenty-First Century*, 1:79.

9. Robertson, "The Holy Spirit," in *The Westminster Confession into the Twenty-First Century*, 1:76.

planned salvation, God the Son accomplished salvation, and God the Spirit applies salvation. The Holy Spirit is involved in every aspect of applied salvation.

It is by bringing us into vital union with Christ that the Spirit applies to us the benefits of salvation. What Joseph Pipa wrote about Calvin's teaching is just as applicable to the teaching of the Standards: "Union with Christ is essential to every aspect of the Christian life and the Spirit is essential to that union."[10] As the Confession states, "All saints that are united to Jesus Christ their head by His Spirit, and by faith, have fellowship with Him in His graces, suffering, death, resurrection and glory" (26.1). Therefore, "the members of the invisible church by Christ enjoy union and communion with Him in grace and glory" (WLC, Q. 65); "The communion in grace which the members of the invisible church have with Christ is their partaking of the virtue of His mediation, in their justification, adoption, sanctification, and whatever else in this life, manifests their union with Him" (WLC, Q. 69); and, "The communion in glory which the members of the invisible church have with Christ, is in this life, immediately after death, and at last perfected at the resurrection and day of judgment" (WLC, Q. 82).

The Larger Catechism puts it this way: "Christ, by His mediation, hath procured redemption, with all other benefits of the covenant of grace.... We are made partakers of the benefits which Christ hath procured, by the application of them unto us, which is the work especially of God the Holy Ghost.... Redemption is certainly applied and effectually communicated to all those for whom Christ has purchased it, who are in time by the Holy Ghost enabled to believe in Christ according to the gospel" (Q. 57–59).

Calvin explains why salvation must be personally applied to us if it is to be effective in saving us: "We must understand that as long as Christ remains outside of us, and we are separated from Him, all that He has suffered and done for the salvation of the human race remains useless and of no value for us.... The Holy Spirit is the bond by which Christ effectually unites us to Himself."[11]

10. Joseph Pipa, "Calvin on the Holy Spirit," in *Calvin for Today*, ed. Joel R. Beeke (Grand Rapids: Reformation Heritage Books, 2009), 60.

11. Calvin, *Institutes*, 1.7.5.

Robert Bruce's statement is a beautiful summary of what the Standards teach on the effects of the subjective work of the Spirit:

> What does the Spirit do as soon as He comes into us? He chases away darkness out of our understanding. Whereas before I know not God, now I see Him, not only with a general knowledge that He is God, but I know that He is God in Christ. What else does the Holy Spirit do? He opens the heart as well as the mind. Those things on which I bestowed the affection of my heart, and employed the love of my soul, are now, by the working of the Holy Spirit, made gall to me. He makes me hate them as much as poison. He produces such an inward disposition in my soul that He makes me turn and flee from the very thing on which I poured out my love before, and instead to pour it out upon God. This is a great perfection, but nevertheless, in some measure He makes me love God better than anything else. He changes the affections of my soul.[12]

The Standards also emphasize the relationship of the Holy Spirit to the covenant of grace. The Confession teaches us that the inner work of the Spirit is promised in this covenant, for in the covenant of grace, God "freely offers unto sinners life and salvation by Jesus Christ, requiring of them faith in Him, that they may be saved; and promising to give unto all those that are ordained unto life His Holy Spirit, to make them willing and able to believe," and thus receive all the benefits of the covenant of grace (7.3). Therefore, it is only in that covenant that the benefits of Christ's mediation are applied to us.

The benefits of salvation that Christ procured for us on the cross and that the Holy Spirit applies to all those ordained to eternal life include union with Christ, regeneration, effectual calling, faith, repentance, justification, adoption, sanctification, perseverance, assurance, good works, and glorification. The Standards explain how the Spirit is related to each of these benefits (see WLC, Q. 66, 67, 74–76, 79–83, 87, 90). Thomas Ridgeley commented:

> The Father is beheld and enjoyed, as his glory shines forth in the face of Christ, as bestowing on his saints all the blessings which he has promised in that everlasting covenant which was established with and in Christ, as their head and saviour; his

---

12. Robert Bruce, *The Mystery of the Lord's Supper*, trans. and ed. Thomas F. Torrance (London: James Clarke, 1958), 95.

purposes of grace, and all his promises having had their full accomplishment in him. The glory of Christ is beheld as the person to whom the whole work of redemption, together with the application of it, was committed, and by whom it is now brought to perfection. The Holy Ghost is beheld as the person who has, by his power, rendered every thing which was designed by the Father, and purchased by the Son, effectual to answer the end which is now attained, by shedding abroad the love of the Father and Son in their hearts, dwelling in them as his temple, and beginning, carrying on, and perfecting that work which is so glorious in its effects and consequences. In these respects the saints have perfect and distinct communion with the Father, Son, and Holy Ghost; which far exceeds all they can have here, and is infinitely preferable to all the delight which arises from that enjoyment which they have of the blessed society of perfect creatures to whom they are joined.[13]

Question 151 of the Larger Catechism explains that the Holy Spirit's work is so vital and so holy that offending "the Holy Spirit, His witness, and His workings" aggravates the guilt of the offender (see also WCF, 19.7; 20.1).

Although the Holy Spirit was active in the Old Testament church, a more extensive and copious effusion of the Spirit was reserved to the New Testament. This abundant outpouring of the Spirit, beginning with the day of Pentecost, was foretold in Isaiah 44:3 and Joel 2:28, 29. As Robert Shaw wrote:

Upon the ascension of Christ, and the commencement of the Christian dispensation, the extraordinary and miraculous gifts of the Spirit were communicated, not only to the apostles, but often to common believers; and the ordinary gifts and gracious influence of the Spirit are still conferred in richer abundance than under the former dispensation. Hence the Apostle Paul represents it as an eminent part of the glory of the New Testament...dispensation that it is "the ministration of the Spirit" (2 Cor. 3:8).[14]

---

13. Thomas Ridgeley, *A Body of Divinity...Being the Substance of Several Lectures on the Assembly's Larger Catechism* (Philadelphia: William W. Woodward, 1815), 3:398 (on Q. 90).

14. Robert Shaw, *The Reformed Faith: An Exposition of the Westminster Confession of Faith* (1845; repr., Inverness, U.K.: Christian Focus, 1974), 204.

The Westminster Confession agrees: "[Believers'] ability to do good works is not at all of themselves, but wholly from the Spirit of Christ. And that they may be enabled thereunto, besides the graces they have already received, there is required an actual influence of the same Holy Spirit to work in them to will and to do of His good pleasure; yet are they not hereupon to grow negligent, as if they were not bound to perform any duty unless upon a special motion of the Spirit" (16.3).

The relation of the Holy Spirit to justification is a subject largely neglected today, but the Standards make four points about this role of the Spirit: He applies the benefits of salvation to us (WLC, Q. 58); He makes justifying faith a saving faith (WLC, Q. 72); He applies Christ to the elect, justifying them (WCF, 11.4); and He infuses grace in sanctification (WLC, Q. 77). So, then, the Holy Spirit unites us to Christ and makes us partakers of all the blessings of Christ's redemption, including the actual application of the righteousness and life of Christ to those in whom He creates faith, truly making us complete in Christ.

In his *The Doctrine of Justification*, James Buchanan included an excellent chapter on this subject entitled "Justification: Its Relation to the Work of the Holy Spirit," in which he wrote:

> If the work of the Spirit in us consists merely in the effectual application of the work of Christ for us, and in making us partakers of all the blessings of His redemption, it follows that Regeneration and Justification are simultaneous, and that no man is justified who is not renewed, nor is any man renewed who is not also justified. This is a most important truth, and one that is sufficient to neutralize the two great errors, which have been maintained by opposite parties on this subject. The one is the error of the Antinomians, who have spoken of Justification as being antecedent to, and independent of, Regeneration by the Holy Spirit [as the carnal Christian heresy teaches today].... The other is the error of the Popish writers, and some of their followers in the Protestant Church, who have spoken of Justification as dependent, not on the finished work of Christ alone, but on our personal obedience and final perseverance; and have virtually postponed it till the judgment of the great day, as if it were not the present privilege of believers, and of every believer on the instant when he is united to Christ—or as if he did not receive

Christ for his sanctification, and even for his perseverance, as well as for the free pardon of all his sins, and the gracious acceptance of his person and services.[15]

Justification by faith and the promise of the Spirit by faith are the two focal points of Paul's gospel, as we see in Galatians 3:14. The doctrine of the Holy Spirit is a vital and essential complement to the doctrine of justification. Justification opens the way into new life; the Holy Spirit creates and develops that life. In justification, God removes the guilt and the sinner's liability to judgment; in regeneration and sanctification, the Spirit gradually removes the corruption of sin. In justification, God imputes righteousness to the believer; in sanctification, the Spirit infuses righteousness into him. In justification, God changes the legal standing of the sinner before Him; in sanctification, the Spirit changes his actual condition. All whom God declares righteous, the Spirit makes righteous.

The work of the Spirit *in* us is as necessary for our salvation as the work of Christ *for* us, but for different reasons. The Bible explicitly connects justification and the Holy Spirit in several texts, such as 1 Corinthians 6:11—"And such were some of you, but you were washed, but you were sanctified, but you were justified in the name of the Lord Jesus Christ and in the Spirit of our God."

So we see that although a distinction is to be clearly made between our justification and sanctification, both of these blessings of salvation are connected with the work of Christ and the work of the Spirit in different ways. The role of the Holy Spirit in justification is to bring the sinner into union with Christ; create in the sinner justifying faith; apply Christ to the believer; and give and develop that life of righteousness which justification makes legally possible.

Thus, we see that the life of the believer depends always on the constant work of the Holy Spirit within him. If God's people are to enjoy the benefits of salvation and live holy lives, they must remain in unbroken union and communion with the Spirit.

Although the believer struggles with his sin, and although that battle may be fierce, dependence on and faith in the Spirit of Christ guarantees growth in righteousness and Christlikeness. No matter

---

15. James Buchanan, *The Doctrine of Justification: An Outline of Its History in the Church and of Its Exposition from Scripture* (1867; repr., Edinburgh: Banner of Truth, 1961), 401–402.

how weak the believer feels in himself, he may be assured of the powerful work of the Spirit within him. "A continual and irreconcilable war" goes on in the believer, "the flesh lusting against the Spirit and the Spirit against the flesh" (WCF, 13.2). However, "through the continual supply of strength from the sanctifying Spirit of Christ" (WCF, 13.3), believers will get the victory over sin and continue to grow in grace and in the knowledge of Christ.

The Holy Spirit and the Means of Grace

God has been gracious in giving us ordinances that are means of grace to assist us in our Christian walk, most particularly the Word of God, the sacraments of baptism and the Lord's Supper, and prayer. The Larger Catechism explains in Question 154 that "[t]he outward and ordinary means whereby Christ communicates to His church the benefits of His mediation, are all His ordinances; especially the word, sacraments, and prayer; all which are made effectual to the elect for their salvation." Means of grace are not only Christian duties performed in obedience to God; they are also promises from God by which He assures and conveys to His people His presence and His saving, sanctifying grace by the work of His Spirit.

The Holy Spirit and the ministry of the Word

The Standards consistently emphasize the Spirit of God and the Word of God, as we have seen. The Holy Spirit works the Word of God into the believer, and the Word is powerless in us without the Holy Spirit; hence, the Bible is described as "the sword of the Spirit which is the Word of God" (Eph. 6:17). This truth is especially seen in the Spirit's relation to the reading and preaching of the Word of God. The Larger Catechism says:

> The Spirit of God maketh the reading but especially the preaching of the Word, an effectual means of enlightening, convincing, and humbling sinners; of driving them out of themselves, and drawing them to Christ; of conforming them to His image, and subduing them to His will; of strengthening them against temptations and corruptions; of building them up in graces, and establishing their hearts in holiness and comfort through faith unto salvation. (Q. 155)

The preacher of the Word has no control over the Word. Although preaching proceeds from frail men, nevertheless, when the preached Word is accompanied with the power of the Spirit, it accomplishes God's purposes in the hearts of all the hearers, saving some and hardening others.

As Calvin has written: "The Holy Spirit so inheres in His truth which He expresses in Scripture, that only when its proper reverence and dignity are given to the Word does the Holy Spirit show forth His power.... By a kind of mutual bond the Lord has joined together the certainty of His Word and of His Spirit so that the perfect religion of the Word may abide in our minds when the Spirit, who causes us to contemplate God's face, shines."[16]

The Holy Spirit and the sacraments

The sacraments of baptism and the Lord's Supper "become effectual means of salvation, not by any power in themselves, or any virtue derived from the piety or intention of Him by whom they are administered, but only by the working of the Holy Ghost, and the blessing of Christ, by whom they are instituted" (WLC, Q. 161).

The Holy Spirit, with the Word, makes the sacraments means of grace that really "signify, seal, and exhibit [convey] unto those that are within the covenant of grace, the benefits of His mediation; to strengthen and increase their faith, and all other graces, to oblige them to obedience; to testify and cherish their love and communion one with another; and to distinguish them from those that are without" (WLC, Q. 162).

The sacraments become powerfully effective means of God's saving grace by the working of the Spirit of Christ. Only He can make the sacraments effective in the lives of those for whom they were intended. He makes the sacraments "represent," "exhibit" (WLC, Q. 177), and "confer" (WCF, 27.3) Christ, the grace of God, and the benefits of Christ's mediation.

If the Holy Spirit is absent from the sacraments and other means of grace, Calvin wrote, they "accomplish nothing more in our minds than the splendor of the sun shining upon blind eyes, or a voice sounding in deaf ears. Therefore, I make such a division between Spirit and sacrament that the power to act rests with the former, and

---

16. Calvin, *Institutes*, 1.9.3.

the ministry alone is left to the latter—a ministry empty and trifling, apart from the action of the Spirit, but charged with great effect when the Spirit works within and manifests His power.... The Spirit transmits those outward words from the ears to our soul."[17]

It is the work of the Spirit that makes baptism a sign and a seal, an instrument that confirms the elect's participation in the benefits of salvation. Among other benefits, it is a sign and seal of "his engrafting into Christ, of regeneration" (WCF, 28.1). This has been misinterpreted by the federal vision theology to imply baptismal regeneration. However, baptism does not effect regeneration. Because baptism is a sign and a seal, the spiritual reality that is symbolized is presupposed; baptism does not create the reality. Baptism creates neither union with Christ nor regeneration; it presupposes that which it confirms, just as Abraham's circumcision was a seal of the righteousness of the faith that he had while uncircumcised (Rom. 4:11).

Also, it is by the work of the Spirit in the Lord's Supper that grace is exhibited and conferred. It is by the work of the Spirit that the Lord's Supper is effective in bringing spiritual nourishment from the exalted Christ, who is really and spiritually, though not physically, present in the Lord's Supper. It is the work of the Spirit that makes the Confession's statement true:

> Worthy receivers, outwardly partaking of the visible elements in this sacrament, do then also inwardly by faith, really and indeed, yet not carnally and corporally, but spiritually, receive and feed upon Christ crucified, and all benefits of His death: the body and blood of Christ being then not corporally or carnally in, with, or under the bread and wine, yet as really, but spiritually, present to the faith of believers in that ordinance, as the elements are to their outward senses. (29.7)

The Holy Spirit and prayer
The Larger Catechism defines prayer as "an offering up of our desires unto God in the name of Christ, by the help of His Spirit; with confession of our sins, and thankful acknowledgment of His mercies" (WLC, Q. 178). It then explains how the Spirit helps us in praying:

---

17. Calvin, *Institutes*, 4.14.9.

We not knowing what to pray for as we ought, the Spirit helpeth our infirmities, by enabling us to understand both for whom, and what and how prayer is to be made; and by working and quickening in our hearts (although not in all persons, nor at all times, in the same measure) those apprehensions, affections, and graces which are requisite for the right performances of that duty. (Q. 182)

This is obviously a reference to Romans 8:26–27, which teaches us that the Holy Spirit is essential to true prayer. Without the Spirit's help, we cannot pray. As D. Martyn Lloyd-Jones said, "Without the Holy Spirit prayer is mechanical, lifeless, difficult…prayer is an awful task, but with Him everything is changed and it becomes free and glorious and the supreme enjoyment of the soul."[18]

The Holy Spirit and the Non-Elect

We should discuss briefly one last issue regarding the Spirit mentioned in the Confession—His work in the non-elect: "Others, not elect, although they may be called by the ministry of the Word, and may have some common operations of the Spirit, yet they never truly come unto Christ, and therefore cannot be saved" (10.4).

What are these "common operations of the Spirit" that even those who will never be saved may experience? The scriptural support for this difficult statement is found in Matthew 7:22, Matthew 13:20–21, and Hebrews 6:4–6. The Assembly especially had the last text in mind. It states: "For it is impossible for those who were once enlightened, and have tasted of the heavenly gift, and were made partakers of the Holy Ghost, and have tasted the good word of God, and the powers of the world to come, if they shall fall away, to renew them again unto repentance; seeing they crucify to themselves the Son of God afresh, and put him to an open shame."

Besides the fact that the Holy Spirit sustains all human life, the Confession here is concerned with what the Spirit may do in the non-elect who will never be regenerated and saved. Robertson wrote on this issue:

Those who remain hardened in their sinful condition may nonetheless, be "called by the ministry of the Word" through

---

18. D. Martyn Lloyd-Jones, *God's Way of Reconciliation: Studies in Ephesians Chapter Two* (Grand Rapids: Baker, 1972), 273.

the working of the Holy Spirit (WCF, 10.4). Just how far the working of the Spirit goes into the soul of these who reject the gospel must remain a mystery beyond the knowledge of men. But the Scriptures indicate that they may "become partakers of the Holy Spirit," Heb. 6:4. They may taste the heavenly gift, they may taste the goodness of the Word of God, and in some undescribed way they may participate in the reality, of the Holy Spirit, Heb. 6:4, 5. This description must serve forever as a warning to the presumptuous who would dare to treat lightly the things of God, though it should not be allowed to terrify them who have experienced more than merely a taste of these realities.[19]

Grieving the Spirit

Sins forbidden in the first commandment include "resisting and grieving of His Spirit" (WLC, Q. 105). This answer explains Scripture's warnings: "Ye stiff-necked and uncircumcised in heart and ears, ye do always resist the Holy Ghost, as your fathers did, so do ye" (Acts 7:51); "And grieve not the Holy Spirit of God, whereby ye are sealed unto the day of redemption" (Eph. 4:30).

In Stephen's sermon that led to his martyrdom, he addressed his hearers as "stiff-necked and uncircumcised in heart and ears," charging that they were "always resisting the Holy Spirit" because they were persisting in their refusal to believe and obey God's Word, like their Old Testament fathers (Acts 7). He was echoing what God had said about Judah in the day of Jeremiah (9:26).

Because the hearts of Stephen's hearers were closed to God, their ears were closed to the Word of God; thus, they resisted that Word with all their might. To resist the preached Word is to resist the Spirit of that Word, who alone can work that Word into the heart. To resist the Holy Spirit is to cut oneself off from the only One who is able to apply the benefits of salvation. The Holy Spirit drives home the preached Word to the hearts of its hearers. He who resists the Word of God resists the Spirit speaking in that Word, whose Word it is.

Furthermore, Paul warns us in Ephesians 4 about "unwholesome words"—communication with others that lacks dignity, purity, or

---

19. Robertson, "The Holy Spirit," in *The Westminster Confession into the Twenty-First Century*, 1:82.

love, and is not "good for edification." This is language that not only injures others, but more importantly, also grieves the Holy Spirit of God. Therefore, he urges: "Let all bitterness and wrath and anger and clamor and slander be put away from you, along with all malice. And be kind to one another, tender-hearted, forgiving each other, just as God in Christ also has forgiven you" (Eph. 4:31–32).

What is it to grieve the Holy Spirit of God? And why is grieving the Spirit such a terrible thing?

First, because the people of God in Christ are the temple of God where the Holy Spirit lives (1 Cor. 3:16, 17), "to pollute the souls of believers by suggesting irreligious or impure thoughts to them is a profanation of the temple of God and an offence of the Holy Ghost," wrote Charles Hodge.[20] Second, the Holy Spirit who condescends to live in the believer's heart, is grieved and offended whenever we sin in the way Ephesians 4:30–32 describes. Therefore, reverence for the Holy Spirit who lives in other believers and in our own hearts should prevent our ever giving utterance to a corrupting thought. When the Spirit of God is offended, He is grieved. Not only is His holiness offended, but His love for us is also wounded.

Grieving the Spirit is heinous because He is the third Person in the blessed Trinity, and because He is the One who has sealed us for the day of redemption. Therefore, to grieve the Spirit is to show immense ingratitude to the One whose indwelling confirms that we are the children of God and who secures our eternal salvation (Eph. 1:13–14). To grieve Him, therefore, is to grieve Him on whom our salvation depends. As Hodge has written:

> Though He will not finally withdraw from those in whom He dwells, yet when grieved He withholds the manifestations of His presence.[21]

Conclusion

The Westminster Standards are unmistakably clear that we cannot make ourselves Christians. Only the Holy Spirit can make anyone a Christian. We cannot believe in Jesus without the Holy Spirit. We cannot think or live like Christians without the Holy Spirit. We can

---

20. Charles Hodge, *A Commentary on Ephesians* (1856; repr., Edinburgh: Banner of Truth, 1964), 199.

21. Hodge, *Ephesians*, 199.

neither preach the Word of God effectively nor hear it beneficially without the Holy Spirit. We will never believe that the Bible is the Word of God or understand it properly without the Holy Spirit. We cannot pray without the Holy Spirit. We cannot be good husbands, wives, fathers, or mothers unless we are filled with the Spirit, and we are filled with the Spirit only as the Word of God dwells richly in us. So, then, we must not resist or grieve the Spirit of Christ. Whenever we do so, we need to cry out to God for mercy and forgiveness.

CHAPTER 17

John Owen on the Holy Spirit in Relation to the Trinity, the Humanity of Christ, and the Believer

Ryan M. McGraw

The doctrine of the Trinity is increasingly misunderstood by church members, and it is often abstracted entirely from personal holiness. The doctrines of Scripture are practical, promoting communion with God as well as personal holiness. When doctrine no longer promotes godliness (Titus 1:1), that doctrine itself disappears.

In this respect, John Owen's teaching on the Holy Spirit potentially meets a great need in the church today. The doctrine of the Trinity was essential to him because it stood at the heart of the gospel and of Christian experience. The Savoy Declaration of Faith, which he helped produce, states that the "doctrine of the Trinity is the foundation of all our communion with God, and comfortable dependence upon him."[1] Owen's theology of the Holy Spirit takes the most fundamental doctrine of the Christian faith—the Trinity—and makes it the foundation of personal piety.

The central message of Owen's teaching on the Holy Spirit is that the eternal relationship between the Spirit and the other two Persons in the Godhead, coupled with the resulting connection between the Spirit and the human nature of Christ, are the foundation of the Spirit's work in believers. We shall consider, first, the relation of the Spirit to the Trinity; second, the relation of the Spirit to the incarnate Christ; and third, the relation of the Spirit to believers resulting from their union with Christ.[2]

---

1. Savoy Confession, 2.3. Cited from A. G. Matthews, *The Savoy Declaration of Faith and Order, 1658* (London: Independent Press, Ltd., 1959), 79.

2. This article is largely popular. My interest is not primarily historical, but to bring Owen into contemporary theological discussion and practice. In doing so, I have, in part, followed the model set by Alan Spence, *Incarnation and Inspiration:*

The Relation of the Holy Spirit to the Trinity

The Trinity is the thread that runs through Owen's entire theology.[3] He wrote his work on the Holy Spirit to counter the false teachings of the Socinians, Quakers, and anti-supernaturalists,[4] and to treat comprehensively the Person and work of the Holy Spirit in a manner that, in his view, no one else had done.[5] He published this work

---

John Owen and the Coherence of Christology (Edinburgh: T&T Clark, 2007). For a few works that establish Owen's historical and theological context, see Peter Toon, God's Statesman: The Life and Times of John Owen (Grand Rapids: Zondervan, 1973); Carl R. Trueman, John Owen: Reformed Catholic, Renaissance Man (Aldershot, U.K.: Ashgate, 2007); Richard A. Muller, Post-Reformation Reformed Dogmatics: Prolegomena to Theology (Grand Rapids: Baker Book House, 2001); Carl R. Trueman and R. Scott Clark, eds., Protestant Scholasticism: Essays in Reassessment (Carlisle, Cumbria: Paternoster, 2005); Willem J. Van Asselt, Introduction to Reformed Scholasticism, trans. Albert Gootjes (Grand Rapids: Reformation Heritage Books, 2011); John Coffey and Paul C. H. Lim, eds., The Cambridge Companion to Puritanism (Cambridge: Cambridge University Press, 2008); and Philip Benedict, Christ's Churches Purely Reformed: A Social History of Calvinism (New Haven: Yale University Press, 2002).

3. For Owen's Trinitarianism, see Carl R. Trueman, The Claims of Truth (Carlisle, Cumbria: Paternoster, 1998); Kelly Kapic, Communion with God: The Divine and the Human in the Theology of John Owen (Grand Rapids: Baker Academic, 2008); Brian K. Kay, Trinitarian Spirituality: John Owen and the Doctrine of God in Western Devotion (Eugene, Ore.: Wipf & Stock Publishers, 2007); Robert Letham, "John Owen's Doctrine of the Trinity and Its Significance for Today," in Where Reason Fails: Papers Read at the 2006 Westminster Conference (Stoke-on-Trent, U.K.: Tentmaker Publications, 2006).

4. John Owen, Pneumatologia, in The Works of John Owen (repr., Edinburgh: Banner of Truth Trust, 1976), 3:7–8, 36–39. For a brief survey of this controversy, see Joel M. Heflin, "Omnipotent Sweetness? Puritanism Versus Socinianism," in Puritan Reformed Journal 1, 2 (July 2009): 64–95. For the Socinian controversy as it related to Thomas Goodwin and Owen in particular, see Mark Jones, Why Heaven Kissed Earth (Göttingen: Vandenhoeck & Ruprecht, 2010), 69–71. See also Philip Dixon, Nice and Hot Disputes: The Doctrine of the Trinity in the Seventeenth Century (Edinburgh: T&T Clark, 2007).

5. Owen, Works, 7:22. Geoffrey Nuttall observed: "When John Owen, in the preface to his Pneumatalogia, declares, 'I know not any who ever went before me in this design of representing the whole economy of the Holy Spirit,' he is neither ignorant of, nor antagonistic to, the work of the early Fathers. Indeed, he explicitly combines 'the suffrage of the ancient church' with the 'plain testimonies of the Scripture' and 'the experience of them who do sincerely believe' as the foundation on which 'the substance of what is delivered' securely rests.... What is new, and what justifies Owen in his claim to be among the pioneers, is the place given in Puritan exposition to experience, and its acceptance as a primary authority, in the way indicated in the passage just quoted. The interest is primarily not dogmatic, at least not in any theoretic sense, it is experimental. There is theology, but, in a way which has hardly been known since St. Augustine, it is theologia pectoris." Geoffrey

gradually in several parts. Volume 3 of the Goold edition of Owen's *Works* marks the first installment of this project. This volume primarily treats the person of the Holy Spirit in relation to the Trinity, the Spirit in relation to Christ, and the Spirit's work in producing holiness in believers. Volume 4 concludes his labor by addressing the work of the Spirit and the authority of Scripture, illumination, prayer, spiritual comfort, and spiritual gifts. In his view, the triune God meets the redeemed sinner in the Person and work of the Holy Spirit, and the sinner approaches the triune God through Him. This makes Owen's treatment eminently practical. His practical emphasis resulted from the unity of the works of the Godhead in time and the fact that the Spirit proceeds from the Father *and* the Son.

The external works of the Trinity are undivided
(Opera Trinitatis ad extra indivisa sunt)

Owen began with the unity of God and of His works. Because God is one, the external works of the Trinity are undivided. This means that the works of God in time are always works of the entire Trinity. No divine Person is excluded from any work of God. In its Latin expression, this largely Augustinian principle has dominated the Western understanding of the Trinity.[6] This means that whether we consider creation, providence, the incarnation of Christ, or anything that God has done, we must consider all three Persons of the Trinity as the objects of faith and worship. This is why it is wrong to isolate the work of the Holy Spirit from the work of the Father and the Son.

However, this principle recognizes that while all three Persons in the Godhead act simultaneously—expressing the fact that each is fully divine—each divine Person acts distinctly in every work of God.[7] The Father always represents the authority of the Godhead, the Son is the instrument by which the Father accomplishes

---

F. Nuttall, *The Holy Spirit in Puritan Faith and Experience*, with a new introduction by Peter Lake (Chicago: University of Chicago Press, 1992), 7.

6. Owen, *Works*, 3:93, citing Athanasius and Basil; see also 66–68. For Owen's dependence upon both Eastern and Western Trinitarianism, Letham wrote elsewhere, "Owen is not so much an innovator as a brilliant synthesizer." *Where Reason Fails*, 11. For the manner in which Western Trinitarianism pervaded Owen's thought, even in his views of communion with the three Persons, see Trueman, *The Claims of Truth*.

7. Owen, *Works*, 3:93.

His purposes, and the Holy Spirit finishes or perfects every work of God.[8] According to Owen, we can never understand the peculiar work of the Holy Spirit unless we first have an adequate notion of the unity of all three Persons in every act of God in time.

"...and the Son..." (filioque)

Western Christians who use the Nicene Creed confess regularly that they believe that the Holy Spirit proceeds from the Father and the Son. While this phrase has marked a dividing line between the Western and the Eastern churches, it is important to note that the procession of the Spirit from the Son as well as from the Father was integral to Owen's Trinitarian piety.[9] Following the unity of the Trinity in every divine action, he treated the distinction and the relation between the Persons, both in eternity and in time. His primary target was Socinian anti-Trinitarianism.[10] In this context, he insisted upon the necessity of the so-called *filioque* clause of the creed.[11] This clause has come under attack recently in the West for at least two reasons. First, some have argued that the eternal generation of the Son and the eternal procession of the Spirit are speculative doctrines that go beyond Scripture, and that they have no practical bearing on how we understand the gospel.[12] Second, others have asserted that as long

---

8. Owen, *Works*, 3:94–95. See examples on pp. 95–99. Thomas Manton noted similarly, "There is a chain of salvation; the beginning is from the Father, the dispensation through the Son, the application by the Spirit; all cometh from God, and is conveyed to us through Christ by the Spirit." Thomas Manton, *Sermons on John XVII*, in *The Complete Works of Thomas Manton* (repr., Birmingham: Solid Ground Christian Books, 2008), 10:205.

9. See Robert Letham, *Through Western Eyes: Eastern Orthodoxy: A Reformed Perspective* (Tain, Fearn, U.K.: Christian Focus Publications, 2007), 221–42. It is beyond the scope of this essay to treat Owen's defense of the *filioque* clause. I simply state that authors such as Letham who are critical of the phrase have largely bypassed the period of seventeenth-century Reformed Orthodoxy and the fruitful manner in which men of that time connected the *filioque* clause to the *fons deitatis* principle mentioned below.

10. Owen's Dutch contemporary, Herman Witsius (1636–1708), referred to the Socinians as "the very worst perverters of Scripture." Herman Witsius, *The Economy of the Covenants Between God and Man*, trans. William Crookshank (1822; repr., Grand Rapids: Reformation Heritage Books, 2010), 1:166.

11. Owen, *Works* 3:92, 116–18, 162, 190–91, 195–96, etc.

12. For instance, Robert L. Reymond has pressed this assertion in virtually every book he has written. In Robert L. Reymond, "The Trinitarianism of the Westminster Confession of Faith: Nicene or Reformed?," in *Contending for the Faith: Lines*

as we understand the relationship between the Son and the Spirit in terms of the teaching of Athanasius, we may discard the *filioque* clause with little consequence.[13]

According to Owen, our understanding of the work of the Trinity in redemption hinges upon the *filioque* clause.[14] He taught in common with both the East and the West that the Father is the *fons et origio deitatis* ("the fountain and origin of the deity").[15] This does not

---

in the Sand that Strengthen the Church (Tain, Fearn, U.K.: Christian Focus Publications, 2005), 117–124, he asserts that contrary to the opinion of some, he has not changed his position.

13. See Douglas F. Kelly, *Systematic Theology, Volume One: Grounded in Holy Scripture and Understood in Light of the Church* (Tain, Fearn, U.K.: Christian Focus Publications, 2008), 577.

14. Owen, *Works*, 3:157.

15. Owen, *Works*, 3:19, 43, 60, 92, 94, etc. These citations include language such as, "the fountain and original of the Deity" (43), "*fons et origio Trinitatis*" (60), and "*fons et origio Deitatis*" (94). On page 197, he explained this idea in terms of Christ receiving His personal subsistence by means of the Father communicating to Him "the whole entire divine nature." In other words, the thought of receiving personal subsistence from the Father and an eternal communication of the deity of the Father are inseparable. The Son and the Spirit are both God in and of themselves, and the Father eternally communicates both essence and personal subsistence to them. The divine order of subsistence actually pervades the whole of Owen's work on the Holy Spirit, but it is most concentrated in the first two hundred pages or so. In volume 4, he gave the following summary: "The person of the Father is the eternal fountain of infinitely divine glorious perfections; and they all are communicated unto the Son by eternal generation. In his person *absolutely*, as the Son of God, they are all of them *essentially*; in his person as God-man, as vested with his offices, they are *substantially*, in opposition unto all types and shadows; and in the glass of the gospel they are *accidentally*, by revelation,—*really*, but not *substantially*, for Christ himself is the body, the substance of all." *Works*, 4:169.

The Father is the origin of an eternal communication of what are, in the case of creatures, the incommunicable attributes of deity to the Son and to the Holy Spirit. With respect to the Son in Himself, this means that He is God equal with the Father. With respect to His office as Mediator between God and man as well as His work as the revealer of the Father, He sets the deity on display according to His offices. See also Thomas Goodwin, *Sermons on Ephesians 1–2*, in *The Works of Thomas Goodwin* (repr., Grand Rapids: Reformation Heritage Books, 2006), 1:15, 26. Owen's contemporary Edward Leigh wrote: "The personal property of the Father is to beget, that is, not to multiply his substance by production, but to communicate his substance to the Son. The Son is said to be begotten, that is, to have his whole substance from the Father by communication. In like manner, the Holy Spirit eternally proceeds from the substance of the Father, through the Son." *A System or Body of Divinity* (London: A.M. for William Lee, 1654), 206. While John Calvin believed that the Father was the fountain of the personality of the Son, but that the Son was of Himself (*autotheos*) with reference to His deity, Mark Jones asserts that most of the Reformed Orthodox

mean that the deity of the Son or the Spirit is inferior to the deity of
the Father, but that both deity and personal subsistence are communicated eternally from the Father to the other two Persons. There are
no degrees of deity and there is no subordination of the Persons to
one another. Nevertheless, the Son is related to the Father in terms of
"eternal generation" and the Spirit is related to both the Father and
the Son by "eternal procession." In the latter case, the Spirit proceeds
eternally from the Father through the Son. These eternal relations
within the Godhead are deduced largely from the manner in which
the Persons work in the world. In other words, it was not arbitrary
that the Son was incarnated rather than the Father or the Holy Spirit.[16] The Father would not be the eternal Father without an eternal
Son, and the Son would not be God equal with the Father unless He
was "eternally begotten."[17] It is not fitting for the Father to be begotten; this work is proper to the Son alone. Similarly, the fact that the
Father sent the Spirit on the day of Pentecost through Jesus reflects
the eternal order within the Godhead.[18] The significance of these
things will be clarified below. The primary point is that the order of
the persons in the Godhead is both eternal and irreversible.

The peculiar work of the Holy Spirit

The order of subsistence determines how we understand the work of
the Holy Spirit. In creating the world, for instance, the Father acted
by means of the Son, who is His Word. The Spirit perfected the work
of God by bringing order to creation when He hovered over the face

---

did not follow him on this point. Jones concludes, "That most of the Reformed
Orthodox were both 'Nicenists' and 'Autotheanites' seems to be a fairly accurate
description in light of the evidence above." *Why Heaven Kissed Earth*, 116.

16. Owen, *Works*, 3:116–18.

17. Owen asserted that anti-Trinitarians do not even hold the deity of the
Father in common with the orthodox, since we cannot understand an eternal Father
without reference to an eternal Son, and that this Son cannot be eternal unless He
participates in the full divinity of the Father. See *A Brief Explanation and Vindication
of the Doctrine of the Trinity, Works*, 2:382: "Whoever denies Christ the Son, as the Son,
that is, the eternal Son of God, he loses the Father also, and the true God; he hath
not God. For that God which is not the Father, and which ever was, and was not the
Father, is not the true God." Similarly, the Westminster divine, Francis Cheynell,
wrote, "Moreover, if the Father have not a *divine* and *eternal* Son how is he a *divine*
and *eternal* Father?" *The Divine Triunity of the Father, Son, and Holy Ghost* (London,
1650), 54 (emphasis original).

18. Owen, *Works*, 3:114, 118.

of the deep. Owen believed that one unique aspect of his work was his treatment of the work of the Holy Spirit in the "old creation."[19] The reason was that he treated extensively Adam's dependence upon the Holy Spirit in his obedience prior to falling into sin. The "old creation" refers to the created order prior to the Fall. By contrast, the "new creation" refers to the covenant of grace, whether under its Old Testament or its New Testament dispensations.[20] Owen's treatment of the work of the Spirit in the "old creation" illustrates how he used the *opera trinitatis* principle; all three Persons of the Trinity worked simultaneously when They said, "Let us make man in our image, according to our likeness" (Gen. 1:26). Since the Spirit perfects the works of God, the Spirit in particular made Adam in the image of God.[21] This is inferred partly through hindsight from the New Testament, which assigns the task of renewing believers in the image of God to the Holy Spirit. Owen concluded that the Spirit is the direct author of every good thing that people enjoy in this world, including what is called "common grace."[22]

In practical terms, this means that we must understand all of the works of God, including the gospel, in Trinitarian terms. We must regard all three Persons of the Godhead together, as well as each Person distinctly. Ephesians 2:18 was one of Owen's favorite passages: "For through him we both have access by one Spirit unto the Father."[23] This verse encapsulates the heart of his Trinitarian piety. He added that the Holy Spirit is the only Person of the Godhead that we deal with "immediately" in this life.[24] He is the point at which the Father comes to us through the Son, and He is the means by which we come to the Father through the Son. If we connect the work of the Spirit to the Father, but not through Christ, we will be tempted to come to the Father apart from the Son. This would alter our relationship to all three Persons in the Godhead, which would distort the

---

19. Owen, *Works*, 3:7, 93, 125.

20. Owen, *Works*, 3:125. Manton includes a similar idea in *Works*, 10:133.

21. Owen, *Works*, 3:101.

22. Owen, *Works*, 3:103–104.

23. "Both" refers to Jews and Gentiles. This passage appears often in Owen's works. The idea presented in it is the foundation of his work on communion with God, and it is the primary text for his two sermons on communion with God in public worship in volume 9, among other places.

24. Owen, *Works*, 3:157.

gospel itself. In this light, it is not accidental that the Scriptures refer to the Spirit as both the Spirit of the Father and the Spirit of Christ (Rom. 8:9, 11).

If Owen is correct here, much of the confusion connected to the Person and work of the Holy Spirit at present illustrates how we have lost the practical significance of historic Trinitarian theology. Various forms of Christianized mysticism seek to experience the Holy Spirit in detachment from Christ. Liberal theology desires to call God "Father" apart from the Person and work of the Son, and without the regenerating power of the Spirit. Only a robust Trinitarian gospel brings sinners to a loving Father, through faith in the Son's work as Mediator, by the powerful operation of the Spirit in our hearts. Reversing or amending this order means the death of biblical Christianity.

The Relation of the Holy Spirit to the Incarnate Christ

If the Spirit is linked intimately to the Son in the eternal Godhead, then His work should naturally be connected closely with the incarnate Christ. According to Owen, the relationship between the Spirit and the humanity of Jesus is both the foundation of and the prototype for His work in believers.[25] Few authors have developed this theme adequately.[26] By looking at the ways in which the Holy Spirit operated upon the human nature of Jesus Christ, we understand how the Holy Spirit works in redeemed humanity in union with Christ.

Owen addressed ten ways in which the Spirit operated upon Christ's humanity.[27] I have reduced them to the work of the Spirit

---

25. Owen, *Works*, 3:368.

26. See Sinclair Ferguson, *The Holy Spirit* (Downers Grove, Ill.: InterVarsity Press, 1996), 37, note 2. Spence has argued that Owen's connection between the work of the Spirit and the humanity of Christ is vital for contemporary Christology. Spence, *Incarnation and Inspiration*.

27. The ten facets of the work of the Spirit upon the humanity of Christ that Owen expounded are: 1. The work of the Spirit in the miraculous conception of Jesus (*Works*, 3:162–68). 2. His work in sanctifying the human nature of Christ (168–69). 3. His ongoing work in Christ's actual obedience (169–71). 4. The manner in which He endowed Jesus with the supernatural gifts that were necessary to fulfill His office (171–73). 5. His operation in Christ's miracles (174). 6. Serving as the conduit of communion between the divine and human natures of Christ for His support and comfort in His work (174–75). 7. Effecting the atonement upon the cross (176–79). 8. Preventing the natural corruption of Jesus' body while He was in the tomb (179–80). 9. Though the resurrection of Christ is assigned to all three Persons in Scripture,

in Christ's incarnation, His life and ministry, and His death. In each case, it is vital to remember Owen's assertion that the Spirit perfects or completes every divine work.

The work of the Spirit in Christ's incarnation

The angel stated that the Holy Spirit would overshadow the womb of the Virgin Mary and that the "holy thing" in her would be born of God (Luke 1:35). The Father prepared Jesus' body in His eternal counsel (Heb. 10:5), the Son assumed it, and the Spirit effected the union of His deity and humanity in one Person (Matt. 1:18, 20; Luke 1:35).[28] This parallels almost exactly Owen's treatment of the work of the Godhead in the creation of the world. In both cases, the Spirit perfects or completes the work.

Closely tied to the work of the Spirit in the incarnation of Christ is the Spirit's work in Christ's "sanctification." Sanctification here means "set apart as holy." This meant far more, in Owen's view, than declaring that the Son of God incarnate was holy. Christ's sanctification is parallel to the work of the Holy Spirit in Adam under the "old creation." No creature can render obedience to God in a manner that is worthy to merit everlasting life. Under the covenant of works, Adam could acquire the promise of eternal life only by virtue of his covenant relationship to God.[29] Adam's true failure in the garden was that he stopped depending upon the Holy Spirit in order to obey God. Even a perfect creature is a creature still, and must depend absolutely upon the Creator. The humanity of Christ was no exception. Christ's sanctification by the Holy Spirit furnished His human nature with a "habit" of holiness, by which He was equipped to perform every

---

it is peculiarly the work of the Spirit (181–83). 10. The same Spirit who in the incarnation made the human nature holy made it glorious following His resurrection (184).

28. Owen, *Works*, 3:163. The Scripture references are Owen's.

29. Similarly, Westminster Confession of Faith 7.1 states that mankind could not enjoy God as his blessedness or reward without a "voluntary condescension" on God's part by way of covenant. We must not confuse Owen's position with that of Roman Catholicism, which asserted that there was something inherently defective in Adam's flesh that required supernatural grace in order to acquire righteousness. Instead, Adam's righteousness was natural even though he needed to depend upon the Holy Spirit in his obedience. Compare to Francis Turretin, *Institutes of Elenctic Theology*, trans. George Musgrave Giger, ed. James T. Dennison, Jr. (Phillipsburg, N.J.: P&R Publishing, 1992), 1:470–73, Topic 5, Question 11.

"actual" act of obedience.[30] Thus, the Spirit both united the divine and human natures of Christ, and He prepared Christ's human nature to fulfill all righteousness as a dependent creature.

The work of the Spirit in Christ's life and ministry

The Spirit was Christ's constant companion in His life and work. According to Owen, this meant that by the Spirit, Christ grew in obedience at every stage of human development. Though Christ was never ignorant or negligent of what He should have known or done,[31] yet He learned new duties and exercised new obedience appropriate to every stage of life. His theoretical and experimental knowledge grew simultaneously.[32] His obedience as a twelve-year-old differed from His obedience as a twenty-year-old; both differed in expression from His obedience during His public ministry. In Owen's view, the statement in Luke 2:40 that Jesus grew in wisdom and stature and in favor with God and men fulfilled Isaiah 11:1–3.[33] This prophecy states, "And there shall come forth a rod out of the stem of Jesse, and a Branch shall grow out of his roots: and the spirit of the LORD shall rest upon him, the spirit of wisdom and understanding, the spirit of counsel and might, the spirit of knowledge and of the fear of the LORD; and shall make him of quick understanding in the fear of the LORD." The Spirit filled the human nature

---

30. In Owen's view, with reference to Jesus, "sanctification" is "an original infusion of all grace into the human nature of Christ" (3:168). This re-enforces the point that even Adam in innocence would have needed the Holy Spirit to fulfill the terms of the covenant of works. Even sinless human beings need "supernatural endowments of grace.... This was the image of God in Adam, and was wrought in Christ by the Holy Spirit" (3:168). Isaiah 11:1–3 is a prediction that Christ would obey God by the power of the Holy Spirit. In this view, the fall involved losing "the original grace of God" (3:244). Owen argued that there were at least three ways in which the sanctification of believers by the Spirit is connected to Jesus Christ: "We are crucified with him *meritoriously,* in that he procured the Spirit for us to mortify sin; *efficiently,* in that from his death virtue comes forth for our crucifying; in the way of a *representation* and *exemplar* we shall assuredly be crucified unto sin, as he was for our sin." *Of the Mortification of Sin in Believers; The Necessity Nature and Means of it: With a Resolution of Sundry Cases of Conscience Thereunto Belonging,* in *Works,* 6:85. Christ merits sanctification for believers by His death in order to create within them a disposition to mortify sin. For more references to this twofold sanctification, see *Works,* 3:370, 432, 497, 517, 540, 545, 551–56. See also Manton, *Works,* 10:203.

31. Owen, *Works,* 3:170.

32. Owen, *Works,* 3:170.

33. Owen, *Works,* 3:170.

of Christ with every grace necessary to live a perfect human life. Jesus' personal righteousness is not simply identical to His divine nature.[34] He not only possessed perfect divine righteousness, but also perfect human righteousness. His human righteousness was rooted in His relationship to the Holy Spirit.

In addition to the graces of the Spirit, Christ received the gifts of the Holy Spirit to enable Him to fulfill His mediatorial office. The gifts and graces of the Holy Spirit are not always united. Judas Iscariot and King Saul possessed gifts from the Spirit without the grace of the Spirit.[35] Yet Christ had all of the gifts and the graces of the Holy Spirit. In particular, He received the gifts of the Spirit at His baptism.[36] This included His ability to do miracles and to finish His Father's work.[37]

The work of the Spirit in Christ's death

Relying primarily upon Hebrews 9:14, Owen argued that Christ's atonement was a work of the undivided Trinity.[38] The Son offered Himself to the Father by means of the Holy Spirit. Owen stressed that at least two things were necessary to make the cross an acceptable atonement. First, the sacrifice had to be voluntary on the part of the Son and not imposed by law. Second, the offering had to be rendered by the Holy Spirit. The Holy Spirit was the "altar" upon which Christ offered His sacrifice to the Father.[39]

---

34. See Westminster Larger Catechism, question 38.

35. See also Thomas Goodwin, *Exposition of Ephesians 1 and 2, Part 1*, in *The Works of Thomas Goodwin* (London: 1681), 1:49–50.

36. Owen, *Works*, 3:172. Witsius (citing Owen, among others) added that Christ's baptism was a sacramental seal of the terms of the eternal covenant between the Father and the Son. Witsius, *Economy of the Covenants*, 1:172, 176–77. The Spirit did not simply come upon Christ as a righteous man, but as a covenantal Head and representative of His people.

37. Owen, *Works*, 3:174.

38. "How much more shall the blood of Christ, who through the eternal Spirit offered himself without spot to God, purge your conscience from dead works to serve the living God?" For Owen on the atonement, see Edwin Tay, "The Priesthood of Christ in the Atonement Theology of John Owen (1616–1683)" (PhD diss., University of Edinburgh, 2009).

39. Owen, *Works*, 3:176. This does not mean that the Son was not obligated as Mediator both to obey the law of God and to bear the curse of the law on behalf of His people. Witsius noted that the root of every aspect of Christ's work was a

In conclusion, Owen taught that the ministry of the Holy Spirit was essential to every stage of Jesus' incarnate life and work. As a result, Jesus is the prototype of the work of the Holy Spirit in every believer. The Spirit sanctified Christ from His mother's womb, He descended upon Christ at His baptism, He drove Jesus into the wilderness to be tempted by the devil, He was with Jesus in His teaching and preaching, His power was active in every miracle, He led Christ to the cross, and He was involved in Christ's resurrection. As a result of all of these things, the Spirit descended upon believers from the ascended Christ on the day of Pentecost. The Spirit is justly called the "Spirit of Christ!"[40]

The Relation of the Holy Spirit to Believers

Owen's primary aim in His work on the Holy Spirit was the personal holiness of believers.[41] The latter half of volume 3 treats this subject extensively. Holiness is the Spirit's work, but it is rooted in the believer's union with Jesus Christ. Union with Christ is the means by which believers partake of the graces of the Holy Spirit. This union makes sanctification possible.[42] Below are a few seed thoughts from Owen on the work of the Spirit in the lives of believers.

First, the Spirit unites believers to Christ. Owen noted that the Holy Spirit is Christ's "great legacy to his disciples."[43] Uniting believers to Christ is the first parallel to the Spirit's work in Christ's humanity. As the Spirit united the human and divine natures of Christ in one Person, so He unites believers to the Person of Christ.[44] This does not mean that believers are deified. It means that all that Christ did by and through the Spirit belongs to them. Believers not only partake of the benefits of Christ's life and death, they partake

---

"voluntary covenant engagement" with the Father. Witsius, *Economy of the Covenants*, 1:181.

40. For Owen's expansion of this conclusion, see *Works*, 3:184–88.

41. Owen wrote later, "Our principal duty in this world is, to know aright what it is to be holy, and to be so indeed." *Works*, 3:370.

42. Owen added that union with Christ consists of sharing with Him the indwelling of the Holy Spirit. *Works*, 3:478.

43. Owen, *Works*, 3:156.

44. According to Owen, the Spirit is the substance of the promise that the Father gave to Christ. This promise was fulfilled first in Christ's Person and then in sending the Holy Spirit to His people. This is connected to Owen's view of the *filioque* clause. *Works*, 3:191. See also 3:478.

of the Holy Spirit through union with Christ. This means that every work of the Spirit in the life of a believer is connected inextricably to Christ. If the Spirit's work in Christ is the foundation of the Spirit's work in believers, then the Spirit never works in believers apart from Christ. The "Spirit of Christ" is a Christ-centered Spirit.

Second, the Spirit regenerates and gifts believers. As the Spirit sanctified Christ at His birth and then subsequently enabled Him to obey the law throughout His life, so the Spirit sanctifies believers in their regeneration and then enables them to progress in holiness.[45] With respect to the Spirit's gifts—though some possess His gifts without His graces—Christ procured them for the church by means of His death, resurrection, and ascension.[46] While no single believer possesses all of the gifts of the Spirit, the church as the body of Christ possesses them as a whole. He received the Spirit without measure (John 3:34) so that His people could receive the Spirit and His gifts by measure.

Third, the intimate link between the Spirit and Christ has ramifications for reading the Bible. Owen wrote, "Take away the Spirit from the gospel and you render it a dead letter, and leave the New Testament of no more use unto Christians than the Old Testament is of use unto the Jews."[47] In striking fashion, he added, "He that would utterly separate the Spirit from the word had as good burn his Bible."[48] The Spirit makes the truths of Scripture live in Christians' hearts.[49]

---

45. He defined sanctification as a progressive work as follows: "It is the universal renovation of our natures by the Holy Spirit into the image of God, through Jesus Christ." *Works*, 3:386. A little later, he highlighted the Trinitarian nature of sanctification by noting that the Father takes care for this work, Christ is the fountain from which it proceeds, and the Holy Spirit is the "efficient cause" of it. *Works*, 3:393.

46. In this connection, Owen made extended reference to Ephesians 4:17–18. *Works*, 3:249–53. For an extended treatment of his views on spiritual gifts, see *Works*, 4:420–520.

47. Owen, *Works*, 3:26.

48. Owen, *Works*, 3:192.

49. For his treatment of the work of the Holy Spirit in providing both the objective grounds for belief in the Scriptures as well as the subjecting and saving understanding of the Scriptures, see *The Reason of Faith; or An Answer unto that Inquiry, 'Wherefore We Believe the Scripture to be the Word of God;' With the Causes and Nature of that Faith Wherewith We do so: Wherein the Grounds Whereupon the Holy Scripture is Believed to be the Word of God with Faith Divine and Supernatural are Declared and Vindicated*, in *Works*, 4:4–115. For the manner in which the work of the Spirit is embedded into his definition of true theology, see Owen, *Theologoumena Pantodapa,*

Conclusions

Keeping in mind that his historical context differs from our own, we may draw lessons from Owen's teaching by way of analogy.

First, the doctrine of the Trinity should be central in our personal assurance of salvation. If the doctrine of the Trinity is nothing more to us than a "fundamental" doctrine of Scripture, without bearing daily on our Christian experience, then spiritual problems arise. For instance, we tend to divide the Person and work of the Holy Spirit from the Father and the Son. Even when we do not doubt the Son's willingness and ability to save sinners (the Father, sadly, is often another matter!),[50] we may doubt whether we have the marks of saving grace in us. Therefore, we begin by looking within ourselves to see whether we can detect the marks of the Holy Spirit's work. This is not entirely wrong. We must look to the fruit of the Spirit in our lives, and it is the Spirit with whom we deal immediately. However, if we detach the work of the Holy Spirit in our lives from the work of the Son and of the Father, then we will end in despair. The Spirit is the Spirit of Christ, and He always works to glorify Christ.

When we doubt the work of the Holy Spirit within us, then we must follow the Spirit as He drives us back to Christ. We must draw from Jesus every supply of grace and ability necessary to live the Christian life. Only as we look to Christ will we behold the smiling face of the Father and discover His unsearchable love.[51] It is then alone that we

---

Sive de Natura, Ortu, Pregressu, et Studio Verae Theologiae, Libri Sex; Quibus etiam Origines et Processus Veri et Falsi Cultus Religiosi, Causus et Instaurationes Ecclesiae Illustriores ab Ipsis Rerus Primordiis Ennarantur; Accedunt Digressiones de Gratia Universali, Scientiarum Ortu, Ecclesiae Notis, Literarum Origine, Antiquis Litteris Hebraicis, Punctatione Hebraica, Versionibus S.S., Ritibus Judiaicis, Aliisque (Oxford: Printed for Thomas Robinson, 1661), lib. I, cap. II, 7. He described true theology subjectively as the rebirth of man's mind by the Holy Spirit. *Theologoumena*, 487.

50. "Few can carry their hearts and minds to this height by faith, as to rest their souls in the love of the Father; they live below it, in the troublesome region of hopes and fears, storms and clouds. All here is serene and quiet. But how to attain this pitch, they know not." Owen, *Works*, 2:23.

51. "If the love of a father will not make a child delight in him, what will? Put, then, this to the venture: exercise your thoughts upon this very thing, the eternal, free, and fruitful love of the Father, and see if your hearts be not wrought upon to delight in him. I dare boldly say, believers will find it as thriving a course as ever they pitched on in their lives. Sit down a little at the fountain, and you will quickly have a discovery of the sweetness of the streams. You who have run from him, will not be able, after a while, to keep at a distance for a moment." Owen, *Works*, 2:36.

will see the fruits of the Spirit's work in holiness. Sometimes we treat the fruit of the Spirit in our lives like an apple that is detached from a tree. It may appear to live for a time, but as long as it is detached from the tree it is not truly alive. How, then, can we look for the fruit of the Spirit in our lives apart from the person and work of Christ? The fruit of the Spirit grows upon the vine that is Christ. If we lack the fruit of the Spirit, we must go back to the vine for life and vitality. We must go to Christ to supply all that we need. We need to trust in Him for sanctification as well as for justification, and then we will be neither barren nor unfruitful in the knowledge of God (2 Peter 1:8). When we fail to trust in Christ for the fruit of the Spirit because we doubt we are in Christ, have we not forgotten that the Spirit produces fruit by uniting us to Christ? We must regard the Persons of the Godhead in their proper order of operation. If we desire a steady assurance of salvation, then we must root our faith in a robust practical Trinitarianism.

Second, the church desperately needs Trinity-saturated preaching and teaching. Robert Letham asserted, "A Trinitarian mind-set must become as integral to the preacher as the air we breathe."[52] The greatest prayer of every minister with respect to his preaching, and the highest longing of the church for her ministers, should be for the presence and power of the Holy Spirit. Yet what are we praying for and what do we endeavor after in our preaching? The order of operation in the Godhead answers this question. The great end of preaching is to proclaim the love of the Father (John 3:16). The Father's love is revealed in Christ only (1 John 4:7–10). The Spirit came on the day of Pentecost to enable people to experience the love of the Father, through faith in and union with Jesus Christ, by means of preaching. Christ summarized the Spirit's work by stating that He would convict the world of sin for not believing in Christ, of Jesus' righteousness because He was vindicated when He returned to His Father, and of judgment because Christ judged the ruler of this world on the cross (John 16:8–11). Christ summarized the Spirit's mission, saying, "He shall glorify me, for he shall receive of mine, and shall show it unto you" (John 16:14).[53]

---

52. Robert Letham, *The Holy Trinity: In Scripture, History, Theology, and Worship* (Phillipsburg, N.J.: P&R Publishing, 2004), 443.

53. Owen argued that the order of subsistence of the ontological Trinity (including the *filioque* doctrine) as well as the resultant order of operation in the economic Trinity should shape the labors of church officers. *Works*, 3:195–96.

Ministers, if we desire the blessing of the Holy Spirit upon our ministries, let us keep the mission of the Spirit before us. Let us preach in order to glorify Christ. If we expect the blessing of the Spirit apart from proclaiming Christ, then do we not expect Him to contradict His own revealed will? Any sermon in which we do not drive our hearers to Christ by the help and the power of the Holy Spirit is a sermon in which we declare tacitly that the Spirit's services are unnecessary! A Christless sermon is a Spiritless sermon. For this reason, Reformed homiletics has commonly stressed why and how men must preach Christ crucified in all of their pulpit labors.[54] We must reflect in our preaching the order in which the divine persons operate.

Third, we must recognize that the Holy Spirit is the sum and substance of true prayer. Owen noted that while Jesus told His disciples in Matthew 7:11 that the Father would give "good things" to those who asked Him, the parallel in Luke 11:13 states that the Father shall give "the Holy Spirit" to them. The reason for the shift in language is that "the Holy Spirit" and "good things" are synonymous.[55] This highlights the necessity of praying for things that agree with God's revealed will in Scripture (1 John 5:14–15). The Holy Spirit might not increase our outward prosperity in this world, but He will always promote our communion with the Father, through the Son. This reminds us that we must openly worship, acknowledge, and give thanks to the Holy Spirit for every good gift of God in our lives.[56] Should our hearts not be filled with thanksgiving and praise to God when we recognize that the Spirit is not only the author of "spiritual" blessings in our lives, but of every blessing that we enjoy? Let

---

54. Owen, *Works*, 3:150–51, 200. Thomas Foxcroft (1697–1769) wrote, "Christ is the center of revelation and the adequate subject of preaching; and he must be the substance and bottom of every sermon." *The Gospel Ministry* (1717; repr., Grand Rapids: Soli Deo Gloria Publications, 2008), 5. The great William Perkins (1558–1602) summarized: "The heart of the matter is this: Preach one Christ, by Christ, to the praise of Christ." *The Art of Prophesying* (1606; repr., Edinburgh: The Banner of Truth Trust, 1996), 79.

55. Owen, *Works*, 3:155. See also 109, 398–99. Goodwin made the same observation. See Thomas Goodwin, *Works*, 1:42.

56. Owen added that the Holy Spirit aids believers in prayer primarily in three ways: 1. He gives spiritual insight into the promises of the covenant. 2. He leads us into an experience of our true needs. 3. He creates within us a desire to preserve and to nourish the new nature. Such prayers are an "exact copy" of the work of the Spirit within believers in their sanctification, thus making the Spirit of supplication and of sanctification inseparable. *Works*, 3:398–99.

us be explicitly dependent upon the third Person of the Trinity in every prayer. Let us pray to the Father, in the name of the Son, by the power of the Holy Spirit.

Finally, Owen noted that to the extent that we enjoy communion with the Holy Spirit on earth, we have begun to enjoy heaven now.[57] The Spirit is not simply the seal of our redemption; He is our down payment. A down payment is not merely a pledge of future installments, but also involves partial ownership in the present. Communion with the triune God is the true joy and hope of heaven. In the Person of the Holy Spirit, Christians have begun to experience heavenly joys upon earth. Let us not grieve the Spirit through ungodly living! Let us cultivate communion with the Holy Spirit by pursuing holiness! Let us pray that the Spirit would give us a taste of heaven on earth by glorifying Christ in our hearts, and by revealing the Father's love to our souls through Christ!

---

57. Owen, *Communion with God*, in *Works*, 2:240. He asserted that holiness "is the first-fruits of heaven." *Works*, 3:376. These two ideas are connected in that it is the peculiar office of the Holy Spirit to make the saints holy and to prepare them for the society of heaven. See Thomas Goodwin, *Works*, 1:42.

CHAPTER 18

The Holy Spirit and Revival

John Carrick

On September 23, 1857, there occurred in New York City an event of seemingly relative insignificance. A prayer meeting had been arranged by the city missionary of New York City, Jeremiah Lanphier, a man of some forty years of age and a devoted servant of the Lord Jesus Christ. The Lord had laid upon his heart that something additional was needed. He had been preaching God's Word and seeking God's face in prayer, but he longed to reach the masses of unconverted men and women, young people, and children of New York City, and the Lord led him to arrange for a noon-day prayer meeting for businessmen to come together to plead with God for revival.

Therefore, on September 23, at noon, this prayer meeting convened. When the hour of noon struck, nobody had arrived, but by 12:30, six men had come to seek God's face in prayer. The number of six increased to twenty a week later. One week later still, the number increased to approximately thirty-five, and a week later—which, interestingly, in the providence of God coincided with a financial crash—one hundred people gathered in Fulton Street, New York City, to seek the face of God in prayer. Before long, these weekly meetings became daily. Then they began to be held not only in Fulton Street but in other parts of New York City; within six months, ten thousand people were meeting daily in New York City, as well as in other parts of the United States, in prayer, seeking the great blessing of revival.

Revival is a phenomenon. It is not the norm; it is unusual—extraordinary. God goes out of His way, as it were, and rends the heavens and comes down in great blessing on His church.

J. Edwin Orr, an expert on revival, has spoken of the New York revival of 1857 as "an incredible movement of the people to pray."[1] It was initiated through prayer and carried on through prayer. Hundreds and thousands of people were converted in prayer meetings. The net result, according to historians, was that approximately one million people pressed into the kingdom of God at that time. The fires of revival spread across the Atlantic. They reached Ulster, Wales, and parts of Scotland, as well as England and parts of the Continent. It is estimated that perhaps as many as a further one million people were converted on the other side of the Atlantic, resulting in approximately two million conversions in all in this remarkable outpouring of God's Spirit.

It is important to note that revival always begins in the church. God revives and enlivens His church. He pours out His Spirit, and seemingly lethargic, even moribund, church members suddenly become alive with a new power. In the remarkable New York City revival, this power was manifested supremely through the astonishing movement of the people in prayer.

Where in the Scriptures do we find the phenomenon of revival? I believe we could go to many different passages, but I want to touch briefly on just one. We see here, I believe, the significance of a little phrase in Acts 3:19. The apostle Peter, preaching just after the healing of the man lame from his mother's womb, says, "Repent ye therefore, and be converted, that your sins may be blotted out, when the times of refreshing shall come from the presence of the Lord" (Acts 3:19). Notice that little phrase, "the times of refreshing." I believe this brief phrase deals with the whole concept and reality of God's reviving of His work. They are times of refreshing that come from the presence of the Lord.

The context of this exhortation to repent and the reference to the times or seasons of refreshing is that of the healing of the man lame from his mother's womb. Peter and John are about to enter into the temple at the hour of prayer, the ninth hour—three o'clock in the afternoon. But sitting there by the Beautiful Gate of the temple is a man who is a cripple. He is begging for his living, as he must, when his eyes fasten on Peter and John. He hopes for some alms from them. But Peter says to him, "Silver and gold have I none; but such

---

1. J. Edwin Orr, *The Light of the Nations* (Exeter: Paternoster Press, 1965), 105.

as I have give I thee: In the name of Jesus Christ of Nazareth rise up and walk" (Acts 3:6). Thus, through the power of the risen Christ, the apostle Peter is able to raise up this poor crippled man and restore him to perfect soundness.

The people are filled with wonder and amazement at this miracle that is performed in the name of the Lord Jesus Christ. But Peter focuses not so much on the miracle as on the Lord Jesus Christ. He preaches Christ. He emphasizes the mighty God of Abraham, Isaac, and Jacob. He is the One who has glorified His Son Jesus: "Ye denied Him; ye crucified Him; but God has raised Him up. God has glorified Him; and He is the one responsible," says Peter, deflecting any attention away from himself, "for raising up this poor crippled man in this astonishing way." Hence, as he preaches to the people and tells them to repent, Peter refers to the times of refreshing that come from the presence of the Lord.

I want to mention, in passing, that the word "when" in the King James Version is not the ideal translation. It should be "that," "so that," or "in order that." In other words, Peter says, "Repent ye, therefore, and be converted, that your sins may be blotted out, so that the times of refreshing shall come from the presence of the Lord."

I want to consider these times, these seasons of refreshing, which God in His sovereign goodness chooses to bestow on His church and, therefore, on the world; I want you to notice that implicit in what Peter says is a description of the entire period between the two advents. This period will be marked, says Peter, by times or seasons of refreshing from the presence of the Lord.

What exactly does Peter mean when he refers to "refreshing"? The word in the original is interesting. Literally it means "cooling." Remember that this is a hot, Middle Eastern climate, and, therefore, the time of cooling is, in fact, that of refreshing. The idea here is that of times of relief and recovery. Think of a hot, arid, desert climate where the sun beats down relentlessly day after day. How welcome are the cooling breezes that come from the north and bring relief and recovery to those who are oppressed by the heat in those conditions.

My mind goes back to the first week in July 1999. Some of you may remember that during that time temperatures in the United States soared into the 100s. People were dying. There was a tremendous demand for air conditioners. People were dousing themselves with water. They were buying cold drinks. There was a concern even to stay alive because of the oppressive nature of the heat. How refreshing a time of northerly breezes would have been, bringing a cooling of the temperature at such a time.

"Now," says Peter, in effect, "there are such times in the spiritual realm. There are times when God comes, times when God pours out His Spirit and grants this relief, this recovery, this refreshment to His church—these times of cooling that come from the presence of the Lord, as the church passes through the wilderness of this world. As the sun beats down upon her in persecution, in tribulation, in trouble, and in the day of small things, there are times of spiritual enjoyment and refreshment."

What exactly do we mean by "revival"? The word is misused today and is often misunderstood. I think that it is important that we should understand what Peter says on the day of Pentecost, because there is an inextricable connection between true revival, the day of Pentecost, and the Spirit that is given on that occasion: "But this is that which was spoken by the prophet Joel; and it shall come to pass in the last days, saith God, I will pour out of my Spirit upon all flesh.... I will pour out in those days of my Spirit" (Acts 2:16–17, 18). Joel puts the emphasis on the pouring out of the Spirit of God. Peter repeats it—he is citing Joel. This outpouring of the Spirit is, I believe, not limited to the day of Pentecost. There are other, later outpourings of the Spirit of God in revival at certain times and seasons.

Dr. Martyn Lloyd-Jones describes revival in this way: "Revival is an outpouring of the Spirit. It is something that comes upon us, that happens to us. We are not the agents, we are just aware that something has happened."[2] It is a visitation or an outpouring of God's Spirit. It is essential, I believe, that we connect revival to the immediate activity of the Third Person of the Godhead.

The term "revival" is often misused and even abused today. You might be driving along the road when a church notice board catches your eye. On it, you see advertised: "Revival! Revival: November 4, 5, and 6 at 7:30 p.m.!" That is, I believe, a misuse of the term. It is synonymous here with an evangelistic campaign, a series of evangelistic

---

2. D. M. Lloyd-Jones, "Jonathan Edwards and the Crucial Importance of Revival," in *The Puritans: Their Origins and Successors* (Edinburgh: Banner of Truth, 1987), 368.

meetings. There is nothing wrong with such things. They can be used in the providence of God and in His kingdom. But they are not the same as revival. We can never pre-announce revival. It is something that happens, something that God sends. This misuse of the term has led, I think, many to a dismissal of revival, to a disillusionment, perhaps, with it, to a failure to understand what it is. But I would emphasize that this misuse of the term is scarcely two hundred years old. It dates from the early decades of the nineteenth century and, in particular, from the "new measures" controversy involving Charles Grandison Finney.

It is important to note that prior to the 1830s, revival was understood quite differently. Until that time, the church was imbued with an Edwardsean concept of revival. The church has lost sight of and needs to recover this tradition, which emphasized what Jonathan Edwards describes as "remarkable communications of the Spirit of God" and "remarkable effusions, at special seasons of mercy." He says in his *History of Redemption*:

> It may here be observed, that from the fall of man, to our day, the work of redemption in its effect has mainly been carried on by remarkable communications of the Spirit of God. Though there be a more constant influence of God's Spirit always in some degree attending his ordinances; yet the way in which the greatest things have been done towards carrying on this work, always have been by remarkable effusions, at special seasons of mercy.[3]

Edwards is widely regarded as "the theologian of revival." He experienced revival twice—in 1734–35 in Northampton, Massachusetts and in the Connecticut River Valley, and in the 1740s in the Great Awakening, when he was joined by George Whitefield, the Tennant brothers, and others. He wrote extensively on revival. No one analyzed revival more than he.

In the above quotation, notice the concept of periodicity, the idea that revival is occasional or sporadic. It does not occur all the time. It is not the norm. It is something that God sends and gives at certain times and seasons. He speaks of "a more constant influence of the Spirit of God." But in addition to this more constant influence of the

---

3. Jonathan Edwards, *The Works of Jonathan Edwards* (Edinburgh: Banner of Truth, 1974), 1:539.

Spirit, there are special times, remarkable seasons of special mercy and grace. Revival is clearly something uncommon, quite out of the ordinary. Lloyd-Jones says, "A revival is something that comes, lasts for a while, and then passes."[4]

Consider that also implicit in Edwards's view of revival is the concept of degree—the degree or the measure in which the Spirit of God is given. A constant influence of God's Spirit always attends His ordinances, but in addition to this, there are remarkable effusions. His terminology here clearly denotes the idea of periodicity and also the concept of measure or degree.

Edwards illustrates these concepts in his *History of Redemption* as he traces the mighty works of God through the Old Testament and on into the New. In the first place, he refers to the days of Enos, the grandson of Adam: "Then began men to call upon the name of the LORD" (Gen. 4:26). There is something new here, something unusual, something different in degree. Edwards says: "And this in the days of Enos, was the first remarkable pouring out of the Spirit of God that ever was. There had been a saving work of God on the hearts of some before; but now God was pleased to bring in a harvest of souls to Christ."[5]

We see, then, this seasonal element—the element of unpredictability. No man knows the times or seasons that God has put in His own power. Therefore, we can never announce a revival. It is something that simply happens. We can look back historically upon it, but we cannot announce it in advance.

Peter's words in Acts 3 are spoken in the midst of such times. On the day of Pentecost, there are some three thousand conversions; shortly afterward, there are another five thousand conversions. These conversions are inextricably connected with the giving, the outpouring of the Spirit of God. Edwards says, "God also has his days of mercy, accepted times, chosen seasons, wherein it is his pleasure to show mercy, and nothing shall hinder it; times appointed for the magnifying of the Redeemer and his merits, and for the triumphs of his grace."[6] This is the peculiar work of the Spirit of God.

---

4. D. Martyn Lloyd-Jones, *Revival* (Basingstoke, Hants, U.K.: Marshall Pickering, 1986), 105.

5. Edwards, *Works*, 1:539.

6. Edwards, *Works*, 2:294.

Let me remind you of the fundamental work of the Spirit of God. It is to testify to Christ, to glorify Christ. How does He do that? By convincing men of sin, of God's righteousness, and of the judgment to come. He testifies to the Lord Jesus Christ; He glorifies Christ. He leads men to Christ unerringly and irresistibly, and thus they enter the kingdom of God. That is the great task of the Holy Spirit—to lift up, to magnify the Lord Jesus Christ in the conversion and the sanctification of men.

Let me demonstrate this historically. Peter speaks of times, seasons of refreshing, when God greatly blesses His church. Think of the Reformation of the sixteenth century. We tend not to think of the Reformation primarily in terms of revival, but I believe it was, among other things, just that—a mighty movement of God's Spirit across the face of Europe, beginning essentially in 1517 (though there were, of course, precursors before that year in the providence of God). Martin Luther nails his Ninety-five Theses to the church door in Wittenberg in 1517, and before long the progress proves to be absolutely astonishing as the gospel is disseminated across the nations of Europe. Yes, it is a mighty work of reformation, but a mighty work of revival also. The gospel goes forth in power. Men are convicted; they are converted. They are humbled under the mighty hand of God and they press into God's kingdom. God's kingdom comes with power at such times. This great revolt, this mighty revolution of the sixteenth century that we call the Protestant Reformation, was, I believe, among other things, a reviving of God's work.

Take the Great Awakening of the 1740s. There was, of course, a kind of precursor to the Great Awakening. We could, in fact, include it in the Great Awakening. I am referring to the revival in Northampton under Edwards's ministry. It began in December 1734 and continued until about May 1, 1735, a period of some six months. In that time, God poured out His Spirit in great and wonderful blessing upon that town. Other towns and villages in the Connecticut River Valley were also affected. Of the two hundred families in Northampton, some three hundred souls, in Edwards's judgment, pressed into the kingdom of heaven at that time. This is how he describes it: "In the main, there has been a great and marvelous work of conversion and sanctification among the people here.... And we are evidently a people blessed of the Lord! For here, in this corner of the world, God dwells, and manifests his glory."[7]

In 1740, Edwards was joined by the young Whitefield, whose seraphic preaching of the Word of God on both sides of the Atlantic was such that men rushed to hear him. Edwards is describing revival when he says this concerning the Great Awakening: "God appears unusually present"[8] and "God is then extraordinarily present."[9] There is an emphasis on the presence of God in revival. Listen again to our text: "seasons of refreshing from the presence of the Lord." The idea is seasons of cooling and refreshment, which are marked by the presence of God, so that men become conscious of the presence of God in a remarkable and unusual way. Indeed, historians estimate that approximately fifty thousand people were converted in New England during the Great Awakening—as many as one in five—and entered into God's kingdom. Edwards speaks of "so glorious and wonderful a display of His power and grace in the late outpourings of His Spirit."[10]

It is undeniable that some resisted the Great Awakening. Some were opposed to it, such as Charles Chauncy, and even some believers. The Old Side, for instance, tended to resist the Great Awakening on the whole. But this is Edwards's defense of the Great Awakening: "The great weakness of the greater part of mankind, in any affair that is new and uncommon, appears in not distinguishing, but either approving or condemning all in the lump."[11] This, of course, is a common error in the thinking of men, a tendency innate in our minds by nature, either to approve or condemn all in the lump. There is something we do not like; we dismiss it in its entirety. We like it; we approve of everything. "No," says Edwards, "this is wrong. We need to be more discriminating. We need to distinguish between the wheat and the chaff. We must neither approve nor condemn all in the lump, but distinguish between things that differ." There can be no doubt that this great man of God, this theologian of revival, this man with a remarkable, astonishing, discriminating mind, uses a scalpel to distinguish that which is good and of God from that which is not.

---

7. Edwards, *Works*, 1:364.
8. Edwards, *Works*, 1:393.
9. Edwards, *Works*, 1:393.
10. Edwards, *Works*, 1:427.
11. Edwards, *Works*, 1:371.

This is what Edwards says as he defends the essence of the Great Awakening:

> Whatever imprudences there have been, and whatever sinful irregularities; whatever vehemence of the passions, and heats of the imagination, transports, and ecstasies: whatever error in judgment, and indiscreet zeal; and whatever outcries, faintings, and agitations of body; yet, it is manifest and notorious, that there has been of late a very uncommon influence upon the minds of a very great part of the inhabitants of New England, attended with the best effects. There has been a great increase of seriousness, and sober consideration of eternal things; a disposition to hearken to what is said of such things, with attention and affection; a disposition to treat matters of religion with solemnity, and as of great importance; to make these things the subject of conversation; to hear the Word of God preached, and to take all opportunities in order to it; to attend on the public worship of God, and all external duties of religion, in a more solemn and decent manner; so that there is a remarkable and general alteration in the face of New England in these respects. Multitudes in all parts of the land, of vain, thoughtless, regardless persons, are quite changed, and become serious and considerate. There is a vast increase of concern for the salvation of the precious soul, and of that inquiry, "What shall I do to be saved?"[12]

Edwards concedes that there were blemishes. He does not approve all in the lump, nor does he dismiss or reject all in the lump. He discriminates carefully. But he is very careful also to insist that, in the main, this was a great and astonishing work of God's Spirit. Indeed, he describes it as "a strange revolution"[13] that led to "a visible reformation"[14] among the people of God.

At the same time as the Great Awakening in this country, there was a remarkable revival in England. God had raised up the young Whitefield. At the age of twenty-one he was preaching to thousands in the open air. Before long, John Wesley and other great evangelists joined him, and God wrought a remarkable evangelical revival in England.

---

12. Edwards, *Works*, 1:374.
13. Edwards, *Works*, 1:379.
14. Edwards, *Works*, 1:279.

It is important to note that the Puritan era had long disappeared over the horizon. In 1662, some two thousand godly ministers had been ejected from their livings, and the period between 1662 and the 1730s or 40s was one of terrible decadence and increasing corruption in England.[15] But there can be no doubt that in the 1730s and 40s, something astonishing happened. The Oxford historian John Richard Green writes in his *Short History of the English People*:

> A religious revival burst forth…which changed after a time the whole tone of English society. The church was restored to life and activity. Religion carried to the hearts of the people a fresh spirit of moral zeal, while it purified our literature and our manners. A new philanthropy reformed our prisons, infused clemency and wisdom into our penal laws, abolished the slave trade, and gave the first impulse to popular education.[16]

It is not only Green who makes this point; the French historian Élie Halévy (1870–1937) writes, "Evangelical religion was the moral cement of English society." He contrasts what happened in France in 1789, and all that preceded it, with what happened in England in these decades. He makes the point that, but for this evangelical revival, England might well have suffered a revolution analogous to the bloodbath of the French Revolution in 1789.

I come now to what is known as the Second Great Awakening in the early nineteenth century. We are dealing now with the years 1800 to 1825—some historians say 1800 to 1831—a period of twenty-five to thirty years when there were periodic revivals of religion. Iain Murray, in his helpful work *Revival and Revivalism* (notice that he distinguishes between the two), points out that the Second Great Awakening differs from the first Great Awakening in that it was greater in length, more extensive geographically, and also more extensive denominationally. Thousands upon thousands of people entered into the kingdom of God and into the churches of Christ. We see again what Murray calls "this mysterious periodicity,"[17] which is

---

15. See Arnold Dallimore's fine account of this in his biography of George Whitefield: Arnold A. Dallimore, *George Whitefield: The LIfe and Times of the Great Evangelist of the Eighteenth-Century Revival* (Edinburgh: Banner of Truth, 1989), vol. 1.

16. John Richard Green, *A Short History of the English People* (London: Macmillan, 1907), 736–37.

17. Iain H. Murray, *Revival and Revivalism* (Edinburgh: Banner of Truth, 1994), 201.

itself a reflection of the sovereignty of God. He is the One who gives revival. He is the One who sends it at certain times and seasons, and they lie within His power.

Interestingly, there were some precursors to this period of awakening between 1800 and 1825 or 1831. A very interesting and significant precursor occurred in Virginia and North Carolina, known as the Great Revival of 1787–89. Murray makes this interesting observation concerning this revival: "The Great Awakening had largely missed Virginia in the 1740s and left her one of the most materialistic of all the colonies, but in the Virginia of the 1780s an impetus for biblical religion affected large numbers of people and prepared the way for a major spiritual change in the South. For the first time, religion became identified in the public mind with evangelical Christianity."[18]

We need to remember that in the early nineteenth century, America was on the move. There was a movement westward. There was a developing frontier in Tennessee and especially in Kentucky, "the Mother of the West." Men, women, and children were migrating westward by hundreds and thousands. In this context, we find the beginnings of what are known as "camp meetings."

According to Murray, these camp meetings originated in the context of Presbyterian communion seasons. We can easily imagine the scene. Masses of people are there in their tents and wagons. The Word of God is preached and proclaimed. There is prayer. There are prayer societies. There can be no doubt that there is revival. Equally and emphatically, there are excesses and disorders, especially during the Second Great Awakening. There are fallings. There is hysteria.

This brings us to a very important point made by J. I. Packer that revival is a mixed work. Revivals vary in purity, in power, and in methodology. But we should neither approve all in the lump nor condemn all in the lump. There is no doubt that thousands upon thousands of people were converted during the Second Great Awakening. We also acknowledge some of the weaknesses and excesses that marked this awakening.

John B. Bole writes:

The Great Revival altered the course of Kentucky and southern history.... Evangelical Protestantism was placed on such a

---

18. Murray, *Revival and Revivalism*, 87.

foundation that never again was Protestant dominance threat-ened in the South.... Much that is associated with the southern character may be linked to conservative religion, and the Great Revival, beginning in Kentucky, and spreading into the remain-der of the South, was largely responsible.[19]

In the 1830s, however, there arose a man by the name of Charles Grandison Finney. Finney is often referred to as "the father of mod-ern evangelism." In 1834–35, Finney gave a series of lectures, later published as *Lectures on Revivals of Religion*, and began to forge his "new measures" controversy. The other leader in the controversy was the great Asahel Nettleton, described by some as "a second Whitefield." It has been estimated that under the preaching of this great man of God, thirty thousand people were saved.

What were the new measures? They included the anxious seat, the altar call, and decisionist evangelism. Nettleton rightly resisted these innovations and showed how dangerous they were. The problem was that Finney's theology was not merely Arminian, it was basically Pelagian. He says that God commands men to repent; therefore, they must be able to repent. That is a classic Arminian argument. There is, in Finney, a complete disregard of the utter inability of the sinner to save himself, his utter inability to respond to the gospel apart from the saving work of God's Spirit. Gardiner Spring said "The principal advocate of these new measures and these Pelagian errors, was the Rev. Charles G. Finney."[20]

Finney says, "Regeneration consists in the sinner changing his ultimate choice, intention, preference."[21] Could there be a more Arminian, a more Pelagian expression of conversion? Under Finney, conversion is reduced to a decision of the will. He introduces deci-sionist evangelism, with all that it involves, and this Pelagian element clearly affects his theology of revival. Finney insists that "a revival is not a miracle."[22] In other words, it is not an extraordinary work of God's Spirit. Instead, "A revival is the result of the right use of the appropriate means."[23] In other words, men can stir up a revival.

---

19. Cited in Murray, *Revival and Revivalism*, 173.
20. Gardiner Spring, *Personal Reminiscences* (New York: Charles Scribner, 1866), 221.
21. Charles G. Finney, *Systematic Theology* (London: William Tegg, 1851), 411.
22. Charles G. Finney, *Revivals of Religion* (London: Oliphants, 1943), 20.
23. Finney, *Revivals of Religion*, 21.

They simply have to use the means, and if they use them in a correct manner, a revival will result. We can easily see that Finney erodes the whole idea of the sovereignty of God in revival, and the concept of revival as a sovereign work of God's Spirit is replaced by the concept of an evangelistic campaign or a series of evangelistic meetings.

Murray makes this observation in *Revival and Revivalism*: "There can be no question that by 1900 the impression was almost universal that Charles Grandison Finney had introduced revivals in 19th century America."[24] But he had not. Finney introduced revivalism, the new measures that undermine true revival, indeed, undermine evangelism.

Murray, in distinguishing revivalism from revival, writes: "Revivalism contains no real element of mystery.... Revivalism is marked by the predictable."[25] Revival is always marked by the unpredictable. It is a sovereign work of God, something God gives, something God sends at special times and seasons. W. G. McLoughlin compares Edwards and Finney and their respective influences in this way: "One saw God as the center of the universe, the other saw man. One believed that revivals were 'prayed down,' and the other that they were 'worked up.'"[26] In other words, Edwards saw God as the sole cause of revival; Finney saw man. Edwards believed that revivals were prayed down. If they were sent at all, it was in response to prayer. He did not have an *ex opere operato* view. Finney believed revivals were worked up.

I come back briefly to the 1857–58 revival in this country, which is often referred to as the 1858–59 revival in Great Britain. It was the same revival in its trans-Atlantic phases. Notice again the role of prayer in that great revival. John L. Girardeau was ministering in Charleston, South Carolina, largely to African-Americans. He had a wonderful ministry of the gospel among black people. At this time, he had introduced, as had many others in different places, special prayer meetings. He was asked, "What about special preaching services?" He resisted initially. But then there came a point in the revival when he said, "The Holy Spirit has come; we

---

24. Murray, *Revival and Revivalism*, 297.
25. Murray, *Revival and Revivalism*, 380.
26. William G. McLoughlin, Jr., *Modern Revivalism: Charles Grandison Finney to Billy Graham* (New York: Ronald Press, 1959), 11.

will begin preaching tomorrow evening."[27] For eight weeks, night after night, Girardeau preached the gospel because he recognized that the Spirit of God had come and that he must make use of this remarkable opportunity, this special season of refreshing from the presence of the Lord.

Lloyd-Jones points out, "So the two main characteristics of revival are, first, this extraordinary enlivening of the members of the church, and second, the conversion of masses of people who hitherto have been outside in indifference and sin."[28] Thus, once again, we see that revival always begins not in the world but in the church. No one can quicken something that does not have life. The church is quickened. The church is enlivened. As a result, quickening spreads to those who are outside the church.

Orr observes, "The awakening of 1857–58 was the most thorough and most wholesome movement ever known in the Christian Church."[29] This is a remarkable accolade.

Let me comment on the trans-Atlantic quality of that particular revival. Wales has often been described as "the Land of Revivals." Between 1762 and 1862, there were at least fifteen major, outstanding revivals in Wales connected with the great preachers God, in His providence, had raised up in that country. Read *Some of the Great Preachers of Wales*. It is a remarkable work showing how God's Spirit rested on the labors of these men.

This great revival reached Wales in 1858, and Eifion Evans has estimated that as many as one hundred thousand people entered into the kingdom of God at that time. Evans asserts that the Welsh revival was "born in prayer."[30] It was stimulated by the prayers of God's people, which were stimulated by the news of revival. This stimulated prayer in other places. For this reason, this revival was not limited to New York City. Before long, the revival of 1857–58 spread from the north to the south, from the Atlantic to the Pacific, and affected all the major towns and regions of this mighty nation.

---

27. Cited in Murray, *Revival and Revivalism*, 420.

28. D. Martyn Lloyd-Jones, "Revival: An Historical and Theological Survey," in *The Puritans: Their Origins and Successors* (Edinburgh: Banner of Truth, 1987), 2.

29. Cited in Murray, *Revival and Revivalism*, 332.

30. Eifion Evans, *Revival Comes to Wales: The Story of the 1859 Revival in Wales* (Bridgend, U.K.: Evangelical Press of Wales, 1979), 40.

We come now to the revival in Wales in 1904–1905. This, too, was a remarkable revival, although it was marked by some weaknesses and blemishes. David Lloyd George (the prime minister of Great Britain at the time of the First World War), who was not a believer, said that this movement of God's Spirit was, in his view, like a mighty earthquake. He said it was like a tornado sweeping the country.[31] It has been said that one of the great features of this revival was the universal, inescapable sense of the presence of God.

It is undeniable some significant mistakes were made in the 1904–1905 revival. Evan Roberts, the leader, became far too mystical and subjective. There was a neglect of preaching as the revival developed. I remind you, again, that revival is a mixed work. We must neither condemn all nor approve all in the lump, but finely discriminate between that which is good and that which is bad, between the wheat and the chaff, as Edwards himself does.

Let me remind you again of the origin of these times of refreshing. They come "from the presence of the Lord" and they bring the presence of God. Revival is something that God gives, something He sends. That means we can never organize a revival. This idea that we can announce that a revival is going to occur on November 4, 5, and 6 is a complete misuse and abuse of the term. No, revival is something God gives. We might as well speak of organizing a thunderstorm, earthquake, volcanic eruption, or tornado! These acts of God are analogous to times of revival, seasons of refreshing from the presence of the Lord. No man knows the time, the place, or even the instrumentalities that will be used.

So, revival is, in the final analysis, a matter of the sovereignty of God. He chooses the men; He chooses the times; He chooses the places; He chooses the instruments. They are outside of our hands. All we can do is beseech Him. It is the sovereignty of the Spirit! Remember how the Lord Jesus Christ puts it: "The wind bloweth where it listeth" (John 3:8). That is to say, the wind blows where it wills. Have you ever reflected on the sovereignty of the wind—the power of the wind, the direction of the wind, the temperature of the wind? You and I have utterly no control over these matters. They all lie outside of our control and in the hands of God. It is

---

31. Eifon Evans, *The Welsh Revival of 1904* (Bryntirion, Wales: Evangelical Press of Wales, 1969), 114–15.

the same with God's Spirit. He moves where He will. So, there is a sovereignty of the Spirit in revival in terms of time, place, and instrumentalities.

Revival is, therefore, peculiarly a work of the Spirit of God. Yet, characteristically, the Spirit does not focus on Himself. As Packer puts it, "He shines as a spotlight upon the Lord Jesus Christ." His aim is always to testify to and glorify the Lord Jesus Christ. To that end, He convicts and convinces men of sin, of righteousness, and of judgment to come.

We see here the significance of the prophet Joel and his great prophecy: "And it shall come to pass afterwards, that I will pour out my Spirit upon all flesh.... In those days I will pour out my Spirit" (Joel 2:28–29). I believe that this concept of the outpouring of the Spirit, which is so integral to the great Edwardsean tradition that affected America, Scotland, and other parts of the world, is very important to our understanding of what happens in revival. Dispensationalists dismiss the concept. George Smeaton notes this in his work on the Spirit of God, where he takes the dispensationalists to task over this very issue:

> And no more mischievous and misleading theory could be propounded, nor any one more dishonoring to the Holy Spirit, than the principle adopted by the Plymouth Brethren, that because the Spirit was poured out at Pentecost, the Church has no need, and no warrant to pray any more for the effusion of the Spirit of God. On the contrary, the more the Church asks the Spirit and waits His communication, the more she receives.[32]

It is a fact that some Reformed men are strange bedfellows with our dispensationalist brethren in that they do not want any prayer for God's Spirit. They dismiss the notion, as the dispensationalists do, that we have any right, warrant, or need to pray for the influences of God's Spirit. But listen to the Lord Jesus Christ: "If ye then, being evil, know how to give good gifts unto your children: how much more shall your heavenly Father give the Holy Spirit to them that ask him?" (Luke 11:13). We have, I believe, every right and every warrant from Christ's own teaching to ask for the Spirit of God. "If

---

32. George Smeaton, *The Doctrine of the Holy Spirit* (Edinburgh: Banner of Truth, 1974), 288–89.

ye then, being evil…"—and we are; nevertheless we know how to give good gifts to our children—"…how much more shall your heavenly Father give the Holy Spirit to them that ask him?"

Moreover, the great aim—and we say this with an eye upon our Pentecostal and charismatic friends—should be not to focus on the things on which they tend to focus, but on the fact that the Spirit of God testifies to and glorifies Christ, and that He convinces men of sin, of God's righteousness, and of the judgment to come.

So, then, the Word of God and the history of the church show that we have these times of refreshing—times when God moves in unusual, uncommon, extraordinary ways. As we live in a day of small things (although we do not despise that), it behooves us to remember the days of great things, the days when God made bare His mighty arm, when He stretched forth His mighty hand, when He rent the heavens and came down, and brought remarkable blessing on His church—always to testify to Christ, to glorify Christ, and to bring hundreds and thousands of sinners who were dead in their trespasses and their sins into the kingdom of God.

Do you believe that there are such times? Do you believe that there have been such times? Do you believe that in God's sovereignty there could be such times again? Do you ever read about revival? Do you ever pray for revival? You who preach God's Word, do you ever preach about revival? There is, sadly, in Reformed circles a resistance sometimes to the concept of revival. These things ought not to be. We recognize that revival is a mixed work. We do not approve of everything; we do not condemn everything. There are blemishes. But we recognize also that there are times and seasons of remarkable power, of the presence of God manifest among men.

So, we should pray that God's kingdom might come. There is, of course, as the Lord Jesus Himself shows, a very real place for praying in our prayer meetings for the one who is sick, the one who is in need, the one who is seeking a job, the ones who have temporal, material needs. But is it not the case that, all too often, our prayer meetings are saturated with requests of that nature and we forget to pray for that which our Lord puts first—the coming of His kingdom with power in mighty revival? That, surely, should be our great priority, while not for one moment dismissing secondary matters. They also are important, and we have a right to pray for them. But it is more important that God's kingdom should be extended and come with great power. Therefore, I urge you to bid God awake, to arise, to pluck His hand out of His bosom, to visit us, to quicken us, to rend the heavens, to come down, to pour out His Spirit, to testify of the Lord Jesus Christ, and to glorify Him by convicting men and women in their hundreds and their thousands of sin, of righteousness, and of judgment to come. Amen.

PASTORAL STUDY

CHAPTER 19

The Holy Spirit and the
Unique Power of Preaching

Joseph A. Pipa

The Bible teaches that preaching has a unique function; God applies His accomplished redemption by preaching. John Stott wrote that preaching is the applicatory act of redemption:

> It is by preaching that God makes past history a present reality. The cross was, and will always remain a unique historical event of the past. And there it will remain, in the past, in the books, unless God himself makes it real and relevant to men today. It is by preaching, in which he makes his appeal to them through men, that God accomplishes this miracle. He opens their eyes to see its true meaning, its eternal value and its abiding merit. "Preaching," writes Dr. Mounce, "is that timeless link between God's great redemptive Act and man's apprehension of it. It is the medium through which God contemporizes his historic self-disclosure and offers man the opportunity to respond in faith." But it is more even than this. God not only confronts men through the preacher's proclamation; he actually saves men through it as well. This St. Paul states categorically: "Since, in the wisdom of God, the world did not know God through wisdom, it pleased God through the folly of the *kerygma* (preaching) to save those who believe" (1 Cor. 1:21). Similarly, the gospel is itself "the power of God unto salvation to every one that believeth" (Romans 1:16, 17).[1]

Preaching, therefore, is the chief means of grace and should occupy the central place of the church's ministry. The Heidelberg Catechism points out that preaching is part of the exercise of the keys of the kingdom of heaven:

---

1. John R. Stott, *The Preacher's Portrait* (Grand Rapids: Eerdmans, 1965), 53.

Q. 83. What are the keys of the kingdom of heaven? A. The preaching of the holy gospel and church discipline, by these two the kingdom of heaven is opened to believers and closed to unbelievers.

Q. 84. How is the kingdom of heaven opened and closed by the preaching of the gospel? A. According to the command of Christ, the kingdom of heaven is opened when it is proclaimed and publicly testified to each and every believer that God has really forgiven all their sins for the sake of Christ's merits, as often as they by true faith accept the promise of the gospel. The kingdom of heaven is closed when it is proclaimed and testified to all unbelievers and hypocrites that the wrath of God and eternal condemnation rest on them.

The Westminster divines highlighted the importance of preaching in the Larger Catechism:

Q. 155. How is the word made effectual to salvation? A. The Spirit of God maketh the reading, but especially the preaching of the word, an effectual means of enlightening, convincing, and humbling sinners; of driving them out of themselves, and drawing them unto Christ; of conforming them to his image, and subduing them to his will; of strengthening them against temptations and corruptions; of building them up in grace, and establishing their hearts in holiness and comfort through faith unto salvation.[2]

To accomplish this function, God adorned preaching with a unique authority. When a commissioned man preaches the infallible Word of God, God the Spirit takes the spoken proclamation of the divine, inerrant Word of God and speaks uniquely through him. As Pierre Marcel said:

In other words, preaching is not an empty noise, but a power; not a pure and simple declaration of his will, but indeed the very accomplishment of that will (Isa. 55:11). Such is the testimony of Christ and the scriptures concerning the preached word, which, by its very nature as word of God, is and remains as effective as the word by which God creates and sustains the world or that word by which Christ calms the tempest (Mark 4:39), heals the sick (Matt. 9:6), casts out demons (Matt. 8:16),

---

2. See also Romans 16:25–26; 1 Peter 1:23–25.

and raises the dead (Luke 7:14; 8:54; John 5:25,28; 11:43; etc.). The word by which God works in the oral and spiritual realms by the preaching of the gospel is equally effectual and powerful, because, under his orders and by virtue of his will, it is a word of God.[3]

The Reformers' position on the unique authority of preaching is summarized in the Second Helvetic Confession, chapter 1: "Wherefore when this Word of God is now preached in the church by preachers lawfully called, we believe that the very Word of God is preached, and received of the faithful; and that neither any other Word of God is to be feigned nor to be expected from heaven: and that now the Word itself which is preached is to be regarded, not the minister that preaches; who, although he be evil and a sinner, nevertheless the Word of God abides true and good." Chapter 18, concerning when evil ministers should be heard, states, "For we know that the voice of Christ is to be heard, though it be out of the mouths of evil ministers; forasmuch as the Lord himself said, 'All therefore whatsoever they bid you observe, that observe and do; but do not ye after their works' (Matt. 23:3)."

For preaching to accomplish God's purpose, however, the Holy Spirit must act in a unique way. Paul wrote that preaching possesses this divine efficacy when blessed by the Holy Spirit: "And my speech [*logos*] and my preaching [*kerygma*] was not with enticing words of man's wisdom, but in demonstration of the Spirit and of power [power of the Spirit]" (1 Cor. 2:4).

The cause of the efficacy is not simply moral persuasion. There are those who think that the power of preaching lies in the persuasive power of the words. We know that in effectual calling God makes the Word persuasive, but the Word does not possess any persuasiveness apart from the work of the Holy Spirit. Others suggest that there is an inexorable spiritual law that the preached Word operates automatically apart from the Spirit. This is the position of the Lutherans. Such a position detracts from the sovereignty of the Holy Spirit in His work.

The Bible clearly teaches that the efficacy of preaching depends on the Holy Spirit, who is sovereign in making the work of preaching

---

3. Pierre C. Marcel, *The Relevance of Preaching,* trans. Rob Roy McGregor (Grand Rapids: Baker, 1977), 21, 22.

efficacious. Jesus says, "The wind bloweth where it listeth, and thou hearest the sound thereof, but canst not tell whence it cometh, and whither it goeth: so is every one that is born of the Spirit" (John 3:8). The Spirit must join Himself to the preached Word and act with it. John Calvin insisted on the importance of recognizing the sovereignty of the Spirit: "This does not mean that the grace of the Holy Spirit and his influence are tied to preaching, so that the preacher can, whenever he pleases, breathe forth the Spirit along with the utterance of the voice. We are, then, Ministers of the Spirit, not as if we held him enclosed within us, or as it were captive—not as if we could at our pleasure confer his grace upon all, or upon whom we pleased—but because Christ, through our instrumentality, illuminates the minds of men, renews their hearts, and, in short, regenerates them wholly."[4]

The work of preaching, therefore, should be made dependent on the Spirit. Both in his preparation and proclamation, the preacher must actively depend on the Holy Spirit.

The Spirit and Preparation

With respect to preparation, the preacher needs the Spirit to open his eyes to the meaning of the text of Scripture. Marcel wrote: "Since the mysteries of God are accessible only to the spiritual man, the Holy Spirit mediates to each of us the discovery and the understanding of the truth…. The preacher can speak in the name of God and proclaim the word only if that word has been first explained to him by the Spirit. To this end, he must invoke the Holy Spirit each day and when he prepares to preach."[5] The Spirit must illumine the preacher to understand the passage on which he intends to preach. Therefore, the pastor must pray over his preparation. Too often we prepare in our own strength. We know how to exegete and write sermons; therefore, we do not do so in dependence on the Holy Spirit. We need to approach the work of preaching earnestly asking God to explain the text to us.

Not only must we pray over the text of Scripture in order to understand it correctly, but we are also to pray over the content of the sermon; we must pray that the Spirit might give us His message

---

4. John Calvin, *Commentary on 2 Corinthians, 3:6* (Grand Rapids: Eerdmans, 1964), 41–43.

5. Marcel, *The Relevance of Preaching*, 91.

for our people. In connection with praying for the message, we must be praying for our people. Richard Baxter exhorted in *The Reformed Pastor*:

> Our whole work must be carried on under a deep sense of our own insufficiency, and of our entire dependence on Christ. We must go for light, and life, and strength to him, who sends us on the work.... Must I daily plead with sinners about everlasting life and everlasting death, and have no more belief or feeling of these things myself.... Prayer must carry on our work as well as preaching; he preacheth not heartily to his people, that prayeth not earnestly for them. If we prevail not with God to give them faith and repentance we shall never prevail with them to believe and repent.[6]

As Baxter pointed out, we need to be in regular prayer for those to whom we will preach. If we are not praying for them, we will not be able to speak to them with power. We should have the regular habit of praying weekly for our hearers by name and need. Also, we should be praying for those visitors who come—that God will send people in whose hearts He is at work. Members of the church should be praying for the same things during the week.

The Spirit and Proclamation

With respect to proclamation, the prepared sermon can become the powerful Word of God only when it is blessed by the Holy Spirit in the act of preaching. As Paul asserts in 1 Corinthians 2:4, "And my speech and my preaching was not with enticing words of man's wisdom, but in demonstration of the Spirit and of power." We must note the difference between the sermon prepared in the study and the sermon preached. Both works are necessary, but they are separate acts. Marcel said, "They make a capital error, who think that the preacher, because he is present and the service begins, possesses his sermon [that he is prepared to read it if it is written, to give it from memory, to improvise with the help of an outline, etc.], and that is enough that this ready-prepared sermon be rendered in a few minutes in order for the preaching of God's word to be heard."[7] The sermon is what

---

6. Richard Baxter, *The Reformed Pastor* (Edinburgh: The Banner of Truth Trust, 1974), 122–23.

7. Marcel, *The Relevance of Preaching*, 93.

we prepare in the study; preaching is the act in the pulpit. One may have a good sermon and bad preaching or a bad sermon and good preaching. Most of us have experienced the reality of having a good sermon on paper—in our notes—but in the act of preaching it was dull and lifeless. We also have experienced and heard sermons that were not technically good, but the preaching was powerful. Our aim is to have both a good sermon and good preaching.

The Unction of the Spirit

The work of the Spirit in the act of proclamation is called "unction." The term means "anointing" and refers to the Spirit's work on the preacher as he preaches. Marcel defined unction:

> When, in preaching, a man abandons himself to the freedom of the Spirit, he discovers that his faculties are developed above normal: freedom is given not only to the soul but also to the tongue, his mental penetration is deeper; his ability to picture things in his mind is greater; truth works a greater power in his soul; his faith is more intense; he feels himself involved in a living and compact reality. His feelings are much more sensitive and spontaneously permeate his heart. He comes to think the thoughts of Christ, to experience the feelings and emotions of Christ.... The Spirit endows his word, his expression, with a natural freshness and vitality which gives the word a new and original appearance and which belong only to the spoken style.[8]

Marcel continued: "The preacher who abandons himself to the power and freedom of the Spirit has the experience that from the time he begins to speak (when he was trembling a few moments before—and he will tremble if he knows to what God has called him!), he is independent of circumstances, freed from every fear, of the fear of the public or of the judgment of certain ones whose incredulity or critical bent he knows. In accordance with the promise, he receives the gift of being free."[9]

William Perkins dealt with unction under preaching in the "demonstration of the Spirit." He said that this demonstration "becomes a reality when, in preaching, the minister of the Word conducts himself in such way that everyone—even those who are ignorant of

---

8. Marcel, *The Relevance of Preaching*, 100, 101.
9. Marcel, *The Relevance of Preaching*, 101.

the gospel and are unbelievers—recognize that it is not so much the preacher who is speaking, but the Spirit of God in him and by him (Mic. 3:8; 1 Cor. 2:4; 14:24, 25; 4:19, 20). This is what makes his ministry living and powerful (Luke 11:27)."[10]

D. Martyn Lloyd-Jones pointed out that there is also unction on the congregation: Preaching "should always be a transaction between preacher and listener with something vital and living taking place. It is not the mere imparting of knowledge, there is something much bigger involved. The total person is engaged on both sides; and if we fail to realize this our preaching will be a failure."[11] Marcel explained the result of the Spirit's unction on a congregation:

> These are facts of experience, not only for the preacher (or the Christian who is called to bear witness), but also for the hearer whose heart the Lord opens to be attentive to the word (Acts 16:14). The Spirit begins to speak a language suited to each soul he cherishes, and for everyone present he makes the preaching of the word relevant. The believers find themselves equally freed from every subjective estimation concerning the pastor as man, his failings, his awkwardness, his age, etc. Preaching by the Spirit, this man becomes for them the man of God in the relevance which God accords that face to face situation. No law of collective psychology can account for these effects. They are the results of the free work of the Holy Spirit.[12]

Those of us who preach have experienced the phenomenon of hearers approaching us (sometimes angrily) and asking, "Who told you about me?" Or the hearers testify that we preached as if we understood exactly what they were thinking. Such responses are the product of the anointing of the Holy Spirit.

As I have already said, the Spirit works sovereignly. He gives various measures of outward manifestations of power as He pleases. At times, He works powerfully in individuals when the preacher has felt no evidence of power or unction. But preaching always accomplishes God's purposes (Isa. 55:10, 11). At times, God immediately

---

10. William Perkins, *The Art of Prophesying* (Edinburgh: The Banner of Truth Trust, 1996), 71, 72.

11. D. Martyn Lloyd-Jones, *Preaching and Preachers* (Grand Rapids: Zondervan, 1972), 54–55. Cf. 42–43 and Marcel, *The Relevance of Preaching*, 65.

12. Marcel, *The Relevance of Preaching*, 101.

converts men and women under the preaching of the Word, as He converted Saul of Tarsus (Acts 13:48; 16:14). Most often, He works more slowly, as He did in Nicodemus. We also must remember the sobering truth that sometimes He uses preaching to harden sinners: "Now thanks be unto God, which always causeth us to triumph in Christ, and maketh manifest the savour of his knowledge by us in every place. For we are unto God a sweet savour of Christ, in them that are saved, and in them that perish: To the one we are the savour of death unto death; and to the other the savour of life unto life. And who is sufficient for these things?" (2 Cor. 2:14–16). But when all is said and done, the glory belongs to God (Rom. 11:33–36).

Seeking Unction
What are we to do to seek the Holy Spirit's unction?

Pray for unction
First, we must pray for unction. The minister must prayerfully seek the ministry of the Spirit both during his preparation and for his proclamation. He needs to meditate prayerfully on his sermon, asking God to apply it to his own heart and life. Particularly before entering the pulpit to lead corporate worship and preach, the minister needs to plead with the Lord to grant the ministry of the Holy Spirit in unction. There is no more important work in the preaching of God's Word.

The work of prayer also belongs to the congregation. We need to train our congregations to seek the Lord daily in private and family worship for the preparation and proclamation of the Word of God. God's blessing on preaching should be the primary thing for which God is beseeched in the church's prayer meeting. In fact, every church needs to have a commitment to the prayer meeting if it expects the Holy Spirit to work in its midst. We must teach our people to pray for us as we study and for themselves as they hear. We must teach them to pray for the act of preaching, that God will come down powerfully on the preaching of His Word.

Depend on the Spirit
Second, we must approach the work of preaching with a conscious dependence on the Holy Spirit, aware that if He does not bless the preaching, it will be spiritually useless. Albert Martin said that we quench the Spirit (1 Thess. 5:19) when we have "a carnal and slavish

attachment to the labors of the study."[13] The preacher must handle himself in such a way that the Spirit is free to intervene in the course of preaching. It is a capital error to think the preacher possesses the sermon and delivers himself of what he concocted in the study. Martin concluded, "We ought to come to our pulpits with a prayerful expectation that, in the gathering of the people of God in the context of the promised special presence of Christ, Christ Himself will grant unplanned and unpredictable dimensions of His activity by the Spirit, which will require something other than a carnal and slavish attachment to the labors of the study, regardless of the form—manuscript, notes, memorized text—in which we bring the fruit of that study into the pulpit."[14] Marcel expanded:

> If the word which is going to be uttered is to be the preached word of God, it must be uttered with the assistance and power of the spirit. Before the "sermon" begins, nothing exists either for the preacher or for the believers concerning this word so long as it is yet to be preached. It still depends entirely on the freedom of the Spirit and is to be submitted to him. Only the intervention of the Spirit can lift that word to make it neither a lecture, a recitation, a discourse, an elocution, nor a meditation, but a preaching, a word spoken in the vitality of the Spirit, and therefore preached. If the Spirit is absent, there is, in a manner of speaking, a sermon, but no preaching.[15]

The preacher must actively depend on the Spirit in the act of preaching and allow Him freedom of action. Christ instructed His apostles that when they were called on to give an answer for their faith, they did not need to worry about what they would say: "But when they deliver you up, take no thought how or what ye shall speak: for it shall be given you in that same hour what ye shall speak. For it is not ye that speak, but the Spirit of your Father which speaketh in you" (Matt. 10:19–20). Although this primarily speaks to our need to give an answer for our faith when we are called upon to do so, a secondary application is to the work of the preacher. Marcel said:

---

13. Albert N. Martin, *Preaching in the Holy Spirit* (Grand Rapids: Reformation Heritage Books, 2011), 54.

14. Martin, *Preaching in the Holy Spirit*, 55.

15. Marcel, *The Relevance of Preaching*, 94.

[This is an] injunction and promise valid in all circumstances for every preacher! This does not, therefore, here mean an indirect dependence, a repetition of what Christ has already said during preparation and before the worship hour. Preparation and even redaction constitute only a preliminary part of preaching. It means rather that the preacher, in church, is to yield himself a malleable and living organ for what Christ by the Spirit wills him to say to those who hear. If Christ is left free, he will constrain the preacher to add, delete, and modify (in form or even in content) such and such portion of that which he had intended to say, which he cannot now say. If the preacher is and remains dependent upon his manuscript or upon his memory, there is not just one prisoner—there are two: the preacher and the Spirit, and through the Spirit Christ. The written or memorized text of the sermon at this moment exercises its dominance; Christ through the Spirit is not free. To sound out the scriptures in the study, to prepare, to write, to reflect, to pray, on the one hand, and to preach, on the other, are distinct acts which employ the distinct and complementary interventions of the Spirit. One cannot replace the other.[16]

If we have properly prepared and have a good outline, we may prayerfully depend on the Holy Spirit to give us the exact words we will utter. Our desire is to speak "not in the words which man's wisdom teacheth, but which the Holy Ghost teacheth; comparing spiritual things with spiritual" (1 Cor. 2:13).

For this reason, historically the Reformed have been committed to extemporaneous preaching. Extemporaneous preaching is not unprepared preaching; it is trusting the Spirit for the words of

---

16. Marcel, *The Relevance of Preaching*, 95. Marcel defends this use of Matthew 10 in a footnote: "Some critics have asked me about the legitimacy of applying this promise and assurance to ordinary preaching. I readily recognize that the Biblical text refers to a particular circumstance. But verses 16 and 17a are applicable to every preacher's actual situation, even in the Church. And it is incontestable that the spiritual attitude which Christ requires of his apostles in verse 19, an attitude of complete confidence in the presence and aid of the Holy Spirit, and, as Calvin emphasizes, of distrust of their own powers, is the attitude of every preacher who is conscious of the charge which God has laid upon him. As for the promise in verse 20, it is corroborated in a general sense and is applicable to every preacher by numerous New Testament texts and by the experience of all those who in the ministry of preaching have taken it seriously."

expression. In a letter to the duke of Somerset, Calvin declaimed against the reading of sermons:

> What I have thus suggested as to the manner of instruction is only that the people be so taught as to be touched to the quick, and that they may feel that what the Apostle says is true, (Heb. iv.) that "the word of God is a two-edged sword, piercing even through the thoughts and affections to the very marrow of the bones." I speak thus, Monseigneur, because it appears to me that there is very little preaching of a lively kind in the kingdom [England], but that the greater part deliver it by way of reading from a written discourse.... But all these considerations ought not to hinder the ordinance of Jesus Christ from having free course in the preaching of the Gospel. Now, this preaching ought not to be lifeless, but lively, to teach, to exhort, to reprove, as Saint Paul says in speaking thereof to Timothy, (II Tim. iii.). So indeed, that if an unbeliever enter, he may be so effectually arrested and convinced, as to give glory to God.... You are also aware, Monseigneur, how he speaks of the lively power and energy with which they ought to speak, who would approve themselves as good and faithful ministers of God, who must not make a parade of rhetoric only to gain esteem for themselves; but that the Spirit of God ought to sound forth by their voice, so as to work with mighty energy. Whatever may be the amount of danger to be feared, that ought not to hinder the Spirit of God from having liberty and free course in those to whom He has given grace for the edifying of the Church.[17]

Charles H. Spurgeon enforced this point:

> In the pulpit do we really and truly rest upon the aid of the Spirit? I do not censure any brother for his mode of preaching, but I confess that it seems very odd to me when a brother prays that the Holy Ghost may help him in preaching, and then I see him put his hand behind him and draw a manuscript out of his pocket, so fashioned that he can place it in the middle of his Bible, and read from it without being suspected of doing so. These precautions for insuring secrecy look as though the man was a little ashamed of his paper; but I think he should be far more ashamed of his precautions. Does he expect the Spirit of

---

17. John Calvin, *Letters of John Calvin* (Edinburgh: The Banner of Truth Trust, 1980), 95–96.

God to bless him while he is practicing a trick? And how can He help him when he reads out of a paper from which anyone else might read without the Spirit's aid? What has the Holy Ghost to do with the business? Truly, He may have had something to do with the manuscript in the composing of it, but in the pulpit His aid is superfluous. The truer thing would be to thank the Holy Ghost for assistance rendered, and ask that what he has enabled us to get into our pockets may now enter the people's hearts. Still, if the Holy Ghost should have anything to say to the people that is not in the paper, how can He say it by us? He seems to be very effectually blocked as to freshness of utterance by that method of ministry. Still, it is not for me to censure, although I may quietly plead for liberty in prophesying, and room for the Lord to give us in the same hour what we shall speak.[18]

John Piper has a procedure he uses to keep him mindful of his dependence on God as he approaches the act of preaching. He does five things summed up in the acronym APTAT. First, "I *Admit* to the Lord my utter helplessness without him." He confesses that he can do nothing without God's grace and strength. Second, "I *Pray* for help. I beg for the insight, power, humility, love, memory, and freedom I need to preach this message for the glory of God's name, the gladness of his people, and the ingathering of his elect." Third, "I *Trust* not merely in a general way in God's goodness, but in a specific promise in which I can bank my hope for that hour." Fourth, "I *Act* in the confidence that God will fulfill his Word. I can testify that, although the fullness of blessing I long to see has been delayed, God has met me and his people again and again in the display of his glory and the creation of glad submission to his will." And fifth, "I *Thank* God. At the end of the message I express gratitude that he has sustained me and that the truth of his Word and the purchase of his cross have been preached in some measure in the power of his Spirit to the glory of his name."[19]

My approach to preaching is to empty my mind of all concern with what I am about to say. I am aware that if the Spirit deserts me, I have nothing of profit to say. I cast myself on the Spirit for thoughts, affections, words, and strength to express the truth He

---

18. Charles H. Spurgeon, quoted in Marcel, *The Relevance of Preaching*, 95, 96.
19. John Piper, *The Supremacy of God in Preaching* (Grand Rapids: Baker Book House, 1990), 44–46.

would have me to express in my sermon. As I preach, I continually seek the Spirit's aid. Afterward, I pray over the sermon and ask the Spirit to continue to make it profitable to the hearers.

In summary of how we conduct ourselves in the pulpit, Thomas Boston gave us a "checklist":

Before preaching, we should:
- Pray to be tied to the Scriptures and put away from human wisdom
- Pray that our hearts may be melted with the sad state of our people.
- Pray that our souls will be warmed with zeal for God's glory.
- Pray for clarity.
- Pray for bodily strength.
- Pray against all distractions.

After preaching, we should:
- Go aside to pray, following the example of Christ (Mark 6:34–46)!
- Pray that the Word may not be like water spilled onto the ground. Pray that the Word may not be "snatched away" as in the parable of the sower.
- Pray for pardon in the failings of our preaching.
- Pray that conviction of sin would set in and consume our hearers and drive them to Christ![20]

Live a holy life
The third thing that is necessary in seeking unction is a holy life. True spiritual eloquence depends on a holy life. Although we are to heed the lawfully ordained man when he is speaking biblically even if his life does not match his words, there is no spiritual power without godliness.

Perkins gave five reasons why godliness is necessary for a preacher. First, the minister must set the example of what he preaches because biblical doctrine is difficult to understand and practice (Phil. 4:8; 1 Tim. 4:12; 1 Peter 5:3). Second, only the godly man can understand the inward sense of Scripture as he experiences the Word in his

---

20. Thomas Boston, *The Art of Manfishing* (Fearn, U.K.: Christian Focus, 1998), 91–95.

heart (Gen. 18:17–19; Ps. 25:8, 9; Amos 3:7). Third, God hates the combination of godly speech with ungodly life (Ps. 50:16, 17). As Gregory of Nazianzus (ca. 329–ca. 389) said, "It is as strange to see someone who is supposed to guide others on the way wandering out of the way himself, as it is to see a physician with signs of disease in his own body." Fourth, ministerial sins bring great offence to the gospel: "Ordinary people do not distinguish between the ministry and the minister. They are not able to see the importance of the ministry without first assessing the person of the minister. Herod heard John Baptist willingly, not because he was a good minister, but because he was a good man (Mark 6:20)." Gregory of Nazianzus struck the right note again when he said, "He that teaches sound doctrine, and lives wickedly, reaches with one hand what he knocks away with the other." John Chrysostom (347–407), commenting on Matthew 20, said: "The doctor of the church by teaching well and by living well instructs the people how they ought to live well; but by living ill he instructs God how to condemn him." And again: "It is an easy matter to show wisdom in words; teach me to live by your life, this is the best teaching. Words do not make as great an impression on the soul as works do!" Fifth, an unholy minister is not worthy to stand before God (Lev. 10:3; Isa. 6:6–8; Jer. 15:19). "That is why the judgments of God remain for wicked ministers to tremble at (1 Sam. 2:17, 25)."[21]

Martin wrote that we can grieve the Spirit (Eph. 4:30) by our unholy lives: "If we would have biblical grounds to expect the immediate agency and operation of the Holy Spirit in and on us in our preaching, we must be able to say with the apostle Paul, 'I know nothing by [against] myself' (1 Cor. 4:4). Further, we must also be able to say with the apostle, 'And herein do I exercise myself, to have always a conscience void of offence toward God, and toward men' (Acts 24:16)."[22]

Perkins points out six aspects of ministerial holiness. First, a minister must maintain a good conscience (Acts 24:16; 2 Cor. 1:12; 1 Tim.1:19): "Without this, the mouth of the preacher will be closed (Isa. 56:10)." Second, he must possess an inward feeling of the doctrine to be delivered: "Wood that is capable of burning is not set alight unless fire is put to it. Similarly anyone who would encourage

---

21. Perkins, *The Art of Prophesying*, 72–73.
22. Martin, *Preaching in the Holy Spirit*, 73.

godly affections and desires in others must first have godly affections himself. Thus, whatever response a particular sermon requires should first be stirred up privately in our own minds, so that we can kindle the same flame in our hearers." Third, a minister must fear God, "so that, filled with a reverent sense of the majesty of God, we will speak soberly and with moderation." Fourth, he must love the people (1 Thess. 2:7): "To encourage this affection, the minister must pray seriously and fervently for the people of God (1 Sam. 12:23)." Fifth, he must live blamelessly before the church and the world: "The minister must also be worthy of respect for his constancy, integrity, seriousness and truthfulness. He must know how to respect others in private or in public, in keeping with the character of his congregation." Sixth, he is to be temperate, "inwardly restraining any strong feelings. Both his outward style of behaviour and his gestures ought to be moderate and straightforward. In this way he will be marked by dignity and authority. Consequently he must be neither covetous, nor a heavy drinker, nor litigious, nor a pugnacious character, nor given to bursts of anger. Those who are younger men must devote themselves to godliness, and reject the lusts of youth (1 Tim. 4:7)." As we seek unction for our preaching, we need to seek a daily anointing, that we will live godly lives and that those around us will see the work of the Spirit within us.[23]

Preach Christ

The fourth important ingredient in seeking unction is to preach Christ. Martin emphasized this element: "The Holy Spirit is grieved when there is an insufficient measure of preaching Christ in our sermonic endeavors."[24] The Spirit's ministry is to exalt Christ; He delights in shining the floodlights on the Person and work of Christ. Paul's determination was to know nothing except Jesus Christ and Him crucified. Our sermons must be full of Christ. Martin suggests questions by which we may evaluate our sermons: "Where was the person and work of Christ in that sermon? Have I traced back to Christ, the source of all the grace and power for sufficiency to perform the duty, all the duties I have articulated? Have I drawn motives for obedience from our hearers' relationship to Christ? Have

---

23. Martin, *Preaching in the Holy Spirit*, 74.
24. Perkins, *The Art of Prophesying*, 50.

I traced back to Christ, who is the great fountainhead of all redemptive privilege, the privileges of grace I have expounded?"[25] If we are to enjoy the Spirit's blessing on our preaching, our sermons must be full of Jesus Christ.

Each of us needs urgently to seek the unction of the Holy Spirit in his preaching. Let us use these steps that the Bible teaches.

Practical Effects of Unction

The presence of Spirit-given unction is seen in the style and delivery in preaching.

Style

The commitment to the role of the Holy Spirit in preaching led our fathers to emphasize plain preaching. Perkins related the plain style to unction: "Now we must think about the actual preaching itself. Here two things are essential: (i) the hiding of human wisdom, and (ii) the demonstration or manifestation of the Spirit."[26] He added: "To preach in the demonstration of God's Spirit is to preach with such plainness, and yet with such power, that even the least intellectually gifted recognize that it is not man but God himself who is teaching them. Yet at the same time, the conscience of the mightiest may feel not man but God reproving them through the power of the Spirit."[27] He called plain style spiritual; it enables the audience to judge that the Spirit is speaking through the words and gestures of the minister.[28] Spiritual speech is marked by words that are simple and clear, expressing the majesty of the Spirit. The minister's language must be plain so that the people will understand him: "Spiritual speech is speech which the Holy Spirit teaches (1 Cor. 2:13). It is both simple and clear, tailored to the understanding of the hearers and appropriate for expressing the majesty of the Spirit (Acts 17:2, 3; 2 Cor. 4:2–4; Gal. 3:1)."[29] This plain style predominates in all Protestant preaching, with the exception of that of high Anglicans.

---

25. Perkins, *The Art of Prophesying*, 51.
26. Perkins, *The Art of Prophesying*, 71
27. Perkins, *The Art of Prophesying*, 86.
28. Perkins, *The Art of Prophesying*, 72, 73.
29. Perkins, *The Art of Prophesying*, 72.

The purpose of plain style is not simplicity for the sake of simplicity, but simplicity for the sake of communication. It is a philosophy of communication that seeks to speak to the people so that they can readily grasp the truth of the sermon. A. F. Herr wrote, "The plain style is sober, simple in expression, as direct as possible, and free from ornamentation of either fantastic ideas or verbiage…it appears, on the whole, to be the spontaneous creation of the spirit of the Reformation."[30]

Marcel added: "In form and language, preaching should be stripped of everything which does not tend to edify. Superfluous theological discussions, useless or subtle questions which would confuse believers, are excluded."[31] Calvin spoke plainly and simply in order to be understood by the common people. He opposed all pulpit discourse that exalted the preacher and not God:

> If he who speaks wishes to please, if he wishes to demonstrate his abilities, if some mad desire transports him so that he is oblivious of the salvation of his hearers, he is guilty of rank sacrilege, since he uses the word of God for a purpose that is not sacred. It is indeed true that men gladly have itching ears, for something new. It makes no difference what! So intense is our desire that many who undertake to teach for the sole purpose of feeding their ego and being praised ferret out and present frivolous questions. If the questions have some appearance of subtlety, they are satisfied and cease to bother about edification.[32]

Commenting on 1 Corinthians 2:13, Calvin wrote:

> By the words "taught by human wisdom," Paul means those which savour of human learning, and are polished according to the rules of the rhetoricians; or are purposely and proudly overloaded with philosophy in order to rush hearers into admiration. But the words "taught by the Spirit" are suitable for a style which is sincere and simple, rather than empty and ostentatious, and one more in keeping with the dignity of the Spirit. For in order that there may be eloquence, we must always be on the alert to prevent the wisdom of God being spoiled by a forced and common brilliancy. But Paul's way of teaching was such

---

30. A. F. Herr, *The Elizabethan Sermon* (New York: Octagon Books, 1969), 89–90.
31. Marcel, *The Relevance of Preaching*, 95.
32. Marcel, *Relevance of Preaching*, 80n19.

that in it the power of the Spirit shone forth, pure and simple, without any external assistance.[33]

The plain style is not dull, drab, or unadorned, but rather direct and in the language of the hearers. Rhetoric, therefore, takes a back seat to truth. Reformed preachers thought it would violate their hearers and the Word of God to bypass the minds of the hearers with the tricks of rhetoric. They did not want to encrust the clear teaching of the Word of God with metaphysical wit. John Owen, after describing a number of the rhetorical flourishes of the metaphysical styles, wrote:

> Such things become not the authority, majesty, greatness, and holiness, of Him who speaks therein. An earthly monarch that should make use of them in his edicts, laws, or proclamations, would but prostitute his authority to contempt, and invite his subjects to disobedience by so doing. How much more would they unbecome the declaration of His mind and will, given unto *poor worms*, who is the great possessor of heaven and earth![34]

The plain style includes four things. First, the hiding of human wisdom "both in the content of the sermon and in the language." We seek to proclaim God's Word, not our knowledge, skill, and erudition, so that "the hearers ought not to ascribe their faith to the gifts of men, but to the power of God's Word (1 Cor. 2:1, 2, 5)."[35] I do not mean that the sermon does not deal with the full content of a text and all the great truths of God's Word, but we are not to make display of our intellect and learning—we are not to carry all the facts of preparation into the pulpit. Therefore, we are to avoid lengthy quotations from commentators and theologians, as well as abstract theological discussion.

This commitment does not mean that we should be lazy. We should use the highest means possible, both in our academic preparation for ministry and for each sermon; we ought to prepare diligently.

Perkins pointed out the relation of plainness in content to power:

---

33. John Calvin, *New Testament Commentaries: 1 Corinthians* (Grand Rapids: Eerdmans Publishing Company: 1973), 60.

34. John Owen, *An Exposition of Hebrews* (Marshalltown, Del.: The National Foundation for Christian Education, 1960), 1:52.

35. Owen, *An Exposition of Hebrews*, 1:71.

Since even the uneducated person sees his faults revealed, it follows that he understands what is said; and if he can understand it, then it must be plain. Then, in addition, notice the power: his conscience is so convinced, his secret faults so unveiled, and his heart so ripped up that he says, "Certainly God speaks in this man."

This is the real evidence and proof of God's Spirit. It is taken as high commendation in the world's eyes when men say of a preacher, "He is a real scholar," because he is scholarly, well-read, has a retentive memory and a good delivery. So it is, and such commendation (if deserved) should not be despised. But what commends a man to the Lord his God and to his own conscience is that he preaches with a plainness suited to the ability, and so powerfully to the conscience, of a wicked man that he realizes that God is present in the preacher.[36]

Second, the plain style includes a simple vocabulary. We are to use simplicity in wording. We should use the vocabulary of the common people, not make our words a display of our learning. We adopt a crucified style adjusted to the weak. Our aim is for people to leave marveling at God's greatness and not at our ability. Most newspapers and magazines today are written with a middle-school-level vocabulary. We need to preach at that level. This commitment does not mean that we fail to use the great theological terms of the Bible: election, justification, sanctification, propitiation, and so on. We must not cheat our people by not exposing them to the great words of Scripture. But we should remember periodically to define them as we use them. We might stretch our people by using a more difficult word and explaining it in the next sentence. However, it is best to avoid the use of Latin, Greek, and Hebrew terms.

A third mark of plain style is concreteness of expression. We should explain biblical truth and doctrines in the language of the market, office, and classroom. We need to develop our use of metaphors and similes. A metaphor is a figure of speech in which a term that ordinarily designates an object or idea is used to designate a dissimilar object or idea in order to suggest comparison or analogy. For example, 1 Corinthians 3:9 says, "For we are labourers together with God: ye are God's husbandry, ye are God's building." A simile

---

36. Perkins, *The Art of Prophesying*, 86, 87.

is a figure of speech in which two essentially unlike things are compared, introduced by "like" or "as." Many of Christ's parables use similes: "The kingdom of heaven is likened unto a man which sowed good seed in his field" (Matt. 13:24). Such figures give arms and legs to truth, making it extremely memorable.

Fourth, the plain style is natural. It is good to listen to other preachers and have models, but we must be ourselves in the pulpit. We should not try to preach like our favorite preachers. Rhetorical devices are helpful, but we must not become studied or artificial. Above all, we must be sincere. If we speak naturally from our hearts, we may not be as eloquent as others, but that is the type of plain speaking that God greatly blesses.

The Directory for the Public Worship of God summarizes the basic elements of plain style:

> Plainly, that the meanest may understand; delivering the truth not in the enticing words of man's wisdom, but in demonstration of the Spirit and of power, lest the cross of Christ should be made of none effect; abstaining also from an unprofitable use of unknown tongues, strange phrases, and cadences of sounds and words; sparingly citing sentences of ecclesiastical or other human writers, ancient or modern, be they never so elegant.[37]

Delivery

Delivery also is connected to the Spirit's role in preaching. We should seek to develop the use of our voices, both in terms of range and volume. It is good to begin in a moderate range with moderate volume, then become more fervent and vehement as emotions build, particularly in exhortation. We should vary our voice range in order to make emphasis and to keep attention. It is helpful to develop a diversity of pace and make use of pauses.

With respect to gestures, Perkins said, "There should be a gravity about the gestures of the body which will in their own way grace the messenger of God...the arm, the hand, the face and eyes may express and (as it were) speak the spiritual affections of his heart."[38]

---

37. *Directory of Public Worship*, in *Westminster Confession of Faith* (Glasgow: Free Presbyterian Publications, 1994), 381.
38. Perkins, *The Art of Prophesying*, 75.

A man who enjoys the unction of the Spirit will preach with obvious zeal and passion. This zeal will manifest itself differently in each man, according to his gifts and personality, but each man must preach with a passion. Baxter insisted on the need to have one's heart stirred up:

> I confess I must speak it by lamentable experience, that I publish to my flock the distempers of my own soul. When I let my heart go cold, my preaching is cold;...and so I can oft observe also in the best of my hearers that when I have grown cold in preaching, they have grown cold too; and the next prayers which I have heard from them have been too like my preaching.[39]

Later he gave this counsel:

> O sirs, how plainly, how closely, how earnestly, should we deliver a message of such moment as ours, when the everlasting life or everlasting death of our fellow-men is involved in it! Methinks we are in nothing so wanting as in this seriousness; yet is there nothing more unsuitable to such a business, than to be slight and dull. What! Speak coldly for God, and for men's salvation? Can we believe that our people must be converted or condemned, and yet speak in a drowsy tone? In the name of God, brethren, labour to awaken your own hearts, before you go to the pulpit, that you may be fit to awaken the hearts of sinners. Remember they must be awakened or damned, and that a sleepy preacher will hardly awaken drowsy sinners. Though you give the holy things of God the highest praise in words, yet, if you do it coldly, you will seem by your manner to unsay what you said in the matter.... The manner, as well as the words, must set them forth....
>
> Though I move you not to constant loudness in your delivery (for that will make your fervency contemptible), yet see that you have a constant seriousness; and when the matter requireth it (as it should do, in the application at least), then lift up your voice, and spare not your spirits. Speak to your people as to men that must be awakened, wither here or in hell.[40]

The Westminster Larger Catechism, in answering the question, "How is the word of God to be preached by those that are called

---

39. Baxter, *The Reformed Pastor*, 61.
40. Baxter, *The Reformed Pastor*, 147ff.

thereunto?" gives a good summary of the elements of Spirit-anointed preaching:

> They that are called to labour in the ministry of the word, are to preach sound doctrine, diligently, in season and out of season; plainly, not in the enticing words of man's wisdom, but in demonstration of the Spirit, and of power; making known the whole counsel of God; wisely, applying themselves to the necessities and capacities of the hearers; zealously, with fervent love to God and the souls of his people; sincerely, aiming at his glory, and their conversion, edification, and salvation. (Q. 159)

Conclusion

God the Spirit makes preaching His major medium. Preaching is the public, authoritative, verbal proclamation of the Word of God that explains and applies this Word. The one who preaches is to be commissioned by Christ through His church. When such a one preaches the Word in the power of the Spirit, Christ is present and speaks through him. By the Spirit's sovereign power, God will convert and sanctify.

As the church believes and acts on these truths, she will be able to preach to a culture that is unwilling and unable to listen. God will continue to work through the foolishness of preaching to build His church.

APPENDIX

The King James Version:
Its Tradition, Text, and Translation

Michael Barrett

The year 2011 marked the four hundredth anniversary of the first edition of the King James Version (KJV) or Authorized Version (AV) of the Bible. From its inception to the present, the King James Version has testified to the unfailing providence of God in preserving His Word and in providing a vehicle for disseminating that Word to the entire English-speaking world.

The influence of the KJV has been incalculable. It helped shape the very language into which it was translated. The KJV's mark on the English language is immeasurable in terms of its use in classic literature and its origination of idioms so commonly used even in everyday speech. It became the principal primer for learning; for many, to read the Bible was the chief reason for learning to read. Although the incentive to literacy is now more secular than sacred, familiarity with the language of the KJV is still an important component in literary education. In addition, and most significantly, the King James Version served the advance of Christ's kingdom wherever English was spoken and read.

Faith comes by hearing and hearing by the Word of God (Rom. 10:17). For centuries, for English-speakers, the KJV was the Word heard. Although aspects of the English language have changed over four hundred years, causing many today to regard the AV as a venerated but irrelevant relic, its value, influence, accuracy, beauty, and understandability remain. Notwithstanding its age, there is no good reason to disregard it or to relegate it to the past. So, reflection on the history, influence, and reliability of the Authorized Version is in order. Its tradition is rich; its textual basis is verifiably sure; and its translation is accurate. In every way, the KJV is an outstanding version of the Scriptures, worthy of continued use as well as historic veneration.

Its Tradition

As is so often the case regarding the workings of divine providence, events and circumstances affirm God's control in using obstacles and opposition to accomplish His purpose in such a way that all glory is His. The history of the English Bible that culminated in the publication of the KJV is checkered with human hindrances and divine superintendence.

The KJV translators stood on the shoulders of those who, often in peril of their lives, labored to bring God's Word to the public domain from the secrecy and seclusion of Romish control. The Word of God fueled the Reformation, and as the fires of Reformation spread, so did the desire for the Scriptures. William Tyndale's work undisputably laid the foundation upon which others built, including the translators of the King James Version. Tyndale was charged with heresy and warned not to preach in public, but he was driven by his desire to see the Bible translated into English so that every man could read God's Word for himself. In response to a priest attacking his doctrine, Tyndale uttered his now-famous words: "If God spare my life, before long I shall cause a ploughboy to know the scriptures better than you do." God did not spare his life long enough for him to see his prophecy fulfilled, but the Lord did spare him long enough for him to set in motion the means whereby his desire was fulfilled exceedingly abundantly, more than he could ever have dreamed. His translation (1526, 1534) influenced the Coverdale Bible (1535), the Matthew Bible (1537), the Great Bible (1539), the Geneva Bible (1560), the Bishop's Bible (1586), and the King James Version (1611). It is commonly calculated that ninety percent of Tyndale's Bible has been preserved in the Authorized Version. With the widespread acceptance and use of the KJV, Tyndale's prediction was fulfilled to every place on the planet where English is spoken or read. A work begun under the threat of persecution (the human hindrance) prospered because it was preserved and blessed by God (the divine superintendence).

Although each of the antecedent English Bibles has its own story generating praise for God's good providence in making His Word accessible, the production of the King James Version is a testimony to the way God uses men's hostility to accomplish His purpose. If not a matter of overturning outright hostility, it certainly illustrates God's ability to turn a king's heart to achieve an end not in the mind of the king himself. In many ways, King James I was an unlikely character to be associated with a Bible so singularly blessed by God. The son of Mary, Queen of Scots, James was awkward as a youth and not particularly regal as an adult. But regardless of his less-than-commanding appearance and demeanor, he followed his mother's rival, Queen Elizabeth I, to the throne of England. Behind his back, of course, it was murmured around England that "King Elizabeth" was to be followed by "Queen James." However, what he lacked in regal bearing, he made up for in intellectual accomplishment. He was well trained in the classics, and even had hands-on experience in biblical studies, including translation.

The relationship between church and state was a pressing issue from the beginning of James's monarchy. At the beginning of his reign, a group of Puritan ministers presented him with a petition requesting that certain concerns about the church be resolved. After a delay caused by a deadly epidemic in the country, the Hampton Court Conference convened in 1604 to address the concerns. For the most part, the conference failed to resolve any issues. But on the last day, John Rainolds made a most unexpected proposal. Rainolds was a Puritan, a Hebrew scholar, the president of Corpus Christi College at Oxford, and not particularly liked by the king. He proposed a new translation of the Scriptures that would be acceptable to all Protestants. Some summarily dismissed the suggestion because there were already multiple versions available, some of which were remarkably good. Surprisingly, however, James was favorable to the proposal and gave it his moral but not financial support.

He did so with a couple of caveats that give some insight into the reason for his support. He had a deep disdain for the Geneva Bible, which he considered to be the worst of all the English translations. His dislike was not so much for the translation as for the notes, some of which he interpreted to be subversive to the monarchy and the state church. Consequently, he sanctioned the new translation project so long as there would be no notes and nothing that would promote Puritan and Calvinistic doctrine. So, ironically, the king's hatred of doctrines that we hold dear led to the translation of the

Bible we cherish. What an example this is of God turning the heart of a king!

The operation of divine providence is evident in the entire project; without that divine superintendence, the work would never have been completed. The planned procedure, humanly speaking, did not have much prospect for success; it was going to be a committee project. Whereas earlier English versions had been the works of individuals, who often labored in secrecy because they were in peril of their lives, this was going to be a collaborative effort of forty-seven scholars and churchmen divided into six groups: two at Oxford, two at Cambridge, and two at Westminster. The chance of any two scholars agreeing on anything was slim. When we multiply that slim chance by the number of scholars within each group and then that by the factor of each group having to approve the work of the others, it is clear that the probability of finishing was not great. Generally, assigning a project to a committee marks its certain death. That we have the KJV at all witnesses to God's good providence. Without disputation, the KJV is the most remarkable work ever accomplished by a committee.

Notwithstanding the official sanction and amazing circumstances associated with the production of this new English version, the KJV did not receive immediate widespread acceptance. Particularly, the Geneva Bible, with its strongly Calvinistic and anti-monarchal comments, remained the popular choice among most Puritans—at least until the mid-seventeenth century. Significantly, the Geneva Bible, packed by the Pilgrims on the *Mayflower*, was the first English version to reach North America. But before long, the KJV, though never officially authorized by the throne, became popularly authorized by its overwhelming acceptance both by the clergy and the people.

From that time, the KJV became the standard text of the English Bible, and its history and tradition cannot be separated from the history of the church in the English-speaking community throughout the world. The KJV enjoyed that rich tradition until relatively recently, when its language and text have been questioned by a new generation of scholars and churchmen. Many, while recognizing the significant history of the KJV, contend that it has no future. The translation that has done so much in shaping and influencing the English language and its literature is now regarded as archaic, antiquated, and inadequate for communicating to the contemporary English-speaking community.

I reject this assessment and argue that there is no good reason to abandon the use of this version that owns such a celebrated heritage and tradition. I reluctantly admit that the plethora of modern English versions, some produced by liberal critics and some by evangelicals, has destroyed the monopoly held by the KJV for centuries, but I do not believe the KJV will ever be dethroned as the standard English Bible to which all others will be compared and by which all others will be evaluated. Whereas modern versions use contemporary language to give expression to God's Word, the KJV alone had and has the kind of weight that has affected the language itself. Expressions and idioms from the KJV abound in current usage and are employed even by those who are clueless regarding their origin. "Feet of clay," "reaping the whirlwind," "scapegoat," "thorn in the flesh," "labor of love," "my brother's keeper," "lamb to the slaughter," "fly in the ointment," "powers that be," "salt of the earth," "sour grapes," "a law unto themselves," "falling flat on one's face," "a broken heart," "a drop in the bucket," "seeing eye to eye," "putting words in one's mouth," "the root of the matter" — these are just a few of the KJV-originated words and phrases that come to mind, and the list could go on and on. It is hard to determine the KJV's range of influence objectively, but there is enough evidence to suggest that accusations against its readability may be exaggerated.

Undeniably, some of the vocabulary and syntax patterns are archaic. This is not surprising, for it is the nature of language to evolve over time. Four hundred years is ample time for semantic shifts to occur and for grammatical conventions to change. But these changes are neither severe nor incomprehensible; they serve to aid the church, particularly in the liturgy of public worship. Interestingly, the translators intentionally rejected some contemporary idioms of their day in favor of retaining archaic expressions in order to produce a Bible with a sound of dignity, particularly for its public reading. If a dignified wording was a concern then, how much more is it now? So much of contemporary worship today is humanized and brought down to common levels. When pressures from popular culture define so much of public worship, it is imperative to promote and maintain in worship a distinction, dignity, and reverence that directs our hearts and minds to the majesty and uniqueness of our God. The beauty, elegance, and cadence of the KJV—not to speak of its translation accuracy—create dignity, contribute to our perception of the matchlessness of God's Word, and help us worship the Lord in the beauty of holiness. Whether in ministerial reading or in congregational responsive reading, the KJV is peerless in fostering a spirit of reverence before the Word of God.

The supposed difficulty in understanding the language of the KJV can be remedied by habitual exposure to it. Understanding anything requires a circle of knowledge that includes specialized jargon. To someone unfamiliar with baseball, the statement "the batter drew a walk" is incomprehensible. Similarly, a stranger to baseball's rules might find it odd that fans would jeer a pitcher for throwing balls when throwing a ball is his job. But it does not take long to figure out the language and rules of the game. For someone my age, listening to younger people talking about computer technology or techniques is confusing. But if I listen long enough, I can figure out what it means to blog, even if I do not know the derivation of the word.

So, there is a jargon with which we must be familiar if we are to understand the Bible. This is not a unique phenomenon caused by the age of the KJV. The Septuagint, the Greek translation of the Hebrew Old Testament, created a biblical jargon understandable to those who knew the Bible but liable to misunderstanding by those who did not. There are several instances in which the translators infused a Greek word with un-Greek significance to include the nuances of the Hebrew word it translated. This practice resulted in word meanings that would have been understood in the biblical context but misunderstood in a secular context. Similarly, the language of the KJV is understandable if given the chance. It does not take much exposure to figure out that "to wit" means "to know," "to prevent" means "to precede," "quick" means "alive," or "conversation" means "behavior."

Learning the language of the KJV requires thought, but that is never a bad thing when coming to the Word of God. It is better to retain a translation that has influenced culture positively, as has the KJV, than to dumb down a translation to reflect the culture. Even more significant than cultural or literary influence is the contribution the AV has made to the sober worship of the Lord. The KJV remains the best liturgical text to meet the needs of the sanctuary. Let the tradition continue.

Its Text

In evaluating any version of the Scriptures, the text from which it is translated is a crucial factor. In the providence of God, the Hebrew and Greek Testaments used by the translators of the KJV have proven to be the most accurate and verifiably reliable texts available both then and now. The Masoretic text printed in the Rabbinic edition of Daniel Bomberg (1524/25) was the basis for the Old Testament, and the Greek text of Theodore Beza (1598), designated as the *Textus Receptus* or Received Text, was the basis for the New Testament.

But these published editions did not fall from heaven into the hands of the translators. They represent a long history of transmission from the original inspired manuscripts through multiple copies and finally to the printed text. All along the way, God guarded and ensured the preservation of His Word. This divine preservation is the necessary and logical corollary to divine inspiration. Foundational to confidence in Scripture as the Word of God, whether in the texts of the original languages or in the texts of versions, is the fact that God inspired His Word. Divine inspiration involves both a process and a consequent product. Peter describes the process: "Knowing this first, that no prophecy of the scripture is of any private interpretation. For the prophecy came not in old time by the will of man: but holy men of God spake as they were moved by the Holy Ghost" (2 Peter 1:20–21). Peter's remark does not concern the hermeneutics of Scripture but rather its origin. In another well-known passage, Paul describes the consequent product of the supernatural process of inspiration: "All scripture is given by inspiration of God, and is profitable for doctrine, for reproof, for correction, for instruction in righteousness: that the man of God may be perfect, thoroughly furnished unto all good works" (2 Tim. 3:16–17). God used men as His instruments of communication, but the words communicated were formed by the Holy Spirit bearing the human authors along in such a supernatural manner that what they wrote was the "breathed-out" Word of God. I cannot explain the mechanics of inspiration, but neither can I deny its fact.

The process of inspiration is past and finished. It was a supernatural operation of God's Spirit limited to those men, beginning with Moses and ending with John, whom God selected to be His instruments in the writing of the biblical books. The process of inspiration ceased at the close of the canon. This is a vital truth for those of us who are cessationists, for so long as there is inspiration, the door is open for continuing revelation. The product of inspiration, the infallible, inerrant corpus of truth—the divinely breathed-out words of Scripture—is the starting point for the progression of preservation that leads to the Bible we possess.

Whereas inspiration involved an extraordinary, supernatural work of God, preservation involves the operation of God's providence—His ordinary work, but His work nonetheless. Inspiration guarantees the preservation and recognition of both the canon and text. Books are not canonical because the church recognized them as such; the church recognized them as canonical because they were, immediately in consequence of their inspiration. Likewise, the text of Scripture has been preserved because of its inspiration. The church has not determined the text; it has been the means through which God has protected His Word and ensured its perpetuation, just as Israel, the Old Testament church, received and safeguarded the laws and promises given at first (Rom. 9:4). Although thousands of years separate us from the past process of inspiration, in God's providence we have a massive amount of evidence that assures the recognition of the words breathed out by the Holy Spirit. God's Word was inspired in terms of process; it is inspired in terms of the product.

We do not possess the actual documents written by the human authors of Scripture, but we do possess thousands of witnesses to the original texts—manuscripts, ancient versions, and patristic writings. How that evidence is interpreted is crucial. My principal reason for retaining the KJV after all these years is the text from which it is translated. I believe that the extant evidence justifies the conclusion that the Greek edition used by the KJV translators represents the best tradition preserved in the majority of witnesses to the text of the New Testament. The KJV's predecessors were based on the same basic text, but with the exception of the New King James Version, its successors have used a different textual basis. In the providence of God, which text to use was not an issue for the seventeenth-century translators; they used the only text available to them. But what was the only text then remains the best text tradition now. That is not surprising, since it represents the text perpetuated by the church, to whom God entrusted His Word.

Confessedly, my conclusion rests on my opinion as to how to account for the evidence. Others who believe in inspiration and preservation as dogmatically as I have a different opinion as to how and where God preserved His Word. Evaluating their theory can wait for another day; my concern is to celebrate the AV.

The principal difference of opinion concerns the New Testament text. The history and transmission of the Old Testament text is interesting and important but not as controversial as that of the New Testament. Virtually all scholars regard the Masoretic text of the Old Testament to be authoritative, and it is the text used by most of the modern translations. The New Testament text is another story.

The AV translators used the Greek edition of Beza. But there was a long history of transmission before the Greek New Testament was published and printed. As late as AD 200, Tertullian wrote that the originals of some of the New Testament letters were still located in the churches to whom they were written, which implies that there were already copies of those letters elsewhere. In fact, we have portions of the New Testament dating to Tertullian's day and one fragment from about seventy years earlier. On the one hand, that is amazing; on the other hand, it is not. The desire for the dissemination of the Word accompanied the spread of the church. But until the invention of the printing press in the fifteenth century, every new manuscript was a handmade copy of another. Notwithstanding how tedious the process was, it produced thousands of Greek manuscripts of the New Testament in the Greek-speaking world. For many years, that Greek-speaking world was the world of the New Testament, and presumably the Bible spread wherever the church was. However, in time Latin replaced Greek in the West, which led to Latin translations, culminating in Jerome's Vulgate in AD 404. The Latin version in the West meant practically that there was little reason to continue copying the Greek text. Greek, however, remained the language in the East, and consequently, Greek manuscripts continued to proliferate in what became the Byzantine Empire. It is not surprising, therefore, that the majority of extant Greek manuscripts come from these locations, where the Greek-speaking church continued the preservation of the Word in the form in which it was originally given. Some manuscripts have been discovered that date earlier than many of those coming from the Byzantine Empire and have readings differing significantly from those in the church-used and church-preserved text, but discovery is not preservation. Preservation implies continuity and unbroken tradition. Genuine readings can be traced throughout the history of the church.

For centuries, partly due to Rome's idolatrous elevation of the Vulgate, the West had neither interest in nor access to the Greek New Testament. The providence of God changed that. The Renaissance generated the interest, and the rise and dominance of Islam afforded the access. Studying the originals behind the classics was an earmark of the Renaissance; this included study of the Scriptures. Hebrew and Greek scholars began to proliferate. The spread of Islam in the East caused churchmen to migrate to the West, taking the Scriptures with them. So, providentially, the Greek text that had prevailed from the early church was the text that entered Europe at the time when God was about to initiate the Reformation, that epic movement that was going to direct the course of the church from that time on.

In addition, God's providence put in place a mechanism that made hand copying obsolete and opened the way for the effusive spread of His Word, both in the original languages and in translation. The printing press served God's purpose in the advance of the Reformation. It also gave birth to a new business: publication. Publishers knew the importance of being the first to the press in order to secure the advantage in the marketplace.

In the early sixteenth century, the race was on to publish the first Greek New Testament. The forerunner appeared to be Cardinal Francisco Ximenes from Spain with the Complutinsian Polyglot (Hebrew, Aramaic, Latin, and Greek). It was printed in 1514 but not published until 1522. Forben, a printer in Basel, Switzerland, was aware of the Polyglot and was determined to beat it to publication. He approached Desiderius Erasmus, a learned Greek scholar, and commissioned him to prepare a text for publication. Erasmus agreed, and using the few manuscripts kept in the library at Basel, he won the race to publication in 1516. The edition went through various printings and edits until it was standardized by the French printer Robertus Stephanus in 1546/49. Then John Calvin's successor, Beza, produced a Greek Testament (1565–98) that was essentially the same as that of Stephanus's; it became the standard Greek Testament used by Protestants, including the translators of the KJV. It was not until an edition published in 1633 by the Elzevir Brothers that the expression *Textus Receptus* was used. Included in the introduction were these words: "Therefore you have the text that is now received by all." That designation then attached itself anachronistically to the earlier editions.

From a purely human perspective, the production of the Greek Testament was a successful business venture. But God ruled over the entire process. The few manuscripts available to Erasmus represented the text tradition that had prevailed from the early church and had been preserved in what we now know to be the vast majority of witnesses to the inspired text of the New Testament. When compared with the majority of extant Greek manuscripts, the Received Text agrees ninety-nine percent of the time. What a testimony this is to the providence of God in preserving His Word! The few manuscripts available for use in the sixteenth century to produce the edition used in the seventeenth century to translate the KJV just happen to reflect the text tradition that is verifiably sure. This is a good and important reason for retaining the use of the AV. Ultimately, the merit of any translation of the Bible depends on the text from which it is translated.

I have not addressed the technicalities of textual criticism except to emphasize the importance of widespread and unbroken tradition in determining the superiority of readings. That the Received Text agrees with the majority text in the majority of places is significant. It represents the Greek text that was preserved throughout the Greek-speaking church for centuries. It is the basis of the English, French, Dutch, and German translations so vital in the Reformation churches. All of this ecclesiastical recognition is hard to ignore. The textual foundation of the KJV is verifiably sure.

Its Translation

The beauty of language is that the message communicated in one language can be communicated in another. Language, like everything else, is subject to divine providence, and this has significant implications regarding the Scriptures. Although the biblical authors did not write in English, we can assuredly affirm our English Bible to be God's Word. Indeed, the translators of the AV affirmed "that the very meanest translation of the Bible in English…containeth the word of God, nay, is the Word of God."[1] The words are not the same, but the message expressed in the Hebrew, Aramaic, and Greek words of the Old and New Testaments can be conveyed in English and indeed in any other tongue. God breathed out every Hebrew, Aramaic, and Greek word in the Scriptures, but the message He revealed through those words is not so intrinsically subsumed in those words as to prevent the message from being expressed and understood with words of another language. Scripture's message is so important that the original languages "are to be translated into the vulgar language of every nation unto which they come" (Westminster Confession of Faith, 1.8).

Equally important to the need for translation is the manner of translation. Given the magnitude of the message, it is imperative that the message of the original and the message of the translation be the same. Translating accurately and faithfully requires that the translator be proficient in both the original and target languages. The six committees engaged in the project commissioned by King James were comprised of competent scholars in biblical languages and men most capable of crafting the English language.

The translators operated under a set of fifteen rules designed to ensure uniformity and to achieve illusive consensus regarding each part before final approval of the whole. The rules detailed the procedures they would follow in the translation process and created safeguards to guarantee agreement, accuracy, and acceptability. The number of required "hoops" seemed to doom the project from the beginning, but contrary to expectation, the process worked well to produce an English Bible that became the standard by which and to which all other translations would be compared.

The first rule governing the committees was that they were to use the Bishop's Bible as the basis of their revision, deviating from it only when absolutely necessary. Rule fourteen allowed them to consult and use other versions that were judged to be superior to the

---

1. "An Answer to the Imputations of Our Adversaries," in "The Translators to the Reader: Preface to the King James Version 1611."

Bishop's. Rule fourteen consistently trumped rule one; the Tyndale, Coverdale, Great, Geneva, and even the Rheims-Douay Bibles were consulted along with the Bishop's. Tyndale's version had the greatest impact. The translators said, "we never thought from the beginning, that we should need to make a new Translation, nor yet to make of a bad one a good one...but to make a good one better, or out of many good ones, one principal good one."[2] But although the KJV is a revision of earlier English versions, the committees relied heavily on the Hebrew and Greek testaments as well. In their address to the readers, the translators frequently reference the importance of the original languages. It is appropriate to refer to them as translators and to their work as translation.

Without knowledge of all the issues of differing translation philosophies and techniques that are currently prevalent and part of academic disciplines, the translators employed methods that can be evaluated and labeled by modern criteria. I argue that the KJV is in the category sometimes referred to as complete equivalency. Simply stated, this means that the translation was as literal as possible—giving due regard to the words, grammar, figures of speech, etc. of the original, yet as free as necessary—ensuring that the message intended by the original was not obscured.

For instance, by using italics to identify words in the translation that have no counterpart in the original, the translators revealed their high regard for the original text as well as their desire to help the reader by smoothing out passages that otherwise would be awkward. Even the use of what are now the archaic second-person pronouns (thee, thou, ye) allows the reader to see something that is clear in the original texts but obscured by the modern usage of "you." Thee, thou, and ye may sound outdated, but they reflect the original Hebrew and Greek precisely and often have interpretative significance, which readers of modern English versions will miss. Giving the readers of a translation the same opportunity of understanding and response as the readers of the original should be the goal of translation and is a mark of a good one. I think that is why, too, the KJV translators from time to time put alternative translations of difficult or ambiguous statements in the margins. These

---

2. "The Purpose of the Translators," in "The Translators to the Reader: Preface to the King James Version 1611."

alternatives give the readers the opportunity to think through the obscurities inherent in the originals.

The merit of any translation is determined by how well it achieves the purpose of translation: conveying the message recorded in one language into another. A good version translates without explaining, maintains the original's content and intent, retains interpretation issues, and permits an equivalence of response between the original and target audiences. It is accurate in regard to lexical and grammatical fidelity. It is sensitive to and reflective of the various styles of biblical writers. And in addition to faithfulness to the original, it is readable, both in terms of private devotion and study, and public worship. If these are the marks of a good translation, then the KJV is an indisputably good translation. It has served its purpose well for four hundred years. It continues to serve its purpose well.

Conclusion

The publication of the King James Version in 1611 was a landmark. The version has left its mark for four hundred years on literature, speech, culture, religion, and, most significantly, the hearts of millions. It has earned its place as the most influential book ever printed, and with the passing of its four-hundredth-anniversary year, venerating it is appropriate. It is old, but it is not outdated.

Contributors

MICHAEL BARRETT is Academic Dean and Old Testament Professor at Puritan Reformed Theological Seminary in Grand Rapids, Michigan. He previously served as President of Geneva Reformed Seminary in Greenville, South Carolina. He also serves as an ordained minister in the Free Presbyterian Churches of North America. He is the author of several books, mostly in the area of Old Testament studies.

JOEL R. BEEKE is President and Professor of Systematic Theology and Homiletics at Puritan Reformed Theological Seminary in Grand Rapids, Michigan. He also serves as a pastor of the Heritage Netherlands Reformed Congregation in Grand Rapids, and as editorial director of Reformation Heritage Books. He is the author of several dozens of books and a few thousand articles published in journals, periodicals, and encyclopedias.

GERALD BILKES is Professor of New Testament and Biblical Theology at Puritan Reformed Theological Seminary. He has written a book on Christ's parables and several articles on biblical-theological themes. He also serves as a pastor in the Free Reformed Churches of North America.

JOHN CARRICK is professor of Homiletics at Greenville Presbyterian Theological Seminary. He has served as minister of Cheltenham Evangelical Church and Matthews Orthodox Presbyterian Church. He is the author of several books and articles published in various periodicals and journals.

IAN HAMILTON was installed as minister of Cambridge Presbyterian Church in 1999. He graduated from Edinburgh University in 1979 and became the minister of Loudoun Church of Scotland, Newmilns, Ayshier the same year and served there for almost twenty years. He has written several books and dozens of articles.

GEORGE KNIGHT is Adjunct Professor of New Testament studies at Greenville Presbyterian Theological Seminary. Dr. Knight has served as professor at several colleges and seminaries in the United States, and as Assistant Pastor or Association Pastor in several PCA churches in the U.S. He has also served as GPTS's Board Chairman since 2005, and has authored several books and contributed dozens of articles to periodicals and encyclopedias.

RYAN McGRAW is the pastor of Grace Presbyterian Church (PCA) in Conway, South Carolina. He is the author of three books, as well as numerous articles and book reviews. He is also the president of the GPTS Alumni Association.

JOSEPH MORECRAFT is an ordained minister in the Reformed Presbyterian Church in the United States. He has pastored churched in Virginia, Tennessee, and Georgia, and has been the pastor of Chalcedon Presbyterian Church since 1974. Dr. Morecraft is also the author of several books and hundreds of articles on multiple topics.

JOSEPH PIPA serves as President and Professor of Historical and Systematic Theology at Greenville Presbyterian Theological Seminary. He has pastored in several Presbyterian churches and served as the Director of Advanced Studies and Associate Professor of Practical Theology as Westminster Seminary in California. He has written or edited numerous books and contributed to a number of journals and periodicals.

WILLIAM SHISHKO is Adjunct Professor of Applied Theology at Greenville Presbyterian Theological Seminary. He serves as pastor of the Franklin Square OPC, in Franklin Square, New York. He is also a frequent contributor to several periodicals.

MORTON SMITH is Professor of Systematic Theology at Greenville Presbyterian Theological Seminary. He has served as pastor in Springfield and Roller Presbyterian Churches, Carroll County, Maryland, and as professor and guest lecturer in several seminaries in the United States. He also served as Moderator of the General Assembly of the Presbyterian Church in America in 2000. He is also a prolific author and contributor to several publications.

JOHN THACKWAY has served as Pastor at the Holywell Evangelical church in Fairlea, Holywell, since 1991. He also serves as editor of *Bible League Quarterly*, for which he has written extensively.

GEOFFREY THOMAS has served as minister of Alfred Place Baptist Church in Aberystwyth, Wales, since 1965. He also serves as Visiting Professor of Historical Theology at PRTS. He is the author of several books and more than a thousand articles.

WILLIAM VAN DOODEWAARD is Professor of Church History at Puritan Reformed Theological Seminary. He previously served as Professor at Patrick Henry College and Huntington University. Dr. VanDoodewaard is an author and writer for numerous academic journals and other periodicals. He is an ordained minister in the Associate Reformed Presbyterian Churches.

MALCOLM WATTS is minister of Emmanuel Church, Salisbury, in England. He is also Chairman of the General Committee of the Trinitarian Bible Society and the Bible League Trust, and visiting Lecturer at the London Reformed Baptist Seminary and at PRTS. He is the author of several books and scores of articles.